D0016873

RENEWALS 458-4574

DATE DUE

ILL# 25432327			
GAYLORD			PRINTED IN U.S.A.

THE BUSINESS OF SHIPPING

THE BUSINESS OF SHIPPING

Seventh Edition

LANE C. KENDALL
and
JAMES J. BUCKLEY

CORNELL MARITIME PRESS
Centreville, Maryland

WITHDRAWN
UTSA LIBRARIES

Copyright © 1973, 2001 by Cornell Maritime Press, Inc.

All rights reserved. No part of this book may be used or reproduced in any manner whatsoever except in the case of brief quotations embodied in critical articles or reviews. For information, contact Cornell Maritime Press, Inc., Centreville, Maryland 21617.

Library of Congress Cataloging-in-Publication Data

Kendall, Lane C., 1912–
    The business of shipping / Lane C. Kendall and James J. Buckley.
        p. cm.
    Includes bibliographical references and index.
    ISBN 0-87033-526-X
    1. Shipping.   I. Buckley, James J., 1950–   II. Title.

HE571 .K4 2000
387.5′068—dc21   00-060311

“Them Damaged Cargo Blues” by James A. Quinby on page 334 is reprinted with permission from an article by Daniel A. Tadros in *Tulane Maritime Law Journal* 17, no. 1 (fall 1992), 17–18, entitled “COGSA Section 4(5)’s ‘Fair Opportunity’ Requirement: U.S. Circuit Court Conflict and Lack of International Uniformity; Will the United States Supreme Court Ever Provide Guidance?”

Library
University of Texa
at San Antonio

Manufactured in the United States of America
First edition, 1973. Seventh edition, 2001

To the memory of
Lane Carter Kendall
1912–1999

Contents

Preface to the Seventh Edition

The purpose of this book has not changed since Lane Carter Kendall wrote the first edition in 1973—to describe the business side of a commercial enterprise whose operating area encompasses the entire world and whose influence affects the lives of every man, woman, and child.

I met Lane Kendall in the early 1990s. It was immediately apparent to me that we shared a deep and profound appreciation for marine transportation, though we approached it from very different perspectives. It quickly became our practice, one to which we both looked forward, to meet weekly to talk about transportation issues. I shared my experiences as viewed from the railing of a ship and he shared his as viewed from ashore. He felt that our diverse but complementary backgrounds would enhance the book and invited me to coauthor the sixth edition, published in 1994. It was a challenge that I gratefully accepted.

We began to work on this seventh edition in 1998, outlining some of the changes that we felt should be made. The majority of the chapters from the sixth edition would be retained, though updated to reflect current activities in the industry. Several new chapters would be added to show the many changes brought about by the dynamics of the industry. Added sections would include chapters that describe the significance of marine transportation, the regulatory environment faced by shipping companies, vessel management companies, and vessel bunkering. Another chapter would describe new technologies being adopted by the maritime industry. In addition, the size of the glossary would be increased to include many more useful references. Enthusiastically, we both began our work on this edition, but with great sadness, I finished the task alone. I will miss Lane.

It was our aim, and will continue to be my aim, to describe the workings of the various divisions of ship owning and operating organizations. The procedures followed in the different aspects of the business have been described and explained. Wherever possible, I have provided background information, including the underlying principles of management by which decisions are reached.

My years in the maritime industry—serving aboard various types of U.S. flag ships at sea, in many capacities at ports and terminals ashore, and now in the classroom—have been very rewarding. They have also required a lot of hard work because of the competitive nature of the industry.

The names of those who have assisted me through the years are far too numerous to list. However, their generosity in sharing their hard-earned knowledge and priceless wisdom is greatly appreciated. I acknowledge my debt to the guides and mentors who helped to shape my career and contributed to my growth through friendly and constructive criticism that saved me from many mistakes. To all persons, I extend my heartfelt thanks.

Any errors, of course, are mine, and I assume full responsibility.

James J. Buckley

Preface to the First Edition

This volume has been written to describe the business side of a commercial enterprise whose field is the entire civilized world. Historically, the theory and knowledge of shipping management, as distinguished from the practical skills of seamanship, have been transmitted from one generation to the next by word of mouth. Little has been put on paper, primarily because the finest exponents of the art of steamship management have been too busy with their day-to-day concerns to do so. The "working level" personnel often are superbly competent, but rarely qualify as literary craftsmen.

It has been my aim, in preparing this analysis of the principles of the "business" of commercial shipping, to describe that which transpires in the various divisions of a ship-owning and operating organization. Insofar as possible, the procedures followed by the men and women in the offices have been described and explained, as well as the principles of management by which their decisions are reached.

In the process of learning the principles and practices as set forth in these pages, I have spent a happy lifetime in association with ships. It has been my good fortune to work in large and small American steamship offices, to operate a major cargo terminal, to participate in establishing the policies of a world-girdling American steamship organization, and to teach young men these principles learned in practice as well as by precept.

My years with ships and seamen have been filled with much toil and many strains. They also have been crowded with pleasant associations and fascinating experiences. I have found that with increased knowledge of the endless ramifications of the steamship business my interest in each day's work has deepened and grown more rewarding. May I hope that those who read this book will also gain greater understanding of a worthwhile way of life, and thus heighten their appreciation of the achievements of each passing day?

The names of those who have helped me through the years are far too numerous to list here. Some who contributed importantly to my knowledge were nameless to me, but their generous sharing of what they knew is no less warmly appreciated. Friends and correspondents in every type of shipping office around the world have contributed in one way or another to my education. Many of the chapters in this volume have been read by senior executives of steamship companies who found time to criticize and to offer valuable suggestions for improving the content. To all who have aided so generously, it is my pleasure to acknowledge my heavy obligation. Any errors, of course, are my own, and I assume full responsibility for them.

Lane Carter Kendall

THE BUSINESS OF SHIPPING

Introduction

People often ask, "Why did you write this book? For whom is it intended?"

The answers to these two pertinent questions may be found in the following sketch of an imagined visit to a ship by three persons: an accountant who has served the ship owning company for five years but never has had the opportunity to go aboard a ship; a lawyer who has just been assigned to a maritime case; and a cadet from a merchant marine academy reporting for his first tour of sea duty.

This diverse party approaches the ship with awe. At more than a thousand feet long and with a navigation bridge one hundred feet above the water, the ship is indeed an impressive sight to behold. The visitors' senses are only beginning to take in all of the sights, sounds, and smells of a bustling marine terminal. The ship tour begins with a rather long, steep climb up the ship's accommodation ladder (often referred to as the "gangway").

As the trio approaches the top, they notice a small, khaki-clad woman in her midthirties wearing steel-toed work boots and a white hard hat. She is speaking intently into a hand-held radio. As the group steps on deck, she finishes her conversation and extends her hand in welcome.

"Good afternoon! Welcome aboard. I'm Audra, the chief mate, and I have the privilege of representing the master, Captain Jason Waters, who is ashore with the agent obtaining customs clearance for us to sail as scheduled as soon as we finish our cargo work here." (See chapter 13.)

She explains that the chief mate (often referred to as "the mate") is the senior deck officer, head of the deck department and second in command of the vessel. "The agent," she says, "does many things besides assisting with vessel clearance matters." She explains that the agent, along with other members of the vessel husbandry team, arranges for tugs to assist with maneuvering and for pilots to bring the ship in and take it back out to sea. The agent procures fuel and possibly fresh fruits and vegetables as well. (See chapter 12.)

The chief mate notices a questioning look from the cadet, who is staring at the stack marking. As if anticipating the question she says, "As you came aboard, you probably noticed that the markings on the stack are not those of our company. That's because we have taken this ship on what is called a bareboat charter. That's similar to renting an empty house. We have the ship for six months, and though the owner retains legal title, we are the temporary proprietors of the ship. We provide the crew and everything needed, and we are fully responsible for operations. If we decide to keep the ship for some time after our six-month period is up, we'll paint the stack with our house markings. In our case, our company provides the crew, but it is becoming more common for a vessel management company to handle all the details of ship operations, including hiring the crew." (See chapter 10.)

"The field of chartering is a specialized branch of the shipping business," she continues. (See chapter 4.) "The operation is much too complex to explain in a few words, but the fact is simple to state: each year, thousands of ships are employed under different types of charters to transport hundreds of millions of tons of dry and liquid bulk cargoes. The world couldn't get along without the services of these vessels, called tramps, which ply no fixed routes, but go where the cargo is to be found and carry it to ports stipulated by the cargo owner." (See chapter 3.)

Over the noise of the giant overhead cargo cranes, the informal lecture continues: "Ships are designed to meet the needs of a trade. (See chapters 20 and 21.) This containership and others like her provide a specialized service vital to the intermodal movement of goods. (See chapters 16 and 17.) You'd be surprised at all the special purposes for which ships are used. Just to name a few, there are live sheep carriers, wood-chip carriers (salvage from lumber yards), oceanographic and geological research vessels, bulk cement carriers, liquefied natural gas carriers, refrigerated cargo carriers, passenger ships carrying pleasure-seeking passengers all over the world (see chapter 7), automobile and truck carriers, plus a variety of tankers carrying every kind of bulk liquid from exotic chemicals to asphalt and jet-engine fuels." (See chapters 8 and 9.)

After a comfortable elevator ride, the party arrives on the navigation bridge of the ship. "From our position here on the bridge, we can look out over the terminal," says the chief mate. "You'll notice a string of trucks at the gate; they are delivering containers to be shipped to the different ports this company serves. They have come from many different points, and at our terminal is a list of the expected times of their arrival. The boxes from the trucks are checked against the list, approved for entry, and inspected for evidence of damage or tampering. They are taken to a place of rest, where they stay until brought under the cranes to be hoisted aboard ship for stowage." (See chapters 14 and 15.)

"How customers are found, what contracts are made, what prices are charged (see chapter 17)—all this is part of the traffic department's responsibility," explains the mate. (See chapters 5 and 6.) "The sales staff is furnished with all of the necessary information from the shipper. Everything being satisfactory, the company issues a bill of lading—that's the contract under which the goods will be carried between stated ports—and also a statement of exactly what is to be carried and in what quantities." (See chapters 18 and 19.)

The mate explains that the load planners take this information and, using their computer skills and maritime knowledge, determine exactly where in the ship the container will be loaded. These planners must consider the weight and size of the box, the destination port, the number of similar boxes consigned to the same port, and whether special attention is required to care for the cargo.

The mate leads the visitors to the offshore side of the bridge. "From this side of the bridge," she says, "you can see a small tank-barge floating alongside us. This is the bunkering barge, bringing us the fuel we need for the upcoming voyage. Bunkering has become a special responsibility of the senior managers because fuel oil is now very expensive." (See chapter 11.)

"Let's go down to the main deck," suggests the mate. "I want you to notice the trucks at the stern (after end) of the ship. They are delivering a great number of packages from our suppliers, who have been negotiating with our procurement office. Because we need such a wide variety of stores, we use three main sources rather than trying to deal individually with each vendor. For major purchases or very large quantities, we buy directly from the manufacturer. For most of the other supplies, we purchase from a ship chandler—a sort of ship's general store. Recently, we have been contracting with the chandler to serve as a consolidator of dozens of small lots rather than have each lot sent individually to the ship. The consolidator contracts with a freight forwarder to ship the collected items to a designated port. Procurement involves the expenditure of many thousands of dollars and in recent years has attracted the attention of our senior managers." (See chapter 12.)

"I hope you observed the number of people going around the ship with tool boxes, bags of spare parts, or thick manuals. They may give the impression that they are working without direction or concern for anyone," says the mate, "but actually, what you are seeing are highly trained, motivated, experienced, and dependable seafarers. They are intensely aware that all their actions are interrelated, and that the safety of the ship, and indeed their own lives, may depend on the proper performance of their duties. They know exactly what needs to be examined, renewed, refurbished, or subjected to trial. Our industry is highly regulated by many different offices and agencies, and it's important that we meet all of the requirements in order to maintain an efficient and safe operation." (See chapter 2.)

"In the engine room, there are other workers, equally skilled, equally well-disciplined. They examine a variety of mechanisms; they watch the bunkering process to ensure that what was ordered is what is being delivered, and they verify that repair jobs have been completed satisfactorily. In these ways, they are contributing to the exercise of due diligence."

As the group makes its way back to the gangway, the mate reflects on the importance of marine transportation in world economies. "Many raw materials and finished goods can be transported only by water," she says. "If not for ocean transportation the world would be a very different place indeed." (See chapters 1, 3, and 22.)

"Before you leave and return to your offices and your regular pursuits (except for our cadet, who is going to experience shipboard life for the first time), I want to present you with this book, *The Business of Shipping*. I think you'll find the answers to any questions that may have been raised by your visit. In any case, you'll find full descriptions of each activity I touched upon during the tour and a lot more!

"This book was written for each of you and also for me. I'm a professional seafarer, but I learned a great deal by reading this book. It broadened my understanding of the industry; it allowed me to see how I contribute to the business, and it influences a great deal of what I do during each day.

"Finally, I think it also was written for that reader who has heard a ship's whistle or seen ships in port, but has never experienced any direct connection with ships.

"We'll sail in about two hours," she says. "Captain Waters will be returning shortly, and I want to check that everything has been made ready for the voyage. Thank you for coming to visit us. It's been a real pleasure to tell you about the ship and our work," she concludes.

Two members of the group head down the gangway after expressing their appreciation for the mate's time and patience in answering their many questions. Upon reflecting on the tour, the visitors begin to appreciate the interesting aspects, challenges, and complexities of the business of shipping.

CHAPTER ONE

The Significance of Maritime Transportation

The business of shipping involves the physical movement of goods and passengers from ports of supply to ports of demand as well as those activities required to support and facilitate such movement. The transportation of goods by ship is the economic lifeblood of many nations, whether they are situated on a coast or not, and marine transportation has always been absolutely essential to the economy and well-being of the United States.

With roughly three-quarters of the surface of the earth covered by water, marine transportation necessarily plays a major role in international commerce. Marine transportation has many characteristics that make it the logical choice for the movement of raw materials and finished products required by an expanding world market. It is estimated that 95 percent of the import and export tonnage of the United States moves by ship.[1]

Many commodities that are essential to manufacturing processes are very heavy (dense), and have low unit value, such as coal or iron ore. Their movement in vast quantities over great distances is made possible only because ships are available at low cost. Shippers of high value cargoes take advantage of the comparatively inexpensive rates charged for overseas movement as well as the abundant cargo space and acceptable delivery speeds.

For the purposes of this book, the marine industry, demand-derived and service-oriented, includes all activities supporting marine transportation—not only governmental and commercial rules, regulations, and financial investment, but also a catalog of other services ranging from the design and building of ships to the methods of scrapping them. Every phase of economic activity is involved: banking, construction and repair, insurance, brokerage, stevedoring, ship supply, and other services too numerous to describe here.

Throughout its history, marine transportation has been important to the economic growth and development of the United States. It has given vital support in times of national emergencies by providing sealift capacity to supplement that available from the navy. It has helped to balance international trade figures through revenue earned from freight. Unfortunately, water transportation is largely ignored by many people, because it is not seen, and its functions in national life are neither understood nor appreciated.

The history of the United States demonstrates that in many ways it is an island nation. The first Continental Congress recognized the contribution of the marine industry to the ultimate success of the American Revolution. That body realized that its only practical choice for transporting the goods demanded by the fledgling economy were the ships of the national flag fleet.

Water transportation played an important role in intercolony and interstate development before an adequate road system was built. Cities evolved because their sites gave access to rivers or oceans. To protect and nurture this vital activity, the Continental Congress adopted legislation granting reduced tariffs on goods imported in American ships. It also limited registration under the American flag to vessels built in the United States. As a direct result of this program, in 1795 approximately 92 percent of imports and 86 percent of exports were carried in U.S. flag vessels.[2]

The nineteenth century was characterized by world strife, international trade expansion, devastating internal conflicts, direct governmental involvement in trade patterns and transportation, and significant changes in transportation technologies. Individually and in combination, these issues had a profound impact on the U.S. maritime industry. Throughout the century, the demand for goods generally continued to grow. Waterborne transportation was still the only efficient and cost-effective way to move goods. Beginning in 1820 and continuing through the end of the century, a subtle change began to take place. Many of the goods moving in international trade, which had once been carried almost exclusively by U.S. flag vessels, were now being shipped in foreign flag vessels. The federal government protected U.S. domestic water transportation by enacting *cabotage* legislation that protected domestic cargo shipping[3] and also passenger service.[4] Currently, these regulations are under attack by various organizations that assert the United States would be better served by the elimination of existing cabotage laws.

The Civil War had a devastating effect on the U.S. flag fleet. Confederate raiders aggressively attacked ships flying the American flag. Some frightened owners transferred their fleets to foreign registries. Following the war, many of these transferred vessels were not returned to American Registry. The national government, preoccupied with recovery from the wounds of that long conflict, paid little attention to the plight of the merchant marine. The completion of the transcontinental railroad in 1869 (with significant financial support from the government) had the practical result of ending the intercoastal trade serviced by the swift clipper ships. Until the opening of the Panama Canal in 1914, the progressive decline in the once important and lucrative intercoastal trade was conspicuous.

The last quarter of the nineteenth century witnessed tremendous changes in the technology of sea transportation. Especially in England, shipowners were substituting iron (and later, steel) for wood in the hulls of their vessels and were replacing sails with reciprocating steam engines. United States shipping interests adhered to wooden construction for their sail-powered schooners. Some progressive owners invested in the new types of ships, but the pace was slow. Foreign flag competition in international trade continued to grow and as the century ended, the role of the U.S. merchant marine in this service was minuscule.

The twentieth century was a period of great change. In the early years, the U.S. Congress enacted several significant laws affecting shipping. Working conditions of seamen were improved,[5] and greater attention was paid to the safety of life at sea.[6] The cabotage laws were revised and strengthened.[7] Military cargoes were restricted to ships of U.S. Registry.[8] When the United States entered the First World War, a major shipbuilding program began, but the war ended before many ships were delivered. These products of American shipyards were sold to operators at bargain prices, and mail contracts, an early form of government subsidies to shipowners, were provided to assist in meeting operating costs. In 1936, a new system of subsidies was made effective with the passage of the Merchant Marine Act of 1936. The intent of this law was to encourage the construction of modern, competitive ships and to operate them, with necessary financial assistance, in direct competition with lower-cost foreign flag shipping lines.

As the clouds of World War II descended, the U.S. government started the greatest shipbuilding program in history, and before the guns were silenced in 1945, thousands of new ships were servicing the military. The contribution of the American merchant marine to final victory was summed up by General (later President) Dwight Eisenhower: "When final victory is ours, there is no organization that will share its credit more deservedly than the American merchant marine. We were caught flat-footed in both world wars because we relied too much upon foreign owned shipping. I consider the merchant marine to be our fourth arm of defense and vital to the stability and expansion of our foreign trade."

Throughout the first half of the twentieth century, the world watched the birth and rapid development of new modes of transportation. Although some pipelines had been built in the later years of the previous century, they came into their own shortly after 1900. Liquid bulk products are moved efficiently and economically through these pipelines; the impact on railroads and coastwise shipping has been very significant.

Following the success of the pipelines came the development of the long-distance trucking companies, offering common carrier service to all parts of the nation. As truck design improved, the road system was expanded and quickly put into maximum use by truck operators. One very obvious effect has been the almost complete elimination of the domestic coastwise shipping business, except for a few specialized tankers and some tug-and-barge operations.

From 1930 onward, air carriers provided passenger transportation on a limited number of routes. After 1945, they became true participants in the domestic trades. As payload capacity increased, the air carriers were able to siphon off the very high-rated (and valuable) cargoes formerly hauled by express steamships and railroads. No longer limited to operation in the continental United States, these carriers have expanded their cargo services to all parts of the world. The impact on waterborne transportation has been dramatic.

The newest mode of transportation, that of electronic transportation,[9] is in its infancy. Yet there are strong indications that this mode is growing rapidly and will soon become a major player in the transportation of such extremely time-sensitive material as documents and information. The information superhighway of the Internet, along with electronic data interchange (EDI), facsimile accepted documents, automatic equipment identification (AEI) tagging, electronic mail (e-mail), local area networks (LAN), and modem transmissions of documents and data are all examples of the interesting innovations in transportation technology. Electronic transportation has been able to compete successfully with air transportation for some of its business, but as of this writing, it has acted solely to complement water transportation.

The twentieth century witnessed some tremendous changes in vessel efficiency as well as significant improvements in terminal design and operation. Ships have increased in length from 300 or 400 feet to more than 1,000 feet; their speed has increased from 10 or 12 knots up to 40 knots, and their capacity has grown from 10,000 tons to more than 500,000 tons. New technological breakthroughs have changed the way vessels are operated. Ships are being designed as specialty ships with little or no cargo gear of their own. No longer is the sextant routinely used to determine the ship's location nor is Morse code used for communications. Today, satellite technology serves to determine a ship's position as well as to effect effortless and dependable communication with other vessels or shore stations. Computers assist in making automated control practical for virtually all aspects of vessel operations, with the resultant reduction of crew size from 35 or 40 people to 20 or fewer.

Terminal design and operations have experienced the most profound changes. Terminals, like the new ships, are becoming specialized and automated. The advent of the forklift to move unitized goods around the terminal was a dramatic improvement over men with hand trucks, but it was only the beginning. Next came the container and LASH (lighter aboard ship) vessels that took the unitization concept to a new, higher level of performance and efficiency. Terminal labor also improved, by necessity, as the new, sophisticated equipment required a labor force with a set of base skills much different from what was required when terminal work was almost all manual labor. The combination of all of these changes improved vessel and terminal efficiency, thereby making a much shorter turnaround time possible for the ships.

As changes were made in the technology and operation of ships and terminals, significant changes were also made in the basic philosophy of business practices, some of which affected transportation. Today, the business community recognizes that inventory management is a significant cost factor; interesting inventory techniques like just-in-time (JIT) are applied in order to utilize resources more efficiently. Transportation is recognized for its very important role in the timely acquisition and delivery of raw materials and finished goods. Transportation, by its very operation, also provides a short-term warehousing function. Today's astute business manager is always on the lookout for innovative ways to use the transportation services of all carriers to enhance business opportunities, resulting in more insistent demands that transportation perform its services on time, every time, and without damage. Intermodal transportation requires that the individual modes, long conditioned to compete with each other, begin to work together to form partnerships that will benefit businesses through better, faster, and more efficient transportation.

As the millennium turned, the total tonnage of goods moved by ship had grown with the increased demand for foreign goods and materials, but the percentage carried on U.S. flag carriers had decreased. Now there is practically no movement of dry cargo on the U.S. coastwise routes; most of the tonnage that is transported between the states is petroleum and its derivatives. About 95 percent of all the international trade tonnage of the United States is being carried by water transportation. Because the United States is essentially an island nation, the business of shipping is now, and will continue to be, vital to national defense and economic growth.

CHAPTER TWO

Regulatory Involvement in Maritime Transportation

For centuries, national governments have exercised some form of regulation and control of waterborne transportation serving their needs. The major maritime countries of the world today engage in widespread regulation, which involves significant expenditures of time, effort, and money. This heavy burden is accepted in realization of the vital role played by national flag merchant fleets in the growth and development of their countries' economies. Governments also recognize that national defense depends to a measurable extent upon the logistical support such fleets can provide.

Appreciating these basic facts, governments of maritime nations consider that transportation, especially that provided by waterborne vessels, is a public service industry affecting every level of society. Transportation overcomes the inconvenience of distance. This is illustrated by the steel industry, which relies upon iron ore from one area, manganese from another, often faraway source, and chrome ore mined in an even more distant region. Telephone lines, so vital in the life of the United States, are fabricated from copper imported from countries on the far side of oceanic horizons. England, an island nation, annually imports scores of millions of tons of foodstuffs to feed its population as well as great quantities of raw materials to meet the needs of its factories. Without support from seagoing vessels, the well-being and prosperity of many nations would be affected negatively. It follows, therefore, that each government, by force of circumstance, must ensure that shipping is adequate to meet the demands of its economy and that it supports the country's objectives.

Governments are able to do things that private carriers are not able to do. For example, in an effort to offer greater mobility to its citizens, a government may decide that more extensive transportation services are required, even if they are operated at a loss. For facilities such as airports, which are too costly for private carriers to finance, a government may undertake the projects. Governments also support research in, and development of, modes and uses of transportation that exceed the capability of private enterprise. To achieve all these objectives, governments impose regulations.

Within the borders of a single nation, control of transportation is comparatively simple. Where monopolies in the provision of transportation services have developed, government regulation—ideally admonitory rather than controlling—serves as the substitute for competition to ensure that adequate service is provided at reasonable (i.e., competitive) levels. Where excess competition between carriers, especially in the pricing of services, threatens to destroy these activities and consequently disrupt economic development, government may intervene by imposing regulations concerning the flexibility of rates and fares.

Where waterborne transportation extends beyond a nation's borders, as is the case in international shipping, the ability of a single government to regulate or control this transportation is restricted by the interests of other national governments. An individual government may impose regulations upon its export trade and on carriers flying its flag, but even these rules are affected by pressures from other maritime nations.

Some governments have adopted the position that a strong national flag merchant fleet is important to national defense and the protection of its commercial interests overseas. Many situations have required transportation that could be provided only by ships, ideally registered under the state flag. To ensure that this capability would be available when needed, these governments have enacted legislation (a form of regulation) to support their maritime industries.

Transportation regulation may be divided into two major categories: safety regulation, which establishes standards and rules for construction, maintenance, and operation in all its modes; and economic regulation, which is intended to stabilize practices for entering and exiting the trades, maintaining services, and setting rates and fares. In addition, governmental support and protection of the national flag merchant fleet may take the form of direct subsidies paid to operators and shipbuilders, indirect subsidies in the form of port development and dredging of channels, flag preferences (i.e., cabotage, or restriction of domestic trading to ships of that nation exclusively), and special legal privileges or benefits.

TYPES OF REGULATORY INVOLVEMENT

Governmental or regulatory involvement falls into two general categories: oversight imposed by the international maritime community for the safety of vessels and protection of the environment and oversight imposed by a national government for the protection and development of its national flag merchant fleet.

The International Maritime Organization (IMO) is a specialized, self-governing agency of the United Nations, autonomously supported by its member states.[1] To become a member, a country must ratify the IMO Convention, which was originally written in 1948, and pay an annual assessment proportionate to the tonnage of its flag fleet.

The objectives of IMO, as stated in Article 1 of the original convention, are "to provide machinery for cooperation among Governments in the field of governmental regulation and practices relating to technical matters of all kinds affecting shipping engaged in international trade; to encourage and facilitate the general adoption of the highest practicable standards in matters concerning maritime safety, efficiency of navigation and prevention and control of marine pollution from ships." IMO is an international forum where member states can discuss and establish minimum standards to which all members must adhere. It does not, however, have the authority to enforce the regulations agreed upon and ratified by member states. Rather, it relies on the member states themselves to codify IMO's conventions or protocols into their local laws and then enforce those laws as appropriate under their legal system.

At the head of IMO is the General Assembly, made up of all member states. This group meets every two years in regular sessions to approve the work being done in committees, to make budget decisions, and to elect members of the Council, which consists of thirty-two member states and acts as the IMO governing body between General Assembly meetings. Five permanent committees report to the Council: the Marine Environment Protection Committee, the Maritime Safety Committee, the Facilitation Committee, the Legal Committee, and the Technical Cooperation Committee.

Since its creation, IMO has adopted more than forty conventions and protocols including Safety of Life at Sea (SOLAS, 1974),[2] International Regulations for Preventing Collisions at Sea (COLREGS, 1972),[3] Standards of Training, Certification and Watchkeeping for Seafarers (STCW, 1978/95),[4] Prevention of Pollution from Ships (MARPOL, 1973/78),[5] and Oil Pollution Preparedness, Response and Cooperation (OPRC, 1990). IMO has also adopted several hundred codes and recommendations including the International Safety Management Code (ISM, 1993),[6] the International Code of Safety for High-Speed Craft (1994), Guidelines for the Control and Management of Ships' Ballast Water (1998),[7] and the International Code for the Safe Carriage of Grain in Bulk (1991). In addition to its role in developing and adopting the various conventions or codes, IMO has been very active in providing technical assistance for programs for port state control arrangements, maritime training, and safety.[8]

Industry-sponsored organizations also are concerned with the safe operation and management of ships and the protection of the environment. The International Ship Managers' Association (ISMA) in its Code of Ship-management Standards,[9] the International Organization for Standardization (ISO) in its 9000 series standards,[10] and Det Norske Veritas (DNV)[11] have developed standard-driven initiatives relating to quality management within the shipping industry.[12] Individual companies that own or manage ships and are affiliated with the ISMA are bound to meet the standards of the ISM Code as they are phased in.[13] They have the option of conforming to other rules of the ISO or DNV that apply to the service or trade in which their ships participate.

An important safety factor for vessel operation is communication equipment, both radio and satellite. The international community has been involved in regulating vessel communication since 1906, when the first radiotelegraph conference met in Berlin and approved the use of SOS as the international radiotelegraph code signal for distress.[14] Since then, there have been numerous conventions addressing all aspects of radio communications between ship stations at sea and between ships and shore-based stations. The latest requirements for safety radio communications involve the implementation of a global maritime distress and safety system (GMDSS), which was implemented in 1999.[15]

Most of the environmental regulations in the codes noted relate to oil pollution and the dumping of various products into the oceans of the world. A number of governments in the world are concerned with more than just the pollution of ocean water. Some governments, for example, have established, or are trying to establish, regulations that cover the emission of gases from the stacks of machinery-powered vessels,[16] the vapor emission from oil and chemical tankers during loading operations, and the disposition of ballast water at the loading port. Ballast water, vital to shipping because it is used to ease the stresses on a ship's hull and to keep her stable, has also inadvertently carried living marine organisms from one part of the world to another. Upon discharge into a new ecosystem, some transported organisms have flourished, often at the expense of indigenous species.[17]

To protect a country's domestic water transportation fleet, many maritime nations have established some type of cabotage law.[18] The word cabotage comes from the French root word meaning "to sail coastwise or by the cape;"[19] it refers to all laws requiring that goods carried between ports in the country ("domestic trade") be carried on national flag vessels. Around the world, the value of cabotage laws is under discussion, and a small number of countries are either eliminating or modifying their current cabotage laws.

To protect their domestic fishing industry and offshore mineral concerns, many countries have established territorial waters and/or exclusive economic zones at various distances from their coasts. Offshore areas up to hundreds of miles from the coast often are reserved by governments primarily to protect their fishing or oil-drilling activities. By such action, these governments control all natural resources known or discovered in their exclusive zones.[20]

The international shipping business is very competitive. For a variety of reasons, ships built in one country may be much less expensive than those built in another. Crewmembers from one country may have significantly lower wages than crewmembers from another. Recognizing these facts and attempting to equalize the competition while assuring employment for their national shipyard and seagoing labor force, some governments have paid operating subsidies to carriers engaged in international trade and to shipyards building vessels for those trades. In recent years there has been considerable debate around the world as to the real value of these types of subsidies. However, subsidies do exist and the subsidy issue will continue to be debated.

In contrast to these subsidies, which are paid directly to the carriers and shipyards, there are indirect subsidies. These provide government funding to an industry for projects such as building locks in rivers, dredging channels, maintaining aids to navigation (for example, buoys or lighthouses), or vessel traffic systems (VTS). These types of government subsidies encourage growth of the nation's commerce by providing the means by which waterborne commerce may be controlled without regard for the nationality of the vessel.

Primarily as a source of revenue, a number of smaller maritime nations not engaged in international waterborne commerce have opened their registries to ships built, owned, and operated by persons who are not citizens of those countries. Among the inducements they offer are simplified, inexpensive documentation to register ships; freedom to employ crewmembers of any citizenship; less onerous vessel inspection; and significant tax advantages. Ships registered in these countries are said to be flying "flags of convenience (FOC)."

UNITED STATES REGULATORY INVOLVEMENT

The fledgling U.S. government recognized the benefits of having a strong national flag merchant fleet, and from the time of the first Continental Congress, it worked to foster and protect the U.S. flag fleet. Initially the government did not have sufficient money to support the merchant fleet directly, but it provided indirect subsidies in the form of lower tariffs on goods carried by U.S. flag vessels. Domestic shipyards were supported by the requirement that only vessels built in American shipyards could fly the national flag.

The United States was, for all practical purposes, dependent on waterborne transportation for protection and economic development. In 1795, partly because of government interest, approximately 92 percent of American imports and 86 percent of American exports were carried in U.S. flag vessels.[21] Throughout the years that number has been eroded to a point where today less than 4 percent of foreign waterborne commerce is carried in U.S. flag vessels.[22] Although the percentage of goods carried on U.S. flag vessels has dropped dramatically, the government has been very active in the regulation of its commercial fleet.

From a safety regulation standpoint, both foreign and domestic water transportation is affected by the United States Coast Guard (USCG), an arm of the Department of Transportation (DOT). When the government adopts one of the international maritime conventions or codes, these rules are codified in the Code of Federal Regulations (CFR). For maritime interests, most of the regulations are contained in Title 46 CFR (Shipping) for vessel safety requirements, personnel licensing, and lifesaving equipment; Title 49 CFR (Transportation) for hazardous materials regulations; and Title 33 CFR (Navigation and Navigable Waters) for navigation requirements. The USCG conducts vessel inspections of U.S. flag vessels and issues Certificates of Inspection (COI) for all vessels passing inspection. The Coast Guard also conducts safety inspections of foreign flag vessels to determine if they are in compliance with the SOLAS convention. In addition, the Coast Guard is responsible for a myriad of other activities including drug interdiction, maintenance of navigation aids, enforcement of the laws affecting fishing and the exclusive economic zone (200 miles offshore), Coast Guard VTS service, port safety and security regulations, marine environmental response, search and rescue operations, marine casualty investigation, and the documentation and licensing of U.S. mariners.[23]

The National Transportation Safety Board (NTSB), established as an independent agency of the federal government in 1975, has the mandate to ensure that all types of transportation in the United States are conducted safely. The board investigates accidents, conducts studies, and makes recommendations to government agencies and the transportation industry on safety measures and practices.[24] It investigates all major marine casualties. After the investigation is complete, its findings are issued together with recommendations for preventing repetition of the same type of accident. These recommendations are not mandates. They are furnished to the USCG, which makes the final determination concerning any appropriate changes in the regulations.

The Merchant Marine Act of 1920 established the American Bureau of Shipping (ABS) as the official classification society for U.S. flag vessels. The ABS establishes construction and equipment standards for ships. Every vessel that meets all ABS standards and requirements is said to be "in class" and will be issued Hull Certificates and Machinery Certificates as evidence of compliance. In order to retain classification, the vessel must go through annual inspections somewhat similar to the USCG inspection. It is a requirement of marine underwriters that vessels maintain classification, and therefore no insurance policy will be written for a ship that does not meet ABS standards.

The Merchant Marine Act of 1936 (as amended) divided the responsibility for the U.S. international merchant fleet between the Federal Maritime Commission (FMC) and the Maritime Administration (MARAD). The FMC supervises economic activities of the merchant marine, while MARAD is responsible for the promotion of the merchant marine, including administration of those programs that subsidize American shipping.

The FMC is an independent agency consisting of five members appointed by the president and approved by the senate. It is responsible for ensuring that U.S. international water transportation business is conducted in a fair and equitable manner. All common carrier tariffs, conference tariffs and activities, terminal tariffs, and service contracts must be filed with the FMC. If a dispute arises, any party, whether a U.S. carrier or not, may file a complaint with the FMC. The FMC conducts investigations as it deems necessary and renders a binding decision. The FMC has the power to subpoena witnesses, impose monetary fines, or revoke tariffs.

MARAD is an agency within the Department of Transportation that administers programs to aid in the development, promotion, and operation of the U.S. merchant marine. Its responsibilities include overseeing the U.S. subsidy programs through the Maritime Subsidy Board, approving mortgage guarantee applications under Title XI of the Merchant Marine Act of 1936 (as amended), monitoring the capital construction funds,[25] maintaining statistics for the merchant marine, and managing the federal maritime academy at Kings Point. MARAD also oversees the state maritime academies' training ships and training programs, conducts research and development for ship design and cargo handling gear, promotes the use of U.S. flag merchant ships, and manages the nation's reserve fleets.[26]

The U.S. government has tried several methods of providing subsidy money to U.S. flag ships serving international trade. The first type was in the form of mail contracts—really a poorly disguised subsidy paid to owners of steam-propelled vessels operating on certain trade routes. These generous contracts were moderately successful, but they were abused by many contractors. In 1936 they were canceled and replaced by subsidies established in the Merchant Marine Act of that year. The subsidy program is administered by MARAD through the subsidy board. The 1936 act provided for a construction differential subsidy (CDS) and an operating differential subsidy (ODS). Both of these subsidies were designed to put the U.S. flag merchant ships on a parity with their foreign competition. Since October 1, 1983, the construction differential subsidy has not been funded, and therefore it has not been available to U.S. carriers. The last operating subsidies expired in 1997, but they had been replaced in 1996 when Congress passed the Maritime Security Act. This act approved a $1 billion, ten-year plan for operating subsidies.[27] Approximately forty-seven U.S. flag ships receive this subsidy.

The agency responsible for the economic regulation of the U.S. domestic fleet is the Surface Transportation Board (STB). For many years, the Interstate Commerce Commission and the Federal Maritime Commission provided the economic regulation for the U.S. domestic fleet. When the Interstate Commerce Commission was terminated in December 1995, the Surface Transportation Board took over many of its duties.

The Federal Communications Commission (FCC) regulates interstate and foreign communications by radio or satellite. It requires that U.S. operators comply with all FCC radio regulations. It also ensures that U.S. regulations conform to all international radio conventions. The FCC licenses all marine radio stations, conducts annual radio station inspections, and licenses vessel radio operators.[28]

The National Cargo Bureau (NCB), by its charter, is dedicated to the safe loading, stowage, securing, and unloading of cargo on all vessels and to the safety of shipboard cargo-handling gear. The bureau accomplishes its goals through the application of uniform standards and by performing a variety of services to shipping. Some of the services the NCB offers include recommending safety regulations to appropriate governmental organizations, working with other nations to achieve safety, providing a central source of commodity handling information, providing safety training courses in stability and hazardous materials, making cargo and cargo gear inspections, issuing cargo gear certifications, and conducting special cargo surveys. The NCB provides a valuable service to both U.S. and foreign registered vessels.

As stated earlier, cabotage laws are those laws that protect the carriage of domestic cargo, and they have been an important part of federal legislation since 1817, when the first U.S. cabotage law was passed. This law was called the Navigation Act and required that cargo moved between two U.S. ports be carried in U.S. flag vessels. The passenger trade also was protected when the Passenger Service Act was passed in 1866. During World War I there were not enough ships to carry all the domestic cargo so foreign flag vessels were permitted to participate in U.S. domestic trade during that war. To reaffirm the nation's cabotage laws, Section 27 of the Merchant Marine Act of 1920, commonly known as the Jones Act after its sponsor, Senator Wesley L. Jones, was passed. The Jones Act is still in effect; however, considerable pressure exists to eliminate or to significantly modify all cabotage laws.

Along with many coastal state governments, the federal government is very concerned with protection of the environment. As a result, a number of environmental regulations affecting the maritime industry have been promulgated. After the passage of the Oil Pollution Act in 1990, for example, a number of coastal states enacted regulations governing times of tank vessel transits (for example, during daylight hours only), requirements for bridge equipment of tank vessels, obligatory tug escorts in sensitive areas, and special coastal traffic lanes for tank vessels. Alongside a pier, many ports require tank vessels to employ vapor recovery systems as they load cargo so that the mixture of hydrocarbon vapors and inert gas in the tanks being loaded cannot be vented directly to the atmosphere.

Tankers are not the only vessels feeling pressure from governmental regulations concerning air pollution. A number of federal and state regulations deal with the issue of air quality standards. Many local areas have air quality management organizations that are charged with ensuring that federal and state air quality standards are met. Some of these rules pose significant challenges for ships, as they require the measurement and control of engine emissions. At least one region proposed that ships shut down their main propulsion system during port visits to reduce air pollution. These laws, known as "cold iron" laws, impose a particular hardship on ships using steam propulsion.

Like air quality, water quality is a concern of coastal states. A number of federal and local regulations specify what cannot be discharged into local waters. Restricted items range from sewage, garbage, and plastics to marine paints and coatings and other harmful or hazardous materials. Another water quality problem has become significant in recent years. This concerns nonindigenous species that are deposited regularly into coastal ecosystems from the discharge of vessels' ballast. These species may not have natural enemies in the new ecosystem and therefore multiply unhampered to the point that they destroy indigenous species, thereby posing a threat to the balance of nature in a local area. They may also contaminate the cooling water at power plants and factories. Considerable discussion is taking place worldwide as many agencies seek ways to control the procedure for taking ballast aboard ships, the treatment of the ballast once taken, and the appropriate method of discharging the ballast.[29]

One of the most significant improvements to safety has been the establishment of local vessel traffic systems (VTS) in major ports. These systems advise all shipping in congested port areas to ensure safe movement of all vessels. VTS systems usually consist of a voice communication network used in combination with radar, the visual tracking of vessels, vessel traffic lanes, and rules regarding vessel movement. Most major ports mandate participation in the VTS by large vessels.

The federal government is also directly involved in the operation of a fleet of ships through the Military Sealift Command (MSC). MSC is one of three organizations that provide transportation services for the Department of Defense under the U.S. Transportation Command (USTRANSCOM). The other two organizations are the Air Mobility Command (AMC) and the Military Traffic Management Command (MTMC). MSC is an operating agency for the Department of the Navy; it owns, operates, and charters a large fleet of ships crewed by U.S. citizen mariners. Its mission is to deliver cargoes and provide logistical support for the army, navy, air force, and marines, and to develop and keep fully up to date plans for expansion of sealift capability in a national emergency. It employs approximately 6,000 people, of whom about 80 percent are seagoing personnel.[30]

The importance of marine transportation will be magnified with increased emphasis on the growth of a world economy. Therefore, it is to be expected that governments everywhere will continue—and probably augment—regulation of this indispensable form of transportation.

CHAPTER THREE

Tramp Shipping: Its Management and Operations

During the half century that ended in 1914, most of the transoceanic cargoes of coal, ore, and grain were carried in comparatively small, general-purpose cargo ships. Moving as they did on routings that varied from voyage to voyage, hauling now one commodity and then another, entering and leaving port without fanfare or publicity and often in need of paint, these vessels gained the appellation of "tramp steamers." To the extent that their wanderings and unkempt appearance paralleled those of that fraternity of homeless men know as tramps, the name may have been appropriate. What was not apparent was the careful and constant concern exercised over the ships by their owners, who contested vigorously for the available business and took pride in their ability to deliver the goods.

The purpose of tramp ships is to provide convenient, timely, and economical transportation for the many kinds of goods needed in a complex industrialized society. Converting this declaration of purpose into the reality of cross-ocean movement of many millions of tons of goods typified by ore, coal, grain, and fertilizer is a task demanding skill and a multitude of resources.[1] It is the nature of the tramping industry to seek cargoes where they can be found and to provide the flexibility in transportation essential to satisfy world needs.

Raw materials vital to the existence of industrialized nations are rarely found close to the places where they are needed. Chrome ore, for example, is an ingredient in high-grade steel, but it is found in large quantities only in areas far distant from iron-ore sources and processors. The availability of inexpensive and dependable transoceanic transportation therefore becomes of crucial importance to both the producing and the consuming regions. Perhaps more dramatic because of the greater volatility of demand is the distribution of grain.

From the vast and fertile plains of the United States, Canada, Argentina, and Australia comes a never-ending stream of the golden staple.[2] For generations there has been a steady and predictable movement of grain from those four producing regions to England, northern Europe, and the Mediterranean nations. Irregularly, depending upon climatic conditions

The breakbulk cargo liner *Fushimi Maru* was designed for efficient and economical handling of her cargoes. Courtesy NYK Lines.

beyond the control of man, urgent appeals have come from India, China, the former Soviet empire, and those areas of Africa where famine seems endemic. Tramp ships provide transportation in the established trades and, as required, shift to new routes to alleviate critical shortages wherever they may occur. Should a crop failure in Argentina coincide with a sharply curtailed harvest in China, tramp shipping routes worldwide would quickly be adjusted to adapt to these new circumstances.

Another reason for the continued existence of tramp shipping is that it provides, at low cost, the transportation required to add value to the estimated 4,500,000,000 metric tons of the basic products of agriculture (of which the many types of grain are predominant), forestry, and mining, as well as manufactured raw materials such as cement, petroleum, steel, and fertilizers that move in world commerce.[3]

Not many years ago, the popular ship for these cargoes (except iron ore) was the vessel of 20,000 to 25,000 tons deadweight. The recent development of the so-called Handimax design—a dry-bulk carrier with a deadweight between 30,000 and 50,000 tons—has met with widespread approval. In 1992, ships of less than 50,000 tons deadweight made up 47 percent of the bulk carrier fleet.[4]

As economical as these ships are, they still cost money to operate. The freight rates charged by tramps are low and are always responsive to world economic conditions. When there is a glut of wheat worldwide, the demand for ships is reduced. Reacting to the laws of supply and demand, shipowners fight for the available business by reducing their rates. Should there be a major crop failure (as there was in the Soviet Union in 1974), enormous shipments of wheat from many producing areas suddenly are required. The demand for ships exceeds the number available, and freight rates climb precipitately.

In their unceasing search for lucrative cargoes, owners of tramp ships are aided by a network of brokers, agents, and representatives scattered around the world. Reports from these sources about a good opportunity, reinforced by the owners' evaluations of the market, stimulate prompt and decisive action. Vessels not otherwise committed are ordered to proceed to the critical area, and negotiations with potential charterers are initiated. It is, however, a paradox of the tramping business that the very action of these audacious capitalists, who will risk a voyage of thousands of miles on the chance of winning a single profitable cargo, ensures that the high freight rates will be reduced substantially in a relatively brief period. Only while there is a shortage of ships will the rates be inflated. As vessels gather in the exporting area, the scarcity is alleviated, and freight rates plummet. Instead of the gamble paying a premium to the speculator, the adventurer may be forced to accept noncompensatory freight rates to reduce the losses incident to working the ship to other ports where conditions are more favorable.

Tramp shipping came into being about 1850, when the first steam-powered ships were placed in regular, dependable service. Coal mined in England, especially in Wales, fueled the fires under the primitive, low-pressure boilers. To ensure a supply of this indispensable coal, stations along the sea routes were established, and shiploads of "best Welsh coal" were sent out regularly. Often the coaling stations were in active seaports. It did not take many years for a brisk trade to develop exchanging the raw materials of those areas for the products of English mills and factories. British ships, always assured of outbound cargoes of either processed goods or coal, were dispatched worldwide in quest of whatever cargoes they might find.

Steamships cost more to operate than wind-driven sailing ships, but their increased reliability and speed, and particularly the possibility of predicting within a few days the exact time of arrival of a cargo, erased that pecuniary disadvantage. Furthermore, the decreased time needed to com-

A general-purpose tramp of 26,592 tons deadweight, the 15-knot *Mario G.L.* was built in 1974. Photograph by Jeff Blinn, courtesy Moran Towing Co.

plete a voyage, as compared with the sailing ship, meant that a single steamship could carry more tonnage during a year than could its more beautiful rival. If proof of the economy of the powered vessel were needed, this was to be seen in the records of performance.

In 1900, the ordinary general-purpose tramp steamer had a deadweight of about 5,000 to 6,000 tons and a service speed of approximately 9 knots. At that same time, the best and most modern tramp, which was not the typical ship, had a cargo capacity of 7,000 tons. When operated with a clean bottom and in fair weather (Force 4 on the Beaufort scale of winds), this standard-raising ship had a speed of 11 knots. As described by the novelist William McFee, who served for years as an engineer in such a ship, the hull was 100 meters (328 feet) long, had a beam of 14.4 meters (48 feet), and was fitted with a full rounded bow. She had no tween decks. Three boilers collectively burned 25 tons of the best Welsh coal each day as they supplied steam to the triple expansion reciprocating engine of 1,800 indicated horsepower. One set of cargo booms was installed over each of the four or five hatches. Such a ship would find employment carrying coal outward from England and returning in due course with a cargo of ore in bulk, cotton in bales, or sugar in bags.

From 1900 to 1914, the size of the ordinary general-purpose dry-cargo ships increased slightly to a maximum of 7,000 tons deadweight. Greater engineering efficiency reduced fuel consumption while raising the

The "Fortune" class of 20,000-ton, 15.5-knot, general-purpose carrier was built in Japan to replace World War II Liberty ships. Courtesy Ishikawajima Harima Heavy Industries.

speed of many tramps to about 10 knots. Until the end of World War I, coal remained the almost universal fuel.[5]

Between 1919 and 1939, the size of ships was enlarged gradually to about 10,000 tons deadweight, and oil fuel began to displace coal. During this period, the diesel engine, which had first been installed in a seagoing vessel only in 1912, attracted the attention of forward-looking shipowners.

The extensive ship construction program undertaken by the United States during World War II produced thousands of ships of a single standardized design. Beginning in 1946, the 10,500-ton deadweight Liberty ship was sold worldwide and quickly became the universal general-purpose tramp. Unlike the earlier ships of this size and type, the Liberty had a single tween deck, which enhanced her adaptability for both bulk and package cargoes.[6] Until they were twenty years old (1962 and afterwards), Liberties were used on every international trade route.

Not until about 1950 did the size of dry-cargo ships begin to grow significantly. As the ravages of war were repaired and European shipyards returned to full productivity, the requirements of seaborne commerce were met by new designs that called for longer, wider, and deeper-draft hulls

The "S.D. 14" was designed in England and was the most successful peacetime series–built ship in history. Photograph by Turner, courtesy Austin & Pickersgill Shipbuilders.

with a deadweight of about 14,000 or 15,000 tons. In 1968, a British shipyard, Austin and Pickersgill, introduced its replacement for the aging Liberties. The "S.D. 14"—a title derived from the technical description of "Shelter Decker, 14,000 tons deadweight"—gained widespread acceptance, and a total of 211 ships of this design were built, making this the most successful series-produced ship in peacetime history. It is especially noteworthy that this undertaking was entirely privately financed.[7]

Concurrent with the entry into service of increasingly larger general-purpose tramp ships was the development of the bulk carrier as a vehicle to be used exclusively for the transportation of coal, grain, and ore. Whereas the distinctive iron ore carriers that had been in existence since early in the century were used exclusively in this trade, the new ships were designed to operate efficiently and economically when fully loaded with coal, grain, or ore. Demand for transportation of these goods was sufficiently great and sustained to justify constructing vessels of the unprecedented size of 40,000 tons deadweight. So successful were these units that all upper limits on size were lifted, and ships of previously unimagined dimensions and cargo capacity were designed, built, and put into operation; the largest ore carrier is the Norwegian-owned *Berge Stahl.*[8]

Although restricted in their choice of cargoes and, because of their great size, limited to the larger ports and harbors, these specialized carriers

With all hatches open, the 121,500-tons deadweight bulk carrier *Endeavor* (built 1975) awaits her cargo. Courtesy Overseas Shipholding Group.

are offered on the world market for charters whereby the shipowner allows a person or company to hire (*charter*) the vessel for a specified voyage (*voyage charter*) or a specific period of time (*time charter*). The vessels carry cargoes to destinations named by the charterers. They compete with other ships of their type and with the general-purpose tramps for whatever cargo may be available. This has intensified the traditional struggle for employment of the conventional general-purpose tramp, but it has not eliminated the smaller ship from the maritime scene. Unlike its competitor, the smaller vessel can enter almost any port of commercial significance and can be berthed at existing facilities. Furthermore, when compared to the huge specialized carrier, the smaller size of the general-purpose ship better serves the needs of many charterers.

A manufacturer of fertilizer, for instance, normally processes 15,000 tons of phosphate rock each week and has a stockpile of approximately 50,000 tons. By chartering tramps of 15,000 tons cargo capacity and scheduling them to deliver one shipload of phosphate rock about every six to ten days, the manufacturer keeps the stockpile at a satisfactory level and has sufficient reserve to operate without interruption even if the ships are delayed by as much as three weeks.

The modern general-purpose tramp is intended to serve several different trades. In one year, for example, a fleet of four tramps lifted cargoes of pig iron, black iron, wheat middling pellets, scrap iron, logs, timber, tapioca, wood chips, coconut oil cake, ilmenite sand, iron ore, grain coal, bauxite, and cement.[9] Designed to operate in ports that have relatively shallow depth and only a minimum of port facilities (*wharves, piers,* and *transit sheds* with their supporting *upland areas*), these general-purpose ships are equipped with sufficient booms, derricks, or cranes to make them *self-sustaining* (i.e., capable of being loaded and discharged by using their own gear).

Competition in the tramping trades is at least partly dependent on the ship's registry. The variances in freight rates reflect the differences in the operating costs of ships flying different national flags. The cost comparison table illustrates the cost of operating the same ship, a bulk carrier of 30,000 tons deadweight, under each of three national registries. The cost of fuel is not included.

COMPARISON OF SHIP OPERATING COSTS

Cost Category / Registry	Registry "A"	Registry "B"	Registry "C"
Crew	$2,800,000	$1,500,000	$500,000
Stores	300,000	130,000	110,000
Maintenance and repair	600,000	160,000	130,000
Administration and overhead	240,000	70,000	35,000
Insurance	380,000	210,000	120,000
Taxes and fees	1,264,000	609,000	10,000
Total	$5,584,000	$2,679,000	$905,000

Source: *Fairplay,* January 21, 1988, 11. Figures are typical; they do not represent the experience of individual shipowners.

MANAGEMENT OF TRAMP SHIPS

Until 1956, when international transportation of cargoes loaded in containers began, tramps engaged in the foreign trade of the United States vied with the cargo liners for bulk cargoes such as grain, lumber, and some types of ore. The liners would seek "parcels" of 3,000 to 5,000 tons to fill otherwise unused space and would quote freight rates that were barely adequate to cover the cost of stevedoring. This practice hurt the tramps because they had to accept these same low rates for full loads of 8,000 to 12,000 tons. The disappearance of the breakbulk cargo liner on most of these trade routes has often been accompanied by the entry of the specialized large bulkers, thus perpetuating and accentuating the competition with which the general-purpose tramp must deal.

Depreciation—the annual provision made by a prudent owner to write off the value of the units of his fleet—is based usually on a theoretical twenty-year life for a ship. In the tramp trade, however, earnings are not so consistent that it is feasible each year to put into the depreciation account an even 5 percent of the purchase price, as good financial practice might suggest. Some owners strive to cut the book value of new ships by as much as they can afford in the first two or three years of ownership and after that as earnings permit. The sooner a ship's value is written off, the more quickly the owner may compete for cargoes in the bad years. The purchase price may have been amortized by the time the vessel is twenty years old, but replacement is not automatic. So long as cargoes can be found and the vessel can meet minimum standards of seaworthiness, owners are likely to continue to operate the old ship.

The owner and operator of a tramp ship must bend every effort to effect the best possible employment of the unit. Every manager aspires to arrange a series of charter commitments that follow one another closely and leave little idle time during which the ship earns no revenue. Should the decision be made to keep the ship under voyage charters—where the returns are higher but the risks of finding continuous employment are greater than in the longer-term time charter activity—it is necessary to be extremely selective in making commitments. For example, an excellent rate was offered for a tramp ship to carry a cargo of grain from New Orleans to Calcutta. Before accepting it, the owner sought assurance that the business would not lose money because of the high cost of sending the ship to the area of her next employment. Market research revealed these possibilities after discharging the cargo in Calcutta:

1. To proceed in ballast to Australia to pick up wheat for delivery in either the United Kingdom or the Bordeaux-Hamburg range of the European continent
2. To proceed in ballast from India to Mauritius to load a full cargo of sugar for a port on the Atlantic coast of either Canada or the northern range of the United States
3. To proceed to Marmagoa, India, to take on a load of ore for Japan. From Japan, these were the potential opportunities for employment: (a) to sail in ballast to the Philippines to load copra for Europe; (b) to go to the Philippines for a cargo of sugar for a United States port on the Gulf of Mexico or the Atlantic coast; or (c) to proceed in ballast to British Columbia for either a cargo of grain for Europe or a full load of lumber for the Atlantic coast of the United States.

In the complex world of tramp shipping, owners rely upon representatives (ship brokers) to find cargoes for them to carry. Necessarily, these brokers must have extensive knowledge of the movement of goods in international trade, of conditions prevailing in those areas where ships are in greatest demand, and of possible opportunities arising out of unexpected circumstances. While some brokers look for any cargoes the ships of their principals can carry, other brokers specialize in one certain trade, such as grain, and devote their time to matching offerings of grain to the available ships. In either case, it is essential that owner and broker work harmoniously to keep the ship(s) filled and sailing.

The center of this activity is in London. The physical headquarters are found in the Baltic Exchange, not far from the Thames River and the famous Tower Bridge. Here at the Baltic, brokers, elected individually to membership based on their personal integrity, knowledge, and resourcefulness, meet to work out charters for their principals. It is often more expeditious for the broker, using the information provided by the principal, to find a ship (or a cargo, depending upon which is represented) at the Baltic than to canvass offices by telephone. The very recent availability of greatly improved means of communication, however, has reduced the need for face-to-face communication, and today, fewer brokers are seen on the floor of the Baltic Exchange compared with the period before 1970. A typical but imaginary example of such a transaction follows.

Angus MacAndrew of Glasgow is seeking a cargo for his ship, the *Highlander,* now at anchor in Hampton Roads, Virginia. MacAndrew notifies John Lawson, his broker in London, who consults other brokers on the floor of the Baltic. In short order, he learns from Basil Smith that Li Wong in Shanghai needs a ship to carry grain to China from either an Atlantic or a Gulf Coast port of the United States. Following discussions between Lawson and Smith, agreement is reached as to price and terms and, after the principals approve, the ship is "fixed," the technical term for being taken under charter. Before the sun sets in London, the *Highlander* has been notified of her next employment and is en route to the loading port.

Most chartering procedures commence with discussion of the acceptability of the standard charter party (contract) for the particular trade to which the ship is to be assigned. These agreements have been drawn up primarily by shipowners groups such as the Baltic and International Maritime Council,[10] a multinational association of many tramp ship owners that has its headquarters in Copenhagen. The contracts incorporate the experience gained from hundreds of voyages in individual trades. While these standard charter parties are revised and brought up to date as frequently as possible, the circumstances prevailing at a particular moment may necessitate mutual agreement on minor modifications in some clauses, changes of substance in other clauses, and deletion of inapplicable or unwanted terms. Great care must be exercised to ensure that the changes do not run counter to court rulings, established practices of the trade, or other clauses in the contract. Brokers, of course, are expected to safeguard the interests of their principals.

Once a broker has made a firm offer for a vessel, the potential charterer is assured that until the option is exercised or allowed to die, the quotation remains in effect, despite other more attractive offers. Because the market is volatile, options are usually written for no more than one or two days. Only after agreement has been reached and negotiations completed are the details of the formal contract drawn up.[11] To prevent confusion, especially when international telephone conversations are involved, it has become common practice to confirm all offers and counteroffers by cable or electronic facsimile reproduction of documents (fax), but these written messages do not replace the spoken pledges made by the brokers.

Brokers need to know the level of freight rates prevailing from day to day. Fortunately for them and for shipowners also, reports (or "fixtures") of ships under charter are published daily in bulletins compiled by large brokerage houses or the maritime trade journals. The technical language of these reports conveys the essentials of the transactions in a minimum of words. The fixture of the *Highlander,* for instance, would be publicized in a paragraph like this:

> U.S. Northern Range to coast of China. Motorship *Highlander,*
> British flag, 27,000 tons, 5 percent, heavy grain, $36.50; option two
> ports China $37.50, 60¢ extra for U.S. Gulf loading option; FIOT,
> three days load, SHEX, ten days discharge, SHINC, $10,000 demurrage, $5,000 dispatch; Feb. 1–12.

Interpreted for the nonprofessional, this reports that the motorship *Highlander,* British registry, has been chartered to carry about 27,000 tons of heavy grain, plus or minus 5 percent at the master's discretion to obtain a seaworthy load and still store and fuel the ship adequately without losing too much revenue. The grain will be loaded in a port between Cape Hatteras, North Carolina, and Portland, Maine, and transported to the coast of China for $36.50 per ton loaded. If the charterer elects to discharge the cargo in two ports in China, the freight rate will be increased to $37.50 per ton. Should the ship proceed to a United States port on the Gulf of Mexico to take on her cargo, the charter will pay 60¢ additional per ton. FIOT (free in and out and trimmed) means that all expenses connected with loading, discharging, and trimming are for the account of the charterer. It is the charterer's responsibility to have the cargo ready to be loaded and to arrange for its discharge. Three days, Sundays and holidays excluded (Shex), are allowed to load; ten days, Sundays and holidays included (Shinc), are allowed to discharge. If either of these times is exceeded, the charterer will be assessed a charge (demurrage) of $10,000 per day; if the cargo-working time is less than what is allowed, the shipowner will pay the charterer $5,000 (dispatch) per day. The *Highlander* must not report earlier than February 1 or later than February 12.

A somewhat different situation is faced when a shipowner has an offer for a voyage charter with option to place the vessel under time charter. The following considerations must be taken into account before a decision is reached.

The contract calls for transporting a specified quantity of a certain cargo between named ports; it is limited to the time required to load, to travel from port to port, and to discharge; and it is fulfilled when delivery of the cargo is completed. Should the voyage be lengthened by unexpected heavy weather, the added expense must be borne by the owner. Similarly, unless otherwise provided by the contract, interruptions to cargo-working operations attributable to adverse weather conditions such as heavy rains, snow, or exceptionally high winds are charged to the owner. For self-protection, the owner may stipulate the number of days allowed to load and to discharge the cargo or may require a certain number of tons to be handled in each 24-hour period. Notwithstanding the hazards mentioned, which are not all-inclusive, the great inducement for an owner to offer a ship for a voyage charter is that the freight is usually greater than would be the hire under a time charter, and the opportunity remains for the owner to take advantage of a possible increased demand for ships and the consequent higher vessel income. The time charter does restrict the shipowner's control to some extent, without reducing the responsibility for the operation of the ship. Whether to put the vessel under voyage or time charter therefore requires evaluation of the potential earning of the ship under each type of charter. The following example illustrates the procedure.

A bulk carrier of 64,000 tons deadweight is offered a voyage charter paying $12.00 per ton of cargo loaded. The estimated time to complete the charter is forty days. Operating expenses, including fuel and port fees but excluding cargo loading and discharging costs, amount to $16,400 a day. A total of 61,800 tons is available for cargo after deducting the tonnage required for fuel, stores, and water. Based on that capacity, at the proposed rate of $12.00 per ton, the revenue from the charter would be $741,600, against which expenses of $656,000 would be offset, leaving net earnings of $85,600.

Cargo revenue, 61,800 tons @ $12.00/ton	$741,600
Voyage expense, 40 days @ $16,400/day	656,000
Earnings from the voyage	$ 85,600

The alternative employment is to place the ship under time charter. Neither fuel nor port fees would be charged to the shipowner, whose operating cost would thus be reduced from $16,400 to $12,000 per day. Voyage revenue would be $480,000. To equal the earning under the voyage charter, the owner would have to charge enough to bring in an additional $85,600, for a total of $565,600. Divided by the number of days required to fulfill the contract, the charter hire per day would be $14,140, equivalent to $9.15 per ton of cargo delivered.

Net voyage expense, 40 days @ $12,000/day	$480,000
Earning from voyage charter	85,600
Revenue required from 40-day time charter	$565,600
Charter hire per day	$ 14,140
Rate per ton of cargo delivered	$ 9.15

"Working the market" requires that the charterer must be well informed about the availability of ships and the fluctuations of the market and must take into account that rates vary for the same commodity on different trade routes and at different seasons of the year. The operator must be aware of practically everything the charterer should know besides mastering a wide assortment of facts and details that are part of business life. Attention must be given to conditions in ports and harbors around the world— the charges made for handling ships, the efficiency of dockworkers, the availability of cargo-working equipment, the peculiarities of depths, tides, winds, ice and fog anchorages, and local customs concerning the use of pilots and tugs. Because ships frequently need repairs, it is important that the owner be aware of what facilities are available in the ports to which the ships may be sent. Establishing contacts in anticipated ports of call will ease the acquisition of pertinent data and reports of developments affecting shipping in those waters. Certainly high on the list of concerns of the shipowner is where and how to obtain the proper grade of fuel at times when quality is highly variable.

A notable example of excellent management is to be seen in the case of the *Scandic Wasa,* a motorship of 20,280 tons deadweight. On fuel consumption per day of 25 tons of intermediate fuel oil, the ship had a speed of 14½ knots. She also burned an average of 1½ tons of diesel fuel per day.

The first charter of the *Scandic Wasa* took effect at Amsterdam, when she went under time charter for a voyage to the Arabian Gulf at a rate of $7,350 per day. She was tendered in September. When this charter expired in November, the vessel was placed under another time charter from the Arabian Gulf to Japan via India. The rate was $12.50 per deadweight ton per month, equivalent to $8,450 per day. The duration of the charter was the time needed to accomplish the single voyage.

On her arrival in Japan, the owners of the *Scandic Wasa* welcomed the ship with instructions concerning another time charter. This called for a voyage with cargo from Japan by way of the Cape of Good Hope to a grain loading port on the Rio de la Plata in Argentina. The time charter hire was $10.70 per deadweight ton per month, equal to $7,233 per day.

The voyage from Japan to Argentina was accomplished in due course, but some delays were experienced on the ship's arrival in the river. The next employment for the *Scandic Wasa* was a time charter from Argentina to Italy at a rate of $13.75 per deadweight ton per month ($9,292 per day). Discharged in Naples, the hard-working tramp continued in ballast to the nearby port of Casablanca, Morocco, to pick up a cargo of phosphate rock destined for Avonmouth, England. On completion of that assignment, she sailed in ballast for Detroit, Michigan, where further employment awaited her.

A frequent experience in tramp shipping is the necessity to send the ship on a fairly long voyage (as in this case, when the *Scandic Wasa* went to Detroit) at the owner's expense to reach the port where the next charter becomes effective. Sometimes the charterer can be induced to pay a "ballast bonus" to help in meeting the cost of the voyage to the loading port. This desirable circumstance normally occurs, however, only when there is an existing or anticipated shortage of ships at the loading point or the voyage is to commence at a place off the normal sea routes.

Finding appropriate employment for ships requires considerable management time and effort. The result of good management is a fleet of fully utilized ships that take advantage of both voyage and time charters.[12]

OPERATION OF TRAMP SHIPS

Tramp shipping can be profitable when there is a brisk demand for transportation of cargoes moving in bulk, and it can be disastrous when, for

The size of the 163,760-tons-deadweight ore-oil carrier *Garden Green* (build 1973) is clearly evident. She was 280 meters long, 47.4 meters wide, with a draft of 17.7 meters. Courtesy Overseas Shipholding Group.

reasons beyond any possibility of control by the owner, there is a sudden reduction in this demand. In a sense, the tramp ship's owner is nearly always at a disadvantage in the marketplace, because only very rarely is the supply of ships so small that owners can set prices on a "take or leave" basis. One economist noted that the shipowner is a "price taker," meaning that the charterer usually dictates the maximum for ocean freights. Even granting that bold and venturesome carriers may send their ships to new geographical regions or reassign them to different trades, for the most part the owners' freedom to demand high rates is strictly limited.

Competition from the large bulk carrier began about 1950 and it has had a profound impact upon the tramping industry. Up to 1950, iron ore, coal, grain, and lumber moved in the available ships. When demand for iron ore suddenly exploded, the steel industry chose the big, semi-specialized bulk carrier. Since then, these ships have effectually driven the general-purpose tramp out of the metallic ores trade.

An additional and unexpected problem for the tramp owner was the invasion of the grain trade by tankers. A portable suction device was perfected with which wheat and other grains could be unloaded from ships by pneumatic action rather than by the conventional discharging equipment of the "marine leg" with its endless chain of buckets and a conveyor belt leading to the shoreside receptacles. Experimental loads were placed in tankers and emptied with the "vacuveyors." The experiments were successful, and literally scores of tankers were chartered to carry grain. They were attractive to shippers because the cargo tanks were comparatively small, the hatch openings were of minimum size, and neither shifting boards nor feeders were needed. These advantages were translated into actual cash savings not only in the cost of these fittings, but also in ship time. Modern dry-cargo bulkers have attempted to meet the competition by installing quickly portable shifting boards that are part of the ship's outfit and can be set up or removed in a short time by the ship's crew.

Tramp owners, as earlier noted, depend upon ship brokers to find employment for their ships. To describe the relationship between them, the daily drama of chartering vessels is simulated in this fictional situation.

King Corporation is a wheat exporting firm in Chicago that purchases grain in the American market and then sells it to European customers. It does not, however, own any ships, leaving the burdens of ship operation to specialists, and it relies upon brokers to find suitable ships invariably taken on voyage charters.

A French importer has purchased 200,000 tons of American wheat (heavy grain) through King Corporation and has directed that delivery of the first shipload of at least 60,000 tons be made by March 30. King is to make all arrangements and pay for the transport of the wheat. Both King and the importer require that the vessel chartered must hold the highest rating from the ship classification organization.

Through its New York broker, James Sharp, King seeks an acceptable ship at the lowest possible freight rate. Sharp canvasses the other brokerage houses but finds nothing listed in New York that meets King's requirements. Sharp therefore cables his London counterpart, Thomas White, to ask for assistance, well aware that White can go to the Baltic Exchange and in short order can offer a suitable ship. The cable to White is phrased in these words:

RELIABLE PRINCIPAL OFFERS FIRM CARGO OF 60,000 TO 70,000 TONS HEAVY GRAIN NEW ORLEANS TO ONE PORT BORDEAUX-HAMBURG RANGE, LOADING NEW ORLEANS FIRST HALF MARCH. WILL USE GRAINVOY CHARTER.

White understands from this cable that a ship able to carry not less than 60,000 tons of cargo in addition to fuel, stores, and water must be in New Orleans ready to load between March 1 and 15. The charter party to be used is a well-known document developed specifically for grain ship-ments. White has a copy of the Grainvoy charter party in his office.

Perusal of the list of ships represented by White shows that none of these vessels will be ready within the time limits. White therefore goes to the floor of the Baltic Exchange, where he meets brokers seeking cargoes for their principals' ships and other brokers looking for ships to transport cargoes. White quickly meets Harrison Burnett, who represents Olav Berg, a Norwegian owner domiciled in Bergen. Burnett tells White that Berg's big motorship *Great Viking* will be off-hire in a Texas port about the end of February. White requests a firm offer of this ship, and Burnett accordingly cables Berg, his principal, as follows:

> FIRST-CLASS CHARTERER MAKES FIRM OFFER OF CARGO OF 60,000 TO 70,000 TONS HEAVY GRAIN NEW ORLEANS TO ONE PORT BORDEAUX-HAMBURG RANGE. LOADING NEW ORLEANS MARCH FIRST THROUGH FIFTEENTH. USING GRAINVOY CHARTER. PLEASE OFFER FIRM BY FIFTEEN HUNDRED HOURS LONDON TIME TODAY.

Berg is pondering how to work his ship back to Norway. White's in-vitation to offer the *Great Viking* fits his desires exactly, so he immediately responds to Burnett with this cable:

> NORWEGIAN MOTORSHIP GREAT VIKING, SERVICE SPEED ABOUT 15 KNOTS, 70,000 TONS DEADWEIGHT, 79,500 CUBIC METERS GRAIN CAPACITY. SEVEN HOLDS, GEARLESS, CLASSED HIGHEST AT DET NORSKE VERITAS, NOW DISCHARGING HOUSTON AND EXPECTED READY TO LOAD AFTER MARCH SECOND. SUBJECT TO REPLY REACHING US BY SEVENTEEN HUNDRED HOURS TOMORROW BERGEN TIME, AUTHORIZE YOU TO NEGOTIATE FOR FULL CARGO HEAVY GRAIN 62,000 METRIC TONS, FIVE PERCENT MORE OR LESS AT VESSEL'S OPTION FROM ONE US GULF PORT TO ONE PORT BORDEAUX-HAMBURG RANGE. DISCHARGING PORT DECLARABLE ON SIGNING BILLS OF LADING. CANCELING DATE MARCH TENTH. FREIGHT EIGHTEEN DOLLARS FIFTY CENTS PER METRIC TON, FREE IN AND OUT AND TRIMMED, LOADING AND UNLOADING SIX WEATHER WORKING DAYS, SUNDAYS AND HOLIDAYS INCLUDED. LAYTIME REVERSIBLE. DEMURRAGE FOURTEEN THOUSAND

THREE HUNDRED DOLLARS PER DAY, DISPATCH HALF
DEMURRAGE. ALL DOLLAR QUOTATIONS PREDICATED ON
EXCHANGE RATE US DOLLARS TO NORWEGIAN KRONER
PREVAILING CLOSE OF BUSINESS ON DAY BILLS OF LADING
ARE SIGNED. GRAINVOY CHARTER ACCEPTABLE EXCEPT
LAYTIME FOR LOADING TO COMMENCE AT NINETEEN
HUNDRED HOURS IF NOTICE OF READINESS TENDERED
BETWEEN THIRTEEN AND SEVENTEEN HUNDRED HOURS.
DEMURRAGE TO BE PAID PER DAY OR PER HALF DAY AND
NOT OTHERWISE PRORATED. BROKERAGE COMMISSIONS
PAYABLE MAXIMUM THREE PERCENT OF CHARTER HIRE.

Burnett immediately visits White's office, and the two brokers analyze the message from Berg. The ship can lift the minimum quantity of grain specified by Sharp and can be in New Orleans within the time limit. The obligation to declare the port of discharge at the time the bills of lading are signed by the master is consistent with good chartering practice: the master must know the destination of the voyage he is about to undertake. The freight rate assigned all costs of handling the grain at both loading and unloading ports to the charterer. The time allotted to take grain aboard and to discharge it is adequate given the facilities at the port of New Orleans and the probable destination ports, and it allows for the possibility that one port may be superior to another in its ability to work ships rapidly. By permitting whatever time is saved in one port to be credited toward the working days in the other port, the charterer is encouraged to use the hours effectively. Demurrage is an essential part of any voyage charter and usually represents the owner's cost and a very small margin of profit. Berg obviously is eager for the business, since he offers to pay brokerage commissions a little higher than the normal rate of 2½ percent.

White considers that the terms of the offer are fair and reasonable when compared with the current charter market and sends a cable to Sharp in New York, relaying everything except the rate of commission, which for Sharp's information is quoted as 1 percent. For his part, Sharp notifies King Corporation of the offer and is instructed to make a counter proposal, which is presented to White in this cablegram:

REFERENCE YOUR CABLE OF YESTERDAY OFFERING GREAT
VIKING. SUBJECT TO REPLY REACHING US BY SEVENTEEN
HUNDRED HOURS TODAY NEW YORK TIME CHARTERER
ACCEPTS OWNER'S OFFER EXCEPT LAY DAYS TO BE MARCH

FOURTH TO TWELFTH INCLUSIVE. FREIGHT RATE TO BE
SEVENTEEN DOLLARS AND TWENTY-FIVE CENTS. LAYTIME TO
BE SEVEN DAYS SUNDAYS AND HOLIDAYS EXCLUDED.
DEMURRAGE TO BE THIRTEEN THOUSAND SEVEN HUNDRED
DOLLARS PER DAY PAYABLE DAY BY DAY AND PRORATED
FOR ANY PART OF A DAY.

On receipt of this message, White presents the modifications to Burnett, who, as a broker, has no authority to accept or reject the proposed changes. He therefore relays the cable to Berg by fastest means.

Berg meanwhile has noted that the charter market is weak, and that his original offer of $18.50 is out of competition. A recomputation of the cost of the anticipated voyage shows that a rate of $17.00 would yield an acceptable profit. He knows that once grain loading and discharging operations commence, they proceed without stop. He is aware that he is under pressure to pay dispatch money when the charterer asks for seven days cargo-working time. There also is the demand for the ship to stand idle on Sundays and holidays, which would cut into the profit remaining when the rate is reduced to the proposed figure per ton. All these factors having been given due consideration, Berg sends this cable to Burnett:

REFERENCE YOUR CABLE REGARDING GREAT VIKING.
CHARTERER'S COUNTER OFFERS ACCEPTABLE EXCEPT
LAYTIME REMAINS AT SIX WEATHER WORKING DAYS SUNDAYS
AND HOLIDAYS INCLUDED.

Burnett notifies White of this response, and the information is transmitted immediately to Sharp in New York, who recommends to King Corporation that the terms set by the shipowner be accepted without further negotiation. King is pleased that the freight rate has been reduced and concedes the other modifications. Sharp therefore is instructed to close the deal, which is done by this cable to White:

REFERENCE YOUR CABLE. GREAT VIKING ACCEPTED.
CHARTERER IS KING CORPORATION OF CHICAGO.
AUTHORIZE YOU TO SIGN CHARTER ON CHARTERER'S
BEHALF BUT AS BROKER ONLY. AIRMAIL SIX COPIES
OF COMPLETED CHARTER. THANK YOU FOR YOUR
EFFORTS.

White passes the word to Burnett, who notifies Berg that his ship has been fixed for the voyage. Berg acknowledges this message in the following cable:

REFERENCE YOUR CABLE CONCERNING GREAT VIKING. THIS CONFIRMS THAT TERMS AS APPROVED BY CHARTERER ARE ACCEPTABLE. SHIP WILL BE ORDERED TO NEW ORLEANS TO ARRIVE MARCH FOURTH. AUTHORIZE YOU TO SIGN CHARTER AS MY BROKER. SEND ME THREE COPIES OF CHARTER. THANK YOU FOR THIS BUSINESS.

Burnett relays this confirmation of the charter to White, who closes his file with this cablegram to Sharp:

RECONFIRM FIXTURE OF GREAT VIKING. SHIP ORDERED TO ARRIVE NEW ORLEANS MARCH FOURTH. THANK YOU FOR THIS BUSINESS.

Negotiations having been brought to a successful conclusion, the charter party is filled out by White's staff, and copies are distributed as directed by the principals. The original document, duly signed by Burnett and White, is filed in the vault at White's office and is available to authorized persons anytime.

Berg composes a brief message instructing the master of the *Great Viking* to sail for New Orleans to arrive in that city during the forenoon of March 4, so that loading can commence that same day. This cablegram is followed by an airmail letter enclosing a copy of the charter party and specific instructions for the conduct of the voyage. In the gracious tradition of shipping, this letter is concluded with the statement: "We take this opportunity to express the hope that you will have a pleasant and satisfactory voyage."

For their part in the transaction, the three brokers will each receive 1 percent of the net earnings of the *Great Viking* under the charter, after demurrage or dispatch is paid.

A relatively new development in chartering made its debut in 1985 when the Baltic Freight Index (BFI) and the Baltic International Freight Futures Exchange (BIFFEX) began operations. Through the buying and selling of freight futures, it now is possible for shipowners or charterers to protect themselves against the likelihood that charter hire will decline or rise before the ship is available to lift a cargo or before the cargo is ready for transportation. There is also an opportunity here for private investors to earn money in this futures market.

The BFI (or "the index") is a property of the Baltic Exchange. Each working day, a select group of mostly London-based ship brokers makes independent assessments of the rates for charters of bulk ships of 50,000 tons (Panamax) and more than 80,000 tons (Cape-size), respectively, on eleven routes. These routes and ship sizes are considered to represent most accurately the overall market for chartered ships. The index, however, is dynamic in nature and if it is determined that certain routes or ship sizes are no longer representative of the market, they may be changed. On seven of the eleven routes, the rates are for voyage charters; the remaining four are estimates of the time charter hire for bulkers of 64,000 tons deadweight. The highest and the lowest rates are discarded, and the remainder are weighted and processed to produce the index for the day.

BALTIC FREIGHT INDEX

Sept. 2, 1999

CURRENT: 1038   PREVIOUS DAY: 1039

The Baltic International Freight Futures Market in London offers owners and charterers in the bulk shipping community a forum for futures trading of a freight rate index. The contracts are based on the Baltic Freight Index, announced daily, of 11 routes listed below.

Routes	Commodity	Weight	Dollars/ Metric Ton	Index
U.S. Gulf–N. Continent	L. grain	10%	11.957	1317
Trans-Atlantic Round	Time charter	10%	8,117*	1072
U.S. Gulf–Japan	H. grain	10%	19.407	1404
Skaw Passero–Taiwan/Japan	Time charter	10%	9,006*	1098
U.S. North Pacific–Japan	H. grain	10%	10.350	1171
Trans-Pacific Round	Time charter	10%	5,188*	657
Hampton Roads/Rotterdam	Coal	7.5%	4.419	908
Far East–Europe	Time charter	10%	4,850*	555
Tubarano-Rotterdam	Iron ore	7.5%	4.522	895
Tubaroa-China	Iron ore	7.5%	7,140	1010
Richards Bay–Rotterdam	Coal	7.5%	5.761	1087

   * Dollars per day

   Source: *The Journal of Commerce,* September 3, 1999, p. 11

In November 1998, a new index called the Baltic Panamax Index (BPI) was introduced and now forms the basis of trading. It is based on seven Panamax routes currently included in BFI, which has been the foundation of BIFFEX since 1985.[13]

Because the index goes up and down as it reflects the freight rate market, shipowners and charterers can use futures as a way of hedging against major increases or catastrophic decreases in charter hire at some time in the future. The fluctuating index forms the basis upon which the BIFFEX assesses the calculation for settlements of contracts at the end of each settlement period.

The BIFFEX, which resulted from a merger between the Baltic Futures Exchange and the London Commodity Exchange, works in a way similar to other futures markets, and its trading practices are governed by the London Commodity Exchange and the London Clearing House. Trading is done through the London International Financial Futures and Options Exchange (LIFFE). Freight futures are also available through several electronic systems to allow market users to react quickly.[14]

Tramp shipping exists to provide the transportation required for those articles of low value exemplified by coal. The tramp ship owner must set freight rates that are low enough to encourage the movement of goods yet high enough to cover the expense of operating the ship and, ideally, to earn at least a small profit.

Establishing cost down to the smallest detail is one way in which the owner attempts to achieve this objective. In this connection, costs mean more than simply the obvious out-of-pocket expenses involved in ship operation; also included must be the less conspicuous items such as amortization, interest, and overhead. For example, a general-purpose tramp with operating costs of $300 an hour is chartered to carry a load of 25,000 tons of coal. Loading at the rate of 750 tons an hour will absorb 34 hours. Only 250 tons are discharged per hour, for a total of 100 working hours. The charter rate must include a charge of 134 hours at $300 per hour ($1.61 per ton) to recover costs.

Some owners develop comprehensive tables of ship costs per deadweight ton that include crew wages and subsistence, vessel maintenance and repair, insurance, amortization, interest, and a contribution toward overhead. Whether the ship is lying in port waiting for assignment or steaming across the ocean, these items do not vary substantially. The costs that do change with the employment of the vessel are fuel, port fees, pilotage, towage, dockage and wharfage, and cargo handling. When all costs are compiled, the owner should add a sum sufficient to cover unforeseen contingencies and to provide a profit. If the market is strong, meaning that there are many cargoes and few ships, these cost figures can be used without trimming

Top: A modern tramp with unusual gantry cranes, the *Bulk Eagle* is well adapted to handle commodities like coal and iron ore. Courtesy Munck International. *Bottom:* Shipboard gantry cranes are paired to handle extra-long items. Courtesy Munck International.

when negotiating for a charter. If, however, the market is considered weak because there are many ships and few cargoes, the owner must exercise the most precise judgment in cutting the estimate of cost to meet the figures quoted by competitors. Sometimes it is necessary to accept business at an actual loss rather than incur the expense of laying up the ship.

Under a gross form voyage charter, for example, a bulk carrier is chartered (fixed) to carry 50,000 tons of coal from Norfolk, Virginia, to Rotterdam at the agreed rate of $10 per ton. The shipowner must pay $5 a ton for loading and discharging the coal. Ship operating expenses are $12,500 a day; for the fifteen days required to load, sail, and discharge, the total cost is $187,500. Cargo handling and ship costs aggregate $437,500, leaving a profit to the owner of $62,500. Any delay in the ship's passage or unexpected increase in the cost of fuel or cargo handling reduces the margin of profit significantly.

Computer technology has given the modern shipowner the capability of sophisticated examination of all the elements of cost and potential profit involved in a proposed voyage. Each element of expense can be identified as a component of the venture. For instance, the speed of the ship can be related to the smoothness of the hull and the cost of fuel when purchased in various bunkering ports. The rapidity with which the proposed cargo can be handled in the ports of loading and discharge can have a major bearing on determining of the length of the voyage. The actual number of tons of a given commodity that can be stowed belowdecks is related to the space needed to hold one weight ton. Detentions may be individually unimportant, but cumulatively they can be disastrous. The profitability of the voyage can be affected by many factors: the willingness of dockworkers to work overtime or on holidays and religious festivals, delays in putting the ship alongside the cargo-working berth, loss of time from shortages of pilots or tugs in the harbor, and hours needed to prepare the ship to accept the proposed load.

In working out the finances of the voyage or voyages, the computer can develop, in any desired detail, such items as these: cost of the ship lying in port at anchor and at the berth working cargo; costs of the ship steaming fully loaded at designed speed; fuel consumption at different speeds and drafts; costs of fuel when purchased at different points along the route compared with the time needed for refueling; port and harbor charges, with particular reference to harbor dues on entering the port and accrued day by day until departure; costs of loading and discharging the cargoes contemplated for the complete voyage; and the costs of overtime paid to use ship's crew when cargo is being worked.

Once these data are available, it is possible to decide the details of the proposed employment of the vessel: the itinerary of the ship, showing for each port the arrival time, waiting time, predictable lost time, and anticipated departure time; costs for each port where cargo is worked, including stevedoring and overtime expenses; and total costs of harbor dues and fees. From these basic figures, management can obtain the cost to transport one ton or a full shipload, the total revenue to be earned on the contemplated voyage, and an analysis of the financial results of the planned employment. This last presentation would include depreciation, interest, overhead, ship operating costs, port charges, cargo-handling expense, and the net profit (or loss) at the offered freight rate.

Just as the computer has made management more systematic and less dependent upon instinct and experience, so the advances in naval architecture and marine engineering have influenced profoundly the development of the tramp fleets of the world. The importance and versatility of the general-purpose tramp have already been set forth. In 1993, the preferred carrier in the bulk trades (except iron ore) had a cargo deadweight between 25,000 and 40,000 tons, adequate cargo gear to be self-sustaining, and a sufficiently shallow draft to permit entrance into almost any port. A recent study by an English maritime consultant pointed out that the multipurpose tramp is being squeezed out of business by containerships and also by the large, efficient, and economical bulk carriers. More than 40 percent of the multipurpose ships are more than twenty years old, and very few replacements have been built or ordered. While these ships are kept in operation, there is demand for them in South America, Southeast Asia, and India. They also find employment in moving cargoes that cannot be packed in containers, and in transporting small lots of 10,000 to 15,000 thousand tons.[15]

The medium-sized bulker is a vessel of approximately 50,000 to 60,000 tons deadweight. This ship has no cargo gear and is popular in both the northern transatlantic and the northern transpacific routes hauling coal and grain.

In the specialized iron ore service, the ship most favored in 1993 was the bulker with a capacity between 100,000 and 125,000 tons of cargo. By assigning these ships to voyages between deep-draft harbors, their utility and inherent economy of scale have been exploited successfully.

Although the demand for tramp ships is undergoing some significant changes, they are still the great equalizers of rates and will remain an important part of the maritime transportation industry. Those individuals who operate and manage tramp ships will still be required to have the same high skills that they have always needed in this competitive and demanding aspect of maritime transportation.

CHAPTER FOUR

Chartering

Annually, hundreds of millions of tons of cargo are moved over the sea routes. Raw materials such as oil, grain, ore, fertilizer, coal, sugar, lumber, steel scrap, copra, and fish meal, usually sent in bulk and in lots large enough to fill ships with a single commodity, are carried from producing regions to consuming areas. Finished products such as automobiles, steel, heavy machinery, and refrigerated cargoes also are transported in consignments large enough to load a ship to capacity. The contract for carrying the goods is known by the generic title of "charter party," a term derived from the Latin "charta partita," literally meaning a "letter divided." In the early days, the contract was copied exactly, and the paper on which the two parts were inscribed then was cut in half, so each of the contracting parties could retain one segment. The charter party is a maritime contract by which the charterer, a party other than the shipowner, obtains the use of a ship for one or more voyages, or for a specified period of time.[1]

Vessels transporting goods under the terms and conditions laid down in the charter party are technically "private carriers," which are operated to suit the needs and schedules of the shipper and the vessel owner. By way of contrast, a carrier who offers transportation for any and all goods offered between the specified ports it serves is known as a "common carrier." An important distinction can be made between the private and the common carrier: a ship loaded with the goods of a single shipper is a private carrier, whereas a vessel carrying the property of two or more shippers is a common carrier.

A private carrier performs the service specified by the owner of the goods—that is to say, it loads the particular cargo at the place designated by the shipper, transports it to the destination named in the contract, and delivers the cargo according to the conditions laid down in the contract, or charter party.

Three types of charters are available. The *voyage charter* is a maritime contract under which the shipowner agrees to transport, for an agreed fee (technically known as freight) per ton of cargo loaded, a stipulated quantity of a named cargo between two or more designated ports. The shipowner retains full responsibility for operation of the ship.

The *time charter* is a maritime contract setting forth the terms under which a person other than the shipowner obtains the use of the vessel for a specified period of time to trade within broad but defined limits, carrying any cargoes not positively barred by the wording of the contract. Compensation, known as charter hire, may be at an agreed sum per deadweight ton per month or at a fixed amount per day. The owner remains in all respects the operator of the vessel; the charterer, among other obligations, assumes responsibility for loading and discharging the cargoes; the charterer also pays the cost of fuel, pilotage, and wharfage and dockage, among other items of operational cost.

The *bareboat charter* (or *demise charter*) is a maritime contract by which a vessel is transferred in all but title from the owner to a separate party for a specified period of time. Among members of the legal profession, it is referred to as a "demise charter," the full implications of which will be explained later.[2] The charterer pays compensation (charter hire), either at an agreed amount per deadweight ton per month or a fixed sum per day. All burdens and responsibilities of operation, including hiring officers and crew and maintaining the vessel in good condition, are assumed by the charterer, who legally is said to be the owner *pro hac vice* (for this period).[3]

At least as early as 1900, it became apparent to shipowners and their brokers that they encountered identical problems with the repetitious carriage of the same item—coal, grain, or iron ore, for instance. Agreement as to the responsibility of the contracting parties in these instances came to be almost routine and suggested that standardized charter parties for each trade were both desirable and feasible. Under the aegis of what today is known as the Baltic and International Maritime Council (organized under a different name in 1905 and in continuous existence ever since), a number of charter parties were drawn up, printed, given code names, and distributed widely. As adopted and modified for current usage, these forms consist of a number of paragraphs (or clauses) containing pertinent material. Blank spaces are provided where applicable data can be inserted to supply the specific information relating to the particular transaction. It is understood that individual clauses may be modified, rewritten, or deleted as the negotiators decide. Typewritten or handwritten revisions always supersede printed clauses. Examples of such standardized voyage charter party forms include the Americanized Welsh Coal Charter (1979); Norgrain (1989), used for grain of all types; and the Sugar Charter (1977).

Tasks shipowners could do through their associations also seemed within the capability of the cargo shippers. There were, and are, relatively few shippers associations, and therefore reliance was placed on the fraternity of brokers who represented the cargo interests. Brokers, from experience, knew what their principals desired, and they composed standardized charter parties that reflected these wishes. As with the shipowners' charters, these documents were given code names, printed, and distributed widely. An excellent example of a shipper's charter is the NYPE 93, drawn up by the American Ship Brokers Association in 1993.[4]

An appreciation of the scope of a typical standardized charter party is gained by noting the coverage contained in a few of the clauses. For the voyage charter, the blanks are filled with the names of the contracting parties; the cargo to be lifted; the name, registry, and capacity (in deadweight tons and cubic measurement of space below decks) of the ship; the ports of loading and discharge; the freight rate, and when and where this will be paid. Spelled out in detail is the responsibility of the shipowner for the seaworthiness of the vessel and the care and custody of the cargo, the definitions of time allowed for loading and discharging the cargo, and the rights and obligations of both contracting parties in connection therewith.

Time charter parties differ in many respects from the voyage charter party. Both contracts identify the parties to the contract, but the data about the ship are much more complete, as are the geographic limits of the vessel's employment. The time and place of delivery and redelivery are noted precisely. Compensation is usually expressed as a lump sum payable for each day the vessel is under contract; the place, frequency, and manner in which payments are to be made are set forth clearly.

Bareboat (or demise) charter parties are too specialized to make use of standardized phraseology. The details of this form of maritime contract are presented in subsequent pages.

SEAWORTHINESS

Underlying the terms and conditions in any charter party is the implied warranty of seaworthiness, which requires the ship to be fit to carry out the contract. In a decision handed down by the Supreme Court of the United States in 1903, this definition of seaworthiness was approved:

> *Bouvier's Law Dictionary* defines seaworthiness to be: "In maritime law, the sufficiency of the vessel in materials, construction, equipment, officers, men, and outfit for the trade or service in which it is employed." . . . In the case of *The Sylvia* (171 US 462, [1988]), Mr. Justice Gray said, "The test of seaworthiness is whether the vessel

is reasonably fit to carry the cargo which she has undertaken to transport. This is the commonly accepted definition of seaworthiness. As seaworthiness depends not only upon the vessel being staunch and fit to meet the perils of the sea, but upon its character in reference to the particular cargo to be transported, it follows that a vessel must be able to transport the cargo which it is held out to carry, or it is not seaworthy in that respect."

According to this quotation, seaworthiness is a relative term. It is to be considered in relation to the voyage undertaken, the cargo to be transported, and the stowage of that cargo. It is clear, however, that seaworthiness does not require perfection in a ship.

By long-standing decisions of courts of law, the obligation to provide a seaworthy ship is absolute, though this interpretation has been limited in recent years to requiring the shipowner to exercise due diligence to ensure that the vessel is in all respects seaworthy for the service intended. The seaworthiness of the ship remains under the absolute control of the master.[5]

The implied obligation of seaworthiness differs somewhat in the three types of charter parties. Under the voyage charter, the vessel must be seaworthy for the contemplated voyage and the named cargo and must be in that condition when the first ton of cargo is taken aboard and when the anchor breaks ground or the last line is let go. The obligation is related directly to those perils ordinarily encountered on the proposed voyage with the specified cargo. Damage to cargo caused by circumstances beyond the control of the owner, or resulting from an error of navigation, does not invalidate the warranty. If damage is sustained by the ship, however, the shipowner is required to effect the necessary repairs at the earliest possible moment if the ship is to be considered seaworthy.

In the time charter, the shipowner remains the operator of the vessel and therefore has the full responsibility of maintaining the seaworthiness of the vessel at the commencement of every voyage during the contract period. If, for example, the ship is chartered for three years to carry iron ore from Brazil to Japan, making twelve loaded voyages in the three years, the shipowner must exercise due diligence to ensure that the vessel is seaworthy at the beginning of each of the twelve loaded and the twelve ballast voyages and to effect promptly any and all repairs required to maintain the seaworthiness of the vessel.

Pursuant to the terms of the bareboat (or demise) charter, the owner turns over to the charterer the full responsibility for operating the ship. The owner's obligation therefore is limited to the exercise of due diligence to ensure that in all respects the vessel and her equipment are seaworthy (i.e., fit to carry out the terms of the contract) at the time the vessel is presented. Maintaining seaworthiness becomes the charterer's burden once delivery has been accepted.

Included in the implied warranty of seaworthiness is the doctrine of "stages," which asserts that a ship will be seaworthy at the commencement of each phase of a chartered voyage. When the vessel tenders at the loading port, and the charterer is ready to put the cargo aboard, the ship must be seaworthy at that time. In normal shipping practice, vessels often are "bunkered" (fueled) not for the voyage to port of final destination, but to an intermediate port where the availability of the desired oil is assured and the price is lower than at the loading port. In these circumstances, the requirement is that the ship have sufficient fuel on board to reach the intermediate port, with sufficient reserves to protect against unexpected contingencies. Seaworthiness would be determined by the quantity of fuel in the tanks, the projected voyage to the bunkering port, and the contingency reserve. The third stage commences when the ship, with fuel tanks filled, is ready to sail on the last leg of the voyage.[6]

It is important to note that the possession of a document from a classification society certifying the structural soundness of the vessel does not, in itself, serve as conclusive evidence that the ship is seaworthy.[7] Recent events in the maritime world have shown that often ships are allowed to deteriorate seriously during the five-year life of the classification certificate. The owner, therefore, must exercise due diligence to ensure that the vessel, pursuant to the terms of the contract, is seaworthy in all respects.

When the master notifies the charterer that the ship is ready to load, there is an implied warranty that the cargo gear is in all respects serviceable and ready for use. Furthermore, at the beginning of cargo operations, the ship must be fit to take on board the cargo specified in the charter party. This warranty sometimes is referred to as "cargo worthiness." Modern tramp vessels often are built to carry specialized cargo; the cargo worthiness of the ship therefore must be judged in the light of the technical efficiency of the design and equipment at the time loading operations are initiated.[8]

WARRANTIES

Any charterer who takes a ship for a voyage or a period of time faces the possibility of disputes with the owner over the performance of the ship (fuel consumption, sea speed, reliability) as well as over other details of the contract such as below-decks cargo capacity. To protect both parties, the specifics of ship performance and the amount of space below decks must be set forth and mutually agreed upon before the charter party is signed. The shipowner provides, and is responsible for, accurate data and gives assurance that they reflect the facts concerning the ship. These stipulations are known as the "warranties," and failure to live up to them may make the shipowner liable for breach of the contract.

Most of the warranties are provable without difficulty, but speed and fuel consumption are affected noticeably by weather conditions. Should a dispute arise over either or both of these stipulations, there will be discussions between the contracting parties until a satisfactory adjustment is made. Should no compromise be reached in these areas or in any other part of the charter party, the dispute may be referred to arbitrators. Their decision will have the same force as a judgment handed down by a court of law.

A typical time charter, as reported in the maritime press, provides this information, including the warranties:

> Delivery Rotterdam, transatlantic round voyage, redelivery
> Havre/Amsterdam range, May 5 to 10, *Belmount,* Norwegian flag,
> built 1975, 110,444 metric tons deadweight, 4.6 million cubic feet
> grain, 12 knots on 43 tons heavy fuel oil plus 1.5 tons diesel,
> $11,600 daily.

The warranties for the big Norwegian motorship are that she has a total deadweight of 110,444 metric tons, her enclosed cargo stowage space equals 4.6 million cubic feet (grain measurement), and that she will travel at a speed of 12 knots on a daily consumption of 43 tons of high viscosity fuel oil and 1.5 tons of marine diesel oil.

VOYAGE CHARTER

Pursuant to the provisions of the voyage charter, the owner is obligated to provide a fully operational vessel that is seaworthy, i.e., tight, staunch, and strong, and in all respects fitted to carry the proposed cargo on the proposed route. The charterer in turn is required to provide a full load of the named item and to that end may demand that the owner stipulate, as warranties or verifiable facts, the name and classification of the ship, the flag of registry, and the deadweight tonnage and capacity (in cubic feet or cubic meters) below decks. Operational characteristics such as speed, fuel consumption, and date of last drydocking are not a concern of the charterer and therefore normally would be omitted from the warranties of the voyage charter.

The charter party always stipulates the port in which the ship is to be delivered or, in the terms of the trade, "tendered" by the owner. It also specifies the beginning and the ending of the period of days during which tender of the ship may be made. This period is known as "lay days." In addition, the charter party sets forth the date terminating the right of the charterer to cancel the agreement and to refuse to accept tender of the vessel. The owner is protected against arbitrary action by the charterer by this clause in the contract:

> If the vessel cannot be delivered by the canceling date, the Charterer, if required [by the Owner] is to declare within 48 hours (Sundays and holidays excluded) after receiving notice thereof, whether they cancel or will take delivery of the vessel.

To obtain maximum revenue from the voyage, the owner directs the shipmaster to accept as much cargo as the safety of the ship will permit. The charterer, having set the date when the ship is to be tendered, is expected to have the cargo waiting so that no time is lost once the ship has been delivered to the charterer. Any delay for which the charterer is responsible raises the possibility of the charterer paying demurrage—a penalty for holding the ship beyond the period stipulated.[9]

To satisfy the needs and wishes of charterers, the voyage charter must state precisely the responsibilities of the contracting parties for the loading and stowage of cargo. Under the "net form" of voyage charter, the contract provides that the cargo will be worked at the expense of the charterer: free in and out and trimmed (FIOT). This means that the cargo will be put aboard the ship, properly trimmed to give a seaworthy load, and removed from the ship at the expense of the charterer, who is responsible for the handling of the cargo.

Quite different is the contractual arrangement under the "gross form" of voyage charter. Sometimes referred to as a "liner terms" contract, the gross form stipulates that the charterer is obligated only to provide the cargo at the loading port and to accept it at the port of destination. The freight charged includes the cost of stevedoring and all other voyage expenses. The shipowner bears full responsibility for the proper loading, stowage, and discharge of the cargo.

Under the net form, the relevant portion of the clause stipulates that "charterers are to load, stow and trim the cargo at their expense under the supervision of the captain." This preserves the authority of the master to supervise cargo operations, while placing overall responsibility upon the charterers. Loss or damages from a defective stow therefore would be for the account of the charterers.

The definition of "supervision" varies with the courts of law and the board of arbitration that handles disputes between the contracting parties. The master clearly can dictate the cargo stowage plan before loading commences but has limited authority to modify this plan unless it can be shown that the seaworthiness of the ship is threatened if the plan is executed. The literature on the subject is voluminous, but in general the conclusion is that the master may advise and suggest, being careful to ensure that the responsibility for the proper stowage of cargo remains with the charterer.[10]

In many voyage charters, the clause is amended by adding the two words, "and responsibility" after the word "supervision." If this is done, there is no question about the role of the master and the liability of the vessel owner in connection with the stowage of the cargo or for loss or damage to the cargo resulting from deficiency of the stow.[11]

The owner stipulates in the charter party the amount of time (usually expressed in days) allowed for loading and unloading the cargo. This allowance is known as "lay days" or "laytime."[12] Any period exceeding the stated limits will result in demurrage. The counter to demurrage is known as "dispatch," which is paid by the shipowner to the charterer for loading or discharging in less than the stipulated lay days. The amount payable as dispatch usually is one half of the demurrage rate; the theory is that the shipowner stands to gain less by unexpected early completion of loading and discharge than would be needed to cover the costs of delay.[13]

A basic document used to establish the commencement of lay days is the master's "notice of readiness," which must be presented to the charterer when the ship is in all respects ready to receive the cargo or to comply with the orders of the charterer. In an English case decided in 1972, the presiding judge made the following ruling:

> In order to be a good notice of readiness, the master must be in a position to say, "I am ready at the moment you want me, whenever that may be, and any necessary preliminaries on my part to the loading will not be such as to delay you." Applying this test, it is apparent that a notice of readiness can be given even though there are some further preliminaries to be done, or routine matters to be carried on, or formalities observed. If those things are not such as to give any reason to suppose that they will cause any delay, and it is apparent that the ship will be ready when the appropriate time comes, then notice of readiness can be given.[14]

Applying the foregoing to the following case, the importance of the notice of readiness is made manifest.

A tanker was completing service under one charter, and the master notified the owner at 1100 that the ship would be empty and free to receive new orders at 1500. The owner earlier had negotiated a charter that was cancelable at noon. The master was directed to file a notice of readiness with the prospective new charterer, stating that the tanker was available at 1100. The master also was directed to expedite discharge and to present his vessel at the earliest possible moment. When the ship was not delivered to the new charterer at 1100 and still had not reported by noon, the charterer canceled the contract. The owner sued. The court held that the notice of readiness was precisely that and nothing less; either the ship was ready to accept the new charterer's orders or the notice was meaningless. The cancellation of the charter party was upheld, and the owner was held at fault for improperly tendering the notice of readiness.

Under the voyage charter, the charterer is obligated to load the ship to the agreed capacity. The cubic measurement and deadweight tonnage of the vessel therefore are essential elements of the charter party. Freight (payment) is due and payable when the cargo is delivered at the port of discharge. Should the charterer fail to fill the ship to the capacity shown in the charter party, the charterer would be obligated to pay "dead freight"—the amount of money equal to the difference between freight paid on the cargo actually loaded and what would have been earned had the ship been fully loaded.

Some voyage charter parties stipulate a "lump sum" payment. This amount is payable at the port of discharge regardless of how much or how little cargo actually was transported. Normally, such an agreement is made when the exact stowage characteristics of the proposed cargo have not been determined at the time the negotiations are concluded. For example, there is significant variation in the number of cubic feet per weight ton (known as the "stowage factor") required to stow different kinds of grain. If the type of grain is unknown at the time the charter party is signed, a lump sum agreement would be appropriate.

Negotiations for a voyage charter require that the intent and responsibilities of the contracting parties be set forth in clearly understood language. This is especially important in documenting the arrival of the chartered vessel in the specified port of destination. Two possibilities exist, sufficiently different to cause major controversy if not fulfilled exactly.

In one case, the voyage charter covers the movement of a given cargo from the loading port to the designated port (or ports) of destination. If the ship is ordered to proceed directly to a berth nominated by the charterer, or, alternatively, when such a berth is not available, to that area of the port where ships customarily lie while awaiting movement to a berth, the master may report the vessel's arrival and issue the notice of readiness to work cargo. Whether the ship goes to the berth or the waiting area, the charterer must be able to give orders that are effective on receipt. This form of contract is known in maritime circles as a "port charter party."

Quite different is the burden placed upon the principals agreeing to the "berth charter party." This contract directs the ship to proceed to the port of destination and to go immediately to the berth that the charterer will have made ready and available. The master is obligated to have the ship ready in all respects to work cargo on arrival at the berth. Until the ship is actually moored at the berth, arrival has not been effected, and therefore a notice of readiness cannot be issued.[15]

To illustrate the principles set forth, a simplified and shortened sample voyage charter is shown in the following paragraphs.

> *Owner, Vessel, Position, Charterer.* It is this day mutually agreed between Universal Ships, Inc., Owner of the *Norway Universe,* of XXX Net tons register, classed 100-A-1 at Det Norske Veritas, now trading and expected ready to load under this charter on or about February 14, 1997, and Northern Export Corporation, of Duluth, Minnesota, Charterer:
>
> *Loading Port, Cargo, Destination.* That the said vessel shall proceed to Newport News, Virginia, or so near thereto as she may safely get and lie always afloat, and there load a full cargo of steam coal, which the Charterer agrees to ship, and being so loaded, the vessel shall proceed to Bremerhaven, Germany, as ordered on signing bills of lading, or so near thereto as she may safely get and lie always afloat, and there deliver the cargo.
>
> *Rate and Payment of Freight.* Freight shall be paid on out turn weight as follows: $11.00 per metric ton, 80 percent to be prepaid in New York within five days of signing bills of lading; the remainder of freight to be paid in New York on completion of discharge.
>
> *Lay Days and Canceling Date.* Lay days are not to commence before February 6, 1997, and, should vessel not be ready to load at or before 5:00 P.M. on February 21, 1997, Charterer shall have the option to cancel this charter party. Should the vessel be delayed while en route to loading port, Charterer is to be notified immediately.
>
> *Notice of Expected Readiness.* Owner is to give Charterer at least fifteen days notice of vessel's expected readiness at loading

port, also stating exact quantity of cargo required to be loaded; subsequently, Owner is to give charterers ten days and five days notice of vessel's definite readiness to load.

Preparation of Holds for Loading. At loading port, Owner is to deliver vessel with holds properly swept, cleaned, and dried, and free of residue of all previous cargoes to inspector's satisfaction, and in all respects ready to receive the cargo.

Loading Rate. Cargo to be loaded, stowed and/or trimmed by spout only by Charterer's stevedores at Charterer's risk and expense, at the average rate of 24,000 tons per weather working day or 24 running hours, Sundays, local, and legal holidays excepted.

Discharging Rate. Cargo to be discharged by Charterer's stevedores at Charterer's risk and expense, at the average rate of 12,000 tons per weather working day, Sundays, local, and legal holidays included.

Laytime Reversible. Laytime at loading and discharging ports is reversible.

Time Commences. Time at loading and discharging ports to commence at 8:00 A.M. on the working day following the day the master has tendered in writing during the hours of 8:00 A.M. to 5:00 P.M. during weekdays and 8:00 A.M. to 12:00 M on Saturday.

Demurrage and Dispatch. Charterer is to pay demurrage at the rate of $9,500 per day of 24 running hours or pro rata for a part thereof, for all time used in excess of laytime. Owner is to pay dispatch money at half the demurrage rate for laytime saved.

Winch and Light Clause. Vessel is to supply at both ends, and at all times free of charge to Charterer, winches, steam, electric power, and gear in good working condition and full light for night work on deck and in the holds if required.

Dues, Wharfage, and Taxes. At loading and discharging ports, all dues and/or wharfage and/or taxes on cargo to be for Charterer's account. All dues and/or wharfage and/or taxes on vessel to be for the Owner's account.

Dunnage. Charterer is to provide all required mats and/or paper and/or wood for dunnage and any separations other than by hold.

Stevedore Damage. When loading and/or discharging is effected by Charterer's stevedores, Charterer shall not be responsible for repairing any stevedore damage unless the master has obtained written acknowledgment of same from stevedores, or unless a joint survey has been made, attended by representatives of Owner and Charterer.

Bills of Lading. The captain, Owner, or agents are to sign bills of lading at such rate of freight as presented, without prejudice to this charter party, but not at less than the total chartered freight.

Deviation. The vessel shall have liberty to tow and/or assist vessels in all situations, and also to deviate for the purpose of saving life and/or property.

Description. Flag: Norway. Year Built: 1990. Deadweight: XXX tons. Draft: XXX meters (XX feet). Gross register tonnage: XXXXX. Cubic grain capacity in holds: XXX cubic meters (XXX cubic feet). Number of hatches: seven. Engine and bridge placement: Aft. Vessel gear and where located: 4 cranes, between #1 and #2, between #3 and #4, between #5 and #6, and aft of #7 hatch.

Owner's Responsibility Clause. Owner shall before, and at the beginning of the voyage, exercise due diligence to make the vessel seaworthy and properly manned, equipped, and supplied, and to make the holds and all other parts of the vessel in which cargo is carried fit and safe for its reception, carriage, and preservation. Owner shall properly and carefully handle, carry, keep, and care for the cargo.

General Ice Clause. In the event of the loading port being inaccessible by reason of ice when vessel is ready to proceed from the last port or at any time during the voyage or on vessel's arrival, or in case frost sets in after vessel's arrival, the captain for fear of being frozen in is at liberty to leave without cargo, and this charter shall be null and void.

U.S.A. Clause Paramount. The Charterer's bill of lading shall have effect subject to provisions of the Carriage of Goods by Sea Act of the United States, approved April 16, 1936, which shall be deemed to be incorporated herein.

Brokerage. Two and one-half percent brokerage on the gross amount of freight, dead freight, and demurrage earned is due to Maritime Brokers, Inc.

_____   _____

For the Charterer   For the Owner
Maritime Brokers, Inc.   Universal Ships, Inc.
Ralph Waters   Thomas Steele
As Broker Only.   As Agent Only.

TIME CHARTER

A time charter, as earlier noted, is a contract by which a party is provided with the use of a ship for a specified period of time. The vessel is fully manned, outfitted, equipped, and operated by the owner. The master, officers, and crew are employed by the owner but are considered as the servants of the charterer, whose orders they obey. The charterer directs where the ship shall go and what cargoes shall be carried; the only limitations on either voyages or cargoes are those set forth in the charter party. The owner is responsible for the seaworthiness of the ship at the commencement of each voyage during the life of the charter party. In addition to maintaining the ship, effecting repairs as needed, paying for insurance on the hull and machinery, and supplying engine room spares, the owner must furnish the food for the ship's personnel. Almost everything else is for the account of the charterer, as evidenced by this detailed clause quoted from the BALTIME charter:

> The Charterer to provide and pay for all coals, including galley coal, oil-fuel, water for boilers, port charges, pilotage (whether compulsory or not), canal steersmen, boatage, lights, tug assistance, consular charges (except those pertaining to the Master, Officers, and Crew), canal, lock, and other dues and charges, including any foreign general municipality or state taxes, also all dock, harbor and tonnage dues at the ports of delivery and redelivery (unless incurred through cargo carried before delivery or after redelivery), agencies, commissions, also to arrange and pay for loading, trimming, stowing (including dunnage and shifting boards, excepting any already on board), unloading, weighing, tallying and delivery of cargoes, surveys on hatches, meals supplied to officials and men in their service and all other charges and expenses whatsoever including detention and expenses through quarantine (including cost of fumigation and disinfection).
>
> All ropes, slings and special runners actually used for loading and discharging and any special gear, including special ropes, hawsers and chains required by the custom of the port for mooring to be for the Charterer's account. The Vessel to be fitted with winches, derricks, wheels and ordinary runners capable of handling lifts up to two tons.

Because the time charterer is to defray many of the operating costs of the ship, the shipowner must supply accurate, detailed information concerning the registration, classification, dimensions, carrying capacity (in terms of tons and cubic feet or cubic meters), speed, and fuel consumption of the vessel.

Under American law, the ship must meet these specifications on the day the ship is delivered to the time charterer. The speed and fuel consumption warranties, however, are not intended to mean that the vessel always will perform in the described manner throughout the life of the charter party unless this obligation is set forth unambiguously in the contract. These warranties clearly would not be applicable in bad weather and in restricted waters such as rivers and harbors. The courts have held that the remedy for deviation from the warranties lies in a systematic review of the records of the ship's actual performance in the described weather conditions.

Most of the warranties are provable without difficulty. However, should a dispute arise over any of the stipulations, the matter usually is referred to a panel of arbitrators, as provided in the charter party. The decision of this panel has the same force as a judgment of a court of law.

While the intent of the warranties is to ensure that the ship's performance meets its stated specifications, the wording of the contract reflects the realities of ship operation. The BALTIME form of time charter, for example, states that the fully loaded vessel is "capable of steaming about _____ knots in good weather and smooth seas on a consumption of about _____ tons of fuel oil."

The word "about" has significance in the systematic review of vessel performance. For instance, the warranted speed of "about 15 knots" was considered to have been satisfied when the ship had a sustained speed of 14½ knots. An arbitration panel ruled that the warranties concerning speed and fuel consumption must be read together.[16] Another decision stated that these warranties applied only in the open sea in the described conditions of wind and sea. The case of the *Areti* demonstrates how these rules have been used to adjudicate problem areas. The warranty specified that the steamer could attain a speed of 10 knots on a consumption of 26 to 27 tons of fuel oil per day. The ship's logs showed that the *Areti* had achieved a speed of 9½ knots on a consumption of 24.85 tons of fuel. The arbitrators decided that the word "about" was intended to apply to such variations, and therefore no breach of contract had occurred.

An arbitration in a 1968 case concerned the actual performance of a vessel as compared to the warranted performance. The panel held that a fair average of the true capability of the ship could be obtained by observing speed on those days when the vessel was fully loaded and the weather was Force 4 or less, together with a few other days when Force 5 or Force 6 winds were generally following the ship.[17]

Some charter parties state very specifically that the vessel is engaged "for a period of about twelve months, charterers guaranteeing to redeliver the vessel within three weeks more or less of the period." The court found that the charterers had the option of keeping the ship for as short a time as eleven months and one week or as long as twelve months and three weeks. The charterers, however were obligated to redeliver the vessel within the precise limits set forth; no grace period was allowed.

An arbitration award in 1977 noted that the printed word "about" had been deleted from a charter party that provided for the use of the ship for a period of thirty-five months minimum to thirty-eight months maximum at the charterer's option. The vessel was redelivered eight days beyond the maximum period. The panel of arbitrators ruled that the owner was entitled to damages resulting from the late redelivery, holding that no allowance for overlap was intended. Redelivery earlier than the thirty-fifth month or later than the thirty-eighth month would constitute a breach of the contract for which the charterer would be liable.[18]

Problems arise in ordering the final voyage under a time charter. If the proposed voyage in normal circumstances can be completed within the stated time limits, the owner must comply with the orders for this "legitimate last voyage." Should the voyage, for reasons not foreseen at the outset nor within the control of the contracting parties, result in overrunning the redelivery date, the charterer must pay for the ship's time. Depending upon the phrasing of the charter party, this payment may be at the originally agreed charter hire, or it may be at the daily rate plus the difference between the contract rate and the market rate, if the latter has increased during the life of the charter. The shipowner would not be entitled to damage in addition to the payment for the ship's time.

The picture changes when the charterer orders the ship to undertake a voyage the duration of which makes a delay in redelivery inevitable and therefore in breach of the contract. The owner is not obligated to obey the orders for this "illegitimate last voyage." In support of this action is the court ruling that the order must be for a legitimate voyage at the time the last voyage is to begin.[19]

Both time and bareboat charters normally contain restrictions concerning the types of cargo that may be carried. At the minimum, the stipulation is that "any lawful merchandise not injurious to the vessel" may be put aboard. Some contracts are more specific; one document states: "No livestock [or] sulfur and pitch in bulk to be shipped." Should the owner wish to protect the ship from damage by certain goods, an "exclusionary clause" would be inserted to limit the quantity of such goods to be transported. A typical clause reads: "No livestock nor injurious, inflammable, or dangerous goods (such as acids, explosives, calcium carbide, ferro silicon, naphtha, motor spirit, tar, or any of their products to be shipped)."

The time or bareboat charterer directs where the ship shall sail. Because marine underwriters are very definite as to the areas of the world where they will accept responsibility for damage sustained by ships they insure, the time and bareboat charter parties provide a space in which the limits of the ship's voyaging are stipulated. Furthermore, the charterer is prohibited from ordering the ship to "any place where fever or epidemics are prevalent," nor may the charterer direct the ship into places where there is danger of it being frozen in for the duration of the winter. A typical ice clause reads as follows:

> The Vessel is not to be ordered to nor bound to enter any icebound place or any place where lights, lightships, marks, and buoys are or are likely to be withdrawn by reason of ice on the Vessel's arrival or where there is risk that ordinarily the Vessel will not be able on account of ice to reach the place or leave after having completed loading or discharging. The Vessel is not to be obliged to force ice, nor to follow icebreakers when inward bound. If on account of ice the Master considers it dangerous to remain at the loading or discharging place for fear of the Vessel being frozen in and/or damaged, he has liberty to sail to a convenient open place and await the Charterer's fresh instructions. Detention through any of the above causes to be for the Charterer's account.

If the contemplated employment of the ship entails voyages to ports where ice conditions may be encountered, the terms and conditions under which that activity will be performed must be negotiated and set forth in minute detail in the charter party.

Under a time charter, the charterer has the privilege of issuing bills of lading for cargo carried in the chartered ship. If the vessel is engaged in private carriage, the bill of lading is only a receipt for the cargo; the contract of affreightment is the charter party. Should the ship be assigned to common-carrier operation, the bill of lading would be governed by the statutes regulating carriage of goods by sea, and the charterer's responsibility for the cargo may be limited by these laws. The master is to sign the bills of lading "as presented" by the charterer or its agents, but the bills must be in conformity with the mate's cargo notes. If these notes show that the cargo was received in

The owner invoked the "ice clause" when his ice-strengthened bulk carrier encountered these conditions. Courtesy A/S Hydraulik Brattvaag.

damaged condition or was damaged during loading, this information must be set forth in the bill of lading. The master may not be compelled to sign "clean" bills of lading for defective cargo. In any case, the master should protect the owner by signing the bills only as the agent of the time charterer.

An owner who time-charters his vessel assumes serious financial risks. A time charterer can cause maritime liens to be placed against the vessel in favor of stevedores, bunker suppliers, and tug services, for example. Such liens may be exercised after the vessel has been redelivered (i.e., after the expiration of the contract). The vessel owner must satisfy these liens and recover from the time charterer—if that party is still within reach. A similar burden may be imposed by a dishonest charterer who accepts prepayment of ocean freight on cargo loaded aboard the chartered vessel and issues bills of lading requiring delivery of the goods to the named consignee. If the charterer retains the prepaid freight and defaults on payments of the charter hire, the owner remains responsible for transportation and delivery of the goods. The shipowner's only recourse is to place a lien against the cargo to the value of the unpaid freight and to file a claim against the individual who has defaulted on the contract.[20]

The simplified form of time charter presented below typifies the agreement between the contracting parties.

This charter party is made and concluded in New York, New York, the first day of June 1997 between Clay Bjornsen A/S of Bergen, Norway, Owner of the good Norwegian motorship *Queen Ingrid,* and Ocean Trading Corporation of Newark, New Jersey, Charterer of the said motorship (described as being classed 100-A-1 at Lloyd's Register of Shipping, of about 57,210 cubic meters (1,893,000 cubic feet) grain capacity, 30,093 gross register tons, 14,720 net register tons, and about 49,228 tons of 2,240 pounds deadweight on a summer draft of 12.118 meters (40 feet 5 inches), with a diesel motor of 9,562 kW (13,000 brake horsepower) and a service speed of 14 knots on a consumption of about 41 tons of high viscosity fuel and about 3 tons of diesel oil per 24-hour day. Permanent bunker capacity is 2,014 tons of high viscosity fuel and 208 tons of marine diesel oil, now in service and trading. These particulars are not guaranteed, but are supplied in good faith, and are believed to be correct.

1. *Delivery.* The vessel is to be delivered in Galveston, Texas, not earlier than July 13, 1997, and not later than July 30, 1997, between the hours of 9:00 A.M. and 6:00 P.M. (Sundays and holidays excepted), at such available berth where she can safely lie always afloat as may be directed by Charterer, for a period of fifteen months from date of delivery.

2. *Trade.* The vessel is to be employed in lawful trades for the carriage of lawful merchandise only, between good and safe ports where she can safely lie always afloat. No livestock, nor injurious, inflammable, or dangerous goods such as acids, explosives, calcium, ferro silicon, naphtha, motor spirit, tar, or any of their products, are to be shipped.

3. *Owners to Provide.* The Owner is to provide and pay for all provisions and wages, insurance of the vessel, all deck and engine room stores, and is to maintain the vessel in a thoroughly efficient state in hull and machinery during the term of this contract.

4. *Charterer to Provide.* The Charterer is to provide and pay for all fuel, port charges, pilotage (whether compulsory or not), lights, tug assistance, consular charges (except those directly related to the master, officers, and crew), taxes, dock and harbor and tonnage dues at ports of delivery and redelivery, agencies, and commissions. Owner also is to arrange for and pay for loading,

trimming, stowing (including dunnage and shifting boards), unloading, weighing, tallying, and delivery of cargo, and all other charges, including detention.

5. *Bunkers.* Charterer at port of delivery and Owner at port of redelivery are to take over and pay for oil fuel remaining in the vessel's bunkers, at the current price at the respective ports. The vessel is to be redelivered with not less than 100 tons and not more than 150 tons of heavy fuel and 40 tons of marine diesel oil.

6. *Hire.* The Charterer is to pay as hire the sum of $9,250 per day, or $5.64 per deadweight ton per month, in cash and without discount, every thirty days, in advance.

7. *Redelivery.* The vessel is to be redelivered on the expiration of the charter in the same good order as when delivered to the Charterer (fair wear and tear excepted), at an ice-free port in the Charterer's option between Cape Hatteras and Portland, Maine, between the hours of 9:00 A.M. and 6:00 P.M. (Sundays and holidays excepted). Charterer is to give Owner not less than ten days notice at which port and on which day the vessel will be redelivered.

8. *Cargo Space.* The whole reach and burthen of the vessel, including lawful deck capacity, shall be at the Charterer's disposal, reserving proper and sufficient space for the master, officers, and crew, and all tackle, apparel, furniture, provisions, and stores.

9. *Master.* The master shall prosecute all voyages with the utmost dispatch and may render customary assistance with the vessel's crew. The master shall be under the Charterer's orders as regards employment, agency, or other arrangements.

10. *Directions and Logs.* The Charterer is to furnish the master with all instructions and sailing directions. The master and chief engineer are to keep full and correct logs accessible to the Charterer and its agents.

11. *Suspension of Hire.* In the event that the vessel is unable to perform for any reason for a period in excess of 24 consecutive hours, no hire shall be paid for such lost time. The Owner shall be responsible for delay during the currency of this charter only if such delay or loss has been caused by want of due diligence to make the vessel seaworthy and fitted for the voyage.

12. *Ice.* The vessel shall not be required to enter any port where there is immediate risk of being frozen in, nor shall the vessel be required to force ice. The master shall have liberty to leave a port when, in his judgment, there is risk of being frozen in, whether or not the cargo has been fully loaded or discharged.

13. *Overtime.* The vessel is to work day and night, if required. The Charterer will reimburse the Owner for the cost of overtime paid to officers and crew.

14. *Liens.* The Owner shall have a lien on all cargoes and subfreights belonging to the Charterer for all claims under this charter. The Charterer shall have a lien on the vessel for all moneys paid in advance and not earned.

15. *Sublet.* The Charterer shall have the option of subletting the vessel, giving due notice to the Owner. The Charterer shall remain always responsible to the Owner for due performance of the charter.

16. *Canceling.* If the vessel cannot be delivered by the canceling date, the Charterer, if required, is to declare within 48 hours after receiving notice thereof, whether they will take delivery or will cancel.

17. *Arbitration.* Any dispute arising under the charter is to be referred to arbitration in New York or such other place as may be agreed upon. One arbitrator shall be designated by Charterer and one arbitrator shall be designated by Owner. If arbitrators cannot agree, they are to appoint an umpire, whose decision shall be binding upon both parties.

18. *Commission.* The Owner shall pay a commission of two and one-half percent to the brokers involved.

_____   _____

For the Owner
Olav Bjornsen A/S
by Harold Saylor
as broker only

For the Charterer
Ocean Trading Corporation
by Joseph Merchant
as broker only

BAREBOAT (DEMISE) CHARTER

Of the three types of charter parties, the bareboat or demise charter is the least used, for the reason that it imposes the heaviest burden upon the charterer, who becomes the de facto operator of the ship.

The term "bareboat" refers to the fact that the fully operational ship is delivered to the charterer but is bare—that is, the ship has on board no crew, no stores, little or no fuel, and no navigational charts. The term "demise" refers to the transfer of possession (but not ownership), command, and control of the chartered vessel from the owner to the charterer for the length of time covered by the contract. In commercial circles, the more common term is bareboat charter, whereas legal professionals speak of the demise charter.

Built in 1992, the 322,941-metric-ton-deadweight bulk carrier *Bergeland* was 338.7 meters (1,137.9 feet) long, 55 meters (184.8 feet) wide, and had a draft of 23 meters (77.2 feet). Her speed was 14.5 knots. Courtesy Bergesen d.y. A/S.

Under the bareboat charter, the shipowner is obligated to present a seaworthy vessel that is fit for the service intended. Once the ship is accepted by the charterer, the responsibility of seaworthiness no longer rests with the owner. The shipowner has the right to approve the nomination of master and chief engineer but has no authority over them. The charterer actually hires and pays the master, officers, and crew, who thereby become the servants of the charterer. The voyages to be made by the vessel and the cargoes to be carried are specified by the charterer. All operational expenses are for that party's account. In all but title, the charterer becomes the owner of the ship; in legal terminology, the charterer is designated as "owner *pro hac vice*," meaning for the duration of the charter party.

A major difference between the time and voyage charters and the demise charter is that there are no standardized forms for the latter. Because the circumstances differ in nearly every case, the contracts are written to cover the individual requirements of the contracting parties. Usually drawn up by experts in contract law, each charter party is unique.

In view of the anticipated employment of the vessel, the warranties concerning the vessel's classification, flag, gross and net tonnage (and in certain circumstances, the Panama and Suez Canal tonnage measurements), deadweight tonnage, cubic measurement of cargo spaces below decks, speed, fuel consumption, port of delivery, date of last drydocking,

COMPARISON OF CHARTER PARTY RESPONSIBILITIES

Responsibility	Voyage Charter	Time Charter	Bareboat (Demise) Charter
Basis of charter hire	Tons of cargo loaded aboard ship	Capacity of ship	Capacity of ship
Duration of charter party	Specified voyage	Period of time	Period of time
Nature of employment (geographic limits)	Port to port	By area	By area
Time when owner provides seaworthy vessel	Start of voyage	Delivery	Delivery
Maintenance of vessel's seaworthiness	Owner	Owner	Charterer
Possession, command, operation, and navigation	Owner	Owner	Charterer
Employer of crew	Owner	Owner	Charterer
Master and crew servants of	Owner	Owner	Charterer
Master under direction of	Owner	Charterer	Charterer
Fuel costs	Owner	Charterer	Charterer
Port, harbor, and light fees	Owner	Charterer	Charterer
Stevedoring (cargo-working) cost	Negotiable	Charterer	Charterer
Hull and machinery insurance premium	Owner	Owner	Negotiable
Protection and indemnity insurance premium	Owner	Owner	Charterer
Time when payment is owed to shipowner	End of voyage	Monthly	Monthly
Legal term for compensation under charter	Freight	Hire	Hire

NOTES:

Definition of a charter: A maritime contract by which the charterer, a party other than the shipowner, obtains the use and services of a ship for a period of time or for one or more voyages.

Demise is a legal term and refers to the transfer of possession, command, and control of the chartered vessel from the owner to the charterer, just short of transfer of full title.

Bareboat refers to the absence of managerial and operational facilities on the vessel when delivered to the charterer.

and other particular attributes are of the utmost importance to the charterer. Should the charter permit the vessel to be used in general trading (i.e., without specifying what cargoes are to be carried or what trade routes are to be followed), the contracting parties must be prepared for unexpected contingencies. In broad terms, the responsibilities of the contracting parties toward each other in such circumstances should be set forth.

When the ship is delivered to the charterer, good management dictates that the contracting parties jointly inspect ("survey") the vessel to disclose any deficiencies not already made known to all concerned. Making inventories of such items as furnishings, replacement parts, stores (if any are on board), and the amount of fuel in the tanks should be another joint exercise. At the end of the charter period, the vessel is to be redelivered in the same condition in which originally received, reasonable wear and tear excepted.[21] If the ship is returned in damaged condition, it is the charterer's responsibility to prove lack of culpability. If the charterer is held to blame, the measure of damage must include the cost of the required repairs.

Throughout the life of the bareboat charter party, the shipowner provides and pays for insurance on the hull and machinery. The charterer is expected to obtain marine protection and indemnity insurance to supplement the owner's hull policy, and again good management dictates that this coverage protect the owner from claims by third parties.

Bills of lading for cargo carried may be issued by the charterer. If the master is required to sign these bills, the documents must indicate that the master is the agent of the charterers. The shipowner is not responsible for loss of or damage to the cargo, but the ship may be subject to liens by cargo interests.

Charter hire may be stipulated as a fixed (lump sum) monthly charge, a sum per deadweight ton per month, a percentage of vessel earnings, a fixed base rate with a supplemental percentage keyed to vessel earnings, a sliding rate adjusted from time to time, or an agreed amount per day. The provisions relating to the payment of charter hire designate the place, time and manner of payment (cash, certified check, bank draft, money order, or whatever is mutually agreed), together with the consequences if the charterer fails to make payments according to the schedule set forth in the contract.[22]

CHAPTER FIVE

Liner Shipping: Its Management and Operations

Every shipping company, regardless of country of origin or location of corporate headquarters, is organized to meet its own particular needs and its own specialized functions. Therefore, no uniform pattern of organization exists in the workaday world of shipping. Nevertheless, the functions of the different officials, by whatever title they may be known, are sufficiently similar to permit their identification within the corporate structure.

At the top of the pyramid in a publicly held company is the *board of directors,* usually made up of persons who have financial or managerial interest in the company. The board may have as few as five or as many as twenty or more people elected by the stockholders and responsible to them for proper management of the business. Always included as a voting member of this board is the chairperson. Increasingly in American corporate practice, this person is also the chief executive officer, meaning that he or she takes an active part in the affairs of the company and makes major decisions within the authority conferred by the board. The president of the company may also serve as the chief operating officer and therefore is a member of the board. The treasurer, who serves as the financial advisor, and the secretary, who keeps the minutes of the meetings and authenticates all official documents, very often are members of the board. In all matters of magnitude, especially those involving massive expenditures (for instance, the purchase or construction of ships, or the entry into or withdrawal from a trade route) and the selection of senior executives, the board makes the final decision.

The *president,* as the chief operating officer, is responsible to the board for the proper functioning of the entire organization. This person may have been promoted through the ranks of the company or may have been brought in at or near the top. As the supervisor of all activities, the president does not become involved for any protracted period of time in the working of any specific division. As ships and their supporting operations have become more expensive, the office of the president inevitably has been concerned primarily with the financial aspects of the company, and a primary consideration in the choice of a president is the person's proven ability to make sound financial judgments under difficult circumstances.

The demands imposed by these fiscal burdens upon the president's time have resulted in the delegation of much of the supervision of daily activity to the *executive vice president*, who may be described accurately as the chief of staff. This officer is responsible for seeing that the policies promulgated by the board and the president are carried out. Within the scope of authority for the position, the executive vice president makes all routine decisions and sends to the president's desk only those matters requiring special consideration. The executive vice president must assume the duties of the president whenever that official is absent from the office and in this capacity as "alternate president" must be as well informed as the president about the affairs of the company.

The *secretary* maintains the official records of the corporation, supervises issuance and transfers of stock certificates (if the corporation is publicly held), accepts service of legal papers drawn against the corporation, and represents the company in court when identification of records or other similar data is an issue. The secretary also is responsible for preparing the annual report to the stockholders, usually in conjunction with the treasurer and the executive vice president.

Many of the secretary's duties involve legal matters, and consequently it is usual for this person to be a lawyer. If it is consistent with company policy, the legal section (sometimes known as the house counsel) may be placed under the secretary's supervision. This important segment of the organization usually consists of one or more lawyers who provide legal advice, comment on the significance of court decisions and the impact of new laws, assist trial attorneys in preparing court cases, and take part in negotiations where interpretation of contract terms may be needed.

Acting primarily as financial advisor to the board chairperson and the president, the *treasurer* obtains the requisite information from the comptroller, cashier, accountants, and auditors. The treasurer is able at any time to report on the complete financial position of the company and to discuss areas of fiscal strength and weakness. In some shipping organizations, the offices of secretary and treasurer are merged into one.

To keep control over the multitude of financial records that must be maintained by a shipping company (especially if it holds a subsidy contract with the U. S. government), some organizations include in the executive structure a *vice president for finance.* The auditors, accountants, and bookkeepers, as well as pursers aboard the ship, come under this officer's supervision. As a master accountant, the vice president for finance cooperates with the treasurer in keeping the president, the board of directors, and stockholders informed on financial matters. Because of the obvious overlap in functions, it is usual for the offices of treasurer and vice-president for finance to be merged.

Analyzing the significance of accounts and supervising the operating budget are rather exact sciences, especially as computer technology is applied to financial management. Larger companies today recognize the need for qualified specialists in this area and have established the office of *comptroller* to handle all aspects of fiscal control. This officer is assisted by the auditors, who oversee accounting procedures and inspect financial records. In general terms, the comptroller supervises expenditures in accordance with the budget while overseeing routines of fiscal administration. In smaller companies, the treasurer performs the duties of the comptroller, assisted by the auditor and chief accountant.

From time to time, liner-service operators have occasion to charter ships into and out of their fleets. As described in detail elsewhere in this volume, chartering is a specialized form of endeavor; in those organizations where it occurs with some frequency, full responsibility for this activity, with authority to make final commitments, is assigned to a vice president. Regardless of title or location within the corporate structure, the official who handles charters must keep abreast of the employment of the company fleet and the potential demand for additional tonnage or the development of a surplus. As circumstances warrant, the *chartering vice president* provides extra ships or finds charters for those that are temporarily redundant.

Aside from chartering, the functions of the officials described are substantially the same as those of senior executives of any corporation. Essential to their success are high moral character, strong leadership, and sound business judgment. It is an advantage if these officials have the widest possible familiarity with the maritime industry, since this will assure them of respect in the business community while providing a sound foundation for their decisions.

Maritime transportation is a business with specialized aspects, but is not unique as an economic enterprise. It exists to make a profit and must sell its service (transportation) to the public in precisely the same manner that the tire manufacturing industry must find markets for automobile and truck tires. Terminology differs, of course, but the realities of competition, cost, plant modernization, and promotion are as clearly defined in the shipping firm as they are in any manufacturing firm. The techniques of management are, in their essentials, the same as in other forms of business. Circumstances and factors influencing the activities of a shipping company often are remote from and completely beyond the control of the mari-

CHART NO. 1   ORGANIZATION OF A TYPICAL AMERICAN LINER-SERVICE COMPANY

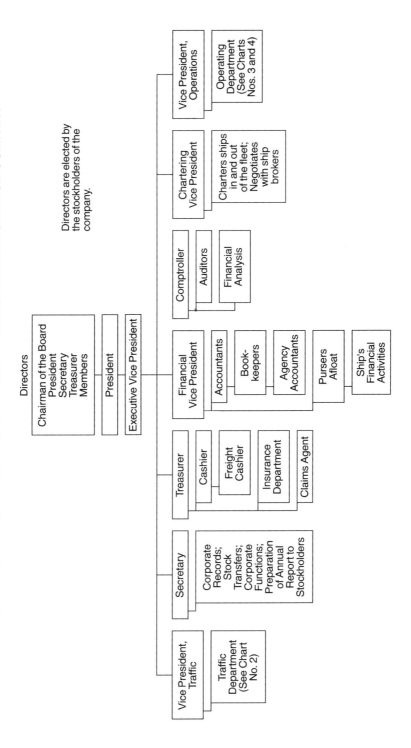

time community, but even here there are similarities with other types of commercial enterprise.

As a case in point, the traffic department of the liner-service company has the same goals as the sales division of a tire manufacturer. Both must sell their respective products, transportation services and tires. The techniques of salesmanship, adapted to the maritime industry, can be applied successfully to "merchandising" transportation. The vice president of the traffic department is responsible for keeping a constant flow of cargo coming to the ships just as the director of sales must find buyers for the tires.

The operating department of a shipowning corporation should be viewed in a similar manner to the production division of the tire manufacturer, for it bears a striking resemblance. Just as the production vice president is required to oversee all details relating to the manufacture of the rubber tires and must adjust output to meet the requirements of the sales force, so the vice president in charge of marine operations must ensure that the ships are kept in good condition, on schedule, and in all respects able to provide the service promised by the sales staff to the shippers.

In shipping as in manufacturing, the traffic (sales) and operating (production) departments are mutually complementary and interdependent. The transportation sales staff must be assured that ships will be available to lift the cargoes they procure; the operating department must have the cargoes to fill the ships they have brought into port. As one executive explained, "The best traffic department in the world cannot survive without a good operating department; the finest operating group has no reason for existence unless it is supported by a good sales force."

TRAFFIC DEPARTMENT

The *vice president, traffic,* directs the department charged with generating the cargo to fill the company ships. This officer reports to the president through the executive vice president, keeping both these officials informed on all matters related to both outbound and inbound cargo. Within the department, the vice president, traffic, sets policy to achieve the goals assigned by the president and the board of directors. As an expert on traffic, this vice president may be called upon to work with carriers to solve matters of mutual concern or to consult with important shippers whose problems are of a magnitude so great that they merit attention from an executive in the organization.

The vice president, traffic, must spend considerable time conferring with fellow executives, especially from the operating and chartering

CHART NO. 2   TRAFFIC DEPARTMENT

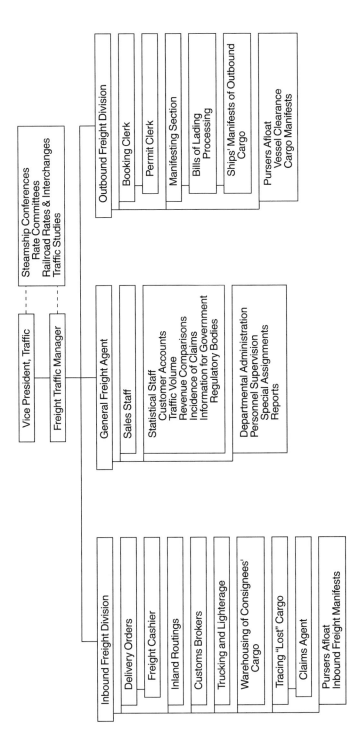

departments, as to the proper scheduling of ships, seasonal changes in demand for shipping space, better employment of the fleet, improvements in design for projected new or modernized tonnage, plans for the acquisition or disposition of vessels, and ways and means of minimizing stevedoring expense. The vice president, traffic, also works with the claims agent, the insurance manager, and the financial manager to develop better ways to handle claims for compensation for damaged or lost cargo. From time to time this vice president will confer with the terminal manager and the superintendent stevedore to consider techniques of cargo handling that might lead to fewer claims. Now and again he or she will be involved in formulating, with the comptroller, freight cashier, and vice president for finance, a policy dealing with the collection of freight charges. The vice president, traffic, will confer regularly with the terminal manager to ascertain that access to the terminal is satisfactory, that control procedures are working properly, and that receipts and deliveries are meeting company promises to shippers and consignees.

Outside the company, the vice president, traffic, may serve as a member of an industry group studying ways to improve packaging of goods or to standardize practices of booking cargo. As the patterns of business place greater emphasis on intermodal transportation, much time is devoted to establishing rates that will cover the costs of inland transportation, and so must be acceptable to railroads, trucking contractors, and the government regulatory bodies.

If the company belongs to an association of shipping lines that regulates competition and sets uniform freight rates, the vice president, traffic, may represent the organization at times when a firm commitment to a certain principle or policy is required. He or she also may be part of a special committee of the association responsible for adjusting freight rates to meet changing conditions and shippers' requests. In addition to these "troubleshooting" assignments, the vice president must always be alert to better ways to carry out the mission of the company, to gain larger shares of the available business, and to augment company profits.

The *freight traffic manager* is the deputy to the vice president, traffic, and is qualified to substitute for that executive when the office is vacant for any reason. As the supervisor of the freight traffic department, this manager ensures that departmental policies are carried out in the most effective manner and that appropriate recommendations are made to higher authority when necessary. The freight traffic manager considers shippers' requests for special calls at ports not on the regular schedule or for the transport of large quantities of unusual cargo.

Immediately under the freight traffic manager is the *general freight agent,* who directs the sales staff (sometimes called solicitors) and handles departmental administration. The job of the sales staff is to handle the contact between the carrier and the shipping public; the company's prosperity depends upon the ability of the salespeople to convince clients that the company deserves their patronage. The coordination of their efforts and the establishment of policies with regard to sales are of great importance and represent a major part of the general freight agent's work. This agent supervises the day-to-day appointments made by the sales staff, suggests ways to deal with difficult customers, and makes sure that the capabilities of the company are set forth correctly. When subordinates make suggestions that have merit but involve changes in departmental or company policy, the general freight agent transmits these suggestions, together with a recommendation, to the appropriate executives. As additional information is obtained which may be useful in selling the services of the company, the agent calls in the sales staff and together, they develop ways to use this knowledge to induce shippers to give their business to the company. Clients who benefit by this effort may become supporters of the line since they appreciate that the sales personnel often bring suggestions which, if accepted, can be financially advantageous to the shipper.

In addition to these responsibilities, the general freight agent directs the keeping of records that show many aspects of the company's business: the total volume of business handled, the total revenue earned, the demands for service to named ports, the desirability of certain commodities in the light of the cost of handling them, the frequency with which claims for damages are made, the business received from individual shippers, the seasonal variations in the volume of cargo offered by shippers and in the tonnage carried by the ships, and even comparisons between voyages and calendar periods. These records have many uses. They may furnish data for some governmental agency concerned with international shipping. Perhaps the president has directed that certain aspects of traffic activity are to be analyzed and the most readily available information would be in these statistical records. Should a traffic study (a forecast of future business trends based on past experiences and present practice) be in progress, the data from these records could be of major importance. These reports are circulated to the senior executives, the comptroller, the operating department, and any other officials who may require them. They are useful as the basis for judgments relating to all aspects of freight traffic.

An important activity of the general freight agent is to maintain close contact with the claims division to learn which commodities and which shippers are involved in claims for damages as well as the probable causes of the alleged damage and the validity of the claims.

As the departmental administrative officer, the general freight agent makes routine and special assignments, sets up training programs for new members of the department, transfers persons within the department for most efficient use of their capabilities, and recommends promotions when earned or dismissals when necessary. Incidental to these supervisory functions, the general freight agent maintains appropriate personnel records.

The freight traffic department is divided into two major segments, the *outbound freight division* and the *inbound freight division,* of which the outbound is by far the larger. The chief of each branch usually holds the rank of assistant freight traffic manager and reports to the freight traffic manager.

The *booking clerk* is a senior member of the outbound division and controls the space in a cargo ship, allocating that space to individual shippers as they make their requests. From the operating department, the booking clerk obtains basic information such as the amount of fuel, water, stores, and equipment to be aboard the ship on the proposed voyage as well as the actual space (in cubic feet) and capacity (in tons) available for cargo. As reservations for space in a breakbulk vessel are received, the booking clerk computes the stowage factors and allots the required number of cubic feet. The sales staff works closely with the booking clerk to ensure that customers are extended the treatment they have been promised. Conversely, when the booking clerk finds that a vessel needs either high-volume lightweight cargo or dense cargo, an appeal is made to the sales staff to assist in making a balanced load by arranging visits to shippers of the kind of cargo desired. The booking clerk is in regular contact with the terminal and notifies the chief stevedore about the type of cargo that has been booked and when it will be arriving. On the basis of the booking clerk's daily reports, the stevedore plans the stowage of the ship, and the terminal manager tentatively lays out the transit shed.

For fully containerized ships, it is not necessary to compute stowage factors for individual shipments nor is the stevedore dependent upon the booking reports. Instead, the booking clerk reserves undesignated "cells" for the containers offered by the shippers and relies upon a carefully programmed computer to determine exactly where each box will be stowed. The booking clerk notifies the terminal of the anticipated receipt of the containers, making certain that all necessary data are furnished for proper identification of the containers. The clerk is in frequent contact with the gatehouse of the terminal to update and clarify earlier information.

Working directly under the booking clerk is the *permit clerk,* who notifies shippers of large lots of cargo (usually defined as 10,000 pounds or more from a single originator), directing them when to send their consignments to the terminal. The "permit system" is designed to favor the shipper of large lots and, by spacing the arrivals of trucks at the terminal, to eliminate the heavy expense of truck waiting time.

Cargo that moves in small lots (often described among breakbulk carriers by the railroad term of "less than carload lot" or "LCL" cargo) normally does not come under the permit system. Experience has shown that little, if any, time is saved for the small lot shipper as a result of attempting to schedule truck movements to the terminal, and a good deal of clerical work can be eliminated. Cargo that requires special handling (a heavy-lift item, for instance) or that must be brought to the ship's side by barge or lighter should be scheduled to prevent congestion and confusion in the loading operations and also to avoid great expense charged to the shipper for delays at the terminal.

When a patron uses a shipping line that handles only cargo in containers, and that patron's individual offerings are in comparatively small lots (referred to by the carriers as "less than container loads" or again "LCL" cargo), the consignments are directed to a section of the terminal reserved for this type of traffic. At this "consolidation station," known as a container freight station (CFS), small lots are processed and loaded into containers by terminal personnel. There is no significant difference in the handling of these shipments between a breakbulk terminal and a container yard.

The manifesting section, under the *chief bill of lading clerk,* is the busiest and largest of the segments of the outbound freight division. Here the shipper delivers, for processing, the bills of lading. These are matched with the dock receipts from the terminal to obtain the actual measurements of the parcels in the shipment together with their actual count and condition (or the size, number, and weight of the container(s) in the shipment). They are then "freighted" by the *rate clerk,* listed on the ship's outbound cargo manifest, signed by the chief clerk for the master, and routed to the freight cashier to hold until the shipper prepays the freight charges and picks up the freighted bills of lading.

The *inbound freight division* is a service agency responsible for ensuring that consignees obtain their cargo without delay and in an orderly manner. The carrier requires that the original bill of lading be surrendered before the cargo is released. This procedure necessitates the timely notification of the consignees of the anticipated arrival of the vessel. Personnel of the inbound freight division also inform consignees of those pertinent regulations with which they must comply prior to taking delivery of their goods. When the goods are removed from the ship, the consignees call at the inbound division offices and exchange the original bill of lading for a "delivery order," which authorizes the terminal to release the cargo to the consignee or a designated representative. Should the goods be destined to an inland city, the department makes arrangements for transportation pursuant to the consignee's instructions. If required, cargo will be warehoused until this transportation is available. No charge is made for this assistance unless the cargo is left on the terminal too long; the expense of trucking, warehousing, customs broker's service, and transportation to the ultimate destination is for the customer's account. If the consignee believes that some or all of the shipment has gone astray, the inbound division initiates the search and keeps the claims agent at the loading point informed of its efforts. Finally, since pursers on the homeward voyage often make up the inbound cargo manifest, the inbound division maintains constant liaison with them to make certain that their work satisfies company and governmental requirements.

OPERATIONS DEPARTMENT

Supervising the operation of the fleet is the *vice president, operations.* While a seafaring background is not mandatory for this official, it is highly desirable because of the intimate contact with the personnel who run the ships, perform the essential stevedoring functions, and make the repairs. Broad experience in management directly related to ship operations may be a satisfactory alternative to service in merchant vessels.

The vice president is responsible to the president, (through the executive vice president) for all matters concerning ship construction, operations, stevedoring, and labor relations. If the company is small, the vice president usually is the officer who handles negotiations with shipyards for building and repair contracts, with stevedores on details of handling cargo in the various ports served by the company fleet, with suppliers of ships stores and outfit, and with representatives of all types of labor unions on many aspects of the working agreements. The larger the company, the greater the likelihood that specialists will handle each of these activities, but final decisions on these matters are made by the vice president. To assist with the many duties required in running the department and to assume the direction of the department whenever the vice president is absent, an *operating manager*, who administers the department, is appointed.

In many companies, the final appointments of masters and chief engineers of the ships are made by the vice president. The marine superintendent

CHART NO. 3 OPERATIONS DEPARTMENT

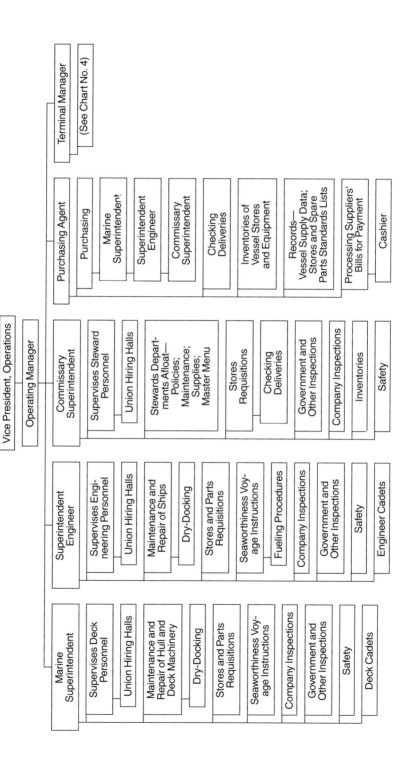

initiates the recommendations for promotion to the rank of master and forwards this through the operating manager to the vice president. Similarly, the superintendent engineer selects the person considered best qualified for the position of chief engineer. After studying these proposals, the operating manager forwards their recommendations to the vice president for final selection. The reason for this action is to assert, in unmistakable terms, that these two seafarers enjoy the full confidence of the highest echelons of management. It also authorizes the two appointees, after they are approved, to talk to anyone below the vice president, when representing the interests of the ship, as equals.

The operating manager is the departmental executive officer and coordinator of all activities in the department. Within the very broad limits of authority of the office, the operating manager makes those decisions needed to carry out company and departmental policies. A most important facet of the duties is the evaluation of the periodic reports prepared by the various divisions of the department. Covering the actual performance of assigned functions, these reports afford a means of determining the efficiency with which the work is accomplished, and they offer opportunities for improvement in the techniques of supervision and management. The results of these evaluations always are made known to the vice president.

MARINE DIVISION

At the head of the marine (or deck) division is the *marine superintendent,* who is responsible to the vice president for the seaworthiness of the ships in all particulars except for the engineering department. The marine superintendent necessarily is both a qualified shipmaster with long experience and a person with demonstrated ability as an executive. The marine superintendent supervises the performance of deck personnel of the fleet through study of vessel logs, conferences with ship's licensed officers, and personal observation. Before each voyage is begun, the marine superintendent issues instructions to the master that include the latest information relating to conditions on the route, appropriate details of special requirements, and pertinent comments on carrying out company policies as they may apply to the forthcoming voyage. The marine superintendent may also inspect ships on their arrival in the home port to ensure that governmental and company standards of maintenance are upheld. All licensed deck officers, except the masters, are hired by the marine superintendent (usually through seafaring unions) who also supervises, through these officers, the performance of the unlicensed personnel. Because of these personnel activities, the marine superintendent must establish and maintain a good working relationship with officials of the maritime unions.

Safety of personnel afloat is of major importance. Some of the larger companies have *safety directors;* smaller organizations often designate the marine superintendent as the official in charge of the safety program for the deck department.

Requisitions from the ships for repairs to hull and deck machinery within the purview of the deck department and also plans for scheduled drydocking, inspections, surveys, and other examinations of the hull pass through the marine superintendent's office. The marine superintendent (or an assistant sometimes known as a *port captain*) always is present when the bottom is sighted and accompanies all inspection parties on their tours. Requisitions for spare parts and consumable supplies for the deck department must be approved by the marine superintendent before they are forwarded to the purchasing agent.

Training of deck cadets is under the supervision of the marine superintendent, who sets company policy concerning their duties and responsibilities while aboard the ship.

ENGINEERING DIVISION

Occupying a position of importance equal to that of the marine superintendent but concerned solely with the engineering activities of the fleet is the *superintendent engineer.* Like the deck counterpart, this official has a background of years of service afloat and has demonstrated the qualifications desirable in an executive. Many of the responsibilities of the office parallel those of the marine superintendents: seaworthiness of the engineering department; supervision of personnel afloat, including training of cadet engineer officers; relations with the maritime unions; inspections and surveys; safety; and oversight of repairs and procurement of spare parts.

Engine abstract logs and voyage reports are submitted to the superintendent engineer by the chief engineers as their ships return to the home port. Examination of these documents reveals with notable accuracy the efficiency of engineering practices of the ship and serves to delineate those areas where improvements are in order. From the listings of repairs accomplished by the ships during their voyages, both by ship's company and contractors in ports of call, the superintendent compiles individual histories of each ship's maintenance program. Some large shipping companies have a maintenance and repair section that is charged with all details relating to accomplishing repairs beyond the capability of shipboard personnel.

In this case, the superintendent engineer serves as the liaison between the ship and the specialists of this section.

The chief engineer of a ship (the maintenance and repair officer) has overall responsibility for the physical condition of the vessel during a voyage. All requisitions for work exceeding the capability of the ship's crew are channeled through the chief engineer and are delivered to the superintendent engineer in the home port. Once contracts for the requisite repairs have been let, actual performance thereunder is monitored by the chief engineer and the department heads concerned (e.g., deck repairs by the chief mate or commissary department by the chief steward).

When a vessel is scheduled for drydocking, the marine superintendent and the superintendent engineer cooperate fully to take maximum advantage of the time on drydock and in the shipyard. Repair lists from the ship serve as the basis for writing the specifications for the work to be performed. The importance of verifying that the specifications have been carried out fully and competently cannot be exaggerated; these superintendents are the technicians responsible to upper management for the seaworthy condition of the ship. The protection of the owner's interests, especially in regard to meeting standards of the classification societies, underwriters, and governmental agencies, must always be a paramount consideration. To this end, appropriate liaison must be maintained with the technical representatives of these bodies to ensure that their inspectors will be on hand at the appropriate times.

Supervising vessel fueling, providing instructions to the ship concerning records of fuel consumption, and establishing the tests to be conducted on fuel taken aboard in places other than the home port are particular responsibilities of the superintendent engineer. These have attained new significance as the uniformity and quality of marine fuel and diesel oil became questionable following the petroleum crisis of 1973. In some instances, the office of the superintendent engineer may prepare the plans for bunkering the ship during a voyage; in any event, the bunkering records kept by this office may be consulted by staff members whenever necessary.

COMMISSARY (STEWARD'S) DIVISION

The *commissary superintendent* supervises all aspects of activities related to the care and feeding of the shipboard personnel. This official, who invariably has a background of seafaring experience as a ship's chief steward, establishes policy for the operation of all aspects of the steward's department (often designated as the catering department) afloat. As ships come into the home port, the commissary superintendent inspects them to ensure that they meet company standards of cleanliness, storage, and record-keeping and that the physical condition of the accommodations and food preparation spaces is satisfactory. Ships' chief stewards are guided and in-structed in the most efficient and effective ways of preparing and serving food; frequently a master menu will be furnished by the commissary su-perintendent for use during the voyage. All requisitions for foodstuffs are submitted to the commissary superintendent for approval before being sent to the purchasing department. All matters relating to safe operating prac-tice are of major concern as are instructions for the proper and safe perfor-mance of duties of steward's department personnel.

A major activity of the commissary division is the procurement of competent seafaring personnel, and therefore the superintendent maintains good relations with the maritime unions. In the absence of government certifications of competence or standards of proficiency in the performance of the duties of steward personnel, the commissary superintendent is free to establish (within the framework of the agreement with the maritime un-ion) appropriate qualifications for selection, promotion, and dismissal of commissary staff.

A very important part of the routine of the commissary superinten-dent's office is checking supplies when they are delivered to the ship. This entails the coordination of schedules with the purchasing division and the assignment of inspectors to examine foods as they are brought to the ship. It is standard practice in U. S. shipping companies to have a qualified inspec-tor from the U. S. Department of Agriculture examine and approve all meat, poultry, eggs, butter, and vegetables before they are accepted by the ship.

PURCHASING DIVISION

The duties of the purchasing division are set forth in detail in chapter 12, "Ship Husbandry—Procurement of Vessel Stores, Supplies, and Services."

TERMINAL DIVISION

The *terminal manager* is in charge of all activities directly related to han-dling the cargo moving into and out of the ships at the company's terminal. Whether the carriers are engaged in the breakbulk or the container trade, the terminal division must employ scores of skilled workers as well as nu-merous clerks; it expends large amounts of money for rent of facilities, operation of equipment, and compensation of personnel. The terminal man-ager should have extensive experience in all phases of cargo handling, demonstrating unusual competence as an administrator and supervisor. The terminal manager is the company's technical advisor on all matters dealing with cargo handling, stevedoring, and management of the marine terminal. The manager's immediate seniors in the executive structure are the operating manager and the vice president, operations. Functionally, the terminal division has four sections: receipt and delivery of cargo, stevedoring, administration, and protection and custodial care.

The *receiving clerk* is one of the key assistants to the terminal manager. This person is in charge of the office through which pass all papers connected with outbound cargo brought to the terminal for loading aboard a ship. The actual examination of the cargo is performed by *checkers,* who are hired by the day as they are needed. When cargo arrives at the terminal, a checker is assigned by the receiving clerk's office to inspect, count, and measure the packages and to insert the appropriate data on the dock receipt. The completed form, initialed by the checker, is returned to the receiving clerk for authentication. The original goes to the delivering carrier as proof that the cargo has been accepted in the condition noted on the dock receipt. Throughout the process of loading the ship, a member of the receiving office staff makes frequent surveys of the cargo spaces to ascertain the exact area in which lots of cargo are stowed.

In addition to handling the documentation described above, the receiving clerk assists the terminal manager in laying out the transit shed for the next ship. Copies of the booking clerk's daily reports serve to indicate the quantity of cargo for each port of call and thereby suggest the amount of floor space to reserve for those ports. Truck traffic into the terminal area is controlled by the receiving clerk, who issues directions to drivers as they arrive consistent with the number of checkers available to oversee the unloading of the cargo from the vehicles.

Terminals operated by containership companies follow almost the same routine, except that the role of the checker is minimized. The exterior condition of the container is inspected carefully, the condition of the seal on the container's door latch is examined, and appropriate data to identify the container are recorded. Containers are weatherproof and are stored in "container yards (CY)," sometimes on wheeled chassis (this operation is known as a "wheeled operation") and sometimes dismounted and stacked two or more high (this operation is known as a "grounded operation"). Thousands of containers are assembled in a large terminal, and a highly sophisticated computer system controls their receipt, inspection, locations in the yard, movements within the yard and to the ship's side, and stowage aboard the ship.

CHART NO. 4   TERMINAL DIVISION

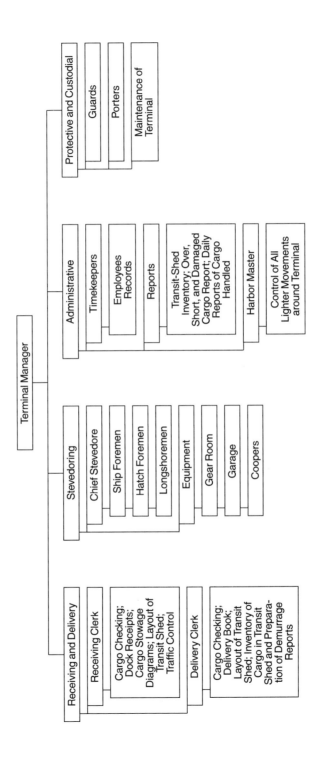

Terminal Manager

Receiving and Delivery
- Receiving Clerk
  - Cargo Checking; Dock Receipts; Cargo Stowage Diagrams; Layout of Transit Shed; Traffic Control
- Delivery Clerk
  - Cargo Checking; Delivery Book; Layout of Transit Shed; Inventory of Cargo in Transit Shed and Preparation of Demurrage Reports

Stevedoring
- Chief Stevedore
  - Ship Foremen
  - Hatch Foremen
  - Longshoremen
  - Equipment
  - Gear Room
  - Garage
  - Coopers

Administrative
- Timekeepers
- Employees Records
- Reports
  - Transit-Shed Inventory; Over, Short, and Damaged Cargo Report; Daily Reports of Cargo Handled
- Harbor Master
  - Control of All Lighter Movements around Terminal

Protective and Custodial
- Guards
- Porters
- Maintenance of Terminal

The *delivery clerk* has functions similar to those of the receiving clerk, except that the delivery clerk is concerned entirely with inbound cargo. As the consignees claim their goods, a checker is assigned to inspect the packages to ascertain their condition at the moment of transfer to the consignee. The checker's report is filed in the delivery office, and the trucker or other inland carrier signs for the cargo in the delivery book, which shows the date and hour when the ocean carrier released the goods. The delivery clerk also aids the terminal manager in laying out the terminal for incoming cargo, using information transmitted from the overseas ports to the inbound freight department. The delivery clerk takes periodic inventory of the transit shed to determine what cargo has not been claimed, and what lots have been on the transit shed's deck in excess of the allowed free storage time. From these records, charges for storage (demurrage) are compiled.

For containership terminals, the responsibility imposed upon the delivery clerk is the same as in the breakbulk terminals, but the details of operation are incorporated into the computer system.

The loading and unloading of ships employed in breakbulk service is a specialized activity normally performed by independent contractors rather than by the shipping company. Once awarded the contract, the stevedoring firm assigns a supervisor to the terminal. This *chief stevedore* or *stevedore superintendent,* although on the contractor's payroll, functions as a de facto member of the terminal manager's staff. This individual oversees the performance of the longshoremen. The details of each day's work as required to meet the schedule set forth by the terminal manager—number of gangs to be employed, supporting equipment needed, specialized workers to be assigned, and safety precautions to be followed if unusual cargo is handled—are the concerns of the stevedore superintendent, not of the terminal manager. The terminal manager ensures that the terms and conditions of the contract are carried out, that longshoremen are not idle, and that the responsibility for damage to cargo that occurs in the terminal is fixed at the earliest practical moment.

Many stevedoring contracts stipulate that the contractor will furnish all gear and equipment. Usually the stevedore company also employs the mechanics and carpenters necessary to maintain these items in proper condition. The terminal provides the space for shops. Where the contract requires the shipowner to provide and maintain the gear and equipment, the terminal manager must exercise positive supervision to make certain that all requisite materiel is in dependable operating condition.

Container terminals represent very large investments of capital. Besides the space needed to store and to maneuver the containers, multimillion-dollar cranes are used to hoist the containers into and out of the ships, and other highly specialized equipment is employed to stack containers in the yard or to shift containers from chassis to the ground and vice versa. Few container companies own these terminals, preferring to lease them from public bodies (port authorities, cities, or state agencies). Relatively few laborers are needed, and those who are hired are considered as skilled operators rather than manual workers. Some containership operators manage their terminals completely with their own personnel, while others contract for everything: terminal space, labor, equipment, and supervision.

Administratively, a great deal of paperwork is processed by the terminal division. Among the numerous reports submitted in connection with each loading and unloading operation of a breakbulk ship, those prepared by the *timekeeper,* the *safety engineer,* and the *stevedore superintendent* are most useful in evaluating the competence of the labor force. The timekeeper's records are compiled daily and show how many workers were employed at any time; the number of hours of straight time and overtime work; and the workers and number of hours assigned to handle premium or penalty cargo (commodities for which longshoremen receive extra compensation). Reports filed by the safety engineer (or the official charged with responsibility for safety of personnel) supply details of safety meetings, accidents, injuries, or equipment failures that occurred and were placed under investigation. From the stevedore superintendents come data on the actual performance of longshoremen in terms of tons of cargo handled per hour, stoppages and the reasons therefor, problems encountered in the stowage or discharge operation, and related details.

Each morning, a report is drawn up to show the amount of cargo handled by the terminal during the preceding twenty-four hours. As a vessel is finished, a report of any cargo that has been overcarried, short-delivered, or damaged is prepared. Inventories of unclaimed lots of cargo are inspected and brought up to date. All these documents are channeled through the terminal manager's office before being disseminated to the divisions concerned. By inspection of these papers, the terminal manager is able to gain a summary of activity during the period covered.

In containership terminals, although the computer is used to bring together all the details, the same types of reports must be prepared regularly to provide the basis for evaluating the performance of the terminal organization. The enormous cost of the ships makes rapid turnaround essential, and maintaining control of the terminal activity is a vital part of attaining that goal.

Some ports have a significant quantity of cargo moved within their limits by lighters—barges with no means of propulsion. Any terminal that has a steady flow of lighter traffic may have among its supervisors a *harbormaster,* who controls the arrival, moorings, and departures of these craft. All lighters come under the harbormaster's supervision as soon as they are moored in terminal waters, and they are shifted when and where the harbormaster directs in order to fulfill the cargo-working plans. When the lighter is emptied, the harbormaster notifies the owner of this fact and orders the lighter to be moved to a point where it can await its owner without interfering with other operations. It is important that prompt notification of the release of the lighter be given to that craft's owner in order to fix the exact time when the terminal's responsibility comes to an end.

Maintenance of the physical plant is a necessary and important activity. Security guards often are assigned the duty of reporting to the maintenance office whenever they observe something that needs attention: a deck plank that should be replaced, an electrical conduit that has been damaged, a break in the protective fencing around the terminal, or piles of debris ready for removal. The maintenance workers who react to these reports sometimes are placed under the supervision of the protective division for administrative control and routine assignments of work. Large-scale projects such as repainting the interior of the transit shed, resurfacing the working area, or installing new lights, automatically invite the terminal manager's personal attention since they entail major financial expenditures and a possible rearrangement of all terminal activity during the job.

As the overall supervisor, the terminal manager must be alert at all times to poor working practices that reduce efficiency or increase the risk of injury to employees. In addition, the terminal manager must always seek better and more economical ways, both in terms of time and of money, to handle cargo. As appropriate, the terminal manager makes suggestions for modification or construction of terminal facilities. Finally, and perhaps most important, the terminal manager participates in the formulation of all programs and policies relating to the terminal and terminal personnel.

The organization of a liner-service company can be as varied as the number of companies that exist. What they all have in common, however, is that their particular structure is designed to allow them to operate efficiently as they carry out their mission. The functions required to carry out the mission will be identical no matter what size the company may be, but individual titles may vary somewhat from company to company. Close examination of any one company's structure will give the observer insight into the management philosophy of the company.

CHAPTER SIX

The Conference System

From the early days of transoceanic shipping until the present, an international flavor has characterized the business of moving goods from one land to another. Merchants of many nations brought their wares to overseas markets, seeking the most profitable transactions. They cherished their own ideas of what constituted proper business practice, and resisted vigorously any effort of one sovereign power to impose its code of commercial morality upon the citizens of another country. This almost instinctive hostility toward regulation was learned early by shipping men and women who had inherited from their predecessors a sturdy independence and a willingness to assume great risks in exchange for great returns. Despite this attitude, however, there was a dim awareness among shipowners that uninhibited competition could be disastrous not only to them but to their customers. The alternative to government control had to be an industry-generated and industry-managed system of supervision and regulation.[1]

Awareness changed into concern when improvements in steam engineering, particularly as they applied to marine installations, made it possible for powered vessels to undertake long voyages. Bitter rivalry between the steamers and the sailing ships became the normal condition of business, and it forced the growth of the idea that shipowners who faced the same problems on the same trade routes and who scrambled for a share of the available business had much to gain by establishing some form of mutually acceptable regulation. By surrendering a fraction of their rights to independent action in exchange for protection from predatory competition, the shipowners hoped to benefit themselves as well as their clients.[2]

The soundness of this idea was put to the test in 1875 when steamship owners in the London-Calcutta trade became involved in a freight rate "war" with the operators of sailing ships moving between these two ports. In their search for a way to end this unhappy situation, the owners called a conference at which was advanced the idea of an industry association to police the trade. Approval of the idea resulted in the formation of the Calcutta Conference.[3] To understand and appreciate the complexity of the issues that faced the shipowners, the events significant to the development of this conference merit attention.

Just at the time the Suez Canal was opened in 1869, steamships were not only becoming more numerous and more efficient, but they were replacing sailing ships on one route after another. Because they did not depend upon the wind, the powered vessels could take advantage of the shorter distance to India made possible by the canal, whereas the sailing ships were thwarted by adverse wind conditions in the Red Sea and were forced to use the route around the Cape of Good Hope, almost 4,000 nautical miles longer. The steamers not only could make the voyage more quickly, but they also could predict with reasonable accuracy the day of arrival at their destination. To offset these disadvantages, the sailing ship owners reduced freight rates, a move met by even greater concessions from the steamship operators. The destructive nature of this struggle immediately became apparent.

The major steamship operators (Peninsular and Oriental Steam Navigation Company, British India Company, and T. and J. Harrison) and some of the smaller carriers met in the 1875 conference and jointly agreed to end concessions to shippers, to adopt uniform freight rates, and to offer identical terms of carriage. It was expected that these arrangements would stabilize shipping practice and ensure more regularity in schedules, less frequent adjustment of rates, and greater convenience for shippers. The importers and exporters, however, resented the loss of concessions and threatened to transfer a larger proportion of their business to the sailing ships, which were offering more favorable terms. The prospect of losing cargoes prompted the conference to develop the "exclusive patronage" contract, which would commit the shipper to give business only to carriers belonging to the conference. The shippers rejected the proffered contract, demanding some guarantee of preferential treatment before they would bind themselves to the conference. Responding to this demand, in 1877 the conference proposed to establish the "deferred rebate," to be paid after a designated period during which loyalty to the conference had been demonstrated.

The arrangement required that shippers desiring to receive the rebate agree to give their business only to the lines that were members of the Calcutta Conference. In return for this exclusive patronage contract, the conference members bound themselves to return one-tenth of all freights paid during a six-month period contingent upon the continuing exclusive patronage of the conference carriers during a further period of six months. Failure to live up to the terms of the contract automatically canceled both the earned refund and the credits being established toward a second refund.

The penalty for "disloyalty" was set forth in the following words, taken from a circular issued in 1885 by the England-China Conference:

> Shipments for London by non-Conference steamers, at any of the ports of China or Hong Kong, will exclude the firm making such shipments from participation in the return, during the whole six-monthly period within which they have been made, or any portion of the freight charged, even though the firm elsewhere may have given exclusive support to the Conference lines.[4]

The working of the new system was described very clearly in this quotation from the report of the Royal Commission on Shipping Rings submitted to Parliament in 1909:

> . . . if at the end of a certain period (usually four or six months) they have not shipped goods by any vessel other than those despatched by members of the Conference, shippers will be credited with a sum equivalent to a certain part (usually 10%) of the aggregate freights paid on their shipments during that period, and the sum will be paid over to them if, at the end of a further period, usually four to six months, they have continued to confine their shipments to vessels belonging to members of the conference. The sum so paid is known as a "deferred rebate." . . . If, during any period, a shipper sends any quantity of goods, however small, by a vessel other than those despatched by the Conference lines, he becomes disentitled to rebates on any of his shipments by conference vessels during that period and the preceding one.[5]

Acceptance of the exclusive patronage contract was a voluntary act on the part of the individual shipper. The alternative was to pay the rate quoted in the tariff without expectation of receiving a partial refund. Inevitably, this meant that the landed cost of the goods at the destination would be greater for one who did not sign the contract than for one who signed. This economic pressure brought many shippers under the contract; by the close of the century the deferred rebate scheme prevailed in practically all the conferences of carriers operating out of the United Kingdom. In many of these trade routes, the conference system with its rigid hold on shippers produced the closest approach to a monopoly that is possible in ocean shipping.

The Royal Commission found that deferred rebates had proven effective in gaining and holding the loyalty of shippers, as evidenced by the large sums the carriers owed to individual shippers. To control this limited monopoly, the commission recommended that conferences be directed to deposit with the Board of Trade copies of all conference agreements as well as rebate circulars and claim forms, all memoranda of understandings with lines outside the conference, and all agreements with shippers' associations that had been recognized by the Board of Trade. To satisfy complaints that customers did not have ready access to tariffs of conference carriers, it was further recommended that tariffs be published and at least one copy be filed with the Board of Trade.[6]

In 1923, the British Imperial Shipping Committee concluded a further study of steamship conferences and found that, to some extent, deferred rebates were necessary in most trades. The system, however, did deprive the shippers of much of their freedom of choice and removed the corrective effect of free competition.

The contention is valid that the deferred rebate is an effective shield from the competition of both independent liner operators and tramps. Few shippers will risk the loss of benefits accrued under the deferred rebate system to take advantage of the comparatively small savings to be gained by employing either the independents or, when the volume of cargo justifies movement in shipload lots, by chartering a tramp. As a useful tool in building up dependable patronage, the value of the deferred rebate was acknowledged in both the English and the American investigations.

American attitudes toward monopolies and competition were quite different from those of both Western Europe and Japan, where monopolies and agreements in restraint of trade were acceptable business practices. In the United States, those arrangements among commercial firms were outlawed and discouraged by the stringent provisions of the antitrust laws. Aware of the restrictive nature of conferences and consistent with the antitrust sentiment prevailing in the United States, a committee of the House of Representatives was appointed in 1912 to investigate the conference system and its effect upon American foreign commerce.

Under the chairmanship of Representative Joshua W. Alexander of Missouri, a subcommittee of the House Committee on Merchant Marine and Fisheries conducted the investigation and held hearings over a two-year period. In 1914, it published its four-volume report and made a number of recommendations for legislative action. Chief among them was that the conference system be exempted from the provisions of the antitrust law, but made subject to continuous scrutiny by a regulatory agency. Two practices of European conferences were condemned: the deferred rebate and the use of the "fighting ship," a vessel used on a sea-lane by a group of operators (for example, a conference) for the express purpose of excluding, preventing, or reducing competition by driving a nonmember carrier off that route.

The Alexander Committee considered that the deferred rebate was intended to establish a near-monopoly of ocean transportation on the trade route in which the carriers operated. The fighting ship was viewed as the weapon of monopoly. Evidence had been presented proving that this practice had been followed, particularly in the North Atlantic, to the detriment of nonconference carriers.[7]

The Alexander Committee's recommendations furnished the solid basis for what became the Shipping Act of 1916. Conferences organized in the United States were to be exempted from the provisions of the Sherman antitrust law on condition that all joint actions be subject to some form of government supervision. The tools of monopoly—deferred rebates, fighting ships, and discriminatory practices—were disapproved. To support its recommendations, the committee declared that trade with foreign nations required that uniform rates be available to any and all shippers, that they be comparatively stable, and that they take into consideration all the elements of transportation. Those carriers that elected to operate outside of the conference framework were not subject to government control unless discrimination was charged by a shipper.

It is important to note that the attitude and thinking of the Alexander Committee, which opposed cartels and other restrictions on trade but recognized that international shipping required special consideration and treatment, have been accepted and supported by the Congress. In a report written in 1961 by the House Committee on Merchant Marine and Fisheries, the need for a carefully controlled exemption from antitrust legislation was set forth in these words:

> The conference, fixing as it does rates and practices, is permitted to exist only as an exception to the antitrust laws of the United States, and such exception is granted only because of the peculiar nature of ocean transportation, and provided certain conditions are met. In order to secure the benefits of such immunity from the antitrust acts, the conferences are required by Section 15 of the Shipping Act of 1916 to file all their agreements with the appropriate regulatory body, which at present is the Federal Maritime Board, and obtain approval of that body. The Board has considerable jurisdiction under the terms of that act to regulate the conferences and see that they observe the restrictions upon which their immunity from the operation of the antitrust acts is predicated.[8]

   Perusal of the various laws enacted by the Congress of the United
States to regulate conferences reveals the persistence of the nineteenth century hostility toward monopolies of any sort. This attitude may be discerned
in the provisions of the Shipping Act of 1984, even though by this date the
influence of these associations of carriers has been curtailed very sharply.
Intra-conference competition, for example, was evident in the frequent announcements to the shipping public that rates on certain commodities were
"open"—that is, each carrier in the conference was free to set rates at any
level that seemed appropriate. (See sample rate increase notice.) Significant
and unilateral improvements in the quality of service also demonstrated the
rivalry between conference members. In combination, these actions sig-
naled that conferences did not pose the threat of monopoly.

GENERAL RATE INCREASE
EFFECTIVE FEBRUARY 1, 1986

The Member Lines of the United States and Gulf Ports/Eastern Mediterranean and North African Freight Conference announce that spiral-
ing operational expenditures necessitate the implementation of a
General Rate Increase, for both Port to Port and Intermodal Rates, effective February 1, 1986, as follows:

   Five percent (5%) on rates up to $165.00 W/M or M
   Five percent (5%) on all weight rated commodities
   Five percent (5%) on all container rates, rounded up to the high-
   est $25.00
   Minimum Bills of Lading and Optional Bills of Lading will also be
   increased by $10.00

Any questions you may have relative to this announcement should be
directed to the Member Lines, their Agents or the Conference Office.

   Constellation Line   Prudential Lines, Inc.
   Farrell Lines, Inc.   Waterman Steamship Corp.
   Lykes Lines

                               R. H. Cabrera
                               Chairman

   An analysis of the liner services of nine major maritime nations conducted in 1957 pointed out that the fleets of the individual carriers were
small. Forty percent of the operators owned twenty or fewer ships each; an

equal percentage claimed ten or fewer vessels. The largest single owner fleet embraced only 2 percent of the total number of ships assigned to liner service. From these facts the conclusion was drawn that no single operator nor any combination of two or more operators attempted to dominate a trade route through control of the largest fleet. The conferences, consequently, could be described as having neither the capacity nor the intention to establish a monopoly.[9]

THE "8900" RATE AGREEMENT
WISHES TO ANNOUNCE:

DUE TO STEADILY INCREASING OPERATIONAL COSTS, THE "8900" RATE AGREEMENT HAS FOUND IT NECESSARY TO INCREASE RATES AND CHARGES IN F.M.C. NO. 9, 10 & 11 FREIGHT TARIFFS. EFFECTIVE MAY 1, 1985, AN INCREASE OF FIVE PERCENT WILL BECOME EFFECTIVE WITH THE DATE THE VESSEL SAILS FROM THE PORT OF LOADING OR THE DATE THE CARGO IS RECEIVED BY THE CARRIER, WHICHEVER BENEFITS THE CARGO.

THE "8900" RATE AGREEMENT COVERS TRADE FROM POINTS IN THE UNITED STATES MOVING THROUGH U.S. ATLANTIC AND GULF PORTS AT INTERCHANGE TO MIDDLE EAST PORTS, WEST OF KARACHI AND NORTH EAST OF ADEN, BUT EXCLUDING ADEN AND KARACHI AND TO INLAND POINTS IN BAHRAIN, IRAN, IRAQ, KUWAIT, OMAN, QATAR, SAUDI ARABIA AND THE UNITED ARAB EMIRATES.

Very truly yours,
THE "8900" LINES
ANTHONY A. DE GIGLIO
VICE CHAIRMAN

As the conference system evolved after 1875, the exclusive patronage contract (also called the loyalty contract) with its accompanying dual freight rate structure was considered indispensable to the existence of the associations. The purpose of the contract was to provide the members of each conference with a steady flow of cargo from shippers whose support would be forthcoming over a reasonably long period of time. In exchange, the members of the conference agreed to reduce the nominal (or "tariff") freight rate by a stipulated percentage—a benefit granted only to those shippers who signed the contract.

In the United States, from the effective date of the Shipping Act of 1916 until 1948, the regulatory authority exercised only the most cursory type of supervision over the contracts on the premise that the basic agreement having been approved, issuance of the contract by the conference automatically was approved. In 1948, the Maritime Commission carefully examined the details of the dual rate system and prescribed modifications to be made by one conference. A major attack on the dual rate system was initiated in 1949 and culminated in 1952 in a decision by the U.S. Supreme Court that the differential between contract and noncontract rates was arbitrary and consequently unlawfully discriminatory. The use of the dual rate structure by two North Atlantic conferences therefore was permanently enjoined. Further legal action culminated in the Supreme Court's ruling, announced on May 19, 1958, in the case *Federal Maritime Board et al. v Isbrandtsen Company, Inc., United States of America, and Secretary of Agriculture,* which held that the use of contract/noncontract rates proposed by the Japan–Atlantic and Gulf Freight Conference violated that provision of the Shipping Act of 1916 prohibiting restrictions to trade and unjust discrimination (in this case, setting up a retaliatory device to stifle competition). The dual rate system was declared illegal.[10]

Congressional hearings conducted between 1958 and 1961 examined all aspects of the conference system. Testimony offered by both carriers and shippers led to the conclusion that conferences were essential in the foreign trade of the United States. The loyalty contracts, with the associated dual rate structure, were given general approval. As the conferences existed at that time, these factors supported their continued operation:

1. The "ease of market entry"—any ship on the ocean may stop at any port and discharge or load cargo. It costs a great deal to establish a liner service, but nothing beyond the investment in a single ship for a tramp owner to participate, as opportunity affords, in a specific trade.
2. The rigid fixed and operating cost structure of the shipping industry. It costs almost as much to sail a ship one-quarter full as completely loaded. This may encourage the independent to cut rates as a means of obtaining cargo.
3. Lack of governmental control over the level of ocean freight rates.
4. A marked difference in the operating costs of similar ships flying diverse flags.
5. An imbalance between inbound and outbound cargo. For example, on the trade routes from U.S. ports on the Gulf of Mexico to the United Kingdom and European continent, the disparity was four to

one in favor of outbound loadings in 1959. This places enormous pressure on the carrier to find homeward cargoes.

6. Overtonnaging of ocean trade routes, which tends to accentuate the already severe competition existing among ocean carriers.[11]

Conferences were intended to provide, through the carriers' own efforts, the stability demanded by international trade but not furnished by national governments. The dependence of liner companies upon regular and repeated patronage is well known and is corroborated by the findings of a recent study of a trade route originating in the United Kingdom. Of the 3,900 different clients of the liner services on that route, only three shippers accounted for 25 percent of the total tonnage carried. The next 25 percent was generated by fourteen customers, and the third 25 percent came from eighty-two patrons. Only 2.53 percent of the shippers using these liners contributed 75 percent of the cargoes. Another line's experience was similar. On the route between northwest England and the Middle East, between 25 and 40 percent of the business originated with twelve shippers.[12]

It is significant that the Senate Committee on Commerce, in its report written in 1961 on the proposed amendment to the Shipping Act of 1916, quoted with approbation the comments of the Alexander Committee in 1914:

It is the view of the committee that open competition cannot be assured for any length of time by ordering existing agreements terminated. The entire history of steamship agreements shows that in ocean commerce there is no happy medium between war and peace when several lines engage in the same trade. Most of the numerous agreements and conference arrangements discussed in the foregoing report were the outcome of rate wars, and represent a truce between the contending lines. To terminate existing agreements would necessarily bring about one of two results: the lines either would engage in rate wars which would mean elimination of the weak and the survival of the strong, or to avoid a costly struggle, they would consolidate through common ownership. Neither result can be prevented by legislation and either would mean a monopoly fully as effective [as], and it is believed more so than, can exist by virtue of an agreement.[13]

Three traditional types of conferences exist today: closed conferences that apportion the capacity of their members' ships to the volume of cargo offered (rationalization), closed conferences that do not practice rationalization, and open conferences that do not limit capacity of member fleets. Only the United States requires, as a matter of law, that conferences admit to membership any common carriers prepared to serve the trade routes covered by the associations. The 1990s brought a new kind of conference, a hybrid of the traditional conference, into existence. This super-conference is known as a global alliance and will be discussed later.

Proponents of the closed conferences with rationalization argue that it is only by limiting competition between carriers to a few dependable performers that the standards insisted upon by shippers will be maintained. Restricting membership in the conference to the number of carriers that will provide transportation for the proffered cargo is efficient and economical. Although conferences offer lower rates to those shippers who sign loyalty contracts, most of the cargo actually is controlled by a small number of shippers who are more concerned about the service they receive than with the relatively small saving afforded by the loyalty contracts. (In this connection, it is noteworthy that the Shipping Act of 1984 prohibits the use of loyalty contracts and dual freight rates.)

The records of two closed conferences that practiced rationalization and offered loyalty contracts support these comments. Over a twenty-year period, marked by times of political instability and operational difficulties, load factors for these conference members came to almost 90 percent of capacity.

More common than these conferences are the associations that have closed memberships but do not attempt to rationalize tonnage. While freight rates and other matters governing transportation of goods are agreed upon jointly, conference members continue to compete with each other for the available cargo. From time to time, because of economic conditions, some restrictions may be imposed, such as sharing cargo tonnage, allocating ports to be served, and arranging schedules to enhance the efficiency of ship employment. These coordinated efforts, even without rationalization, have been beneficial. One conference, for instance, reported that over a span of five years its load factors ranged between 75 and 90 percent in one direction and between 85 and 92 percent in the other direction.[14]

Advocates of the closed conference recognize the desirability of having the concerns of the shippers given full consideration and therefore recommend that so-called shippers' councils be formed to negotiate with the associated carriers. In support of their recommendation, these advocates point to the success of the Australian Meat Shippers' Council, which forced the conference covering the trade between Australia and the United States to lower its rates. A parallel case was that of the Australian wool-shipping interests, which formed the Joint Wool Commodity Group and exerted sufficient pressure on the Australian Northbound Shipping Conference to bring freight rates between Australia and Japan down by approximately 10 percent.[15]

The Australian Overseas Transportation Association is a major council whose functions are (1) to obtain economies in shipping by rationalizing tonnage, (2) to approve freight rates, and (3) to approve agreements between shippers and shipowners. Loyalty contracts and rebates, discounts, and the like are permitted. Founded in 1929, the association includes producers and exporters. Boards having significant influence on conference matters are the Dairy Products Control Board, the Wine Overseas Marketing Board, and the Meat Board. When the association was established, its goal was rationalization through cooperation, which left considerable strength in the hands of the shippers. The closed Australian conferences, based on strong loyalty contracts and rationalization with pooling of cargoes, have not led to the monopolistic abuses feared by some theorists.[16] It should be noted that one reason for the success of these groups is that the export trade in Australia is confined to a few commodities that are shipped in large quantities. This is not the case in many other nations.

Under the closed conference system, internal pressure upon members is exerted to operate only that number of ships required to satisfy the demands of the trade. To maintain a certain frequency of service without putting additional ships on the berth, a number of conference members in recent years contracted for space in each other's vessels. To cite a hypothetical case, company Alfa sails on alternate Fridays, and company Kappa schedules its departures on the same route for the intervening Fridays. Alfa has built up a strong clientele of loyal shippers who control a weekly total of 250 containers, which they insist upon dispatching every Friday but want the Alfa bill of lading and Alfa service at the port of discharge. To keep this business, Alfa contracts with Kappa for 250 container spaces on each sailing. This transaction is known in the trade as "space chartering." Alfa and Kappa retain their individuality. They do not merge any of their activities, nor do they reveal any carrier-shipper relationships. There is no reduction in intercompany and intraconference rivalry. The number of ships serving the trade route is maintained at the level that gives reasonable assurance of survival for conference members and forestalls disastrous freight rate wars. A significant and certainly not coincidental benefit is that the load factor of the conference members' ships is kept at satisfactory levels.

A British report on conferences contained these observations on the relative merits of open and closed conferences:

[T]he "open" conference appears least likely to serve the interests of shippers. It is also least likely to serve that of shipowners; in their evidence to us they agreed that such a conference arrangement typically resulted in low load factors, low profits, and rising freight rates . . . .

The "closed" conference with fully rationalized sailings therefore appears to us most likely to serve the best interests of both shippers and shipowners. We appreciate that we have here come to a different conclusion from those reached by some others who have studied conference arrangements; we believe that they may have given too little weight to the full range of the needs of shippers and to the practical results of unrestricted competition in all fields other than price. We identify the opportunity for providing a planned systematic series of sailings as the feature of shipping conferences which is potentially most beneficial. The full exploitation of that opportunity requires a "closed" conference.[17]

Conferences that may be joined by any common carriers serving the trade routes are precluded from setting up any restrictions on the number of ships or the total carrying capacity of vessels operated by conference members. Agreement is reached on a common tariff of freight rates, and some adjustments may be acceptable for sailing schedules. Competition within the ranks of the conferences, however, remains keen, often manifesting itself in unilateral revocation of published freight rates for particular commodities or independent action to retain current rates rather than adopt the conference's increase.

Advocates of the open conference assert that competition between carriers, held within the framework of the association, results in the lowest cost of transportation and the highest levels of service. In theory this may be true, but in the harsh realm of ship management the theory loses vitality. It is axiomatic that when too many ships seek too few cargoes, two results are inevitable: the revenue to the ship will be reduced to the unprofitable level, and the quality of service will suffer. Shippers have no institutional loyalties and use those vessels that meet their needs most effectively without regard to previous performance. As noted repeatedly in this volume, owners of cargo are concerned only that what they send across the oceans arrives in good condition and on schedule. Whether the carrier makes a profit or sustains a loss is not a matter of interest to either shipper or consignee.

Conferences, especially those that are governed by the U.S. law requiring open membership, have been losing their economic power for de-

COMPANIA PERUANA DE VAPORES (CPV)
(Peruvian State Line)

We regret the decision by members of The West Coast of South America Conference to put into effect 7/8/85 a general rate increase of 8%, both north and southbound to and from Peru and Chile.

CPV considers this increase inopportune at this time and hereby wishes to notify its customers, shippers and freight forwarders that we have already notified the Conference we intend to take "independent action" to and from Peru and Chile with current rates.

We hope this action will induce members of the Conference to reconsider their position and decline the general rate increase.

A member takes independent action against an increase in conference freight rates (New York *Journal of Commerce,* June 18, 1985, p. 18-A).

cades, and they no longer pose any threat to monopolizing a trade. In 1953, Daniel Marx, Jr., identified six factors that restricted the monopoly power of the conference:

1. Interconference competition.
2. Actual or potential competition from other lines which may or may not intend to join the conference.
3. Alternate sources of supply or markets.
4. Actual or potential competition from tramps.
5. Bargaining strength of shippers.
6. Government regulation or intervention.[18]

These factors still exert powerful constraints on the conferences. An important addition to Marx's list could have been made in 1985. This was the significant competition from airlines, which have siphoned off a very large percentage of the highest paying cargo. The economic effect on the waterborne carriers has been to distort the time-honored rate structure under which the revenue from commodities carried at high freight rates actually subsidized the movement of items that could not pay the full cost of sea carriage. It is not an exaggeration to assert that this competition from the airlines has undermined permanently the financial stability of many shipping companies.

The Shipping Act of 1984 directed that all agreements of conferences domiciled in the United States contain these provisions: (1) a statement of the purpose of the association; (2) specific assurance that any common carrier serving the trade route would be admitted (or readmitted) to membership upon application; (3) permission for a member to withdraw, upon reasonable notice to the conference, without a penalty; (4) establishment of an independent neutral body to police the obligations of the conference and its members; (5) a mechanism for consultations to resolve intercarrier disputes by a means other than judicial process and to cooperate with shippers to prevent and eliminate malpractice; (6) procedures to consider promptly shippers' requests and complaints; and (7) authorization for any conference member, upon advance notice of not more than ten days, to take independent action on any rate or service stipulated in the tariff filed with the Federal Maritime Commission.

In addition, the law specified that conferences might not issue loyalty contracts nor set up dual rate structures; they could make no refunds other than those provided for in the published tariffs, nor could they deny cargo space to any shipper who had filed a complaint or had patronized a competing carrier; and they might not employ fighting ships or offer deferred rebates. Discrimination between shippers or ports also was categorically forbidden.

A change from established procedure altered the role of the Federal Maritime Commission in enforcing the law against conferences. Today, the commission is empowered to investigate reports of alleged malpractice and, if sufficient evidence is uncovered, to refer the matter to the United States District Court of the District of Columbia for action. If the allegations are sustained, the district court can enjoin the conference(s) permanently against the questioned conduct. A carrier found in violation of the law or an order of the commission may be fined $5,000 per day for each violation. If the court determines that the violation(s) took place "willfully and knowingly," the penalty could be increased up to $25,000 per day per violation.

Experience with self-policing of the conference system by means of a neutral body has been favorable since the system was established on January 1, 1979, pursuant to a directive from the Federal Maritime Commission that included these stipulations:

1. The basic agreement forming the conference must show how complaints against conference members are to be handled.
2. The self-policing body must have no relationship to the conference members, and must be able to examine, and to acquire, whatever information and documents it needs by making appropriate demands upon the carriers concerned.
3. There must be provision for adjudicating disputes and for levying penalties. Accused parties must be afforded the opportunity to rebut charges made against them.

4. The self-policing agency must file two reports each year with the Federal Maritime Commission.
5. The self-policing agency may not limit the carriers they police from producing documents and information demanded by the Federal Maritime Commission, nor must the self-policing agency deny access by the commission to any data it may have accumulated in connection with an investigation.

In a clarifying statement, the commission announced that these "neutral bodies" would be expected to make "self-initiated, on-site investigations . . . regularly . . . into the activities of each member line." These investigations were to be handled

> . . . with reasonable discretion, and did not have to be identical in nature. As a matter of normal routine, the agencies were to reveal the identities of complaining parties, but this would be waived in those circumstances that might encourage retaliation by or against the member or . . . when it would unfairly prejudice the member's ability to rebut any material allegation made against it.

An example of the authority granted to a neutral body was set forth in a report published by the *New York Journal of Commerce* on September 15, 1983. A conference had contracted with a neutral body for policing service and included in the agreement the power to assess fines. Acting on complaints, the neutral body determined that a carrier member had been guilty of malpractice (although the offense was not described, it was said to have involved rebates from the published freight tariffs), and it assessed a fine of more than $9 million.

Historically, there has been criticism that the conferences do not prevent disastrous freight rate wars. This charge is true. Numerous wars have occurred on all trade routes. One of the more interesting (and one of the longest) was the war between the United States/South and East Africa Conference and the Seas Shipping Company (operating under the trade name of Robin Line. This war started in June 1935 when Robin Line announced its entry into the South and East African trade and applied for membership in the conference. The application was denied on the grounds that there already was sufficient conference tonnage available to meet the needs of the American shipping public. Robin persisted in its plans and announced sailings to South Africa. The conference replied by reducing rates, and in the course of the war, rates fell to $4 a ton, regardless of the commodity. By 1937, all exclusive patronage contracts between shippers and the conference had expired. A major American automobile manufacturer was asked to renew its contract with the conference but was given no assurance concerning the level to which the rates would go at the end of the war. The manufacturer refused to sign the contract, and the conference retaliated by refusing to allot space to the automobiles of this shipper. The manufacturer appealed to the Robin Line for assistance, and an agreement was reached to transport the vehicles to South Africa for $8 a measurement ton. Robin Line also promised that after the war ended, the freight rate would be no higher than it had been in 1935. This had the effect of stifling further gains from the war, which came to an abrupt end on July 1, 1937. It was characterized throughout by bitterness on both sides. It is noteworthy that from the end of the war until the sale of Robin Line to other owners in 1955, there was no dual rate system in the South African conference.[19]

The introduction in 1969 of new, very large, and extremely fast containerships on the routes from Japan, Hong Kong, and Taiwan to both Pacific and Atlantic coasts of the United States precipitated new rivalries that nearly destroyed the entire conference structure in the Pacific. Containerships were placed in service as quickly as individual owners could take delivery, and in a short time a major problem of overtonnaging existed. The fierce struggle for available cargoes was characterized by rate cutting, secret rebating, and wholesale resignation from the conferences followed by recision of the resignations when a modicum of agreement was established. As the volume of cargo dropped substantially during the worldwide business recession that began in 1971, turmoil on the route increased significantly, but under pressure from numerous governments a period of relative calm was reached in 1975. The transpacific trade has been plagued intermittently since then by a series of skirmishes between the carriers, precipitated again by adverse economic conditions in the entire Pacific basin. Several carriers were forced into bankruptcy, conference memberships were reduced, and sailing frequencies were curtailed. In mid-1985, some semblance of peace prevailed, but the basic difficulty of too many ships looking for too few cargoes persisted.[20]

Every discussion on conferences stresses that they give stable rates to the shipping public. This beneficial result is obtained in part from the conferences' practice of making rates that members are able to accept. Reaching agreements on rates often is a tedious process, and during these discussions the shipping public gains from the status quo being maintained. Furthermore, proposed rate changes must be filed with the Federal Maritime Commission, and advance notice of intended increases in rates must be given to concerned parties. The FMC currently accepts electronic filing of tariffs.

As a normal function, conferences from time to time initiate reviews of their rate structures, usually as a result of developments that necessitate earning greater revenues. Typical of this situation was the drastic rise in the cost of bunker fuel oil in 1973, which most conferences countered by adding a surcharge to the rates. Shippers do not have to wait for this kind of conference action to have rates examined; they may submit applications for adjustments in freight rates at any time. These requests are handled by the rate committee, composed of a small group of traffic experts appointed by the conference chair from the membership. The shipper furnishes data relating to the value of the commodity: its selling price at point of importation, the price of competing articles offered on the same market, the number of tons of the commodity that the shipper exports (or imports) in a year, and the freight rate suggested by the shipper as fair and reasonable. Comparison of this information with similar data supplied by the statistical section of the conference staff leads to a recommendation from the committee to the whole conference. If the recommendation is approved, the change must be forwarded to the Federal Maritime Commission for filing. Eventually, new pages showing the revised rates are published and distributed to holders of the conference tariff.

Conferences have sustained a number of misfortunes in recent years in addition to pressures from shipper organizations such as those in Australia, Europe, Japan, and the United States. The overtonnaging of trade routes is a worldwide problem, resulting in the withdrawals from membership of several carriers. Freight rate wars have become almost cyclical in the more important trade routes, a situation not ameliorated by the growing use of intermodal routings, especially those overland movements competing with the all-water transportation of goods to or from the Orient to the Atlantic and Gulf Coasts of the United States as well as to European destinations.

Whereas it may have been true early in the twentieth century that conference carriers dominated but did not monopolize the major trade routes of the world, the situation has changed significantly. Economic pressures caused by the prolonged recession that has afflicted the shipping of all nations since 1973 have forced many carriers either to suspend operations or to sell out to larger and stronger organizations. The enormous increase in the cost of building and operating containerships encouraged the formation of consortia of carriers. Space chartering between carriers that would otherwise be intense rivals proved to be another way for individual carriers to maintain frequency of service without the necessity of operating ships carrying only partial loads. Rerouting vessels to one or two ports at each end of the route and the increasing use of feeder ships has made possible reductions in fleet sizes. International balances of payments and overvalued currencies created unbalanced movements in which vessel revenue was derived disproportionately from one direction rather than from the round voyage. None of these actions and problems, it should be noted, was exclusive to conference members.

The maritime world has certainly changed since conferences came into existence. The traditional trade routes are still plagued with excess capacity, but now the shippers are more organized.[21] They are demanding that the carriers compete in improved services to larger trade areas with bigger and faster ships. Shippers are putting pressure on carriers to achieve greater economies of scale and thus lower per-unit cost, to provide better intermodal connectivity, and to improve terminal operations. As the new environment of the 1990s evolved, it became more difficult for carriers to make a profit. In their attempt to change with the times, increasing numbers of conference members took independent action by lowering their rates to gain market shares. The result of all of the changes was a general weakening of the conference system.

Today, shippers' associations[22] are becoming better organized and more powerful, and they are putting their collective pressure on carriers, conferences, and Congress to change the old conference system. In particular, shippers' organizations would like the industry to move toward deregulation and to end the antitrust immunity for conferences.

On May 1, 1999, the Ocean Shipping Reform Act of 1998 took effect. It permits vessel operators and shippers to sign confidential contracts, requires the disclosure of cargo movements on the docks to U.S. longshore unions, and promotes intermodalism by permitting carriers to offer inland transport services. In addition, it keeps the FMC intact but eliminates the need for paper tariff filing. Rates may now be filed with privately owned tariff bureaus.[23]

Carriers still look to the conference system as a mechanism that allows them to be profitable. As each carrier brings a new generation of containerships into service, the problem of how to fill space becomes a greater concern to it. Some carriers, in their struggle to fill the huge new ships and cope with rate volatility on each trade route, realize that the old conference system does not work very well in today's environment. In their attempt to change with the time, they are experimenting with different kinds of agreements and arrangements that they hope will protect them from predatory practices, keep their ships full, eliminate drastic fluctuations in rates, and make their operations more efficient.

The current trend among carriers is to forge long-term, multilane, global agreements with competitors who rationalize their cargo where it is appropriate. Some of these new arrangements include space-charter or slot-charter agreements, vessel-sharing agreements, hybrid conferences and shipping alliances (known by such names as discussion agreements, alliances, global alliances, consortia, global partnerships), and other agreements where shipping lines share terminals, containers and chassis, other assets, and even some staff.[24] It is interesting to note that these new shipping alliances can be made up of conference members as well as independent carriers, both working together for their mutual survival.

Typical of the new arrangements was an agreement in December 1996 when two major carriers, one an independent and one a conference carrier, joined forces in a transpacific space-charter pact. In the agreement, the Japanese Nippon Yusen Kaisha Limited (NYK Line) leased space on the Korean Hyundai Merchant Marine Company vessels operating between Asia and the U.S. West Coast.[25] While alliances can restructure their schedules and combine resources, they must keep their marketing and pricing separate in order to avoid losing their individual identity and to prevent the risk of prosecution over price-fixing. Alliances do not have the antitrust immunity that conferences enjoy. What this obviously leads to is the situation where the same cargoes move to the same destination on the same ship but at different rates.

One of the significant characteristics of the new alliances is that they each control large capacities. As an example, the Grand Alliance (Hapag-Lloyd, Neptune Orient Lines, Nippon Yusen Kaisha) controls a fleet of approximately 70 ships with a capacity of 400,000 twenty-foot equivalent units (TEUs). The largest alliance in terms of number of ships is the Maersk/Sealand global alliance that controls about 175 ships with a 347,000 TEU capacity.[26] As more companies join the emerging alliances, their fleet size and capacities will surely increase.

An alternative to companies joining alliances is for shipping lines to merge.[27] P&O Containers and Nedlloyd merged to form the P&O Nedlloyd Container Line which offers 112 owned or chartered ships plus a global network of services.[28] It was intended that this merger would allow the new company to be large enough to operate independently in the Europe-Asia Trade. It is a foregone conclusion that there will be other mergers as the industry tries to maintain stability in a very competitive business.

Alliances and mergers will be significant factors in shipping in the immediate future. However, conferences will continue to thrive on those trade routes with smaller volumes of cargoes, smaller ships servicing them, and slower growth potential.

Conferences do serve a useful purpose. They still attract members from the stable group of carriers, and they continue to set and maintain standards of service that are desired by shippers. If they ever posed a threat to monopolize the movement of cargo on trade routes, that day has passed into history, and conferences today are more likely to be seeking ways to ensure that their members will survive the difficult period that has overtaken them. That they can and do perform a useful role has been demonstrated in the past, and it seems that, as they march into the second century of their existence, they will continue to provide certain standards of conduct and service that will be welcomed by those who use the seas to transport their goods.

CHAPTER SEVEN

Passenger Vessel Operations

It has been necessary for people to cross waterways—rivers, lakes, bays, oceans—from time immemorial. This need has been met over the centuries in a variety of ways, from a single strong man wading across a ford carrying a traveler on his shoulders to huge ships accommodating thousands of persons. Between these two extremes, a world-circling business was created, and it has become important in the economic life of modern nations.

With the growth of populations, the demand for transportation across waterways became more insistent. Ferries—powered craft shuttling between two points—were enlarged, their routes were lengthened, and their significance in the life of their communities greatly enhanced. In the closing years of the twentieth century, especially in Northern Europe, many ferry services employed ships as big as their predecessors on the long sea routes.

People have always had the desire to use water transportation to satisfy many of their desires. Some used water transportation, in the form of workboats, to provide food, while others used ships to escape their homelands and seek new freedoms and opportunities in foreign lands. As vessels became safer and more reliable, people began to use them for other, more recreational purposes. Besides the traditional transportation purposes of ferries and passenger vessels, a whole industry has developed around small passenger vessel operations that specialize in bay and river day excursions, dinner cruises along the waterways, and specialty cruises. While these specialized forms of water transportation are growing, this chapter will specifically deal with large, oceangoing passenger cruises.

Liner service, described elsewhere in this volume, connected markets on opposite sides of the oceans. At its height, the age of the ocean liners saw dozens of very large ships crisscrossing the seas in every direction. Most of these liners carried not only hundreds of passengers but also thousands of tons of cargo.

The introduction of jet-propelled, large-capacity aircraft spelled the end of the epoch of the passenger-carrying ocean liner. Shipowners placed their vessels in the cruise trade—defined as transportation of vacationing

The *Queen Elizabeth 2* is the only large passenger ship operated in both liner and cruise service. Photograph by F. J. Duffy.

passengers on voyages to one or more ports of call—and offered sailings of various lengths to meet the demands of the market. From this somewhat unstable base grew the present worldwide multibillion-dollar industry.

Many deviations from the conventional cruise are seen in the offerings to the traveling public. Of sometimes special interest is the so-called adventure cruise, which is a voyage to a little-known or nearly inaccessible place, such as the North Pole or the Palmer Peninsula in Antarctica, or Pitcairn or Easter Island in the Pacific. The appeal of these offerings is directed toward those who have the leisure to indulge their desire to get "to the ends of the earth" and are willing to pay the often high price of such travel.

No matter whether a cruise is to be conventional or an adventure, or any variant between these limits, the objective of every cruise operator must be to give the traveler a pleasant experience. This is accomplished by providing attentive care to each passenger and by having consistently high standards of performance with little (ideally no) awareness by the passenger of the intricate details of management, supervision, service, and operation implicit in delivering on the promise of an unusual vacation.

Almost five million persons, all of them vacationers on holiday traveling to one or more ports of call, embarked on ships sailing from United States ports in 1994. Another million passengers boarded similar ships in the ports of the United Kingdom, Germany, France, Italy, Australia, and Japan. The economic importance of this segment of the shipping industry is enormous. For instance, in 1992 in the United States, 135,000 persons were engaged directly in the management and operation of these ships, while 315,000 other workers were employed in activities related to cruise ship operation. The industry generated $14.5 billion in wages and paid $6.3 billion in taxes to the United States. Scores of ships representing investments of billions of dollars were assigned to this trade.[1]

The cruise business as it exists today began about 1947, and it has been growing through the years since then. The vessels themselves are floating resort hotels equipped with elaborate facilities for passenger recreation and offering well-publicized professional entertainment for the pleasure of their patrons.

The roots of the cruise business in the United States may be traced back to 1867, when Mark Twain and many other Americans voyaged to the Mediterranean in the paddle-wheeled steamer *Quaker City.* Exactly when cruising began in Western Europe is not readily determinable. A "special Mediterranean tour" was operated for British clients in 1844, but repetitive offerings of pleasure voyages were not made until 1889 when the Peninsular and Oriental Steam Navigation Company (P&O Line) sent the *Chimborazo* on a genuine Mediterranean cruise designed specifically for the enjoyment of the passengers.[2]

In 1891, Albert Ballin, the guiding genius of the Hamburg-America Line, diverted the *Augusta Victoria* from her regular transatlantic voyage and sent her on a two-month cruise through the Mediterranean. So successful was this venture that it was repeated annually until 1914.[3]

Until the disappearance of regular passenger liner service during the late 1960s and the early 1970s, most of the ships that participated in cruising out of United States Atlantic ports were assigned for most of the year to shuttle operation between fixed ports. During the winter months, when the volume of passenger traffic dropped to very low levels, it was common practice to divert all but the largest liner service vessels to cruise operation, though only part of their accommodations could be considered acceptable for warm weather travel. In the years antedating World War II, as many as ninety ships were thus engaged. Year-round cruising was not feasible, however, until air-conditioning was installed on ships, ensuring passengers of comfortable quarters whatever the outdoor temperatures.[4]

Cunard Line introduced the *Caronia* in 1949 as a ship intended primarily for cruising but adaptable to liner service whenever there was sufficient demand. This dual-purpose design proved satisfactory, and other steamship owners followed Cunard's lead. Interchanging ships between liner service and cruising ended when jet-propelled aircraft began carrying passengers across the oceans. Steamship shuttle service was overwhelmed by the competition and faded away gradually between 1960 and 1972.

Driven off their regular routes by the airplanes, many passenger liners were placed in year-round cruise operation. Newer ships like the *Caronia* had been planned for this employment and were fitted with the amenities demanded by the cruising public: outdoor swimming pools, broad decks for strolling and playing games, large public rooms with good views to seaward, complete air-conditioning, and private baths for every cabin. These vessels made the transition to their new assignments with considerable success. The older ships were sent to the breakers.

As work weeks have been shortened and vacations (or holidays) have become universal in the industrialized nations, the demand for recreation has intensified. As early as 1954, Greek shipowners sensed this and began to offer short (three- to seven-day) voyages from Piraeus to the nearby islands of the Aegean Sea. These proved to be immensely popular and afforded employment to two dozen ships.[5] A Norwegian operator, Knut Kloster, Sr., put his first ship into the United States cruise trade in 1968. In the next few years, Miami, Florida, was transformed from a moderate-sized port to the world's busiest passenger cruise terminal.[6] In 1972, short cruises from Florida to Caribbean destinations became available, and since then, they have been the magnets drawing patronage to the cruise services.

Between 1970 and 1990, many ships were designed expressly for these short voyages and reflected the demands of the trade. Distances between the islands are limited, and cruises are of short duration. For the greater part of the year, the seas are calm and winds favorable; speed is not important. Depending upon the operators' choices of routes and markets to be tapped, the ships varied in passenger capacity from about 700 to more than 2,000; they ranged in size from 650 to 900 feet long. The general specifications for Caribbean cruise ships, therefore, called for long, full-bodied, shallow-draft hulls powered for a maximum speed of 21 to 22 knots.[7]

Earlier in this chapter, the speed of cruise ships was mentioned. Those vessels intended for primary employment in the Caribbean have been designed with only a small reserve of power to provide the extra speed needed to compensate for delays caused by adverse winds and seas. The practical effect of this restriction on power has been to confine the ships to the Caribbean (or similar) areas.[8]

To meet the demands of the burgeoning trade, fleet owners built larger ships. Within certain fixed limits, as the number of passengers increased, the unit cost of serving those travelers was lowered. The managing director of a shipyard that has constructed many very large cruise ships observed, however, that the economies of scale were achieved only up to a capacity of 2,000 passengers; above that number, the advantages decreased noticeably.[9] That opinion is not shared by Royal Caribbean Cruises as they are building three vessels of 136,000 gross tons with azipod drives each capable of accommodating 3,100 passengers.[10]

The decision to build a new ship for the cruise trade is of the first magnitude. Between signing the contract with the shipyard and delivery to the owners, the interval may be as short as eighteen months or greater than two years. Ships of the larger capacities cost $400 million or more in 1997. The owner must be optimistic that when the ships are placed in service, there will be thousands of persons willing and anxious to pay (in the aggregate) millions of dollars (or marks or francs) to gratify their desires for a vacation voyage.[11]

The alternative to building a new ship is to convert an existing vessel to meet the specific needs of the operator. This procedure may save as much as one-half the cost of acquiring a new ship. One of the most thoroughgoing conversions in recent years was that of Costa Line's *Costa Allegra*. Launched in 1969 as a containership, the *Annie Johnson* was transformed, at a cost of $160 million, into a deluxe cruise ship with a capacity of 800 passengers accommodated in 405 cabins. In the process, the hull was lengthened when a new midbody section (11.5 meters [45.4 feet] long, and 25.75 meters [86.5 feet] wide) was inserted. The main machinery was replaced, and the upper two decks of the new superstructure were fashioned of aluminum to improve vessel stability. The result was described in the owner's booklet distributed in 1992 when the *Costa Allegra* entered the Caribbean trade:

> Surprises await you at every turn. On the pool deck, you'll splash in a stream that flows across the transparent ceiling of the Murano Bar, one deck below. Hallways, public rooms and unexpected corners are enlivened with vivid paintings, infused with the energy and spirit of Europe's great artists. Glass elevators glide past a towering wall mural in the sky-lit atrium. The designer's generous use of glass has given the *Costa Allegra* a refreshing sense of spaciousness.[12]

As operators gained experience in year-round cruise service, they adapted to the perceived needs and desires of their patrons. In 1988, a design consultant observed that the new generation of cruise ships was being built from the inside out to satisfy the requirement that the vessel be a floating pleasure palace. This was considered more important than to create a ship that was aesthetically acceptable when viewed from shore.

Cruise ship owners follow different patterns in commissioning designers for their new units. Carnival Cruises, for instance, used a single architectural firm to do the work on all its ships. The German yard of Joseph L. Meyer, which built two 1,750-passenger ships for Celebrity Cruises, engaged yacht designer John Bannenberg to create the sleek hull. The interior was the product of a "distinguished cadre of recognized interior design firms" domiciled in New York, London, Athens, and Las Vegas. Each of these different offices had a "core concept that formed the basis of individual room designs that worked together to create a cohesive environment of glamour and elegance."[13]

Royal Caribbean Cruise Line built two ships in 1995 that could be employed in areas with greater temperature ranges than those encountered in the Caribbean. The operator planned to assign the *Grandeur of the Seas* and her sister, the *Enchantment of the Seas,* to the Alaska trade in the summer and to the Far East during the North American winter season. Passengers were expected to spend more time in their rooms, which therefore were made more spacious and comfortable than were the cabins of ships deployed only in the Caribbean. Further consideration of passenger comfort was shown in the decision to limit speed to 24 knots; a faster speed would be "uncomfortable for the passengers," according to the owner.[14]

Of vital interest to cruise operators is the determination of what brings a passenger to a ship. A study conducted in 1995 discovered that the principal reason for choice was the reputation of the company (or the ship) as a provider of "good service." Other elements, not necessarily in order of preference, were the following:

Special discounts on fares.
General reputation of the ship operating company.
Individual ship's reputation for serving fine food.
Availability of air/sea combination packages.
Number and desirability of ports of call.
Quality of shipboard entertainment.[15]

The selection of a base port from which cruise ships will operate is conditioned primarily on how conveniently passengers may be transported to that point. For decades, most cruises from the United States Atlantic coast originated in New York, largely because of the network of railroads that fed that metropolis. The obvious drawback to New York as a starting point was that a winter voyage to the Caribbean would begin and end with at least twenty-four hours of steaming through cold weather and often stormy seas.

The 32,396-gross-ton *Royal Majesty* was built in 1992 and typified the medium-sized cruise ships of the period. Courtesy Kvaerner-Masa Shipyards Inc.

When high-speed, jet-propelled aircraft put all cities east of the Mississippi River within two to four hours flying time of Miami, the picture changed dramatically. Most of the ships serving the Caribbean area now are assigned to the Florida ports of Miami, Port Everglades, and Port Canaveral. An incidental benefit to the shipowners was that the airplane widened enormously the region from which cruise patronage might be obtained.

For the long cruises, defined here as those lasting twenty or more days, the operators must draw on the comparatively small pool of retired and semi-retired persons. That these long voyages are difficult to sell is borne out by the facts of operational history. In 1992, the *Queen Elizabeth 2* started her 128-day world cruise with 700 embarked passengers. Only 200 had purchased tickets for the entire cruise. Similarly, only 160 of the *Sagafjord*'s 410 passengers were committed for the 96 days of her cruise. By contrast, the Nippon Yusen Kaisha's *Asuka* was assigned to a 96-day cruise around the world, starting in Japan. All 460 passengers were making the complete voyage. The average age of these passengers was sixty-five years, and their affluence was confirmed by the cost of the cruise: $30,000 to $150,000, depending upon the accommodations.

As an inducement to travelers who did not want to make the complete voyage, shipowners subdivided the long cruises into a series of segments of varying lengths. Voyagers were encouraged to join the ship at ports with conveniently scheduled airline connections and to spend a limited number of days at a preselected port of debarkation. The plan proved to be acceptable to many patrons and was the basis on which the *Queen Elizabeth 2* and the *Sagafjord* obtained most of their passengers.[16]

Longer cruises, exemplified above, represent a challenge to the managerial skill of the operator because they pose a gamble. To win the favor of a notoriously fickle and highly selective public, the traffic managers must devise itineraries to allure those looking for shipboard vacations. They must decide how many hours ashore will satisfy the desires of the passengers for sightseeing and shopping, how may days should be spent at sea between ports so that travelers will not become too fatigued, and how long the cruise should last from start to finish.

Cruise Lines International Association in 1994 determined that these trends in marketing merited special emphasis: more interesting itinerary, voyages timed to suit the schedules of employed persons, cruises appealing to families, "exciting" shipboard activities, theme cruises, and high-class entertainment. Discounting fares for those who can plan far ahead is now a standard procedure, advertised widely in the promotional material distributed by the carriers.[17]

While the demand for cruises was greatest in the United States, it was not confined to this nation. Clients in England, Western Europe, and Japan showed noticeable eagerness to enjoy these seaborne vacations. German, French, English, Scandinavian, and Japanese owners built ships to participate in the United States trade and also to cater to local customers. Croisieres Paquet, a French cruise operator, concentrated its sales efforts on citizens of Belgium, Switzerland, Luxembourg, French-speaking Canada, and (of course) France. Both decor and management of the ships showed strong emphasis on the French style.[18]

A bold incentive to induce "adventurous" passengers to participate in an experimental voyage met with success. During August and September 1984, 98 persons took part in the first passenger ship voyage through the Northwest Passage. Capitalizing on that achievement, the *World Discoverer* transported 140 passengers from Nome, Alaska, to Halifax, Nova Scotia, between August 23 and September 14, 1985.[19]

A remarkable opportunity was afforded to about 100 persons who booked passage in a nuclear-powered Russian icebreaker with passenger accommodations. The enormous power built into the ship permitted her to move steadily through fields of ice six to ten feet thick at a uniform speed of 6 knots; in the open sea, she could cruise at 22 knots. The ship actually drove precisely to the North Pole, and all passengers were permitted to disembark, walk around the magic point, and celebrate with a barbecue lunch on the ice. That it had appeal only for the wealthy leisure group was manifested by the price of the seventeen-day expedition: $17,900 to $22,900 per person.[20]

Shore excursions are available, usually at extra cost, on practically all cruises. Normally, the shipowner/cruise operator specifically and categorically disavows any connection with or responsibility for these sightseeing trips, and all the promotional material contains carefully worded statements to that effect. The disavowal, however, is somewhat technical, because the cruise operator nearly always has selected a single concessionaire at each port of call to provide the tours, tickets for which are sold on board the cruise ship. The alternative is to hire a travel agency with a worldwide organization with the capability to assume full responsibility as an independent contractor.

In either case, the cruise operator must ensure that the concessionaire or contractor performs to its specifications. Obviously it does the shipowner's reputation no good if passengers are dissatisfied with their experiences ashore. After all, they do not have the opportunity to choose among competing excursion operators. For these reasons, cruise ship owners are careful in the selection and appointment of concessionaires.

Selecting the ports of call for the cruise requires the exercise of highly professional judgment. Unless the cruise is intended to appeal to that small coterie of travelers who seek exotic places seldom visited, the itinerary must include a few of those cities that have earned and retained popularity with the public. If a satisfactory mixture of well-known tourist attractions and "unexploited" spots can be attained, the potential clients will probably react affirmatively. For short voyages from the Atlantic coast of the United States, Bermuda and the Caribbean area have been favorite destinations. Longer cruises include such famous attractions as Hong Kong, Honolulu, Nice, London, Singapore, and Stockholm, as well as out-of-the-way points such as Bali, Spitzbergen, and the Straits of Magellan.

Just as ships engaged in passenger liner service were designed expressly to meet the needs of the travelers on a specific route, so vessels used exclusively in cruise operation must be satisfactory for that service. The characteristics of the cruise route and the demands of the passengers are very important in determining the employment of the ship. Very large ships (2,000 or more passengers) must appeal to the mass market, and

The 133-meter (439 feet) long, super-deluxe cruise ship *Seabourn Spirit* was designed to enter shallow and compact harbors. Here she is passing under London's Tower Bridge. Courtesy Seabourn Lines.

schedules for these ships must take into account the limited time of vacationers. Ship operators are under constant pressure to attract patrons in the numbers required to make the venture financially sound.

The Norwegian Cruise Line (until 1988, the Norwegian Caribbean Line) established to its satisfaction that operating a very large ship on short cruises from Florida to the Virgin Islands would be feasible. The superliner *France* was available for purchase. After exhaustive studies to determine what adaptations and modifications would be necessary to make the ship acceptable in the subtropical environment, the decision was reached to acquire the *France* and, after conversion, to put her into year-round operation of seven-day cruises. In June 1979, the Compagnie Generale Maritime transferred ownership to the Norwegian Caribbean Line. A multimillion-dollar conversion included changing the name to *Norway,* and in May 1980 the "new" ship was placed in service.[21]

A number of ships, each carrying about 250 passengers, were built in the 1980s to cater to a different group—wealthy passengers who demand (and are willing to pay for) maximum comfort and personal service. These vessels are operated on seven- and fourteen-day cruises from base ports to off-the-beaten-track destinations and relatively unknown harbors in the

When named in 1980, the *Norway* was the world's largest cruise ship, accommodating 2,400 passengers. Her crew numbered 800. Photograph by Jeff Blinn, courtesy Moran Towing Co.

Mediterranean and Caribbean seas, along the Atlantic coast of South America, and many Pacific Ocean ports. Typically, the ships had two-room suites, each complete with a full bath, remote control television, radio, stereo phonograph, videocassette recorder, refrigerator, and bar stocked with liquor chosen by the occupants. The fare was comprehensive; no additional expenses were incurred for personal services or beverages at the bar. Tipping was prohibited. Meals were served at the convenience of the passengers, and every dish was prepared individually.[22]

A significant trend in the sales management of cruises emerged about 1975 and has become more prominent in the years since then. Instead of

One of the eighty identical suites in the super-deluxe cruise ship *Seabourn Spirit*. The ship was built in 1988 and had a maximum capacity of 204 passenger in 104 suites. Courtesy Seabourn Lines.

stressing the glamourous nature of the ports of call, increased emphasis was given to the luxury and comfort of the ships, the pleasures to be enjoyed in passage from one harbor to another, the professional entertainment provided each evening at sea, the varied nature of shipboard activities available to passengers, and the elegance of the meals served in the dining rooms. The unique feature of the cruise—a vacation afloat while living in a deluxe hotel—became a major selling point, and if the number of persons embarking on cruise ships each year was the criterion, it was what the traveling public wanted.[23]

A further innovation in cruise service was the introduction of luxurious sail-propelled ships. Scientifically designed and computer controlled, the triangular sails were served by skilled seamen, and schedules were maintained, should the need arise, by activating auxiliary engines. The experiment was successful, and these ships now operate from a number of base ports in different parts of the world.

Later entries of sail-powered cruise ships were smaller, barkentine-rigged ships that relied more on manpower than on machinery for handling the sails. The newest of these "sailing ship resorts" were the *Star Clipper* and *Star Flyer,* built in Belgium at a cost of $40 million per ship. Each carried 180 passengers and a crew of 70. Deployed in the Mediterranean, Caribbean, and South Pacific, this fleet of wind-driven ships attracted favorable response from the traveling public.[24]

In both the United States and Western Europe, peak demand for cruises occurs during the winter months when those who can arrange vacations seek respite from the rigors of cold weather and its attendant discomforts. In recent years, shipowners serving the United States cruise markets have found it advantageous to base their ships in southern ports; Miami and Los Angeles are the most popular. Several operators run their ships out of San Juan, Puerto Rico, and other Caribbean ports.

In the case of ships that sail repetitively on fixed routes, like Carnival Cruise Lines' fleet, the emphasis is placed upon the ships and the activities offered on board, as set forth in this quotation from the company's catalog of cruises:

> If Your Kind of Fun means days spent lounging in the sun, nights of thrilling entertainment, exciting tropical ports of call, fine dining, pampering service and an endless variety of activities, then a Carnival cruise is for you. . . .
>
> You'll enjoy unmatched pampering service, from fresh towels delivered twice a day to waiters at your beck and call. You'll savor a wide array of dining experiences. . . .
>
> At night, Carnival offers the broadest entertainment choices of any land or sea resort. . . .
>
> If you're looking for a vacation with a difference, you've found it with Carnival.

Longer cruises represent a special effort by the operator and are usually planned for a selected ship and a particular time. The names of the ships and their owners serve to attract patrons; either these travelers are "repeaters" who have made previous cruises with the ship or the company, or they are persons who have been impressed by the reputation of the operator. Often the reservation books are opened twelve to fifteen months before the departure date; always there is as much publicity and advertising as can be arranged to attract attention and to provide impetus to the sales campaign.

Princess Cruises, directing its efforts toward those who are able to take the long voyages, offered these words:

> You're a traveler who dreams of following in the footsteps of Hemingway, Livingston, and Marco Polo, of penning a postcard in the

The *Wind Spirit* and her two identical sister ships were built in Finland in 1986 and 1987 to carry 148 passengers in luxurious accommodations. The ships were 110 meters (360 feet) long on the waterline, 15.8 meters (64 feet) in beam, and had 21,500 square feet of computer-operated sails. Courtesy Windstar Cruises.

hotel where Rudyard Kipling wrote a classic or of sailing through the Suez Canal aboard a ship descended from the vessels of Princess' parent, P&O, that sailed to India 150 years ago. . . .

You know where you want to go and the best way to get there. That's why only Princess Cruises will do. . . .

No other mode of travel can rival the feeling you get when the lines are cast off and the land is left behind. As you turn your face to the open sea, you slip immediately into the easygoing rhythm of shipboard life you remember so well.

To establish some rules and thereby to forestall cutthroat competition, thirteen cruise ship operators came together in 1979 to form the Caribbean Cruise Association. Similar to the conferences established in other trades, the aim of this group was to adopt a code of ethics concerning promotion and sale of cruise services and to fix certain areas of responsibility for the welfare of the traveling public. Five years later, after an interim merger in 1972 into the International Passenger Ship Association, the Cruise Lines International Association came into existence with administrative offices in New York and San Francisco. This body consisted of the thirty-one major cruise ship operators catering to the tourist trade from the

United States. It functioned in a manner similar to other steamship conferences, and was subject to surveillance by the Federal Maritime Commission because of its relation to American foreign commerce.

A fundamental principle upon which all these carriers agreed was that
the more desirable the accommodations aboard ship, the higher the price charged
the person occupying those quarters. The most modern ships feature cabins
that, by categories, are almost identical in size, decor, facilities, and amenities.
Most of the rooms are designated as "outside," with portholes looking out to
sea. Suites and oversize rooms that can be combined to form a suite are in the
best locations. Inside rooms cost less than outside, and the rate per person is
less for double rooms than for single cabins. Showers are standard; tubs are
available only in the more high-priced rooms.

The tariff of a high-class cruise ship lists per-person fares and the differentials related to the location of the room, its size, and the amenities provided.

Navigation deck	Deluxe stateroom: king-size bed, sitting area, bathtub and shower, outside	$3,095
Navigation deck	Deluxe cabin: two lower beds, sitting area, bathtub and shower, outside	2,575
Main deck	Large cabin: two lower beds, shower, outside	2,095
"A" deck	Large cabin: two lower beds, shower, outside	2,010
"A" deck	Large cabin: two lower beds, shower, inside	1,595
"C" deck (lowest)	Standard cabin: two lower beds, shower, outside	1,870
"C" deck	Standard cabin: two lower beds, shower, inside	1,295

Seating in the dining room of a ship with large passenger capacity is
frequently limited, and two "seatings" may be required to handle all the embarked passengers. There is a perennial argument about the relative desirability of "first seating" and "second seating." Travelers with children and
those who follow early schedules usually elect the first meal hour; those
who consider that dining at later hours reflects a more elegant standard of
life, or who normally lead lives starting later in the day, choose the second.
The food is identical; sometimes it may be a bit fresher at the first meal. Unavoidably, diners at the first seating are aware of subtle pressure to vacate
the dining room to permit it to be prepared for the second.

Besides the revenue from the sale of tickets, cruise operators look to
the ship's bar (or bars, commonly) and shops for significant contributions to
voyage profits. On short trips, bar profits can make the difference between a
break-even operation and a profitable voyage. On long trips, where there is a
great deal of social activity and many private parties, the bar profits can be
substantial. Shops of all sorts are ever more prominent aboard cruise ships.

The "International Promenade" on the *Norway* has shops offering luxury goods at prices rivaling those in the most exclusive stores ashore. Jewelry, porcelain, watches, clothing, sportswear, and children's clothes and toys are features. Passengers are lured into these places by their presence and by the fact that on the high seas there are no tariffs on imported goods. (Whatever is purchased at sea must be declared to customs officials and may be subject to duty when brought into the United States if the value exceeds the "free allowance" accorded to returning residents.)

Some ship operators have elected to contract with specialists to handle all details connected with these stores. If this is done, the concessionaire procures the merchandise, hires the necessary sales personnel, maintains the required inventories, and ensures that stocks are replenished before the commencement of each voyage. Usually the contract stipulates that seagoing salespersons are to have the same accommodations as the cruise staff or the junior licensed officers.

Some shipowners contract with food service organizations to take over all aspects of food services and catering. When this is done, the contractor usually assigns to each ship under contract a supervisor selected for competence and experience. The contracting firm purchases, delivers, and stows aboard ship all food supplies. It plans the food service for each ship, and hires, trains, and supervises the kitchen and dining room staff. The crew's galley, which follows an entirely different menu from that of the passenger-service kitchen, also is the responsibility of the food service contractor.

The shipowner must bear the ultimate burden of proper care of the passengers and may assign a "hotel manager" as the contract supervisor. Discharging exactly the functions implied by the title, the hotel manager reports directly to the master, who traditionally is the official responsible for the safety and happiness of the passengers.

The practice of having concessionaires or contractors operate the dining rooms and bars has not met with universal approval by passengers. Many complaints have been filed against poorly trained, inefficient, and ungracious service personnel. Maritime labor unions in the United States have alleged that workers are obtained for the least possible expenditure of money, with no regard for the qualifications of these persons. The unions also have charged that the contractor's workers are exploited and poorly housed.

Whatever the truth may be, the use of concessionaires does place the reputation of the shipowner in serious jeopardy. In the first place, passengers assume that everyone working aboard the ship is employed directly by the steamship operator and therefore condemn the company for the shortcomings and mistakes of contractor personnel. In the second place, the concessionaire may have been the lowest bidder for the contract and may provide a low grade of service. In the third place, the contractor does the purchasing and inspection of foodstuffs, and the quality of what is procured may not be known to the ship's representatives and contract supervisors until it is offered to the passengers. If the quality of foodstuffs is inferior, this fact could have serious effects upon the popularity of the ship with the traveling public.

An alternative practice gained popularity in the 1990s—contracting with a professional ship management organization, which becomes responsible for one or more phases of the ship's operation. Various modifications of the basic concept validate its usefulness. The contractor may recruit the crew, but the shipowner actually hires these people. (There may be legal reasons to establish the relationship between owner and seafarer.) The contractor may be both recruiter and trainer of personnel in all branches of shipboard activity. The contractor may furnish supervisors to ensure that shipboard personnel performance meets appropriate standards. The contractor may take over the food service division or the housekeeping or maintenance of passenger accommodations. Final responsibility for the safe and efficient operation of the ship, however, remains with the owner.[25]

For those operators who send their ships on a variety of voyages—some long and some short, some repeating earlier experiences and some new in many respects—the normal procedure calls for the traffic department to conjure up an itinerary attractive to the public. The marine operations department then determines what is feasible, given the characteristics and capability of the ship. Of major importance is the depth of water available in the suggested ports of call; unless water depth exceeds the draft of the ship, it will be necessary to take the passengers ashore in tenders. If tenders are required, local conditions of wind, surf, height of waves, and landing area must be scrutinized, as well as the type and condition of the tenders themselves. If the ship must rely on its own boats, or if the tenders available in port are small, the possibility that passengers may be injured getting into or out of the tenders at the ship's anchorage must weigh heavily in the decision to call at, or to eliminate, that port.

Each proposed port of call is given systematic and methodical study, and only those that are acceptable from the viewpoint of the navigators and shiphandlers are approved. The traffic department must adapt its plans to the conditions discovered by the operating department. Once the ports of call are set, the engineering department works out the schedule of the ship's movements to achieve maximum economy and efficiency.

Certain basic principles apply to making cruise schedules. The ship should arrive either at the anchorage, if tenders are to be used, or at the berth, if wharf or pier is available, not earlier than eight o'clock in the morning. Time for the passengers to enjoy the attractions ashore must be proportioned to the size of the place being visited and the interest it may have for tourists. Generally speaking, an average stay of four hours for an island like Saipan is satisfactory; for a well-known city with many attractions like Honolulu or Copenhagen, a call of at least sixteen hours is proper. In a city where shopping is the great lure, as happens in St. Thomas, Virgin Islands, a full business day must be allowed for the pleasure of the passengers.

In areas like the Caribbean and the eastern Mediterranean, where a number of ships sail to the same islands, coordination of schedules is of major importance. Cruise passengers expect to enjoy the attractions of the port and resent overcrowding and overloading of facilities. Preventing such occurrences requires that the cruise operators agree on the sizes of ships and therefore the number of passengers, the number of ships in a harbor at one time, and the length of port stays. George Town, the capital of the Cayman Islands, analyzed the cruise business during the sixty-one days of November and December 1994 and noted that there were only four days during that period when cruise ships were not in the port. The average number of visitors was 3,177 per day; on one day, the figure was 6,000. The business men of George Town petitioned the cruise operators to impose a limit of three ships on any one day, carrying between 5,500 and 6,000 passengers. The preferred number was near the daily average of 3,177. To comply with that request, the schedule for the *Tropicale,* with 1,400 passengers, was planned so she would arrive in the early morning and sail at 1:00 P.M.; the *Enchanted Seas* and the *Crown Dynasty,* with a total of 1,533 passengers, would steam into port in the early afternoon.[26]

Departure time poses a problem because of the possibility of stragglers. Standard procedure is to notify all members of the cruise party that the ship will sail at the appointed hour, and anyone not on board must find his or her way to the next port of call at their own expense. This notice is widely distributed by every possible means of communication aboard ship. It is accepted practice to fix the departure hour to fit the ship's arrival at her next scheduled stop. If the distance to be covered is short—for example, the 104 miles from San Juan, Puerto Rico, to Christiansted, St. Croix, Virgin Islands—departure time might be as late as 2:00 A.M. and cruising speed would be set at 17 knots to ensure arrival at eight o'clock that same morning.

To the cruise passenger, speed is of minor importance, but it is very significant to management. Slower speeds are more economical in fuel consumption, and therefore the lowest speed that will meet requirements is chosen. For instance, from Barcelona, Spain, to New York harbor is 3,728 miles. At 22 knots, this distance can be traversed in seven days and two hours; at 20 knots, in seven days and nineteen hours; and at 18 knots, in eight days and sixteen hours. Very likely, the decision would favor 20 knots, which would permit departure at 7:00 P.M. and arrival at 2:00 P.M., a good hour for the end of the cruise.

Ideally, arrival at every port of call would be in the early morning and departure would be effected after dark, so that passengers might spend the entire day ashore. However, in the real world of winds, tides, and distances, the schedule must be made to fit the circumstances encountered in the port at the time of the proposed call. If tides regulate the hours of entry and departure, or if pilots take ships strictly in the order in which they arrive at the pilot station, the schedule must consider these facts.

Once the itinerary and schedule for the cruise have been determined, the supply division of the shipowner's organization begins its work. The deck and engineering departments of the ship must requisition enough materiel and spare parts to meet every reasonable and foreseeable need, and they must make sure that delivery schedules can and will be met. This is particularly critical when the ship is completing one long cruise and is scheduled to start on another of equal duration within a maximum of twenty-four hours after arrival.

The catering (or hotel) department must order the foodstuffs that will be required for the cruise, based upon the menus that have been prepared. A 1,200 passenger ship assigned to a ten-day cruise requisitioned these quantities:

15,186 pounds of meat
7,900 pounds of poultry
3,547 pounds of lobster
2,720 pounds of assorted prawns
1,150 pounds of crabmeat
4,242 pounds of assorted fish
18,600 pounds of fresh vegetables
4,850 pounds of frozen vegetables
7,900 pounds of potatoes
960 gallons of fresh milk
9,500 pounds of flour
22,000 pounds of assorted fresh fruit
2,700 pounds of assorted pasta
1,960 cans of assorted fruits

1,800 pounds of coffee
1,460 pounds of sugar

Bar supplies were of the same magnitude, as evidenced by this list:

286 bottles of French champagne
690 bottles of American wine
215 bottles of French wine
585 bottles of Italian wine
40 bottles of cognac
60 bottles of Scotch whiskey
5,976 bottles of soft drinks
38 bottles of gin
27 bottles of rum
155 bottles of vodka
95 bottles of assorted liqueurs
55 bottles of bourbon and rye whiskey
3,940 bottles of assorted beers

Whether the cruise is for three days, four days, or seven days—the categories of cruises most popular in the United States—the pattern of operation has become standardized: depart in the early evening and return to the home port by midmorning. Only eight to twelve hours therefore are available to take on stores and supplies for the next sailing. It takes little imagination to comprehend the coordination required between the management staff ashore, the suppliers, the service agencies in or near the port city, and shipboard personnel. A careful schedule of deliveries must be set up and rigidly followed; qualified inspectors must be on duty to ensure that what is being put aboard the ship is what the purchase contract called for, and that it meets specifications and is in the quantity ordered. The operation is complicated by the fact that after several months, some key personnel from the ship's company will be rotated every time the ship comes into port. It is the responsibility of shore management to adjust to this circumstance. The resupply routine is somewhat more difficult in those instances when the turnaround day is Sunday, and some emergency procurement may be impeded because the supplier has closed for the weekend.

Every cruise ship eventually must be refueled. Some ships carry enough oil for two or more consecutive short voyages; others, especially those assigned to longer cruises, may require fuel at the start of every trip. Depending upon the power plant of the vessel, certain types of oil must be provided. A turbine-driven steamer like the *Norway* burns heavy oil (bunker "C"), whereas a vessel with medium-speed diesel motors may operate on marine diesel oil. The newest ships may have slow-speed diesels, most of which have been adapted to use bunker "C" though some work only on diesel fuel. Depending upon the type, quality, and quantity of oil available in the ports of call, one or more refueling points will be selected, and the schedule will include the time needed to refill the tanks.

An important function of the operating department is to arrange to bring the ship into port and to care for her until she departs. That means a pilot must be waiting to direct the cruise ship without delay to a waiting berth, for passengers do not accept apologies when they are delayed in getting ashore. Tugs must be available (if required) at the specified times. (Many newer vessels have bow thrusters, which permit maneuvering without assistance from tugs, a great asset in the berthing and unberthing operation.) Launches or tenders, when needed to ferry passengers to and from shore, should be at the ship's side when the anchor splashes into the water. Cruise vessels are normally accorded "yacht privileges" in ports of call, so formalities of entrance and clearance are reduced to the minimum. Ship's officers must be informed of any local regulations that might be troublesome to the passengers and must make sure that this information is distributed to everyone. In every port of call, the ship must rely on the agent, who is selected before the start of the cruise and is known to be experienced, dependable, and resourceful as well as reasonable in its charges for services rendered.[27]

It is essential that the ship's agent be furnished with complete information concerning the ship's movements, and that the agent in turn ensures that the ship's personnel are instructed in how to communicate with its office. The names of the agents in the different ports of call are published for the benefit of passengers. The importance of the ship's agent is best appreciated in listing the demands placed upon them. They arrange for pilotage, towage, launch service, and stevedoring (if required). They also handle customs clearance and Coast Guard concerns; sometimes they even help passengers to get out of jail.

Employment aboard a cruise ship is very exacting, especially for members of the hotel staff who are in direct and constant contact with the passengers. The master, purser, chief steward, hotel manager, headwaiter, and senior wine steward are chosen not only for their technical competence but also because of their tact, diplomacy, suavity, and patience. Especially on the longer cruises, these people are subjected to almost unending demands for special attention and the resolution of difficulties, real and imagined, experienced by the travelers. Room stewards, bellmen, bartenders, and table waiters are under constant pressure to render prompt and courteous service no matter the circumstances in which their day's work may have been performed. The senior medical officer of a large cruise ship found that many members of the steward's department suffered from ulcers, hypertension, anxiety, and insomnia. He admitted that these health problems resulted in part from the sheer length of the voyages, but he was convinced that the predominant cause was the constant pressure to please everyone, even the most arbitrary and unreasonable passengers.

This pressure to perform is also experienced in the ships assigned to the short voyages. When the vessel arrives in the forenoon and sails in the evening, the time in port is barely sufficient to accomplish the work required to ready the ship for the next trip. Typically, in those few hours, the ship must be cleaned thoroughly, and every cabin must be stripped, wiped down, refitted, and made to look as though it had never been occupied. Damaged fittings and scarred bulkheads must be repaired. Stores must be taken aboard and stowed properly. To achieve what is necessary, shoreside workers meet the ship and perform most of the required repairs and major cleaning. The contribution of the ship's company is restricted by the obligation to release bedroom stewards and stewardesses, bellmen, and receptionists from their cleaning chores about two hours before sailing time so they can change uniforms and take their stations to greet incoming passengers.

Although not a licensed or certificated seafarer and not in the shipboard chain of command, the cruise director is a major and indispensable contributor to the success of the three-, four-, and seven-day "mass market" cruises. There is no tradition that a director be a man or a woman; both have achieved marked success. This person is responsible for running all the shipboard games and entertainments. The basic reason for having a director (and on large ships, assistants to the director) is to encourage the passengers to take part in those games, sports, meetings, sessions, or other forms of amusement or instruction that take place on a typical day at sea. Every activity therefore is scheduled through the director's office; there can be no conflicts in the use of space or equipment. Events involving passengers are scheduled in this office and published in the ship's daily news sheet.[28]

Cruises are gaining in popularity not only because they carry people to overseas points, but also because they offer a completely different style of life for the duration of the cruise. As floating vacations, cruises demand specialized management, and to meet this demand corporations are formed to design, build, own, and operate ships to cater to those who would make an ocean voyage the "thrill of a lifetime."

CHAPTER EIGHT

Industrial and Special Carriers

Included with the thousands of vessels that collectively constitute the merchant marine of the world are many fleets made up of vessels that are neither common carriers nor tramps. Because of their restricted employment or very specialized design, they belong to one of two different categories of shipping. The *industrial carrier* serves the needs of particular industrial enterprises, while the *special carrier* meets the demands peculiar to certain types of cargo.

Industrial carriers are those ships that exist as part of the plant and transportation properties of large industrial organizations and are operated exclusively for them. The "Great White Fleet" of refrigerated ships ("reefers") operated by Chiquita Brands, the world's largest banana supplier, typifies this category. The major purpose of this group of ships is to provide the transoceanic transportation essential to the life of the parent concern. No other users must be considered by the owners, and no obligations are to be met but those laid down by Chiquita Brands, which has full responsibility and control.

Other ships, such as liquid chemical carriers or automobile transporters, are owned by shipping companies that are not affiliated with any industrial activity. These ships—the *special carriers*—have been built to haul a certain cargo with the greatest efficiency and economy; they are made available, either under charter or in regular berth service, to those users who must send their goods across the oceans. For their own reasons, these users choose not to become owners and operators of ships; instead they benefit from the distinctive capabilities of the specialized vessels when the need for their services arises.

Many ships apparently correctly designated as industrial carriers are designed to transport a single commodity and therefore may be considered as both special and industrial carriers. There is nothing contradictory in this finding, so long as the reasons for the existence of these ships are understood.

 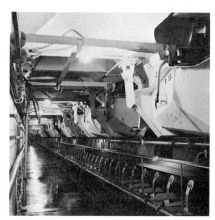

Top left: Melvin H. Baker, a self-unloading bulk carrier. The port for the conveyor is at the stern. *Top right:* Discharging conveyor extended through stern port. *Bottom left:* Discharging coal to inland waterways barges. *Bottom right:* Conveyor system below cargo compartment. Courtesy Nordstroms Marine Systems.

INDUSTRIAL CARRIERS

The industrial carrier is defined as the marine transportation link in the process of manufacture or distribution (or both) of the materials used or produced by an industrial organization. Some carriers handle nothing but raw materials, others transport only finished goods, while still others will be used interchangeably.

Properly managed, an industrial carrier is an integral part of the larger process of manufacture and distribution. It may be owned by the corporation and transport only those cargoes assigned, or it may be chartered for whatever period suits the convenience of the charterer. There is one overriding characteristic: whether engaged in one-way or round-trip voyages with proprietary cargo, or in outbound trips with the return in ballast, the ship carries, in one direction, a full load of the "industrial" cargo. Furthermore, the service performed must be competitive in cost with commercial operators. A possible exception to this rule is that the required transportation is of such a nature and between such ports that commercial operators are not interested.

It is not necessary for ships used as industrial carriers to be operated by the corporation. So long as the ships are ready, willing, and able to perform, it is immaterial whether a commercial ship manager is in charge of the vessel(s) or a corporation official has that responsibility.

As experience is gained, the industry may require modifications in the design of the vessels it is using. Over a time, the ships may become unique specimens, ideal for the purpose intended but not necessarily acceptable in any other trade. There is nothing contradictory in the idea that the industrial carrier is purpose built; it is the use to which the ship is put that determines the category to which it belongs.

A remarkable example of how an industrial carrier can satisfy these purposes is to be seen in the history of the self-unloading gypsum rock carrier *Melvin H. Baker.* Built in 1956 by AG Weser of Bremen, Germany, and owned by Skarrup Shipping Corporation of Monrovia, Liberia, the ship was under charter to the National Gypsum Company for thirty-seven years. Officially classed as an ore carrier, she was 159.95 meters (538 feet) long, 23.02 meters (77.6 feet) wide, and had a draft of 9.45 meters (30 feet). She made 1,759 voyages between Nova Scotia, Canada, and Rensselaer, New York, and delivered more than thirty million tons of gypsum rock. She was withdrawn from service in 1993. The cost of the transportation she provided was said to have been between five and six dollars a ton.

It is important to differentiate between industrial carriers and ships of a certain type in liner service that are built and operated to transport one type of product such as refrigerated fruits, vegetables, and meats. These ships are common carriers, restricted by their design to a limited variety of cargoes. Cool Carriers, for instance, lifts full loads of bananas from tropical sources for delivery in Europe. Outbound to the tropics, the ships carry general cargo that will not damage their structure: automobiles, bagged rice, bagged sugar, wheat, and timber, besides containerized goods.

As already noted, the industrial carrier is controlled by the parent corporation, which sets its own schedules. Vessels, both owned and chartered, are dispatched strictly in accordance with the needs of the industry; no customers have to be informed of sudden changes in sailing times or space allocations within the ships. To a company like Chiquita Brands, which depends upon ships to transport materials required in its operations, this factor alone justifies the maintenance of a controlled fleet. Having a fleet of ships permits Chiquita Brands to route them to those ports where the demand for bananas is at the maximum.

Ownership of an industrial carrier is acceptable economically if the normal pattern of transportation exceeds the capabilities of established operators on the sea routes of interest to the organization, and the investment in ships plus the expense of management are less than the fees charged under chartered tonnage contracts. The industrial carrier brings to the proprietor's corporation the benefit of dependable, efficient, careful, and economical transportation of its cargoes. So long as control of the fleet is vested in the parent enterprise, it is immaterial whether the ships are owned or chartered.

SPECIAL CARRIERS

One of the more interesting and certainly more significant trends in commercial shipping during the twentieth century was the emergence of ship owning companies that restrict themselves to transporting specialized cargoes. These organizations usually tailor their operations to meet the perceived needs of the shippers.

The specialized ship is one designed for the express purpose of carrying, usually in shipload lots, a particular type of cargo, either in bulk or in packages of stipulated size and nature. Among the many varieties of specialized carriers are ships built to transport automobiles and trucks, bulk cement, chemicals in liquid form, coal, iron ore, liquefied natural and petroleum gases, newsprint and other paper products, petroleum and its by-products, wood chips, and refrigerated fruits, vegetables, and meats.

Although this chapter primarily covers the carriage of cargo, it must be noted that there is also a category of specialized ships that do not carry cargo. Instead, they are designed to perform specialized and unique services. Examples of these types of ships include offshore supply vessels,[1] anchor-handling vessels,[2] cable-laying vessels,[3] and research vessels (both oceanographic and geological).

Although transportation by water is the most economical means of movement ever devised by man, there is no single commodity for which the individual cost of carriage does not constitute, in some measure, a barrier to its ready sale in the markets of the world. Carriers are entitled to be compensated for their services, but the shippers expect that this compensation will be as small as possible. The ability to meet this expectation demands the exercise of amazing ingenuity by shipowners, naval architects, and shipbuilders. Particularly in the second half of the twentieth century, the fruits of these endeavors have become important in a wide range of shipping operations, as one specialized design after another has been created to meet specific needs for sea transport. Extraordinarily complex ships have been built to provide safe, efficient, and economical transportation. Paralleling these achievements have been successful attacks upon that age-old problem for the shipowner: how to reduce the time required to work the ship in port and get her back to sea.

Designed to transport most efficiently a single commodity in ship-load lots, the specialized carrier often does well in areas where the conventional ship could not function. An example of specialized carriers meeting a demonstrated need is seen in the transoceanic movement of liquefied natural or petroleum gas. Once the practicality of transportation had been proven, many ships were built expressly for these trades.[4]

In many parts of the world, there is a continuing demand for very large quantities of cement. For decades, it was impossible to ship this commodity in bulk and to discharge it with the self-unloading equipment installed in coal and ore carriers. Cement is extremely fine and powdery in its composition; it packs easily and has a very high angle of repose. Mechanical discharge required that the cement flow to the conveyors, a movement eventually achieved by pumping compressed air into the mass. Using this principle, engineers developed several self-unloading mechanisms by which ships carrying cement in bulk could discharge their cargoes efficiently and economically.

When she was delivered in 1981 to her owners, Empresa Nacional de Elcano, the *Castillo de Javier* was the largest self-unloading bulk cement carrier in the world. She had a deadweight of 44,612 tons and was 189 meters (635.9 feet) long and 31.37 meters (105.4 feet) wide. When fully loaded, she had a draft of 11.91 meters (40 feet). Two oil engines with a combined output of 12,300 brake horsepower gave her a speed of 14 knots. The bulker had six holds, two of which were exceptionally large and were intended for the cement cargoes. Transverse screw conveyors moved the cargo to each side of the hold, where the cement fell through a valve-operated trap door into pipeways laid in the double bottoms. Vacuum pumps sucked the cement out of the ship in two cycles, one from the hold to a reloader chamber and the other from that chamber to the shoreside silo. By means of this system, the ship could be emptied at the rate of 600 tons an hour. The builders, Astilleros Españoles of Bilbao, Spain, claimed that the mechanism they had devised made it possible to carry not only cement in bulk, but also low-density commodities like flour or any granular or pulverized material. A further advantage of the pipeway system was that the tank tops were flat and easy to clean, thereby making it feasible to carry different types of cargo on

The refrigerated cargo ship *Hansa Bremen*, of 19,461 tons deadweight, was built in 1992 and had a speed of 21 knots. Her four hatches were served by the two sets of twin cranes, which could be operated singly or doubled-up for extra-heavy loads.

the return voyage. The ship's utility was enhanced by three 20-ton cranes so mounted that they served all six hatches.[5]

Beginning about 1965, there was a major expansion of the worldwide demand for bananas and other tropical fruits and vegetables. To provide the transportation, the existing fleet of refrigerated ships was augmented significantly. On March 31, 1992, 981 ships with an average size of 326,000 cubic feet made up this fleet. Only 70 of these ships, however, had refrigerated capacity of 600,000 cubic feet or more.[6] The largest reefers were used by those suppliers of perishable foodstuffs who berthed at highly mechanized loading and discharging terminals and had connections to the comprehensive distribution system that delivered the goods to retail stores.

Some reefer ship fleets were operated by corporations that produced, processed, transported, and marketed their fruits and vegetables. Every component part made a specific and vital contribution. Chiquita Brands, the world's largest supplier of bananas, had such an organization; its Great White Fleet is a prime example of an industrial carrier using ships of a highly specialized design. The prototype vessel was introduced in 1992.

The *Chiquita Deutschland,* a 22.25-knot ship, had 645,586 cubic feet (18,283 cubic meters) of insulated cargo space that was both temperature and atmosphere controlled. To care for the variety of other perishable goods handled by Chiquita Brands, the ship was divided into seven groups of compartments in which temperatures could be separately controlled. Refrigerated cargo increasingly moved on pallets rather than in big containers. The *Chiquita Deutschland* therefore had five deck levels in each of three large holds and three levels in the smaller forward hold, all designed for mechanized handling of the pallets. The uniform clearance (deck to overhead) was 2.2 meters (7.4 feet). In addition there was space for containers, with plugs to provide power for their refrigeration equipment.[7]

Lauritzen Reefers of Denmark operates the world's largest fleet of tramp reefers. This company put the *Ditlev Lauritzen,* the first of four identical vessels, into service in 1991. At that time, her capacity of 765,000 cubic feet of below-decks controlled temperature space made her the biggest refrigerated ship in the world. She also had space for 422 20-foot containers. As a specialized tramp, the ship was designed with flexibility to handle all types of refrigerated cargo as well as to load back-haul cargoes such as containers and automobiles exported from Japan. The ship was 160.4 meters (539 feet) long, 23.5 meters (79 feet) wide, and had a draft of 9.8 meters (33 feet). Her 15,300 brake horsepower engine gave her a cruising speed of 19 knots.

Lauritzen's experience in this form of specialized transportation began shortly after World War I. The *Gunderson,* built in 1920, was the first "pure" reefer in the fleet. From then on, under charter to fruit importers, Lauritzen operated a small number of well-designed, relatively high-speed reefers. As the demand for fresh fruits and vegetables increased, the company progressively built more and larger ships until the *Ditlev Lauritzen* class was acquired.[8]

This $50 million ship had five holds, all with five levels, and clearance of 2.2 meters (7.4 feet). The below-deck area was divided into nine zones with a total of 23 cargo spaces. Temperatures could be individually set from a low of −29° Celsius for deep-frozen cargo to +13° Celsius for bananas. Fans circulated air through the coolers and thence downward and longitudinally through the gratings, ensuring maximum ventilation for perishable items such as fruits and vegetables.

Facing the stiff competition of the time, the *Ditlev Lauritzen* was equipped with all the automatic and computer-controlled machinery and labor-saving devices available when she was launched. This elaborate outfit made it possible for the ship to be operated by a crew of six. She entered service with a master, two navigating officers, a chief engineer, a second engineer, two experienced deckhands, and a cook/steward.[9]

Cargo space in a 1993-built refrigerator ship, showing raised flooring for circulation of cooled air. The uniform height between decks is 2.2 meters (7 feet 3 inches). Courtesy Danyard A/S.

In 1993, the *Albemarle Island* began working for the Ecuadorean banana-distributing organization known as NOBOA. Built by Danyard of Aalborg, Denmark, this ship had a hold capacity of 627,683 cubic feet (17,776 cubic meters). In addition, she could accept 148 refrigerated containers, each 40 feet long. With a full complement of reefer boxes, her total capacity for perishable produce was about 33,550,200 cubic feet (950,000 cubic meters). Overall, the *Albemarle Island* was 179.9 meters (590 feet) long, 25.2 meters (83 feet) wide, and on a draft of 9.2 meters (30 feet) had a deadweight of 14,160 tons. Loaded with bananas, the ship had a top speed of 23.1 knots; when carrying bananas and containers, the top speed was reduced to 22.2 knots. In 2000, the elimination of the most commonly used Freon (CFC) refrigerant was ordered by the European Union and the Montreal Protocol because of its effect on the earth's ozone layer. Ammonia, which does not damage the ozone, was chosen as the ship's primary refrigerant. This was the first time in more than twenty years that ammonia had been so used in seagoing ships.[10]

For many years, the storage of fruits and vegetables in shoreside warehouses has been handled in special chambers where the atmosphere is controlled by regulating the oxygen content and humidity of the air that is

The reefer ship *Geest St. Lucia* had a speed of 21.4 knots. In addition to her refrigerated cargo, she carried 439 containers. Courtesy Danyard, Denmark.

cooled and pumped into the airtight chamber. By increasing the nitrogen level and decreasing the oxygen content to a predetermined level between 1 percent and 3 percent, the storage life of produce is extended. This controlled atmosphere reduces the respiration rate of the produce, delays ripening and deterioration, and maintains quality.

Recently, ships have been fitted with controlled atmosphere equipment and can provide surface transportation for exotic produce that formerly had to be sent by air express. The *Granada Carrier* typifies this newest type of reefer ship. She and a sister ship were the first such ships built in Japan. The crew aboard these ships must be carefully instructed concerning safety because the oxygen level of the air in the cargo holds is insufficient to sustain human life. Once the cargo is loaded and cooled, the controlled atmosphere equipment—essentially a nitrogen gas generator—is started. Delivery of good produce is ensured in all ports.[11]

Transoceanic movement of extremely heavy items—railroad locomotives, electricity generators, and mining equipment, for example—has been part of overseas shipping operations for decades. In the years immediately following the end of World War II, the Norwegian firm trading under the name of Belships specialized in handling these offerings. With

When built in 1990, the 19-knot refrigerator ship *Ditlev Lauritzen* was the world's largest. She was equipped for operation by a crew of six. Her below-decks capacity was 21,684 cubic meters (765,650 cubic feet). Courtesy J. Lauritzen A/S.

carefully designed and strengthened derricks, multisheave blocks, powerful winches, and reinforced decks, these ships often joined ("married") two booms (also called derricks) to lift a unit weighing 500 to 600 tons. A great deal of skill was required to handle these colossal weights in the loading, securing, and unloading phases. As Belships proved the validity of the market, other carriers entered the trade, using vessels ranging from about 2,500 tons deadweight to about 15,000 tons deadweight.

The arrival of the containership was accompanied by the development of very large and exceedingly heavy container-handling cranes. These massive units needed to be shipped to overseas destinations. At first, they were transported in pieces and assembled at the final site, but it was not long before the crane buyers began to demand that the units be transported in one piece, ready to be placed on the wharf.

These enormous structures could not be handled in the conventional heavy-lift ships, creating a demand quickly answered by three Dutch operators: Wijsmuller Ship Management BV, of Ijmuiden; Mammoet Shipping BV, of Amsterdam; and Dock Express, of Rotterdam. Each of these organizations designed and built ships to meet the specialized need. The resultant type of ship was given the generic title of "semi-submersible heavy

The *Wakagiku Maru* was designed and built to carry very large and very heavy pieces. The massive cargo gear serves forward and after cargo holds. Courtesy NYK Lines.

transportation vessel." The ships were all planned so that the hull could sink to the level of the loading platform or, alternatively, deep enough in the water for cargo to be floated into position over the deck of the ship. Once the cargo was in position, the ship was raised to the proper height for a sea voyage. Exceptionally large modules of major construction projects and big, awkward (and therefore sometimes relatively fragile) pieces of equipment—drill rigs, offshore platforms, harbor cranes—were carried. All three operators found many customers, and the performance of their unusual ships justified their bold solutions.[12]

Since the middle 1920s, ships have transported unboxed automobiles across the oceans. Vehicles with empty gasoline tanks and disconnected batteries were hoisted aboard by cranes or derricks and lowered to their designated deck, where they were individually chocked and secured in a time-consuming and expensive process. Various ideas were advanced for improving the technique, but it was not until the middle 1950s that any major breakthrough was achieved. The American-designed and -built *Comet* was one of the first ships constructed to carry unboxed automobiles that

Automobiles, palletized breakbulk cargo, heavy equipment, and roll-on/roll-off cargo move in two
directions over this huge ramp of a multipurpose cargo liner. Courtesy Barber Blue Sea.

could be driven on and off the ship with their batteries connected and gasoline in their tanks. The vehicles were secured by patented, fast-working,
and reusable devices. A stern ramp, interior ramps between decks, and a
powerful ventilating system were the special features that revolutionized
the transportation of motor vehicles. Following the success of this experiment, several generations of car carriers were built and put into service, especially in Japan and Sweden.[13] These ships were the first to be called
roll-on/roll-off or RO/RO ships.[14]

   After trying a combination ship that could carry automobiles outbound
and bulk cargoes homeward, Wallenius Lines of Gothenburg, Sweden,
abandoned that idea and concentrated on what came to be called the "pure
car and truck carrier (PCTC)." This company operated a 25-ship fleet worldwide in 1993 and was known not only for the efficiency and dependability

Otello, Wallenius Lines' 1992-built pure car and truck carrier, has twelve vehicle decks. Vehicles are loaded over the stern and side ramps. The many ventilators seen on the weather deck are part of the system installed to ensure safe air conditions when loading and unloading vehicles. Courtesy Wallenius Lines, Stockholm.

of its vessels but also for the fact that they were named for famous operas. The *Aida* was introduced in 1991 and was followed by her sister, the *Otello*, in 1992. These 20-knot ships were designed for functional efficiency rather than for aesthetic beauty. Like other purpose-built car carriers, their square superstructures, which extended virtually the full length of the hull, were about 26.8 meters (90 feet) high. A distinctive feature of the Wallenius ships was the massive stern ramp, mounted at an angle of 25° to the centerline to permit drive-on/drive-off vehicle movement. The interior design featured twelve decks, four of which could be raised to accept loads as tall as 6.5 meters (21.8 feet). The fixed decks were strengthened to carry weights up to 2.5 metric tons per square meter. The high clearance and massive weight tolerance made possible the transportation of tractors, cranes, heavy earth-moving equipment, buses, helicopters, railroad locomotives, and marine engines. When loaded only with automobiles and trucks, these ships carried 6,118 automobiles or 3,208 cars and 531 heavy trucks. The total weight of such a cargo was less than that needed to bring the ship down to her load-line marks, and therefore water ballast tanks were installed to add 4,000 tons of weight as needed for the safety of the ship and cargo.

To simplify the handling of large vehicles, the 17,000-horsepower engine was offset to the starboard side to create a single unobstructed passage through the main hold area. Elaborate safety measures, including a system to flood the cargo spaces with carbon dioxide, were provided. The ventilation system, used at maximum capacity during vehicle loading and unloading operations, effected twenty-five changes of air per hour.[15]

Vehicle carriers were owned almost exclusively by established ship operating companies and were made available to automobile producing and exporting organizations under either charter or contract of affreightment. Regardless of the contractual relationship, the vessel operator supplied the experience and expert technique required to deliver cargoes on schedule and in perfect condition.

It is worth repeating that ships of specialized design are often used by industrial organizations, and the line between the two categories of industrial or special carrier may be very faint. It is the use to which the ship is put that determines whether she is an industrial carrier; it is the design and the principal cargoes the vessel carries that fix the definition of special carrier. However, each provides a vital service and is necessary for the efficient transportation of goods.

CHAPTER NINE

Tanker Management, Operations, and Chartering

Ranging in size from enormous to almost tiny and transporting more tons of cargo of direct concern to more people in more parts of the world than any other type of ship afloat, tankers have become indispensable to the modern industrial economy. They are vital components of the merchant marine, and their management requires the same managerial skills needed by all ships engaged in moving cargoes across the seas. Dedicated as they are to the transportation of liquid commodities in bulk, however, these vessels also demand specialized knowledge and techniques both from the personnel who take them to sea and from those ashore who supervise their activities.

In the history of shipping, transporting oil in bulk is a relatively new enterprise. The first steamship designed and built to carry petroleum in bulk rather than in wooden barrels or metal drums was put into service in 1886.[1] This was the *Glückauf* ("Good Luck"), built in England to the order of Wilhelm A. Riedemann, a merchant of Hamburg, to serve the German-American Petroleum Company.[2] She was a small ship, measuring 300 feet (91 meters) long and with a deadweight of 3,020 tons—hardly noticeable alongside today's gigantic crude-oil carriers. Her place in history, however, derives from the fact that she was the prototype of the world's tankers, with steam-driven pumps segregated from the cargo tanks by steel bulkheads and the engine room at the after end, separated from the cargo tank area by a cofferdam formed by twin bulkheads. This pattern of construction has not been altered significantly over the years.

Since the *Glückauf* was launched, bulk oil carriers have multiplied in numbers, increased in speed and, most conspicuously, grown enormously in size. Change was slow at first; as late as 1920, the standard tanker had a deadweight of only some 12,000 tons, although there were a few vessels of about 20,000 tons deadweight.[3] In 1939, some 16,000-ton ships were in operation, but the majority of tanker-owning companies still leaned toward the "handy-sized" ships of 12,000 tons. The average speed of all these ships was about 11 knots, compared to the 10 knots of the *Glückauf.*

The demands for transportation of petroleum during World War II greatly exceeded the capability of the prewar fleet and called forth new standards for tankers. Bigger and faster ships were essential, and the United States built 532 oil carriers of the T-2 class. With a deadweight of about 16,750 tons and a speed of 14.5 knots, these ships proved conclusively that large, fast oil tankers were economical, efficient, and as versatile as the handy-sized tankers of 12,000 tons.[4]

Once the utility of the T-2 had been demonstrated, growth became characteristic of the tanker-operating industry. In 1947, the first of the really big ships were built. These "colossal" vessels of 25,000 to 27,000 tons deadweight quickly were relegated to lesser positions by the advent of tankers of 32,000 tons and, very shortly thereafter, of 45,000 tons. The peak was reached in 1979 with the completion for the C.Y. Tung interests of Hong Kong of the *Jahre Viking* (originally named *Seawise Giant*), a crude-oil carrier of 569,783 tons deadweight.[5] Owing to a worldwide reduction in consumption of oil a few years later, the demand for very large crude carriers decreased markedly, and no ships of that size have been built since 1979.

Paralleling the growth in the size of the ships was the proliferation of tankers in the world's merchant fleets. On March 31, 1996, there were in existence 3,035 commercial oil tankers, 216 combined carriers (designed to transport in shipload lots oil, dry-bulk commodities, or iron ore), and 321 liquefied petroleum gas tankers more than 5,000 cubic meters in capacity.[6]

Distribution of refined products traditionally was the province of smaller, shallower-draft vessels. These "delivery ships" were limited in size by the depths of harbor channels and berthing areas as well as by the capacities of storage facilities ashore. For many years, a fleet of tankers of 3,500 to 12,000 tons deadweight was employed in the United States coastwise trade. By the mid-1980s, a product carrier of approximately 50,000 tons deadweight had been designed to serve the majority of United States ports.[7] These newer and more efficient ships gradually displaced the older, smaller vessels. The big carriers, generally those of 200,000 tons deadweight or larger, were used exclusively to move crude (or raw) petroleum from the oil fields to the refineries.

During the years when the size and number of tankers in the world fleet were increasing, a concurrent change in the pattern of ownership was taking place. Shortly after the end of World War II in 1945, half of the world's tanker tonnage belonged to, and was operated by, the oil companies. In 1995, shipowners not affiliated with the petroleum producing and refining corporations (and therefore usually designated as the "independents") controlled 91 percent of the world fleet.[8]

Top: The 14.5-knot, 16,650-ton-deadweight T-2 tanker proved her worth in war and peace. *Bottom:* First of the American-flag supertankers, *Esso Zurich* (built 1949) had a deadweight of 26,555 tons and was 628 feet long. Courtesy Standard Oil Co.

This shift in transportation capability was deliberate. The producers allocated to different purposes the capital that would have been invested in tankers and, at the same time, sought to divest themselves of the burdens and responsibilities of fleet ownership. Day-to-day control of those tankers owned by oil companies in several instances was assigned to organizations devoted exclusively to the management of ships.[9]

Although the transportation of petroleum and its derivatives is a specialized branch of maritime activity, the management of tankers is not a unique form of supervision. Tankers, like other ships, must be built, maintained, and repaired. The same facilities that support the tanker industry also

This elaborately equipped ship conversion and repair yard in Bremerhaven, Germany, has one of the largest graving docks in Europe and can service any type or size of vessel. Photograph by Wolfhard Scheer, courtesy Lloyd Werft Bremerhaven.

serve the dry-cargo operators. Shipyards with repair docks large enough to accommodate the enormous tankers and containerships are available only in a comparatively small number of ports and are needed as much by dry-cargo shipowners as they are by tanker operators. The sophisticated machinery and control devices installed in new ships, both tankers and other types, require highly skilled personnel. Recruitment of crewmembers is, therefore, very competitive, because the number of qualified seafarers is finite. Regardless of the kind of ship, the schedules prepared for sailing, bunkering, and drydocking are governed by the same principles.

Some aspects of ship management are distinctive to the tanker business because of the nature and inherent qualities of petroleum and its derivatives. Among these characteristics may be cited the specialized terminals required for loading and discharging the ships, the integration of the schedules of operation of refineries and tankers, and the normally one-directional flow of traffic.

The fact that petroleum traffic flows only in one direction is of major importance in the management of tankers. Except in unusual circumstances,

The integrated tug-barge *Belcher Port Everglades–Belcher Barge #102* was built in 1981 to carry 55,000 tons of oil. The 15,000-horsepower tug fits into a 35-meter notch at the stern of the 195-meter-long barge. Photograph by Aurora Photography, courtesy Belcher Oil Co.

the ships are engaged for a significant portion of their lives in expensive and genuinely nonproductive voyages in ballast back to their loading ports. No really satisfactory alternative has been developed.[10]

Refineries are located far from the sources of crude petroleum and therefore depend upon the tankers to maintain an unbroken flow of the crude oil. Necessarily the operating schedule of the refinery is closely related to the movements of the tanker fleet. Production managers and tanker traffic controllers work together to ensure that there will be no interruption in the delivery of the crude supplies.

Distribution of the refined product may involve the use of tankers. That system, however, is built around the extensive network of pipelines and other forms of land transportation; therefore the role of the tanker is much less critical.

Oil companies depend on the independent tank vessel operators to provide the required transportation. Using chartered tankers to meet specific needs, the producers control the movement of their oil without the responsibility of ship operation. Short-term, single-voyage, or consecutive-voyage charters meet immediate requirements, while time charters lasting six months or more provide the long-term flow of oil. "Spot" coverage is a vital, but marginal, activity arising out of the need to meet unscheduled demands from the production or marketing divisions. "Unscheduled" in this case means an unexpected contingency such as a mishap withdrawing a ship from service, a sudden surge in demand for crude oil or petroleum products, or the breakdown of a refinery.

Tankers are engaged in one of two types of service, known distinctively as "clean" and "black" (sometimes also called "dark oil" or "dirty") trades. Ships in this latter trade carry only crude, residual, and darker oils up to diesel grades.

The clean trades, as the name implies, demand that the ship be very carefully prepared before any cargo oil is pumped into the tanks. Certain jet-engine fuels, for example, must be carried only in tanks coated with inorganic, nonferrous compounds to eliminate contamination from the corrosion of the tank bulkheads. Lubricating oil may be emulsified if water is left on the tank bulkheads; therefore, extra care must be exercised to ensure that no trace of moisture remains to pollute the cargo. It is customary to fill ("press up") the tanks to capacity so that there is minimal void space in which condensation can form.[11] In those instances where several grades of lubricating oil, varying in color from grade to grade, must be pumped through the same piping system, the lightest colored oil is pumped first. This ensures against contamination from any residue encountered in the pipes.

Black (or crude) oils, which are transported only from oil field terminals to refineries or prepared storage facilities, are markedly heavier than refined products. The characteristic high viscosity of the crude oils, which usually must be heated to render them sufficiently fluid to move through the ship's pumping system, requires that each of the cargo tanks be equipped with coils through which superheated water or steam is circulated. The oil thus heated is transferred ashore by the ship's pumps. As the carrying capacity of the tankers grew, so did the capacity of the pumps, measured in tons per hour. In the very large crude carriers (VLCC)—a designation applied to ships of 200,000 tons deadweight or larger—the pumps move at least 10,000 tons of petroleum every hour.[12]

As a consequence of a number of tanker casualties in which the cargo tanks were ruptured and millions of gallons of crude oil were spilled on coastal beaches and in estuarine waters, the need to safeguard the environment became a major consideration of legislative bodies, marine insurance underwriters, and the petroleum industry. As one means of preventing such disasters, the so-called double-hulled tanker was designed. This ship has a complete inner hull that is separated from the outer by approximately ten feet. The theory was that a grounding would pierce only the outer skin and would not imperil the integrity of the cargo tanks.

Although initially there was some debate among tanker operators over the safety factor built into the double-hulled tanker, the trend in that direction is very strong. The first very large crude carriers built to these principles were the *Eleo Maersk,* 299,381 tons deadweight, owned by Maersk Tankers

The double-hull crude oil carrier *Berge Sigval,* 306,430 metric tons deadweight, was built in 1993. She was 332 meters (1,115.5 feet) long, 58 meters (192.6 feet) wide, and had a draft of 22.8 meters (74.9 feet). Her speed was 15.4 knots. Courtesy Bergesen d.y. A/S.

This cutaway drawing shows structural details of a double-hull tanker. Two of the three athwartships tanks are depicted. Courtesy Bergesen d.y. A/S.

of Denmark; the *Arosa,* 291,381 tons deadweight, owned by Arosa Maritime, Inc. of Greece; and the *Berge Sigval,* 306,430 deadweight tons, belonging to Bergesen d.y. A/S of Norway, which was the world's largest double-hulled tanker when placed in service in early 1993.[13]

Safety is the paramount responsibility not only on board ships but also around the terminals where tankers load and discharge. At sea, in the approaches to ports, at anchorage, at the berth when pumping cargo as well as when awaiting orders, and throughout the normal routines of cleaning tanks, performing maintenance work, and standing watches, the utmost vigilance must be exercised constantly by all personnel if accidents are to be prevented. Implicit in meeting these responsibilities are the provisions for the navigation of the vessel: selection of routings, use of pilots, proper communication procedures, supervision of electronic aids to navigation, and selection of adequate berths. Fire, obviously, is an ever-present hazard, and elaborate precautions are taken to reduce this danger. Safety rules and procedures for shipboard and shoreside activities must be consistent, mutually understood, and everywhere respected.

To reduce the possibility of explosions set off by static electricity in the cargo tanks, tankers of 20,000 tons deadweight and larger are equipped with inert gas systems. The inert gas, with an oxygen content of not more than 5 percent by volume, may consist of treated flue gas from main or auxiliary boilers, gas from a gas turbine's exhaust, or gas from a separate inert gas generator. The inert gas is piped into the tanks as the cargo is pumped out, thereby preventing a potentially volatile mixture of air and hydrocarbon vapor that could become critical, subject to an explosion from a single spark.

Following the development of the inert gas system came the technique of crude-oil washing (COW) of cargo tanks, which is more effective in removing sludge than the time-honored method of washing tank bulkheads with streams of hot water under high pressure. The crude oil is drawn from the ship's cargo, and it dissolves the sludge and sediment. Very little crude oil is lost, as the wash-down eventually becomes part of the delivered cargo. Among the benefits of the crude-oil washing system is that cargoes are free of wash water, and the ballast water is clean and nonpolluting.

Of growing concern among port states and tanker operators is the control of hydrocarbon vapors that historically have been vented to the atmosphere during ballasting, tank venting, or cargo-loading operations. Tanker operators must vent these gases in order to reduce the dangerous pressure that builds in the cargo tanks during these operations. Government agencies, however, have determined that the uncontrolled release of these gases into the atmosphere poses a serious health threat to humans and the environment.

In view of the many hazards of releasing the tank gases to the atmosphere, many port governments now require the installation and use of a marine vapor control system at all marine oil terminals. The basic premise of a vapor control system is that it provides a closed-loop loading or ballasting operation for the tank vessel. This is accomplished by means of an onboard network of vapor collection piping that directs the exhausted cargo gas from each of the vessel's cargo tanks directly ashore for processing. With a properly working vapor recovery system, no dangerous hydrocarbon gas mixture will be released to the environment during tank venting, ballasting, or cargo-loading operations.[14] While these systems are effective, their installation, maintenance, and operation are additional cost factors that tanker operators need to consider.

Other aspects of management are provisioning, storing, scheduling, repairing, and bunkering tankers in worldwide service. Few tankers are employed in repetitive voyages between designated ports, and therefore long absences from the home port often occur. To provide adequate supplies of food, stores, and fuel of good quality—and to procure these at reasonable prices for scores of ships in oil-handling ports around the world—

The centralized, computer-oriented, one-man-operated engine control station is installed in a soundproof room. Courtesy Merlin Gerin.

is an undertaking of impressive dimensions. Management must be alert and responsible when voyages are subject to unforeseen deviations, re-routing on short notice, and unexpected delays beyond control of either the ship's personnel or her owners.

Few ports in the United States have sufficient depth of water to ac-commodate tankers of more than about 300,000 tons deadweight. To ob-tain the benefits of the lower unit cost of transportation afforded by the very large crude carriers, oil refiners devised a procedure by which ships of not more than 75,000 tons deadweight met the supertankers in coastal waters; there the cargo was transshipped into the shallower-draft vessels for delivery to shoreside installations.

A more economical and more permanent method of using very large crude carriers was put into operation off the Louisiana coast in 1981. A huge buoy was anchored in water more than 100 feet deep to serve as the

The largest tanker in the world, the *Jahre Viking* was 458.5 meters (1,540.4 feet) long, 68.4 meters (229.8 feet) in beam, and on a draft of 24.61 meters (82.7 feet) had a deadweight of 564,650 tons. Her 50,000-shaft-horsepower steam turbines gave her a speed of 13 knots. Courtesy Jorgen Jahre Shipping A/S.

mooring point for the ship as well as the offshore terminal of a submarine pipeline connected to the storage facilities ashore. Located about 18 miles offshore, this unit, known as the Louisiana Offshore Oil Port (LOOP), can process more than one million barrels of petroleum per day. The tanker is moored by a cable to the buoy ("single point mooring"), which permits her to face into the prevailing wind and sea at all times. Her cargo is pumped through a floating hose to the buoy, where it is directed into the submarine pipeline. The LOOP is only one of a number of these offshore moorings in use around the world.

In 1996, there were 432 tankers of 200,000 tons deadweight or larger. They gave to charterers the benefits of the economy of scale, and, when compared to ships of about 75,000 tons deadweight or smaller, they offered to shipowners the following advantages: per ton of cargo carried, they were cheaper to build; fewer hulls were needed to transport a given quantity of petroleum; fuel consumption per ton of cargo delivered was less; and crews remained about the same size despite the difference in ship size.

These very large crude carriers have to overcome major problems in actual operation. Their great draft, ranging from 18.29 meters (61.46 feet) for a 200,000-ton tanker to the 24.61 meters (82.17 feet) of the 569,783-ton *Jahre Viking,* restricts them to trade among a comparatively small number of ports. Ships with a draft exceeding 22.8 meters (76.6 feet) that are routed to Japan from the Arabian Gulf must use the deep Strait of Lombok rather than the 1,000-mile shorter passage through the shallower Strait of Malacca. Tank cleaning is more hazardous in the larger ships because of the vast size of the cargo tanks and the greater possibility of generating static electricity that could cause an explosion. Only a few drydocks are large enough to accommodate these giants.

TANKER CHARTERING

Until the outbreak of World War II, the procedures followed by owners, brokers, and charterers of tankers were substantially the same as those used in the chartering of dry-cargo ships. Every voyage was an individual project; costs were set forth route by route and port by port. Each aspect of the proposed voyage was discussed in detail. If the contemplated employment required loading at a single port and discharging at a specified destination, the procedure was comparatively simple and straightforward. If, however, calls were to be made at two or more loading ports, and the charterers wished to have the option of discharging in more than one port, the resulting negotiations became complex and time-consuming.

The outbreak of the war changed procedures. The government of Great Britain requisitioned tankers for use—that is, the government dictated what cargoes were to be loaded at which ports, what route was to be followed to specified destinations, and whether there would be any intermediate calls. All operating costs were defrayed by the government, and the owners were paid a flat fee per day for their services as managers. Gradually, as experience justified the action, the Ministry of Transport (MOT) formulated a schedule of rates and distributed this to all concerned. When the United States entered the conflict, it capitalized on the experience of Great Britain, and the U.S. Maritime Commission (USMC) issued a schedule of rates applicable to American ships. Government control of shipping continued in both nations until 1948, during which period the industry adopted the two government rate schedules.

In commercial practice, the convenience and utility of both MOT and USMC schedules came to be universally appreciated as the bases for contracts. Rate deviations were either added to or subtracted from the printed rates shown in the schedules. The two schedules served until 1952, when the London Tanker Brokers' Panel formulated and distributed the Tanker Nominal Rate Scale (Scale No. 1). New York brokers followed suit with the American Tanker Rate Schedule, which was developed to reflect the costs incurred by ships registered in the United States.

Both of the scales used standard ships with fixed characteristics and provided a fixed sum to be paid to management. A number of changes occurred over the years until 1969, when the brokers in London and New York combined their efforts and produced the Worldwide Tanker Nominal Rate Scale, the short title of which quickly became Worldscale. The size of the standard ship had been increased from time to time to reflect the growth in the carrying capacity of modern tankers. The present standard ship characteristics were adopted in January 1989.

At the present time, Worldscale schedules are compiled and issued by offices in London and New York. The British office carries the title of Worldscale Association (London) Limited, while the American office (which is independent of the London association) is known as Worldscale Association (NYC) Incorporated. Membership in these associations is open to shipowners, brokers, and charterers. Each year, on January 1, a new issue of the schedule is sent to all members and is effective as of that date. Annual changes reflect, among other items, port fees and the cost of fuel, averaged on a worldwide basis.

In practice, it is customary to quote tanker freight rates in terms of Worldscale plus or minus a percentage of the specific (published) rate. If the contracting parties agree on the published rate, the quotation is re-corded at "W.100," meaning that the full scale price is paid. Should less than the scale be approved, the quotation would be "W.45," signifying that 45 percent of the published rate had been accepted. Similarly, when condi-tions are appropriate, an increase above the published rate is noted as "W.135," showing that the negotiated figure was 35 percent above that in the scale.

The accompanying list shows the characteristics of the standard ves-sel as well as the standard port time and transit times used as the bases for calculating the nominal freight rates.

Standard vessel	75,000 tons deadweight
Average service speed	14.5 knots
Fuel consumption per 24-hour day at sea	55 metric tons
Fuel consumption per 24-hour day in port	5 metric tons
Allowance for all other fuel purposes	100 metric tons
Grade of fuel oil	380 cSt
Port time	96 hours laytime plus 12 hours for each extra port
Canal transits	Panama Canal—24 hours
	Suez Canal—30 hours
Variable costs	
Bunker fuel prices	Worldwide average compiled during September each year
Port costs	Based on information available up to September 30
Fixed return to owner	$12,000 per day

Note: All freight rates are quoted in U.S. dollars per metric ton. Rates are revised an-nually and become effective on January 1. Interim modifications are made as required.

A sample calculation is presented to demonstrate how a single freight rate would be derived.

CALCULATIONS FOR A STANDARD SHIP
OF 75,000 DWT AND 14.5 KNOTS SPEED

Specifications	
Standard ship	75,000 tons deadweight
Speed	14.5 knots
Fuel, at sea	55 metrics tons per day

Fuel, in port	5 metric tons
Fuel, other	100 metric tons

Voyage distances

From port A to port B	7,500 miles
From port B to port A	7,500 miles
Total distance R/T	15,000 miles

Duration of R/T

Days at sea (distance ÷ miles per day)	43.10 days
15,000 ÷ 348	
Days in port (2 for loading, 2 for discharging)	4.00 days
Total voyage days	47.10 days

Fuel consumption (all purchased in Port A)

From port A to port B	1,185 tons
From port B to port A	1,185 tons
Reserve for voyage, port A to port B	310 tons
Four days in port at 5 tons per day	20 tons
Fuel, all other purposes	100 tons
Total fuel	2,800 tons

Cargo carried

Ship's total deadweight		75,000 tons
Stores, etc.	100 tons	
Water	400 tons	
Total fuel	2,800 tons	3,300 tons
Tonnage available for cargo		71,700 tons

Freight rate calculations

47.10 days @ $12,000 per day		$565,200
Bunkers purchased @ $101 per ton		282,800
Port costs		
Port A	$15,000	
Port B	75,000	90,000
Total voyage costs		$938,000

Freight rate = Total cost ÷ Tons of cargo

= $938,000 ÷ 71,700 metric tons = $13.08 per metric ton

Worldscale rate = $13.08 (charterers accepting this rate would have it reported as "W.100")

This calculation is reasonably straightforward and easy to interpret for those who own or charter a standard vessel. The following example demonstrates the calculations for the same voyage with a vessel that is larger and faster than the standard vessel:

CALCULATION FOR A TANKER
OF 225,000 TONS DWT AND 15.5 KNOTS SPEED

Specifications		
Ship		225,000 tons deadweight
Speed		15.5 knots
Fuel, at sea		110.0 metric tons per day
Fuel, in port		10.0 metric tons per day
Fuel, other		200.0 metric tons total
Voyage distances		
From port A to port B		7,500 miles
From port B to port A		7,500 miles
Total distance R/T		15,000 miles
Duration of R/T		
Days at sea (distance ÷ miles per day) 15,000 ÷ 372		40.32 days
Days in port (4 for loading, 4 for discharging)		8.00 days
Total voyage days		48.32 days
Fuel consumption (all purchased in port A)		
From port A to port B		2,218 tons
From port B to port A		2,218 tons
Reserve for voyage, port A to port B		555 tons
Eight days in port, at 10 tons per day		80 tons
Fuel, all other purposes		200 tons
Total fuel		5,271 tons
Cargo carried		
Ship's total deadweight		225,000 tons
Stores, etc.	200 tons	
Water	500 tons	
Total fuel	5,271 tons	5,971 tons
Tonnage available for cargo		219,029 tons
Freight rate calculations		
48.32 days @ $12,000 per day		$579,840
Bunkers purchased @ $101 per ton		532,371
Port costs		
Port A	$60,000	
Port B	300,000	360,000
Total voyage costs		$1,472,211
Freight rate = Total cost ÷ Tons of cargo		
= $1,472,211 ÷ 219,029 metric tons = $6.72 per metric ton		

Worldscale rate for the standard ship is $13.08. The rate for the larger, faster ship is $6.72, or 51.4 percent of the rate for the standard ship ($6.72 ÷ $13.08 = .514). The quotation would be W.51.4.

To the basic rates set forth in the schedule may be added extra costs imposed by specified ports, shown in the schedule under the heading of "variable differentials," and forming part of the total publication. The addition to the Worldscale rate becomes part of the final rate. For example, a cargo is loaded at Aqaba for Singapore. The local authorities exact a charge of $0.55 per cargo ton. The Worldscale rate is $5.75 for the voyage from Aqaba to Singapore. To this must be added $0.55, to make the rate $6.30. Any differential must become part of the published rate.

The economies of scale are demonstrated clearly in the following table showing the freight rate required by Worldscale to produce the daily payment of $12,000 to the owner:

85,000 DWT tanker, Ras Tanura to Yokohama W.92.75
280,000 DWT tanker, Ras Tanura to Yokohama W.44.40
350,000 DWT tanker, Ras Tanura to Yokohama W.40.50

Annually, the Worldscale Associations compute the rates appropriate for thousands of voyages. The schedule page shows the magnitude of the computations required. These calculations have simplified the negotiation of tanker charters. Petroleum cargoes, because they are liquid, can be pumped at approximately the same speed in all ports of the world, and almost invariably involve a ballast voyage back to the loading port. These factors can be calculated to a nicety. The great variety of dry cargoes in ships of widely different characteristics, coupled with the normal practice of sending the empty ship to whatever port offers another cargo, makes impractical the creation of similar rate schedules for dry-bulk cargoes.[15]

LIQUEFIED GAS CARRIERS

Closely related in many respects to the movement of petroleum and its derivatives is the carriage of liquefied natural gas (LNG) and liquefied petroleum gas (LPG). These gases belong to the first of two unrelated categories: those with vapors that are flammable when mixed with air, and those with vapors that are both flammable and toxic. In the first category are hydrocarbons: butane, butadiene, propane (LPG), propylene, ethylene, and LNG. The chemical gases—vinyl chloride monomer, methyl chloride, ammonia, and propylene oxide—are members of the second category. The principal hazards associated with gases in the first group are fire and explosions; gases in the second group not only may explode or catch fire, but they may have toxic effects on personnel, possibly causing asphyxiation.

The *Lake Charles* (built 1980) carried 125,000 cubic meters of liquefied natural gas in her five spherical tanks. Photograph by Eckstein, courtesy Moore-McCormack Resources.

Routinely, liquefied gas is transported under pressure, but three different methods are used: (1) "fully pressurized," i.e., under pressure but at the ambient temperature; (2) "refrigerated and semi-pressurized," i.e., under pressure but cooled well below the ambient temperature; and (3) "fully refrigerated," which hints at the process by which the gas is cooled to its boiling point at slightly above atmospheric pressure and transported at that pressure. Liquefied gas is bulky; one ton of the gas occupies about four times the space of an equivalent weight of petroleum.

The first shipment of liquefied gas took place in 1928, when the *Megara,* a conventional oil tanker converted for the purpose, transported liquefied petroleum gas at a temperature of 0° Celsius and a pressure of 250 pounds per square inch. Although this movement was successful, it was not exploited.[16] In 1958, the *Methane Pioneer* was introduced. Built as a small dry-cargo carrier, she had been converted into a transporter of liquefied gas. Her separate, aluminum-alloy pressure vessels were insulated by a "wool" made from balsa wood and proved to be entirely satisfactory. Two years later, the *Bridgestone Maru,* a tanker of 25,626 tons deadweight, was designed and built specifically to haul liquefied gas from Indonesia to Japan. Her performance validated many theories relating to the techniques of shipping this new commodity.[17]

Ships carrying liquefied petroleum gas range in capacity from 5,000 cubic meters to more than 100,000 cubic meters of liquefied gas; they are suitable for transportation of gases of the first category and can be fitted to handle ammonia or vinyl chloride. Cargo is carried at nearly atmospheric pressure and the temperature goes down only to −50° Celsius. Consequently, the tanks may be of the freestanding, prismatic type. These are internally stiffened, heavily insulated externally, and fabricated from special steels that will not crack in the low temperatures. All cargo tanks are installed a minimum of 760 millimeters from the outer hull.

Liquefied natural gas carriers vary in capacity from 25,000 cubic meters to 135,000 cubic meters.[18] Most of the ships are able to carry at least 100,000 cubic meters of liquefied gas. In 1998, there were 105 LNG tankers operating worldwide.[19]

Although many different systems for handling this commodity have been proposed since 1958, only two have gained widespread acceptance. One pattern was developed by Moss, a Norwegian shipbuilding firm, in which freestanding, unstiffened spherical tanks were anchored to the inner hull.[20] The other was created by two French companies, Gaz Transport and Societé Nouvelle Technigaz. This system featured freestanding, prismatic pressure vessels, also secured to the inner hull. In both methods, the pressure vessels were wrapped in thermal insulation.[21]

All carriers of liquefied natural gas are built with a watertight inner hull; those with the prismatic tanks are required to have a secondary containment system that will hold any cargo leakage for at least fifteen days.[22]

Transportation of these liquefied gases has become a major economic activity. The principal exporting nations are Indonesia, Algeria, Malaysia, Brunei, and Australia. Japan alone in 1995 absorbed 1.2 million cubic meters—about two-thirds of the export trade. The main European markets are Spain and Belgium. In 1990, 54 million metric tons of liquefied petroleum gas were moved, giving employment to ships ranging in capacities from less than 2,000 cubic meters to the 137,000 cubic meters of the largest carriers.[23]

Liquefied natural gas is delivered to public utilities with large storage tanks, while liquefied petroleum gas is distributed to vendors with much more limited storage facilities. Consequently, the ships that transport butane and the related gases are likely to be small. Even granting that butane at −51° Celsius presents less of a problem in handling than does liquefied natural gas at −160° Celsius, the responsibility to ensure that every voyage is completed without incident is identical. It is a tribute to the skill and vigilance of the ship operators that hundreds of voyages are made safely each year; for example, in 1991, there were 1,446 deliveries of liquefied natural gas, 400 of which went to Tokyo Bay.[24]

Liquefied gas carriers must be designed and constructed not only to meet the needs of the service for which they are intended, but also in accordance with the requirements of the ship classification society, of which Lloyd's Register of Shipping is the oldest and probably the best known. A ship built with membrane tanks and used for transportation of liquefied gases in bulk would be given Lloyd's Register classification of "+100 A-1 liquefied gas carrier." Promulgated by the International Maritime Organization, the International Code for the Construction of Ships Carrying Liquefied Gases in Bulk (IGC Code) provides an international standard for the safe carriage by sea of liquefied gases (and certain other substances) in bulk. To minimize risks to ships, to their crews, and to the environment, the IGC Code prescribes the design and construction standards of gas carriers and the equipment they should carry.[25]

Refrigerated gas cargo inevitably suffers some evaporation, which is known in the trade as "boil-off gas," or BOG. This is not wasted; it is transferred by an electrically powered gas compressor to the boilers, where it supplements the fuel used to generate steam for the turbines. This gas, however, represents a loss to the shipper, and much attention has been given to reducing the BOG. A building program involving seven identical ships was initiated in 1989, stipulating that the ships should have four independent spherical tanks rather than the more conventional five. Among the advantages claimed for this arrangement on these 125,000-cubic-meter ships were low initial cost, reduction of the "boil-off rate" (BOR) from 0.25 percent of the cargo per day to 0.10 percent per day, and ease of operation, maintenance, and repair. In part this improvement was attributed to the heavy insulation applied to the four tanks. This was 210 millimeters thick and consisted of two layers of phenolic resin and polyurethane foam protected with aluminum alloy sheets and fastened to the tank with stud bolts. To minimize the possible transmission of heat from the hull into the tank structure and thus into the cargo, stainless steel "thermal brakes" were inserted between the skirts, which were of aluminum alloy and steel.[26]

The use of BOG as part of the vessel's fuel is taken into account when assessing fuel requirements and shipping costs. However, LNG boil-off cannot be used in diesel engines and all LNG carriers are still built with steam turbine engines, a technology that is now virtually unknown on any other modern vessel. New propulsion systems based on the use of dual fuel (gas/diesel) are being designed and could change the design and efficiency of LNG carriers.[27]

Through this development period, as fewer steam turbine propulsion systems are being operated, there will ultimately be a shortage of steam propulsion manufacturers and qualified operators as well as spare parts for existing steam systems. This is a concern to LNG ship owners but fortunately, companies such as Kvaerner Maritime are developing efficient and economical shipboard reliquefaction units. The idea is to reliquefy boil-off gas and return it to the cargo tank, thus allowing any type of propulsion system to be used to propel the ship.[28]

In July 1992, the world's largest liquefied natural gas tanker was the 136,400-cubic-meter *Ekaputra,* built by Mitsubishi's Nagasaki yard in 1990 and assigned to transport gas from Indonesia to Taiwan at a temperature of −163° Celsius. The 17.5-knot, turbine-driven ship had five heavily insulated Moss-designed spherical tanks from which the BOR was reported to be 0.1 percent per day.[29]

Abu Dhabi National Oil Company took delivery in 1996 of the *Mubaraz,* an LNG tanker of 135,000 cubic meters capacity. This ship was the first of her type to have four (rather than five) cargo tanks. The four Moss-Kvaerner tanks all were of the same size: 44.04 meters internal diameter. They were formed from magnesium and manganese-alloyed aluminum. The ship's 40,000-horsepower geared turbines were supplied with steam generated in boilers fueled by oil or BOG from the cargo. Her service speed was 19.5 knots.[30]

CHEMICAL TANKERS

Liquid chemicals have been transported in bulk across the seas since about 1950. At that time, shippers of large quantities of animal fats, tallow, and vegetable oils began to charter oil tankers, seeking lower transportation charges. As the advantages of bulk shipment of nonpetroleum commodities became apparent, additional liquids, including a number of chemicals of different types, were offered. It soon was learned that some chemicals possessed characteristics that demanded more sophisticated techniques for bulk transportation than the standard oil tanker could offer. A number of tankers were modified to the extent necessary to meet the new requirements. Multiple piping and pumping systems were installed. Cargo tanks were coated to present a smooth, uniform surface that would resist corrosion and also prevent contamination of the cargoes.[31]

While a number of chemicals are no more dangerous to transport in bulk than is liquefied petroleum, others are genuine "high-risk" cargoes and present management, both ashore and afloat, with peculiar problems. The following have special significance:

- The nature and characteristics of the chemical may increase the danger of fire. Carbon disulfide, for instance, has a low flash point and a wide range of flammability; phosphorus ignites spontaneously when exposed to air; adiponitrile gives off poison gases when it burns.
- Vapors from chemicals may be irritating to the ship's personnel. Only ships designed to carry these chemicals can be used in this trade. If cargo is ventilated to the atmosphere, the vents must be elevated above any crew passageways and must be at least 40 feet from the crew's living spaces. The exact height varies with the chemical(s) being transported.
- Some chemicals react when mixed with other chemicals. Very specific regulations have been promulgated concerning the compatibility of these liquids and must be obeyed precisely. Appropriate steps must be taken by those in charge of loading and by the ship's master to ensure that parcels loaded in adjacent tanks and separated only by a single bulkhead do not cause dangerous results should a leak develop in that bulkhead.
- Certain chemicals have the propensity to react violently when contaminated by water. Every precaution must be exercised to ensure that no water of any sort reaches the tank(s) containing these chemicals. This "family" of chemicals should be transported only in tankers that have double bottoms and nonwater ballast tanks adjacent to the spaces in which these liquids are contained.
- Many chemicals have the capability of polluting human and marine life if they are spilled. The most stringent precautions must be observed to prevent any accidental discharge.

To ensure uncontaminated handling of many different types of chemicals at one time, an intricate web of cargo pipes is essential. Courtesy Moss-Rosenberg Shipbuilders.

In time, the offerings of chemicals to be shipped in bulk increased sufficiently to justify building ships designed expressly to transport a wide variety of these liquids, including the exotic and the extremely dangerous substances. A primary requirement was that the specialized tanker have a double bottom for the entire length of the hull. To isolate the different chemical cargoes one from another, inner skins had to be installed in at least some of the tank areas. Pumping and piping systems were planned not only to prevent contamination of the cargo, but also to minimize the possibility that violent reactions could occur from mixing noncompatible chemicals. Although not an integral part of the safety features of the chemical tanker, multiple piping and pumping arrangements contribute significantly to the efficiency of ship operations in the rapid loading and unloading of the assorted cargoes.[32]

All these matters were studied by the International Maritime Organization before it promulgated the Code for Construction and Equipment of Ships Carrying Dangerous Chemicals in Bulk. This code subsequently was incorporated into the International Convention on Safety of Life at Sea, 1994. Concurrently, IMO prepared a list of hazardous chemicals for which specialized care was mandatory; another list specified which chemical

The chemical tanker has a complex piping system, double bottom, double skin, and cofferdams separating the numerous cargo tanks. Courtesy Stolt-Nielsen, Inc.

liquids were not hazardous. Agreeing with a proposal submitted by the delegates from the United States, IMO adopted rules applicable to tankers that were approved for transportation in bulk of three major types of chemicals:

> *Type I* chemicals. The most hazardous chemicals are restricted to ships with double bottoms in way of the cargo tanks. The cargo tanks shall not be closer to the side of the ship than a distance equal to one-fifth of the vessel's beam.
> *Type II* chemicals. Moderately dangerous chemicals shall be carried only in vessels with double bottoms and side cofferdams at least 760 millimeters inboard from the exterior plating of the hull.
> *Type III* chemicals. Nonhazardous chemicals may be moved in ordinary tankers provided that precautions are taken to prevent loss of the ship when she is carrying high-density cargoes. Normally this would be effected by leaving selected tanks empty in order to distribute the weight evenly throughout the ship's structure.[33]

No single vessel can handle every type of liquid chemical; more than 1,300 different chemical products have been identified as potential candidates for transportation in bulk across the seas. Many of these chemicals have characteristics that must be taken into account when selecting the steel for the bulkheads of the cargo tanks. Most chemicals can be carried satisfactorily in stainless steel tanks; a smaller number can be loaded in tanks fabricated of mild steel and finished with layers of zinc and organic coatings.[34]

On January 1, 1996, a total of 1,283 ships, aggregating 8,070,000 deadweight tons, were engaged in transporting more than 200 different types of chemical cargoes. The main product groups included organic chemicals and petrochemicals, inorganic chemicals and acids, vegetable and animal oils and fats, molasses, and special cargoes such as fuel additives and naphtha.[35]

An assortment of rules, international conventions, and local ordinances governed this trade. IMO, stimulated by the rapid increase in the overseas movement of noxious liquids in bulk, adopted Annex II to the Marine Pollution (MARPOL) Convention. Among other directives, this convention stipulated the way chemicals are to be discharged into receiving tanks ashore or dumped into the sea as residual waste. Superefficient methods of stripping tanks were prescribed and stringent regulations written to cover prewash procedures when the more hazardous substances were to be transported.

Operating tankers in this highly specialized trade, conforming to strict rules, safeguarding personnel, meeting competition—all demand that those involved possess experience, good judgment, and wide technical knowledge. Dominating the industry and based on its participation in the business for more than four decades, Stolt-Nielsen S.A. in 1993 controlled more than 100 ships ranging in size from 1,300 tons deadweight to 36,700 tons deadweight. The company took delivery in 1996 of the *Stolt Innovation,* built by Danyard at Aalborg, Denmark. At 36,700 tons deadweight, this chemical carrier was the first of ten identical ships intended for worldwide operations. She was built to carry up to 44 different chemicals at one time. An elaborate piping system made each cargo space independent; as many as twelve tanks could be discharged simultaneously. All tanks were fabricated completely of stainless steel and were suitable to transport all three types of chemical cargoes. An inert-gas generating system protected the tanks, each of which had a hydraulic pump.

Washing tanks between cargoes can be of critical importance in this trade. To facilitate cleaning, the *Stolt Innovation*'s center (largest) tanks were designed with a minimum of structural members and obstructions,

Stolt-Nielsen's *Stolt Markland,* a chemical tanker of 29,999 tons deadweight, was delivered to her owners in 1991. The ship's system of stainless steel piping and pumps permitted 41 grades of cargo to be loaded simultaneously in 23 center tanks, 16 wing tanks, and 2 deck-mounted tanks set aside for highly sophisticated cargoes. Courtesy Stolt-Nielsen Inc.

and each tank was equipped with a fixed, multistage, multinozzle cleaning machine, supported by a drying system employing two dehumidifiers.

Protection against a tank overflow during the loading process was ensured by the installation of a radar-based automatic level gauging system. Cargo temperatures were monitored by sensors. Other features were a closed cargo sampling system, gas detection of all void spaces, and a vacuum mechanism to handle cargo slops.

A medium-speed diesel-electric power plant of 18,170 brake horsepower gave the *Stolt Innovation* a speed of 16.2 knots. She was 176.75 meters (580.09 feet) long overall, 31.2 meters (102.04 feet) wide, and had a draft, at summer load line, of 11.75 meters (38.56 feet).[36]

Transporting bulk liquids of any kind from and to all parts of the world, tankers have become the largest category of ships in the merchant fleet. Their utility and importance are beyond measure.

CHAPTER TEN

Vessel Management Companies

At one time, the owner would travel with a vessel and take care of all of her physical and commercial needs. As business requirements changed and fleet size grew, it was no longer possible, or even desirable, for owners to accompany their vessels. The day-to-day management of a vessel was turned over to the master, who would see to the safe navigation of the vessel and the general management requirements. This system worked quite well in the days of tramp shipping, when transit times were long and communication slow and expensive.

The trend in the maritime industry over the last thirty years has been for shipowners to hire third-party managers to provide a variety of management functions. The impetus behind this trend is as varied as the number of shipowners questioned. One owner says that this trend is the result of the many changes that continue to be made in the operating environment in which ships do business. Each year new regulations are added concerning such things as vessel maintenance and inspections, safety and pollution, vessel manning and crew training, insurance, communications, and documentation. It is becoming more difficult to stay current with all of the changes.

Others say that the trend has been caused by the owners of smaller companies, who find it difficult to survive in today's competitive business environment. They seek ship managers who can offer them the cost benefits of the large fleet owners without sacrificing the company's identity. Still other owners observe that if they contract with firms specializing in vessel management, they are free to concentrate on their core business, which may not be the actual movement of goods by water. Finally, some owners note that the use of ship managers saves them money because the managers have greater purchasing powers and a larger crew resource and training pool. Whatever the reason given, in this increasingly complex business environment many ship owning companies, both big and small, are clearly deciding that it is more efficient to outsource the management of their fleets to third-party ship management companies.

Outsourcing management functions can take many forms. All ship management companies are involved in the technical management of the vessels under contract to them. In addition, if they have the resources and expertise, these contractors may provide other services: vessel crewing and crew training, a variety of financial services, insurance, consultation, new construction supervision, chartering, accounting, sale or purchase of vessels, bunkering, provisioning, and compliance with requirements for certification.[1] Only a few companies have the resources, experience, or skills to provide all these services. The mainstay of the ship management business is technical management and vessel crewing.

During the 1960s and 1970s, there was little control over the establishment and growth of ship management companies. Shipowners had to exercise great caution in evaluating the capability and reliability of the contractors bidding for their patronage. To make themselves more attractive, many ship management companies offered far more than they could deliver. As a result, by the early 1980s, the ship management industry was faced with a very serious image problem.[2]

Trying to improve the quality of their services and ultimately their desirability, a group of ship management companies formed the International Ship Managers Association (ISMA) in 1991.[3] Since its creation, the ISMA has led the fight to promote quality of service in ship management through its quality assurance accreditation.[4] The accreditation process requires all members to prepare and apply for an external audit to demonstrate compliance with the ISMA Code of Shipmanagement Standards (CSS). The standards encompass all areas of general management and safety for vessel operation both onboard ship and ashore. Any company meeting the minimum standards will receive appropriate certification. Through these efforts, the ISMA attempted to bring self-regulation to a very diverse group of businesses and to bring recognition to third-party ship management companies as a legitimate profession.[5]

As an early standard of quality assurance, the Code of Shipmanagement Standards is but one of four quality assurance standards. The other three are the ISO 9002 Standards, the IMO International Management Code for the Safe Operation of Ships and for Pollution Prevention (more conveniently known as the International Safety Management [ISM] Code), and Det Norske Veritas Safety and Environmental Protection (SEP) rules.

The ISMA Code of Shipmanagement Standards is the most comprehensive of the codes and includes the provisions of the other three codes. Some key areas included in this standard are procedures for management responsibility and authority, document and data control, purchasing, process control, safety management systems, contingency plans and environmental protection, vessel certification, maintenance and repair, manning, communications, insurance, accounting, inspections, control of quality records, audits, training, health, safety and environmental policy, alcohol and drug abuse policy, and marketing policy. The ISMA code is very detailed in its sixty pages and therefore leaves less room for interpretation than other codes.[6] Since it includes the provisions of all the others, the ISMA is trying to get its certification process approved by the other quality-regulating organizations in an attempt to reduce the paperwork and the cost for their members.

The ISO 9000 series of quality standards has been used for some time in the manufacturing and service industries worldwide. In fact, many companies that do business on a global scale require that their partners be ISO 9000 certified as a demonstration that some assurance of quality standards has been met. The ISO 9002 standards are those specific standards used for ship management companies, but they do not include standards on such things as accounting, health, safety and environmental policy, alcohol and drug abuse policy, and marketing policies, all of which are addressed in the ISMA program.

In 1993, IMO adopted the International Safety Management (ISM) code. The code is included as a mandatory chapter of SOLAS and came into full effect in July of 1998. Under the ISM Code (IMO resolution A741 [18]), every company must develop, implement, and maintain a Safety Management System (SMS) that includes the following functional requirements: a safety and environmental protection policy; instructions and procedures to ensure safe operation of ships and protection of the environment in compliance with relevant international and flag state legislation; defined levels of authority and lines of communication between, and among, shore and shipboard personnel; procedures for reporting accidents and nonconformance with the provisions of the code; procedures to prepare for and respond to emergencies; and procedures for internal audits and management reviews. This IMO code does not address the issues of purchasing, accounting, and marketing policy that are addressed in the ISMA program. There is no doubt that ship management companies will have to conform to the ISM code since it is required under SOLAS, which in 1997 had been ratified by 122 countries whose fleets comprise more than 97 percent of world tonnage.[7] In the future, port states will undoubtedly require that every vessel entering their territorial waters meet the provisions of the ISM code as a minimum.

Det Norske Veritas Safety and Environmental Protection (SEP) rules are part of a specialized standard that focuses on safety and environmental protection measures in addition to the basic principles contained in ISO

9002. Unlike the ISMA standards, however, the SEP rules are silent on such issues as process control, communications, insurance, accounting, inspection and testing of vessels and equipment, handling, storage, packing, preservation and delivery, and marketing policy.

With so many quality assurance standards to choose from, ship managers are faced with difficult decisions regarding which certificate, or certificates, to obtain. For one thing, not all certificates have the same status internationally. Since adoption of the ISM code was required of all vessels in 1998, that would seem the likely choice, but it does not include some important items covered in other certification programs. Some ship management companies, depending on their trade and circumstances, will need to obtain more than one certificate. The time to prepare for certification, the costs of the auditing process, the cost of maintaining the certification, and the ultimate benefit of having such certification must be carefully weighed.[8]

Technical management is the thread that all ship management companies have in common. As part of their services, most ship management companies also offer to provide ships' crews. The cost connected with shipboard personnel has become a very controversial subject because it is one of the largest items in the operating budget of merchant ships.[9] One estimate puts the cost of crewing a ship at 40 percent of the operating costs (minus bunker and port charges).[10] While supplying qualified seamen to ships may seem a rather mundane and repetitive type of activity, nothing could be farther from reality.

Before a crew can be selected for a particular vessel, the prudent ship management company will need to consider many things. For example, it must determine if the vessel owner has any restrictions concerning nationality of crewmembers or their union affiliation. A careful review is essential to determine what regulations concerning crew requirements have been laid down by the flag state in which the ship is registered.[11] A survey of the vessel is conducted to assess any particular skills required because of the specialized nature of the vessel (i.e., gas carrier, RO/RO, passenger vessel, containership, etc.) or the specialized or unique trade in which the vessel will be operating. Language or cultural aspects may also be considered.

Once developed, the final crewing plan for the vessel will represent a delicate balance between the demand for quality and the necessity to keep the costs down. More often than not, after all concerns are taken into account, the ideal vessel crew will consist of a mix of nationalities, qualifications, experience, and levels of costs.

One reality of crewing, however, is that once the plan is developed, there may not be enough properly qualified mariners available to crew the ship as planned. A 1995 survey of global labor completed by the Institute for Employment Research at the University of Warwick showed a shortfall of 18,000 officers worldwide, but a surplus of 219,000 unlicensed ratings. When the quality of the seafarer population is taken into account, the shortage is more serious. All the officers recorded as part of the available stock are listed as qualified and properly certified under current regulations. In fact, deficiencies presently exist in the training and certification processes of some countries. Under the 1995 revisions to the STCW Convention, some of these officers may no longer be certifiable, which will increase the shortage of officers.[12]

It is no longer enough just to find a qualified crew and assign them to a vessel for the period of their employment. Today, both the vessel owner and the ship management company are concerned about the requirements for crew training. This training requirement can be costly and difficult, but if done carefully and conscientiously, it will result in safer operation and a more competent crew. Under the 1995 STCW Convention, which came into force in 1997 and will be phased in over a five-year period, shipowners and ship managers are required to ensure that the seafarers they employ are properly certified; detailed personnel records are to be kept to document sea service and training programs completed, and ships are to be crewed according to the flag state requirements. Vessels found violating these new regulations may be prohibited from entering the country or even prosecuted by the flag state.

Under these requirements, the master has new responsibility to train crewmembers before the vessel sails. Each crewmember must receive familiarization training in personal survival techniques and instructions in emergency procedures before being assigned to shipboard duties. Except for passengers, everyone onboard the ship—including all hotel and entertainment staff on passenger ships—must undergo survival and safety training. In addition, there is an English language mandate that requires all crewmembers to have at least a rudimentary ability with a common language. Because of the high turnover rate in crewmembers in the hotel services of passenger ships, these training requirements and the costs associated with them are causing considerable concern.

Ship managers also have new responsibilities under the regulations. No longer can they merely check the crewmembers' certificates. They must develop training plans for at-sea periods, and they must document the training that takes place. Much of this function will be done by the master, but the ship manager must have mechanisms in place to make certain that this training takes place and that it is documented properly.[13]

At one time, most major maritime countries subsidized the training of mariners through various training programs. However, a 1995 BIMCO/ISF (Baltic and International Maritime Council/International Shipping Federation) report indicated that a lack of recruitment, preparation, and training of young seafarers caused workforce shortages. It was noted that by leaving their respective national flags and moving into open registries, shipowners have reduced their operating costs with regard to crewing, but at a price. As the national registry shrinks, there is no longer the demand for the country to subsidize maritime training, so the number of qualified seagoing personnel shrinks.[14] Since the open registries do not provide proper training, the available pool of qualified crewmembers is going to drop even more than it already has.

To meet current crewing demand and the new STCW training requirements, some larger ship management companies are investing considerable amounts of money in the creation of their own proprietary training centers. At these centers, crewmembers, generally on their time off the ships, can learn and improve their skills in many areas. Training runs the gamut from the most basic of seamanship and safety skills to advanced topics of bridge team and bridge resource management, radar and collision avoidance, leadership training, conflict resolution, English proficiency, complex decision-making, engineering, and multicultural diversity and communications. These training centers may have very complex training equipment including complete bridge and engine simulators.

The Philippines are currently the major source of maritime labor, with about 20 percent of the world's seafarers. This is of some concern to crew managers in terms of the provision of adequate training facilities and, in particular, the provision of properly qualified seafarers. Other emerging sources for seafarers are China, the Confederation of Independent States (C.I.S), former Eastern Block countries, and some African countries. The country with the ability to provide quality seafarers, who have proper training and who are willing to work for international wages, will gain market shares and have the attention of crew managers.[15]

The long-term outlook for ship management companies is good, but each will face many challenges that they must address to be competitive. As companies continue their development in an ever-changing environment, it is possible to identify some trends that will affect them:

1. Third-party managers who forge partnerships with vessel owners by continuing to build their resources and improve their expertise will have a strong future. In addition, as the small owners find it more

difficult to survive under costly new legislative mandates, they will begin to look at ship management companies as an avenue to compliance, adding the advantages of increased economies of scale in purchasing, improved worldwide networking opportunities, use of global communication systems, and standardized paperwork.

2. The industry will consist of two diverse groups of ship management companies. One group will have quality assurance certification and will command the higher rates. The other group will not have any quality assurance certification, and they will struggle at the bottom of the rate structure.

3. Many ship management companies will merge, some to obtain quality assurance certification, some to improve their market position by broadening their expertise, resources, and services, and some to take advantage of economies of scale.

4. Ship management companies will enter niche markets, concentrating, for example, on containerships, chemical tankers, passenger ships, etc.

5. Ship management companies will examine new sources for qualified crewmembers, put pressure on some existing maritime labor pools to improve their professional quality, and be innovative in providing the constant retraining and upgrading of crew skills as the 1995 STCW requires.

6. Vessel owners will continue to require ship management companies to maintain the highest levels of information technology available.

Vessel management companies provide a valuable service to ship owning companies. They are currently evolving as the regulatory environment of the shipping industry continues to change. It is difficult to say with any degree of accuracy how they will function in the future. However, it is certain they will be on the scene providing the necessary services demanded by owners of all sizes and types of ships.

CHAPTER ELEVEN

Vessel Bunkering

Once the owner decides on the employment of a ship, it is necessary immediately to develop a sailing schedule that shows the date of departure, the ports of call (including the dates and times when those calls will be made), and the anticipated time of arrival at the final destination. In direct support of this schedule is a "bunkering plan," which must show where the ship will replenish her fuel supplies and what quantities will be taken aboard from the suppliers named in the plan. The bunkering plan is made after studying the fuel needs of the vessel, her earning capability, the availability and cost of fuel in ports along the route, and the cost in ship time to load fuel in the selected outport(s). It also takes into account the requirements for the safety of the ship imposed by international treaties, the regulations of a number of quasi-official bodies, and the insistence of the owner that the voyage return a profit or, in bad times, that the losses are kept to a minimum.

In stabilized liner service, which repetitiously sends the ship to the same ports on a fixed schedule and for which the fuel needs of the ship can be predicted with accuracy, the bunkering plan becomes part of the standard routine of ship management.

For the operator or charterer of a tramp ship, preparing the bunkering plan is basic to the computations preceding every proposed voyage, and it is related directly to the earning power of the vessel.[1] This is especially noticeable when the commodity to be transported is heavy ("dense"), and every ton of fuel means one less ton of revenue-earning cargo.

The tentative sailing schedule thus becomes the basis of all planning for the voyage. Once the route has been fixed (including those ports at which the ship is to call), the fuel needs of the ship can be determined, and the bunkering plan becomes the bunkering schedule.

If economic considerations justify the action and the sailing schedule can be adjusted to allow the time for the call, the ship may be sent to a port for the sole purpose of taking on fuel. Experience has shown that it takes about twelve hours of ship time to receive one thousand tons of fuel.[2] If the port imposes fees for calling, this adds to the expense which must be considered in reaching the decision to bunker en route.[3] If, however, the schedule is inflexible, the choice of fueling ports necessarily is limited to those on the assigned route. Whatever the circumstances, every voyage of a powered vessel, whether in tramp or liner service, depends upon both the sailing and the bunkering schedules. Coordination is essential among the traffic manager, who must please the customer(s); the director of operations, who seeks optimum performance; and the treasurer, who looks for a profit from the employment of the ship.

To ensure that all costs have been included in the voyage computations, certain questions must be asked and answered satisfactorily:

1. *To the traffic manager:* Does the proposed schedule meet existing or anticipated competition? Does it respond to the demands of shippers for minimum transit time?
2. *To the director of operations:* Does the proposed schedule take cognizance of changes in the cargo-working capabilities of the ports along the route?
3. *To the director of operations:* Does the proposed schedule take into consideration those factors that adversely affect efficient operations? Does congestion exist in any port(s) because of inadequate facilities?
4. *To the director of operations:* Does the proposed schedule make the best (i.e., the most effective) use of the ship's speed? Is the cargo-working capability of the ship, measured in ship's time, used to maximum advantage? Are the costs of fuel oil and ship time given adequate attention?
5. *To the bunkering manager:* Is maximum fuel economy, consistent with the requirements of the service, achieved by the speeds specified in the schedule?

The cardinal rule of the shipping business is that every aspect of the ship's employment must contribute positively to vessel earnings. By way of illustration, the following example assumes that only three pilots are on duty at the pilot station. They accept ships in the order of their arrival. The fourth ship in line must wait at least five hours for a pilot to return to the station. Hoping to prevent this long wait, Blue Sea Line's vessel cruises at maximum speed for the entire distance from her last port of call. Traveling at that speed significantly increases the consumption of fuel, an expense that must be balanced against the cost of five hours of ship time waiting for a pilot.

The ore-bulk-oil carrier *Eric R. Fernstrom* (built 1971), 101,835 tons deadweight, receives diesel fuel from two barges. Photographs by Jeff Blinn, courtesy Moran Towing Co.

The bunker schedule must comply with these governing precepts: (a) in all respects, international load line treaties must be observed, and the requirements of marine insurance underwriters concerning reserves of fuel oil must be met; and (b) the plan must contribute to the maximum earning power of the ship.

Compliance with load line requirements is basic to any bunkering plan under a penalty of having the ship declared unseaworthy.[4] American shipowners were placed under the obligations of the International Load Line Convention of 1930 when the Congress ratified the agreement in 1931. The actual load lines for an individual ship are fixed by the classification society when the designs and plans for that vessel are submitted for approval. Once the ship is in service, compliance with the load line requirements is mandatory. Violation of these rules renders the vessel unseaworthy and deprives the owner of legal protection against claims for loss or damage. Marine insurance underwriters have resisted successfully any claims for restitution of loss when a ship has been loaded deeper than the assigned marks and thereby has been made unseaworthy. When a vessel crosses from one zone to another, she must be loaded so that when she crosses the limiting zone line, she will meet the minimum freeboard requirements.

The most scrupulous observance of applicable load line and zone areas is required of all those involved in determining how much cargo is to be put into the ship. For example, a tanker is assigned to a voyage from Bahrain Island in the Arabian Gulf to Galway, Ireland, sailing on December 15. At this time of year, Bahrain Island is in the tropical summer zone; the Mediterranean Sea is in the seasonal summer zone, and the Atlantic ocean, from Gibraltar to Galway, lies in the seasonal winter zone, which is the limiting zone. Because fuel prices are lowest in Bahrain Island, the ship is to bunker for the entire voyage in that port. The tanker's load is calculated to be at the summer load line when she clears Port Said for Gibraltar. If fuel consumption between Port Said and Gibraltar does not lighten the ship sufficiently to meet the winter load line, the cargo load must be reduced by the difference between the permissible deadweight and the actual deadweight. Arrival in Galway with a draft exactly at the seasonal winter line could be prima facie evidence that she had less than the prescribed freeboard when she entered the zone at Gibraltar (assuming she did not take on ballast). The cargo load and bunkering schedule are so constructed that, as each load line zone is entered, the ship will be in compliance with the international rules.

Another aspect of the demands for safety of life at sea is the underwriters' mandate that all ships carry a reserve of fuel equal to not less than approximately one quarter of the fuel to be burned between scheduled ports of call. This means that a vessel proceeding from New York to Panama must take on 125 percent of the fuel that will be consumed on the passage to Panama. The ship cannot carry just enough fuel to reach her destination plus 25 percent of the amount needed from New York to some intermediate but unscheduled port where fuel is obtainable. If she is fueled in New York for the round-trip voyage, she would carry enough oil for the trip plus 25 percent of the amount needed to travel from Panama back to New York.

The second precept in drawing up the bunkering plan is to ensure the maximum earning power of the ship. This requires knowledge of the ship's routing, the possible ports where oil may be purchased, and the load line restrictions, as well as an awareness of the freight rate payable per ton of cargo loaded, the daily costs of the ship in addition to fuel, and the characteristics of the cargo being transported. In breakbulk liner service, it is generally true that the cargo is bulky and fills the holds before the ship is down to her marks. Containerships usually carry a number of empty containers, and even when fully loaded, they are rarely down to their marks. There is, consequently, no conflict between the cargo to be loaded and the weight of the fuel oil required for the voyage. In these trades, bunkering often becomes a process of selecting the port (or ports) along the route where fuel of satisfactory quality can be obtained in adequate quantity at a good price.

IMPORTANT NOTICE TO CONTRACT SIGNATORIES

BUNKER SURCHARGE

The Member Lines of the U.S. Atlantic & Gulf/Australia-New Zealand Conference wish to advise the shipping public that the previously announced Bunker Surcharge of 20% per revenue ton due to become effective December 15, 1981 has been reduced to 18%.

The Conference has also published further precautionary increases which will be subject to review and adjustment based on actual cost experience.

Schedule of Surcharges follows:

January 15, 1981	20% Per Revenue Ton
February 15, 1982	22% Per Revenue Ton
March 15, 1982	25% Per Revenue Ton

To meet the requirements of the second precept fully, the great expense of owning and operating a ship must be appreciated. If a fueling point is one or two days travel time from the shortest course between origin and destination, and it is selling oil at a reduced price, this does not (in itself) justify a diversion of the ship. Not only must the intent of the contract of carriage be met and all reasonable speed be made to traverse the sea distance, but the cost to the owner in ship time must be computed.

Marine bunker fuels are of two types: distillates and residuals. Diesel fuel is distilled as a part of the processing of crude petroleum. After the volatile components—gasoline, kerosene, diesel, and naphtha, among others—are extracted, what remains is considered as almost waste and is sold at less than the price of the crude petroleum. This residual oil was of consistently good quality until the petroleum crisis of 1973. In that year, the price per barrel of crude oil suddenly went up from U.S.$2.70 to U.S.$35.00, and oil companies greatly improved their techniques to extract the maximum quantity of the more volatile (and, compared to residual oil, more profitable) components of the petroleum feedstocks. Inevitably the quality of the residue declined.

What was available to shipowners was a residual fuel which technically was "unfinished." To make it satisfactory for use in modern diesel engines required that it be blended with one or more of the by-products of the petroleum and petrochemical industries. Heavy pressure to reduce air pollution resulted in the marine industry establishing certain minimum specifications that fuel was required to meet.[5] The International Organization for Standardization (ISO) issued its recommended specifications, identified initially as ISO-8217. Periodically, these have been updated, and the year of the update now forms part of the identification. Thus, the latest issue is known as ISO-8217/1996.

Marine fuels today are composed of the frequently changed by-products of the oil refining process, and one or more different grades must be blended into the basic stock to create the fuel ordered.[6] Too often, the blending process has been carried out aboard the bunkering barge during its voyage from the refinery or tank farm to the receiving ship.[7] This period, which averages about three hours, is insufficient to achieve the proper blending of the components.[8] The consequences of poor blending may be overcome by ordering the fuel early enough to permit the full process to be completed at the refinery or the supplier's tank farm, and to specify unambiguously in the purchase contract exactly what is required.

Throughout the time of delivery of bunkers to the receiving ship, samples of the fuel must be taken. In the best circumstances, this sampling is taken at the ship's bunker manifold, which is technically and legally where the transfer of ownership takes place. Normally, at the conclusion of the delivery, the sample is divided equally among three containers, each of which is sealed and carefully labeled with the name of the ship, the name of the supplier, the date of delivery, the exact time of day, and the number of the container's seal.[9] One container is kept aboard the ship, one container is held by the delivery barge for the supplier, and one container is sent to the laboratory for analysis.

The function of the laboratory is to determine by scientific analysis that the fuel is fit for use. The most common reasons that the oil might not be approved are these:

1. The fuel is unstable and therefore unusable.
2. The flashpoint is low, making the fuel unsafe.

3. Contamination exists from waste materials such as chemical refuse or discarded automobile lubricating oil.
4. The residual fuel contains excessive quantities of catalytic "fines," which can cause damage to marine diesel engines.
5. The fuel is hard to burn.[10]

Shipowners knew that fuel for the expensive and complex engines driving their ships must be of consistent quality and free of dangerous contaminants. Used automobile lubricating oil is particularly objectionable. The additives in these lubricants have the potential to cause major damage to the engines. Consequently, purchasers of bunker fuel increasingly insist that the bunkers they buy must be free of such contaminants.[11]

Bunker fuel is delivered by volume (i.e., measured in cubic meters) but paid for by mass (i.e., by the metric ton). Three major factors are involved in the process of evaluating the fuel delivered to a ship: density, viscosity, and energy content.

To effect conversion from volume to mass, the density of the fuel must be determined. Because density varies significantly with the ambient temperature, the marine bunker industry has adopted a standard temperature of 15° Celsius for this conversion. Density also serves to calculate the calorific value and the anticipated combustion performance of the fuel.

Viscosity is a measure of the liquid's resistance to flow. It is not an indication of the quality of the fuel. Like density, viscosity is affected by temperature, and sales contracts usually specify that viscosity shall be calculated at 50° Celsius. This temperature is significant for proper pumping and storage; a small change in temperature at the lower end of the scale can produce a large change in the viscosity of the fluid. Viscosity also is a factor in calculating the potential combustion performance of the fuel.

The energy content creates the propulsive horsepower that drives the ship. It is determined by the calorific value of the fuel. Hydrocarbon fuels contain mainly carbon, hydrogen, and, to a lesser extent, sulfur, all of which can be burned to release useful energy. Calorific value is related to fuel density: dense fuel contains more carbon (relatively heavy) and proportionately less hydrogen (relatively light) than a lighter oil. If fuel is purchased on a weight basis, a lower density fuel will release more energy per kilogram than a high density fuel.[12]

As noted above, the energy content of the fuel creates this propulsive horsepower. If there is less energy per kilogram, the standard speed of the ship can be maintained only by consuming more fuel. If no additional fuel is consumed, the speed of the vessel will be reduced in direct proportion to the deficiency in energy.

The owner of a ship operated under time charter, for example, does not pay for the fuel, which is procured by the charterer subject to the approval of the ship's chief engineer. If, at the rate of fuel consumption warranted in the charter party, the lower energy content of the fuel causes a 6 percent reduction in ship speed, the deficiency may be made up by increasing consumption by 6 percent. Should fuel consumption be maintained at the contract level, the ship's speed would be reduced by 2 percent. Although the charterer purchased the bunkers, the owner had warranted performance and fuel consumption. If the owner's warranty stipulated that the fuel had to be of a certain quality, the charterer would be obligated to provide fuel oil of that grade or suffer the consequences.[13]

Another factor influencing the procurement of bunker fuel is the compatibility of different oils. This is especially important when additional supplies are bought and may be mixed with an earlier purchase. The standards for compatibility have been set by the American Society for Testing and Materials (ASTM). Two fuels are said to be compatible if they can be mixed at the prescribed ratio without affecting the ability of the oils to hold certain components (asphaltenes) in suspension. Because heavier oils have had more of the volatile components removed in the refining process, they are more likely to become unstable when mixed and therefore must be considered as possibly incompatible.[14]

Bunkering a ship requires coordination between the shoreside office and the receiving ship. The office selects the port and the supplier, while the ship accepts and uses the fuel. Good bunkering management therefore dictates that these two groups adhere strictly to these basic rules:

- Fuel requirements must be specified exactly. The buyer must make certain that the supplier has accurate and full information, and that what is furnished by the purchaser conforms to the purchaser's records.
- The supplier's paperwork must reflect agreement to meet the stated specifications.
- The water content of the fuel and the acceptability of fuel oil with that percentage of water must be clearly set forth.
- The bunkering line and hose connections must be secure. A prestart meeting must be conducted with proper system lineup, communications, and safety precautions observed. The ship and the supplier must agree on the rate of flow and the pressure to be maintained in the lines.
- All readings of the flowmeter and notations of dips of oil must be witnessed. These readings are to be taken before delivery starts and after delivery is complete.

- New fuel should be segregated until quality is demonstrated.
- A relatively simple shipboard test of the compatibility of the fuel oil blend must be available.
- Following delivery, standard tests are to be conducted for water content, density, viscosity, and flash point of the fuel.
- If a laboratory is to conduct the analysis of the bunkers, the samples supplied must represent the total quantity of the oil received. Containers must be properly, accurately, and completely labeled.
- Complaints, or notice of intention to complain, should be filed with the supplier at the time of bunkering, or as soon thereafter as possible.[15]

To satisfy the demands of shipowners for more satisfactory and dependable suppliers, in August 1992 the purveyors of marine fuels in Singapore (in 1997 the world's busiest bunkering port) adopted the Singapore Bunkering Procedure, the elements of which have since been copied by other bunkering points. A major feature was the requirement for complete documentation: (1) a predelivery note, which clearly set forth the quantity, grade, and basic specifications of the supplies ordered by the purchaser; (2) a receipt from the ship, showing not only the quantity of oil pumped into the vessel's tanks but also the gauging of the tanks and the temperature reading of the oil; and (3) a postdelivery document that verified the receipt and gave the results of the tests made by the ship to determine the quality of the oil.[16]

As the tempo of international shipping increased and the quality of bunkers available in different ports varied so markedly, better and more rapid methods of analyzing fuel became essential. The Norwegian ship classification society, Det Norske Veritas, pioneered bunker fuel testing in 1980. The head office of Det Norske Veritas Petroleum Service (DNVPS) was established in Singapore, with branches in Rotterdam, Oslo, and Teaneck, New Jersey, U.S.A.[17] Lloyd's Register followed in 1982, setting up its Fuel Oil Bunker Analysis Service (FOBAS) in England, Singapore, and Houston, Texas.[18] The American Bureau of Shipping subsequently formed its Oil Testing Service, with branches in six ports.[19] Other commercial firms followed suit.

Typical of the services provided by these testing organizations to meet the needs of both suppliers and purchasers of bunker fuels were the following:

1. Laboratory facilities at strategically located points to ensure rapid and accurate analysis of samples, and the means to notify the concerned parties of the results.

2. Testing procedures designed and implemented to provide early warning of potential damage from inferior fuels.
3. A simple, cost-effective, and convenient device to obtain representative samples for testing.
4. Verification of quantity and correct sampling technique by trained professionals (i.e., impartial evaluators or surveys of both procedures and data).
5. Predelivery testing of bunker fuel components to detect possible inferior quality.[20]

The goals of these operations were to ensure that the buyer was supplied with what was ordered, that the tests of the oil were made from truly representative samples, and that the purchaser was given early warning of poor quality of fuel. In practice, samples taken during the actual process of delivery to the receiving ship were sent to the nearest laboratory, and the results of the analysis were brought to the ship, or transmitted by radio if the ship had proceeded to sea. (To encourage the use of these tests, the costs have been kept low—in 1996, they were about U.S.$0.45 per metric ton of oil delivered, assuming an order or "stem" of about one thousand metric tons).[21]

The suppliers, concerned over the complaints being made against them, rallied to form the International Bunker Industry Association in January 1993. Initially, the association consisted of suppliers, but soon its membership was broadened to include shipowners, charterers, bunker brokers, barging companies, storage companies, lawyers, marine insurance underwriters, equipment manufacturers, shipping journalists, and marine consultants. Within two years of its formation the group had about 400 members from 45 countries. It had the following aims:

1. To provide an international forum to address the concerns of all sectors of the bunker industry.
2. To improve and clarify industry practices and documentation.
3. To represent the industry in discussions with relevant government and nongovernment bodies and to make known to such bodies the concerns of the industry.
4. To assist members in the event of disputes in identifying the options and exploring the alternatives open to them and eventually to provide a panel of suitable experienced mediators and arbitrators.
5. To increase public awareness of matters of concern to the bunker industry.
6. To increase the professional understanding and competence of those who work in the industry.[22]

PRINCIPLES OF BUNKERING

The principles of bunkering may be understood most readily by applying them to several hypothetical voyages.

All aspects of the voyage must be considered. A modern bulk carrier of 63,500 tons deadweight has a speed of 15 knots on a consumption of 37 tons of heavy fuel oil per day at sea and 10 tons per day when in port. With all fuel tanks filled, she can carry 2,870 tons of oil; she also has tanks for 250 tons of water. Stores normally weigh an additional 100 tons. The minimum cargo therefore is 60,280 tons. Vessel earning can be increased by reducing the fuel load to that which is needed for the planned voyage.

The ship is assigned to trade for a year between two ports approximately 6,300 miles apart. Routed nonstop from loading point to place of discharge, the voyage requires seventeen and one-half days at sea plus four days to work cargo. On each voyage, the engine consumes 648 tons of oil at sea and 40 tons in port. The reserve requirement comes to 162 tons, and water and stores amount to 350 tons. The cargo lift is 62,300 tons.

The alternate routing is to go by way of three fueling points, which would lengthen the voyage by three days. The longest leg between fueling points is nine days, requiring 333 tons of oil. Adding the reserve of 84 tons and the 40 tons of fuel to satisfy port needs, the total weight of oil comes to 457 tons. Together with 350 tons of water and stores, the reduction from the ship's total deadweight leaves a cargo lift of 62,693 tons. The shorter voyage, however, makes possible the completion of 9.36 round trips delivering 583,128 tons in one year, while the longer passages leave time only for 8.3 deliveries totaling 520, 352 tons.

Decisions concerning which routing to use are made depending upon the freight rate paid per ton of cargo lifted and the cost of fuel oil at the various procurement points.

Marine insurance underwriters' requirements must be obeyed. The ship always must have on board sufficient fuel to make the prescribed voyage regardless of how much cargo may have to be sacrificed. Once the minimum fuel requirement has been determined, the question of whether to load additional oil or more cargo can be addressed.

Ships in liner service repeat their voyages and usually take on the same quantities of fuel, water, and stores in the same ports every trip. A pattern is thus established that makes bunkering a matter of procurement rather than planning. For example, a vessel operating from New York to Valparaiso, Chile, via several South American ports might find that Cristobal, Panama, offers the lowest prices for good quality fuel oil. The bunkering pattern would call for the ship to sail from New York with sufficient fuel and reserve for the voyage to Cristobal. At that port, oil would be taken aboard for the voyage from Cristobal to Valparaiso and return. The reserve requirement would be computed on the basis of the fuel needed for the last leg of the northbound passage. At Cristobal and bound for New York, the ship would be supplied with enough oil, including reserve, for the passage to New York and then back to Cristobal, where the procedure would be repeated.

Quality, quantity, and cost of bunkers must be evaluated port by port. As soon as the ship has been assigned to a voyage, the bunkering staff must determine what ports are available or desirable as possible fueling points. These major questions must be answered for each port as the bunkering plan is developed:

1. Are supplies in this port plentiful?
2. Is the fuel of the desired type and quality?
3. What is the price of the fuel? Does the price include delivery, if barging is involved?
4. What are the physical arrangements for bringing oil to the ship—pipeline, tug-barge, self-propelled barge, harbor tanker?
5. Can the ship take on fuel while working cargo at her berth?
6. If a barge is used for delivery, will it be brought alongside after dark? How many tons of oil can the barge carry? What is the pumping rate from the barge into the ship's tanks?
7. If fueling must be accomplished at a special fueling pier, what fees are involved? How much time is needed to shift the ship from cargo pier to fueling pier? How fast is oil delivered to the ship from the pier's facilities?
8. What regulations govern the fueling of a ship by barge, alongside a fueling pier, or at anchor in the port?
9. What fees are charged by the port for a ship calling only for bunkers?

Immediately after a fueling port has been designated, the local agent must be notified. The information provided must include the name of the ship, the estimated time of arrival, the estimated quantity and grade of fuel oil required, the length of time the ship is scheduled to be in the port, and the amount of cargo, if any, that will be handled during the port call. Two days before the scheduled arrival, the master must send a message (telephone, fax, etc.) giving the approximate hour of arrival and the number of barrels (or tons) of oil the ship actually will require. This notification permits the agent to make appropriate arrangements to receive and service the vessel. A confirming message usually is sent by the master twenty-four hours before arrival to ensure that the vessel will be accorded the treatment desired.[23]

Oil companies and major suppliers of bunkers offer contracts to shipowners that ensure supplies of a certain grade of fuel oil at a stipulated price for the duration of the contract, which may be for as long as a year. The alternative is for the shipowner to rely on the open market, buying bunkers in those ports that offer the best prices or wherever necessity forces the procurement of fuel. The price will be that which prevails on the day of delivery. The decision to purchase under a contract or to rely on the open or "spot" market would depend upon the nature of the trade to which ships are assigned.

Drawing on its experience in bunkering a fleet of world-circling tramp ships, one owner customarily used contracts only in those bunkering ports where the availability and quality of marine fuels were questionable. For those ports where oil of good and consistent quality always was available in any quantity, spot purchases were satisfactory, often at prices significantly lower than those set by the contract.

The terms of sale, whether reflecting the stipulations of a contract or related specifically to the spot market, vary enormously, depending upon the locality, availability of fuel oil, and competition between suppliers in the bunkering port. Generally speaking, these sales agreements, which set forth in detail the terms and conditions of the transaction, are weighted in favor of the sellers. It is in the buyer's interest to ensure that purchase orders always state clearly the type of fuel needed, and also refer to ISO standards (e.g., 380 cSt ISO 8317/1996).[24] A careful purchaser may also stipulate that the delivered fuel shall contain no chemical waste, waste lubricating oil, or other substance detrimental to the ship's motors, her personnel, or her structure.[25]

Not until 1995 was a serious effort made by a buyer's group to write a contract that gave them a better position. In that year, the Baltic and International Maritime Council (BIMCO) distributed its Standard Marine Fuels Purchasing Contract, code-named FUELCON. This contract provides that both buyer and seller shall have the right to be present (or to be represented) when measurements are taken of the fueling vessel. It also stipulates that the seller is responsible for connecting hoses at the ship's intake pipes. In the event of spillage during the delivery phase, both buyer and seller are to work together immediately to clean up the spill, regardless of who may be responsible.

FUELCON was greeted without enthusiasm when it was introduced. The industry predicted that it would be years before any such uniform contract could be agreed to by the purchasers.[26] In February 1997, however,

Peninsula Petroleum, a bunker supplier serving the Gibraltar area and the Canary Islands, adopted a somewhat amended version of FUELCON as its standard sales contract and broadcast its sentiments in an advertisement in a technical journal: "With FUELCON, we've broken the mold for marine fuel purchasing to create a new and far better deal for buyers."[27]

A comparison of the BIMCO text with the amended form offered by Peninsula Petroleum reveals some of the differences in outlook between sellers and buyers of marine fuels. FUELCON stipulates that the receiving ship "shall provide segregated tankage to receive the contracted quantity of Marine Fuels." The Peninsula version adds to this statement these words: "The Sellers shall not be responsible for any problems whatsoever, caused by mixing the Marine Fuels supplied with any Marine Fuels supplied by other Suppliers or at any other time." Similarly, that portion of the BIMCO version dealing with documentation—requiring the seller to provide information in accordance with IMO/ISO recommendations for viscosity, density, water content, flash point, delivery temperature, pour point, and vanadium and ash content—is deleted in the Peninsula version.

What is significant about FUELCON is that, for the first time, it provides a basic (or standard) platform for negotiation of the contract. Modifications, amendments, and deletions may be made to fit the needs of the individual contracting parties in precisely the same way that charter parties are tailored from the standard, printed versions to a unique statement of agreement. Just as it took years for some of the BIMCO dry-cargo charters to be rephrased, so it may be foreseen that it probably will be some time in the future before a new FUELCON will be issued by BIMCO.

After the planning, calculations, and negotiations concerning price have been concluded, the supplier must be notified when and where to deliver the named quantities of the precisely specified fuel. The chief engineer of the ship that is to receive the bunkers also must be informed, particularly if there are any restrictions on delivery. In some ports, for example, the supplier's employees are not permitted to board the receiving ship, and therefore the ship's engineering personnel must be available and ready to connect the deliverer's hoses to the intake manifolds.

The ship's fuel tanks must be sounded to ensure that they can accommodate the anticipated delivery. It is good practice also for the ship's personnel to sound all the tanks in the delivery barge before and after delivery. New bunkers should be segregated from those already on board; failure to do so would invalidate any claim that the oil did not meet specification.

The ship's chief engineer becomes the buyer's representative as well as the monitor of the delivery process. The chief must confirm to the owner or charterer that the supplier is prepared to deliver the grades and quantities stipulated in the purchase order. He or she also has the right, under most contracts of purchase, to witness the readings on the gauges of the delivery facility (i.e., the bunkering vessel) at the start of transfer operation, and also the readings taken when the last gallon has been pumped into the ship. This point is important because many contracts state that the delivered quantities shall be determined from the seller's official gauge or meter, not from the ship's figures. For these reasons, the chief engineer (as the representative of the owner, who ultimately must pay for the oil) must be satisfied as to the accuracy of the seller's gauges. Readings from dipsticks or meters and also from the thermometers recording the temperature of the oil must be verified and appropriately noted by ship personnel.[28]

In recent years, the position of bunker surveyor has been created to satisfy the need for accurate, impartial, and systematic monitoring of delivery processes and practices (including the taking of samples) as well as objective recording of the restrictions imposed upon personnel of the bunkering vessel or the receiving ship (or both). Ideally the surveyor is a former chief engineer with demonstrated administrative skills who observes every step in the bunkering process, from loading the bunkering vessel to final delivery of the fuel. The surveyor may be an employee of a testing laboratory such as DNVPS or FOBAS or an independent contractor who, for a fee, will represent and protect the interest of the party providing employment.[29] The qualities essential to the surveyor are expert knowledge, technical competence, high ethical standards, and firmness in enforcing the terms of the contract.

In the tanker trades, every ton of fuel taken aboard reduces the payload by exactly that amount. Necessarily, because the ship is delivering her cargo to ports where oil is not naturally available, she must have enough fuel in her tanks to return to the port where the voyage originated. From the viewpoint of the consignee of the cargo, the most satisfactory tanker is the one that requires the least amount of fuel and therefore delivers the maximum tonnage of oil. Crude-oil carriers of 200,000 tons deadweight are preferred to ships of 70,000 tons because the bigger ships deliver 28 barrels of cargo for every barrel of fuel consumed, whereas the smaller ships deliver only 11 barrels of cargo per barrel of oil burned.

Making the schedule for a tanker follows the same processes used for dry-cargo carriers, except that the tanker is self-sufficient in her ability to discharge her cargo. Normal tanker practice is to commence cargo operations as soon as the ship is at her berth, regardless of the hour. If she is to load in this port, the delivery of cargo begins when the hoses from shoreside tanks are connected. If the vessel is to discharge, her pumps are started when all hoses have been matched with shore piping systems. No crews of longshoremen or cargo checkers are needed; usually, terminal personnel handle all details.

The dry-cargo tramp trade is governed in its bunkering and scheduling practices by the same principles that apply to the liner and tanker operations. There is still the need to load cargo as quickly as possible. In the negotiations for a voyage charter, the number of days allotted for loading and discharge is fixed along with a corresponding bonus or penalty for reducing or exceeding these limits. The master and chief engineer must supervise operations and keep accurate records of time used and activities pursued.

When bunkering for a trip under a voyage charter, the tramp ship faces the same limitations as the liner trade: if the cargo is bulky, then the port is chosen where the appropriate fuel can be obtained at least cost; for dense cargoes, the fueling port(s) and the quantity to buy are chosen by comparing the revenue from each ton of cargo carried to the price of fuel oil in each port. An imaginary voyage of the *Lucky Lady* illustrates the process.

The *Lucky Lady,* a 14-knot, diesel-powered breakbulk vessel of 29,538 tons deadweight, has been chartered for a voyage from Hampton Roads, Virginia, to San Antonio, Chile, carrying coal at a rate that barely meets operation expenses. The terms of the charter party require the owner to load not less than 25,000 tons and not more than 27,000 tons of coal. Northbound, the *Lucky Lady* has been fixed for a part load of 12,000 tons of slab copper from San Antonio to New York and at least 16,000 tons of bagged sugar from Callao, Peru, to Boston. The freight rate on the copper is just above the break-even level, but the rate on sugar is very profitable.

The essential facts influencing the decisions required for the bunkering plan are: (a) the ship consumes 24 tons of fuel per day at sea and 8 tons per day when working cargo in port; (b) there is no fuel available in San Antonio; (c) fuel could be purchased in Callao, but at a high price; and (d) the lowest cost fuel is procurable in Panama.

To reduce voyage costs, only sufficient fuel would be purchased in Hampton Roads to reach Panama, where bunkers for the voyage from Panama to San Antonio and return to Panama would be taken aboard. When the *Lucky Lady* came through Panama northbound en route to Boston and New York, she would be supplied for that passage.

The tables show the step-by-step procedure to follow to determine how much of the high revenue cargo could be loaded. It will be noted that the voyage from Panama to Boston is the longest leg of the northbound trip. The fuel needs for that leg therefore govern the loading of sugar from Callao.

All time computations have been rounded out to the next higher figure. Thus, 2.25 days has been raised to 3.0 days. The ship will have on board at the start of each leg a total of 300 tons of stores and water.

BASIC MILEAGE TABLE

Hampton Roads to Panama	1,822 miles
Panama to San Antonio	2,644 miles
San Antonio to Callao	1,328 miles
Callao to Panama	1,350 miles
Panama to Boston	2,200 miles
Boston to New York	211 miles

CARGO WORKING HOURS

	Tons per Hour	Total Hours	Total Days	Ship Days	Fuel Used/ Tons
Loading coal, Hampton Roads	1,200	23	1.00	1	8
Discharging coal, San Antonio	500	54	2.25	3	24
Loading copper, San Antonio	300	40	1.66	2	16
Loading sugar, Callao	300	55	2.25	3	24
Discharging sugar, Boston	300	55	2.25	3	24
Discharging copper, New York	300	40	1.66	2	16

FUEL REQUIREMENTS, STEAMING

Hampton Roads to Panama	5 days 10 hours	(6 days)	144 tons
Panama Canal Transit	1 day	(1 day)	24 tons
Panama to San Antonio	7 days 21 hours	(8 days)	192 tons
San Antonio to Callao	4 days 1 hour	(4 days)	96 tons
Callao to Panama	4 days	(4 days)	96 tons
Panama Canal Transit	1 day	(1 day)	24 tons
Panama to Boston	6 days 11 hours	(7 days)	168 tons
Boston to New York	0 days 14 hours	(1 day)	24 tons

MANDATORY FUEL RESERVE

25% of fuel needed for passage, Callao to Panama and Panama to Boston

STORES AND WATER

On board at the start of each leg of the voyage:
200 tons of water
100 tons of stores

CARGO COMPUTATIONS

Southbound			
Ship's deadweight tonnage		29,538	
Fuel for Panama/San Antonio/Panama			
Cargo working	64 tons		
Panama Canal transits	48 tons		
Steaming	432 tons		
Stores and water	300 tons		
		844	
Available for cargo			28,694
Coal loaded, per contract			27,000
Northbound			
Ship's deadweight tonnage		29,538	
Sailing from San Antonio			
Fuel on board			
San Antonio/Callao	96 tons		
Cargo working, Callao	24 tons		
Callao/Panama	96 tons		
Panama Canal transit	24 tons		
Safety reserve, Callao/Canal/Panama (25% of 120 tons)	30 tons		
Stores and water	300 tons		
Copper, per contract	12,000 tons		
		12,570	
Unused tonnage			16,968
Sailing from Callao before loading sugar			
Ship's deadweight tonnage		29,538	
Fuel on board			
Callao/Panama	96 tons		
Panama Canal transit	24 tons		
Safety reserve (25% of 120 tons)	30 tons		
Stores and water	300 tons		
Copper, per contract	12,000 tons		
		12,450	
Unused tonnage			17,088
Sailing from Panama to Boston and New York			
Ship's deadweight tonnage		29,538	
Fuel on board			
Panama/Boston	168 tons		
Cargo working, Boston	24 tons		
Boston/New York	24 tons		
Cargo working, New York	16 tons		
Safety reserve (25% of 168 tons)	42 tons		

Stores and water	300 tons		
Copper, per contract	12,000 tons		
		12,574	
Available for sugar			16,964

    The bunkering plan and the ship's schedule were developed with all these aspects of the ship's employment in mind. Full advantage was taken of the flexibility granted by the charters for both the coal and the sugar cargoes, and fuel was purchased at the least expensive point. By these devices, the greatest revenue was earned.

    In summary, the economic success of any ship depends upon the prevailing freight rates, the skill with which the schedule is developed, and the manner in which advantage is taken of the capabilities of the ship and the characteristics of the cargo. Customer desires for the shortest transit times and the requirements by the owner that the ship be used effectively and efficiently usually may be combined to satisfy all parties concerned. In the tanker and many dry-cargo tramping trades, it is dense (deadweight) cargo that is carried. Because only cargo produces revenue, the accurate determination of how and when to fuel the ship is vital to owner and operator. That the intricacies and possible pitfalls of planning the scheduling and fueling of the ship have been mastered is one of the signs of professionalism in ship management.

CHAPTER TWELVE

Ship Husbandry: Procurement of Vessel Stores, Supplies, and Services

It is difficult to overemphasize the importance of ship husbandry—the procurement of stores, spare parts, supplies, and services for ships. The seaworthiness of a ship at the start of a voyage depends, in part, upon the complete discharge of these obligations. In addition to such items as paint, maintenance materials, manila and synthetic line, spare parts, and food, ships need the services of specialists of many sorts: pilots, tug operators, customs brokers, surveyors, and maintenance and repair experts for the ship's complex systems. Owners appoint representatives (agents) in overseas ports to obtain berthing assignments, order fuel (bunkers), contract with stevedores, arrange for customs, health, and immigration clearance and many other services required by the ship. These are the elements of ship husbandry; cumulatively, they constitute a significant portion of the responsibility for vessel management.

Modern procurement practices rely on the computer, supplemented and augmented by electronic communication. The system is built around the shipowner's computerized database, a compendium of factual information ranging from the thousands of items in the shipboard inventory to the names and performance records of each and every supplier. The database is updated by a constant flow of entries from many sources: the name of a supplier is added to the list of those approved; a ship reports a small fire that destroyed one hundred items, all duly listed; a revised price list has been received from a seller of manila and synthetic line; a government regulation has become effective concerning the use of certain semi-toxic paints; and a new pilotage fee is being assessed in three major ports of call.

In practice, as the ship consumes supplies and spare parts,[1] the details are fed into the shipboard computer and are relayed automatically to the home office database. The ship's entries always include the unique inventory number of each item and the identification (description) of that item. When replacement is needed, the computerized records show which suppliers stock that item, the lead time required to fill an order, the suppliers' performance records (prompt delivery, excellent condition of material, accurate billing, etc.), and a list of suppliers holding current contracts with the shipowner.

Until relatively recently, the shipping industry relegated the procurement of vessel stores and supplies to a subordinate division of the operating department. There was little, if any, awareness on the part of the higher echelons of management of the implied rules that guide the procurement process, nor was there much concern to improve efficiency in the discharge of what was accepted as almost unalterable routine. Beginning about 1975, the nearly universal adoption by shipowners of modern electronic communications and computer technology brought about major changes which encouraged senior management to oversee and control ship husbandry. As the implied rules of procurement have become better understood, new methods and techniques have evolved. The data concerning ships, suppliers, and handlers of goods have been integrated into an information network motivated and directed by the requirement that the ship be adequately stored and supplied at the commencement of the voyage.

Most important of the rules guiding procurement is the legal, moral, and operational responsibility to provide the ship with not less than the minimum quantity of those items known to be needed for the contemplated voyage. While the control of cost is understandable, avoiding expenditures is intolerable if the safety of the ship and her crew is thereby endangered. Good procurement practice, however, does encourage seeking the best prices for whatever is purchased.

The second rule is an offshoot of the first, for it prescribes that the senior levels of management control the costs of ship husbandry. Careful scrutiny of individual ship inventories compared with consumption reports, examination of the performance of similar ships in the fleet, and reference to the computerized database provide the information required for appropriate decisions related to systematic control of procurement.

A fundamental premise of ship management is that a ship earns her way only when actually transporting cargo (or passengers) from point to point. A certain amount of time necessarily is allocated to load and unload cargo, but any hours beyond those so identified are considered as nonproductive and to be avoided. The many activities that take place aboard a ship during her time in port include repair work, bunkering, and resupply. Ideally, everything is accomplished within the period allocated for cargo work. All concerned with these functions must coordinate their movements, especially those persons responsible for the delivery of stores and supplies. The goal is to have everything the ship has ordered safely aboard before the scheduled hour of departure, in conformity to the implied rule that the process of resupply must not interfere with cargo work or delay the sailing of the ship.

As used in this chapter, the term "inventory" refers to the collection of consumable and expendable stores of every description placed aboard the ship.[2] The size of, and therefore the financial investment in, the inventory varies with the employment and characteristics of the ship. Government and regulatory agencies as well as labor unions prescribe certain minimum levels for stipulated items. The shipboard inventory is also affected by the availability, quality, and cost of stores and supplies in ports along the ship's route.

Adequate stores must be acquired, but costs are kept under constant surveillance. An exemplary system to achieve this goal was developed for a large fleet of world-traveling ships. A fleetwide budget based on categories of stores (fuel, food, paints, maintenance materials, etc.) was adopted. Concurrently, each ship in a group of similar vessels was assigned a comprehensive budget that reflected the fleetwide budget, and the master became responsible for holding costs within the prescribed limits. As periodic reports from the ships were received in the home office, the records of actual operation were matched against the theoretical budgets (both fleetwide and individual) to ascertain whether anticipated levels of consumption and expense had been overly optimistic, realistic, or unduly pessimistic. Overall fleet performance could be evaluated, while each ship's management was compared to the theoretical budget.

Regardless of where the ships might be located, the shipowner must supply them. If supplies were procured from dozens of vendors and each one was directed to send its packages to the ship, delivery of the entire requisition was not necessarily assured. To overcome that difficulty, suppliers were notified to send their goods to a designated receiver. For a fee, this functionary accepted and held the individual boxes and cartons until everything ordered had been delivered. The assortment then was consolidated into shipping units.

The receiver contracted with a *freight forwarder* to arrange the onward movement of the shipping units. The forwarder is a transportation specialist who consolidates many small lots of cargo to fill a seagoing container. The freight rate charged the forwarder for the container is prorated among the individual shippers and almost invariably is less than the individual would have paid for a separate shipment. Even with the receiver's fee and the forwarder's markup, the shipowner saved money while being certain that the ship needs were met. Part of the forwarder's service is to monitor the movement of the container and to report its location whenever queried. Based on this up-to-the-minute information, the owner is able to notify the ship when the requisition will be delivered.[3]

In the highly competitive environment of the shipping business, constant attention must be given to reducing the overhead cost of doing business. Procurement of ship stores and supplies follows certain procedural steps, and careful scrutiny of each of those steps will reveal the actual cost of the procurement process. If a step can be eliminated, money will be saved. As computerization and the use of electronic communications have permeated the industry, numerous economies have been effected. One operator discovered that more than half of the steps in procurement had been made superfluous by these technical advances.

Summarizing, these are the rules that guide efficient and effective procurement:

1. The ship is adequately, but not excessively, stored at the beginning of each voyage.
2. Control of the total cost of husbandry is a function of senior management.
3. The ship's sailing must not be delayed by delivery of stores.
4. Control of ship supply levels is predicated on inventory and expenditure reports from ships.
5. Realistic budgets for procurement of stores and spare parts are based on performance of operating ships.
6. The exact location of shipments of stores and supplies to vessels in distant ports must be known at all times.

Whenever policy is made relative to the acquisition and retention of expensive spare parts, it is appropriate for management to seek advice from specialists such as the engineer and marine superintendents. It may be found that the cherished notion of "if the chief wants it, get it" is justified only in rare instances. For example, the pumps installed in six ships of the fleet performed without a breakdown for ten consecutive years. That same make of pump was to be installed in a new ship. Although the outlook of the chief engineer was pessimistic, it was decided, on the basis of the record, that no spare pump would be acquired. In another case, at least one of the compressors of the refrigerator unit needed a major overhaul after about six months of service. The chief's desire for a replacement unit was deemed reasonable and was granted.

Underlying this somewhat critical attitude is the concern of upper management with the problems associated with the physical possession of large inventories. Many of the original spare parts placed aboard ships are not used. One authoritative estimate was that, in terms of monetary value, approximately three-quarters of the investment in original spare parts was wasted because the parts never were used.

When a new ship is delivered by the builders, she has on board a year's supply of spare parts. She also has a library of manuals that give complete information on each and every piece of machinery. The purchasing office should ensure that its records show exactly what spare parts have been provided, and that it has complete information ("nameplate date") to use when replacements are ordered. These data become part of the home office database.

It is important to note that the regulatory agencies (like the United States Coast Guard and the British Board of Trade) set certain minimum standards of spare parts and reserve supplies to be carried by ships. The classification societies also establish requirements for spare parts. These stipulations, however, have little impact upon the inventory of spare parts because the shipowner sets its own levels for such items. The disparity results from the fact that the regulators and the classification societies are interested primarily in ensuring that the ship will be able to make port in an emergency, whereas the owner is concerned that the ship will remain in full operating condition throughout the voyage.

An indispensable element in company policy concerning the quantity of spare parts to be placed aboard ship is the *allowance list*. This list reflects the owner's experience on the trade route(s) served and meets the requirements of both the regulatory agencies and the maintenance of the normal ship schedules and operations.[4]

Spare parts can be procured most cheaply if they are ordered at the same time the machinery is being manufactured and assembled. When these same spare parts are purchased years later, the manufacturer may have to stop normal production routines in the factory and tool up expressly to fabricate the required item. Although the original manufacturer retains the engineering drawings and specifications for the parts, there may be no supply kept in stock. The parts can be provided, but at a price.

When a ship is purchased secondhand and brought into a fleet, a thorough inventory is required, not only of the spare parts and consumables supplies, but also of all equipment installed in the ship, in order that the purchasing office will have complete nameplate data for future reference. The results of this examination establish what must be acquired to bring the levels of stores, spare parts, and supplies into conformity with the new owner's standards. Taking an inventory on this scale is a major undertaking; one operator estimated that it took a team of ten experienced persons seven working days to accomplish the task.

The basis for all procurement, as well as for long-range planning for acquisition, storage, and control of both spare parts and consumable stores, is the *ship's requisition.* If the vessel is assigned to a long voyage—two or more months between calls at the home port—it is customary to process requisitions so that everything needed for the forthcoming trip will be on board before sailing time. If, however, the ship returns to her home port every two weeks, requisitions will be submitted at the end of the third voyage. While the ship is making the fourth voyage, the needed items are assembled and are ready for transfer to the ship before the start of the fifth voyage.

A fairly standardized pattern of procurement is followed by ship operators. The cognizant department analyzes the ship's requisition, makes changes as required by company policy or experience, and then passes the requisition to the purchasing department. Replacement of *proprietary parts*—parts unique to a particular manufacturer—is accomplished by ordering the desired quantity from that source.

A major consideration in procurement is whether to use *genuine* replacement parts—that is, parts manufactured by the original maker of the major component. Genuine parts, as might be expected, are precisely machined to the dimensions and tolerances fixed by the designer and specified in the engineering drawings. They make perfect replacements, but may be significantly more expensive than *nongenuine* parts (sometimes described as *pirate* parts) made by an independent.[5]

It is not always necessary that the part required by a ship be new. Many pieces of equipment outlast the ships in which they were installed. When these vessels are dismantled, the used parts dealers acquire these parts and offer them for sale. As ships get older, and the original suppliers of machinery or its components either cease production or go out of business altogether, the only source of replacements may be these dealers.[6]

Some items (for example, tools, valve packing, and interchangeable parts) can be obtained from a number of suppliers, and these are purchased only after bids from three or more sources have been solicited and compared. In every case, the goal of the purchasing department is to meet the needs of the ship efficiently, promptly, and economically.

An essential element in the routine of the purchasing department is the establishment and continuous updating of an active and accurate list of spare parts, both on board ship and in company storage places, supplemented by a current list of manufacturers and distributors who have the various types of equipment readily available. This task may be accomplished by incorporation into the computerized database. Vendors of surplus and used machinery are sources of spare parts, as noted above. Great reliance is placed upon distributors who have been authorized by the manufacturers to handle their products. The advantage of dealing with distributors is that items obtained from them meet specifications as to both fabrication and material.

In liner service, where the same voyages are repeated on closely monitored and rigidly followed schedules, experience and established rates of consumption make preliminary planning for purchasing relatively simple. Following are the principles to be observed:

1. *Length of the proposed voyage.* The quantity of consumable stores and spare parts to be placed on board is regulated by the length of time the ship will be away from the home port.
2. *Route and ports of call of the proposed voyage.* If the ship will travel to industrialized areas where needs may be satisfied promptly, purchases may be dictated more by price and convenience than by any other consideration. Should the planned route pass through politically unstable regions, it is the usual practice to store the ship fully in her home port. Vessels engaged in the cross-trades, which do not return to their home ports, are stored in the area where the most satisfactory arrangements can be made after quality, quantity, and dependability have been evaluated.
3. *The number and nationalities of crew and passengers.* The purchasing department must be given full information as to the number of persons to be fed, together with any restrictions on what may be served. For details, see the following section, "Hotel Services."

From time to time, a vessel employed in liner service will experience operating difficulties that cause significant loss of hours. To make up for this lost time and to be ready to sail the ship on the next advertised date, it will be necessary to reduce port turnaround time. The altered port schedule is transmitted immediately to the ship at sea. The requisition for replenishment is sent by electronic communication, and all suppliers are notified of the shortened time in which to make deliveries.

Items on requisition are divided by the purchasing department into appropriate categories such as hardware, cleaning gear, parts, and electrical supplies. Suppliers of the different types of material represented by a category are invited to submit their bids for the quantities specified. Ordinarily, the lowest responsible bid consistent with good quality and economy over the long run will win the business for the purveyor of a single category, even though prices of some items within the category may be a trifle higher than those of a competitor. Quality is under constant scrutiny, and whenever a particular brand is found to be uneven or otherwise undependable, it is dropped from the list of approved products. Dealers—whether manufacturers, agents, or wholesalers—are held to exact compliance with specifications, and failure to meet the terms of the contract as to brand and quality may be judged sufficient reason to terminate the relationship.

HOTEL SERVICES

Hotel services include all external services provided to the ship for the care and comfort of those aboard. This generally is thought of as food procurement but may include laundry and other types of services as well. Passenger ships assigned to long cruises (sixty to one hundred days) take on fresh fruits and vegetables at a number of ports of call. Meat, cheese, wine, and staples like flour and sugar normally are stored at the port where the voyage originates in quantities sufficient for the entire trip. It is, of course, essential that the quality of the foodstuffs so acquired meet the shipowner's standards and be acceptable to the passengers.

Ships engaged in the short cruises of twenty days or less customarily are supplied only in the port of origin. On the three- and four-day cruises, which have become popular in recent years, the ships spend so little time in ports of call (less than eight hours for a visit) that any kind of support activity for the ship is impractical.

Cargo ships scheduled for long voyages usually take on all supplies, spare parts, and stores in the port of origin. Replenishment at ports of call ordinarily is not planned. Containerships, to cite a reason and an example, come into port, discharge, and load their outgoing containers in the course of less than one working day. Unforeseen shortages are made up at the earliest possible time.

The purchasing department must be notified about any special restrictions which may apply to the food that will be offered to the ship's company. Dietary customs and rules must be heeded, as in these instances:

- A ship based in New York City and manned by a crew from the northeastern United States will provide an abundant supply of potatoes. A ship claiming New Orleans for her home port would offer her crew rice rather than potatoes.
- A German flag vessel would feature national favorites such as sauerkraut, knockwurst, and rye bread.

Passengers' tastes are reflected in this cruise ship's buffet table. Courtesy Cunard Line.

- A vessel staffed by an Italian crew would store large quantities of spaghetti, macaroni, and similar products as well as plentiful stores of tomatoes, olive oil, and favored seasonings.

The quality of food offered to passengers, especially on luxury cruises, is of major concern to the operator. Competition in the cruise trade is so intense that any deviation from the highest standards can have a disastrous effect on the prestige of the operator. Meat of all sorts is a staple of the passenger ships' offering, and to a measurable extent it is the basis for menu planning.

In the United States, meat is processed (cut into roasts, steaks, etc.) and packaged by the producer or the wholesaler. The purchasing department contracts with the source for a specified quantity, usually designated by weight, of each type of meat: 200 pounds of beef rib roasts, 100 pounds of pork loin roasts, 75 pounds of leg of lamb. At the packaging plant, inspectors from the U.S. Department of Agriculture approve each piece before it is placed in the carton.

Much the same process is followed for vegetables and fruits. Farmers harvest their crops at the peak of ripeness and send them to the quick-freezing plant. Because they have been expertly prepared, carefully packaged, and then kept at uniform low temperatures, there is no question about the high quality and freshness of these frozen vegetables and fruits.

These marketing practices affect every aspect of both procurement and preparation of foodstuffs. Inventory records are accurate, expenditure reports are exact, and replenishment orders are precise. Storage in refrigerated spaces is orderly and systematic. Refuse (bones, gristle, and unusable fat) is brought down to a level that permits simple and economical disposal.

In geographical regions where sources of food stores and supplies are not processed as described above, the procedures followed are those that have been in vogue for decades. Specialists in the purchase of meats, vegetables, and fruits constantly go to the local markets to acquire the variety, quantity, and quality of the food items listed on the requisition. Purchases are delivered in bulk: carcasses of beef, pork, and lamb are split in half, and may be further cut into forequarters and hindquarters. Vegetables and fruits are received in large baskets. Inventory records and reports of consumption necessarily are based on estimates rather than on box counts. Experienced cooks and stewards, however, can judge with praiseworthy accuracy how much usable meat and how much bone and other waste is in a hindquarter of beef or lamb. They also can predict how many meals can be supplied by the quantities of cabbage and squash (to name just two vegetables) in the ship's food locker.

Regardless of where the ship is being stored, a schedule for the expeditious handling of the items is essential. In many ports of the United States, by long-standing union agreement, stores are put aboard ship by longshoremen. In such cases, the purchasing department must confer with the terminal department to arrange for deliveries that will not interfere with the cargo work nor be scheduled at hours unacceptable to the laborers. The shipboard divisions (deck, engineering, and hotel services) must be informed of these schedules so that verifying officers may be available to receive the goods. Complete, accurate records are required, and they must show the items delivered to the ship, the time of delivery, the condition of the goods, and the count or weight. Bills will be paid or protests filed on the basis of these documents.

CHANDLERS

Purchases of stores and supplies other than spare parts are made from manufacturers, authorized distributors, *jobbers* (merchants who buy from manufacturers in very large lots and sell wholesale to retailers and heavy consumers), and ship chandlers. Generally speaking, the purchasing department of a major ship owning company attempts to deal directly with the manufacturers of those items used in large quantities. Canvas, paints, oils, and greases are typical of such items. Should the manufacturers set their prices at the same level as the prices quoted by the jobber, it is simpler for the shipowner to order from the merchant who has offices in the home port and who accepts orders for quantities smaller than the manufacturer's minimum. For the wide variety of items needed, often in quite small lots, the purchasing department turns to the *ship chandler,* a merchant who specializes in supplying ships with almost anything they might need, in any quantity and at any time.

In the early nineteenth century, ships and fishing boats sailing out of a port relied upon a shore merchant to provide them with galley coal, salt, lamps, and cordage. As the vessels grew larger and the seafarers came to rely more heavily upon the services of this merchant (who came to be known as a ship's chandler), they placed greater demands upon him. Protective clothing, spare parts for equipment aboard ship, replacement units for worn or broken machinery, and paints were added to the purchasing orders for food and other supplies. In the closing years of the twentieth century, the chandler no longer was a single flesh-and-blood person but a large corporation with many employees, sometimes with outlets in more than one city and enormous stocks from which to fill orders at any time.[7]

Other chandlers maintain moderately sized inventories of those items most frequently in demand. For all other material, they rely on a number of suppliers, including manufacturers, who can and do fill requisitions on very short notice.

In addition to fulfilling their traditional role as suppliers, some chandlers also serve as consolidators for a ship or a fleet, as described earlier in this chapter.

A chandler may establish itself in one or more major seaports and erect warehouses to keep in stock large quantities of thousands of items required by its customers. From these resources, it is able at any hour to meet practically any need of the ship.[8] This same chandler may publish periodically a large catalog in which are listed the thousands of items in stock, each with a description, a unique number, and a base price. The catalog is distributed to owners and placed aboard ships. The unique numbers are used when ordering from the catalog; copying the description is obviated by the use of the number. The catalog is expensive to issue, and changes in prices are publicized by the distribution of price lists that show the variations from the catalog's base prices as percentage discounts or percentage surcharges.

At least one such catalog is in worldwide use. It is published by the London-based International Marine Purchasers Association (IMPA).[9] The great benefits of the unique number system were apparent when electronic communication became almost universal in the maritime industry. This is especially evident when the requisition must be translated into a different language.

Ships, in particular those engaged in the tramping trade, often obtain supplies in the outports through the offices of the agents who represent the owners. Shipboard department heads consult with the agent to ensure that requisitions are clearly understood by the local suppliers. Exceptionally careful inspection of all goods so procured must be made at the time of delivery, and shipboard personnel should follow explicitly the instructions of the owner concerning procedures to be followed if a deficiency or shortage is discovered.

Practically every maritime nation has two or more ship chandlers doing business in its major port cities. In many instances, these corporations join together to form national associations. These national groupings in turn become members of either IMPA or the International Ship Suppliers Association (ISSA).

To bring some uniformity to the standards of ship management, the quasi-governmental International Organization for Standardization (ISO) adopts and disseminates rules and regulations that ship managers, including ship suppliers, must meet. Certificates of accreditation on compliance with these standards must be obtained by specified dates, or penalties may be imposed.

To reflect the injunctions of ISO and to enhance the quality of service provided to shipowners by suppliers while concurrently improving relations between the parties, IMPA and ISSA have established their own standards. Certificates of compliance by individual members are required before approval is granted to a vendor to engage in business.[10]

It is worth noting that when inventories of ship supplies and stores are taken, the contents and condition of the ship's *medicine chest,* or pharmaceutical stores, should be examined by a qualified and licensed pharmacist. A Norwegian pharmacy conducted a two-year-long survey of ships under Norwegian international ship registry (Norwegian senior officers, Filipino unlicensed crew) and discovered many deficiencies. For example, some labels on bottles of medicine were printed in languages not used by anyone in the ship's company. Other labels had dosage instructions difficult to comprehend. Some medications had been retained after their shelf life had expired. As a result, the survey recommended that IMO issue a standard master list of specified and carefully identified medicines to be carried by all ships. If this recommendation is adopted, ship crews always will find familiar medicines in the medicine chest. Essential to the success of this proposal is that the pharmaceutical resources be inspected regularly and shortages made up before the ship leaves port.[11]

The current practice of incorporating each ship as a separate legal entity and simultaneously setting up the ship as an individual accounting (or budget) unit emphasizes the need for accurate records showing exactly what was supplied to each ship. The corresponding receipts will confirm that what was ordered was delivered in full. Large scale purchases, sufficient for three or more ships in the fleet, require special accounting procedures set up by the shipowner.

The hull plan and vessel layout must be studied with care, as procurement of supplies will be affected by structural features of the ship. In particular, the purchasing department must determine the location, size, accessibility, and interrelation of shipboard storerooms of all types (paint and other deck stores, engine room spares, commissary dry stores, refrigerated foodstuffs, and hotel equipment and spares). It must also ascertain what facilities have been built into the ship that simplify or complicate the handling of stores. This information will be useful in selecting sizes and weights of packages. For example, if the boatswain's storeroom is located near a hatchway through which delivery can be made with the ship's cargo gear, it may be feasible to order manila or synthetic line on large spools. If the storeroom is accessible only through a narrow doorway, and everything must be hand-carried down a ladder, spool size is limited to that which can be handled by one or two persons.

SHIP AGENTS

A large containership is entering a harbor on the far side of the Pacific Ocean. Her owner is based in London but does not have an office in this port. As the ship approaches her berth, an interesting series of interrelated events take place.

First, two tugs come alongside the vessel, and the docking pilot climbs up the pilot's ladder to board the ship. The tugs nudge the ship into her berth, and workers on the wharf receive the mooring lines thrown by the crew. As soon as the gangway is rigged, the stevedore and his longshoremen prepare to move the containers from ship to shore and vice versa. Several repairmen also are waiting to go aboard to service certain items of equipment. On the offshore side, as the mooring tugs depart, a bunkering barge is brought alongside to replenish the ship's fuel supply.

This neatly choreographed program came about as a result of careful attention to many details on the part of the owner's representative, known worldwide by the title of ship's agent. Selected partly on the basis of a financial package but more because of demonstrated competence, high integrity, resourcefulness, and experience, this person stands in the place of the owner so long as the ship is in port.

The relationship between owner and agent began with proposals from the agent to represent the owner. That was followed by a tentative pro forma disbursements account listing the charges the owner will have to pay in advance of the ship's arrival. The real work commenced when the contract was signed. The Captain of the Port had to be notified of the ship's intended track. The Port Authority (or the owners of the terminal, if it is not a public entity) was asked to provide a berth appropriate for the size of the ship and the quantity of cargo to be processed. The consignees of the cargo had to be notified when they should be prepared to pick up their goods. In the wake of these activities came contacts with a string of other units, public and private, that were interested in the ship: customs inspectors, surveyors, classification society operatives, repair parties, suppliers of various types, the escort to the airport of those crewmembers eligible for home leave, and a doctor to care for an ailing crewmember.

To accomplish all this requires experience and a wide circle of contacts in the local maritime community. Constant liaison with these contacts provides the wealth of current information required to service the ship properly. If there are rumors in the port about a potential strike of tugboat crews, the agent may arrange for a berth from which the ship could depart from the pier without tugs if necessary—a maneuver that would save the owner considerable expense and prevent a delay for the ship. By virtue of its local knowledge, the agent's office is able to serve as the intermediary between the master and the shoreside authorities and offices.

Another essential quality in an agent is flexibility. After all arrangements for the ship's arrival have been made, it is not unusual for an emergency to arise that invalidates everything the agent has done. In such circumstances, the agent's ability to adjust to the new situation, to reschedule activities, and to keep the owners fully advised becomes the measure of competence and capability.

Even after the owner has advanced funds as delineated in the disbursements account, the agent must be financially able to pay for many services and purchases. These expenditures come from the agent's resources and are reimbursed at the shipowner's pleasure. Ideally, the bills are submitted by electronic mail; they are processed and approved by the owner, and the reimbursement funds are cabled to the agent's bank within a matter of days. Reality seldom equals this ideal situation, which explains why the financial stability of the agent must become a major consideration in making the selection of a representative.

The agent also performs a significant number of time-consuming and expensive operations in order to free the master for those responsibilities that only the master can discharge. The following examples show some of the areas where the agent steps in as the local representative of the shipowner.

Two days before arrival, the master notifies the agent to provide $10,000 in local currency, needed to meet crewmembers' requests for money to defray their shore expenses. Also, potable water tanks need cleaning, the radar must be recalibrated, an electrical generator needs to be repaired, fresh vegetables in sufficient quantity to feed twenty people for fifteen days have been requisitioned by the cook, and two crewmembers will arrive at the airport one day before the ship comes into port.

It must not be overlooked that the ship will be working cargo day and night, and there is a good likelihood that the agent may be needed at awkward hours of the day. Availability and accessibility must be part of the agent's service to the ship.

There is no fixed tariff for the functions of the agent. Fees vary from port to port and reflect the services rendered and the amount of money advanced by the agent. The custom of the trade is to assess a fee for each ton of cargo worked during the ship's visit and to add appropriate charges for services not directly related to handling the ship and her cargo. Money is advanced, for instance, at a fixed and published interest charge. Similarly, meeting and caring for crewmembers joining or leaving the ship is performed at prices dependent upon the extent of care required. The charge for the agent's services, however, usually is modest in comparison to the total expenditures by the ship in port.[12]

AGENCY FOR SHIPS UNDER CHARTER

The owner of a ship operated under a voyage charter chooses the agent(s) who will handle its interests in the ports of call specified in the charter party. As the owner's direct representative, the agent, in the name of the owner, has the authority to do whatever may be required to service the ship. In addition to these general obligations and duties, the agent must comply with the stipulations in its contract with the shipowner. A British judge once commented that someone employed to act as the agent of another person "is bound to exercise all the skills and knowledge he has," and is expected to devote all "his zeal and diligence. . . to the sole and exclusive benefit" of the person for whom the agent is acting.

Sometimes charter contracts permit the charterer to appoint the agent. The relationship, however, is between the agent and the shipowner, who pays the agent for services rendered. Technically, the agent is the employee of the shipowner, not the charterer. The Baltic and International Maritime Council (BIMCO) noted that even when the ship's agent was appointed by the charterer, the agent was still expected to act as though chosen directly by the shipowner.

Obviously, the agent is dependent upon the favor of both the shipowner and the charterer for appointments, and therefore will attempt to serve both principals impartially. Circumstances may arise where the agent is called upon to protect the conflicting interests of both the shipowner (its employer) and the charterer (its performance and character reference). The experienced and well-established agent, drawing upon its knowledge of local conditions and its wide contacts in the port, usually is able to resolve such difficulties satisfactorily.

In the owner-agent relationship, it must be absolutely clear that the person acting for the owner is only the agent. Whenever documents are signed by the agent in the normal course of business, the agent should make sure that each document shows that the signature was that of a person acting only as a representative—the agent—of the shipowner. The usual wording is "as agent only" (sometimes shortened to "as agent") and is found immediately below the signature.

There is no uniform scale of fees to compensate for those services related to turning the ship around in the shortest possible time. Customarily, however, charges are related to the tonnage of cargo handled in the agent's port. In addition, there is usually a price for any service exceeding the basic obligations of the agency contract. Periodically, BIMCO issues bulletins to its members citing recent experiences of its members' ships in ports scattered around the world. From such information, shipowners and agents are able to formulate approximations of what fees will be, and, later, the actual cost assessed against a shipowner for a specific service.

AGENCY FOR A LINER SERVICE

Ships in repetitive liner service traversing the same route and serving the same ports voyage after voyage require at least as much service as do chartered vessels. For a variety of reasons, shipowners may elect to employ agents in the ports of call rather than to open a branch office. They may choose to rely on agents who will perform the duties described for chartered ships. Alternatively, the shipowners may decide to contract with a large agency to serve as its representative in one or more ports, duplicating the activities of the home office. In this case, the contract provides for a *general agency* with these responsibilities:

1. To select stevedore and terminal operators as well as the necessary supporting services such as security guards and cargo checkers.
2. To serve as the traffic department, seeking shippers of cargo and dealing with consignees of incoming cargo.
3. To issue a bill of lading, as required.
4. To provide adequate communication services to reflect the booking of outbound cargo and the receipt of inbound cargo; to report on local conditions (including competition) that affect the profitable and efficient operation of the ships.
5. To supervise the operation of the cargo terminal.
6. To submit disbursements accounts for every call of every vessel at the general agent's ports.
7. To attend conferences dealing with procurement of cargo, regulation of ship operation, and other matters affecting the efficiency of the ships.

It must be understood that if the general agency extends to smaller outports, the demands placed upon the local representative may be reduced to arranging for arrival, berthing, cargo handling, and sailing of the ship. It is not unusual for an agency to contract to service two or more ports.

The procurement of stores and services to support a ship is critical for safe and efficient operation. This task is facilitated by chandlers and agents. Although they often work in the background of busy vessel operations, without the assistance of these dedicated professionals it would be impossible to operate vessels on the precise schedules that are mandated by the world's business community.

CHAPTER THIRTEEN

The Logic of Ship Scheduling

To those who frequent the waterfront of any major port city, it is a special thrill to see one of the huge containerships come into her berth precisely on time. It is equally exciting to watch the departure of the proud queen of the seas exactly at the advertised hour. What appears to be a simple, almost routine process involving a minor amount of calculation is actually a complex exercise in coordinated management.

Drawing up a schedule for a ship service requires much more than dividing the number of miles to be traveled by the speed of the ship to establish the time at sea and then adding enough hours in port to unload and reload the vessel. Determining the basic rules to be followed in a liner-service schedule requires a combination of empirical knowledge and interpretive ability. Managers experienced in the ways of ships and ports and the vagaries of the sea collaborate with those who are wise in the ways of traffic and can convert the demands of shippers into the practicalities of ship operation. Their common goal is to meet the needs of shippers while achieving efficient and profitable employment of the fleet.

Schedules are inseparable from the idea of liner service. One or more ships plying a fixed route and making port calls at regular intervals provide the transportation essential to the commercial enterprise of the region. In time, if the ship movements have been dependable over a protracted period, shippers come to expect that vessels always will be available according to the established pattern, and any disruption in that pattern upsets their business practices. Merchants are especially concerned that the ships sail on the advertised day because many international trade transactions are financed by letters of credit stipulating that the goods be dispatched by a certain date. Failure to meet this requirement can interfere with the financing of the deal.

In particular, therefore, the more frequently a fleet can offer a sailing, the more likely it will be to gain the good will of shippers and prosper from their patronage. This premise is valid so long as there is no question concerning the time the goods spend in transit.

For a hypothetical example, the Blue Seas Line owns a number of 20-knot ships. One of the routes it serves is between Landport and Seahaven, which are separated by 4,800 miles of ocean. The vessels traverse the distance in ten days, and require four days in each port to discharge and reload. The aggregate of these times is exactly four weeks. A fortnightly service is maintained, using two cargo liners. If a shipper is exceedingly fortunate in timing the movement of its cargo, it is possible for the goods to arrive at the loading berth only a few hours before a ship sails and to be discharged at Seahaven on arrival day, so that the transit time is ten days. Another shipper, however, misses the sailing from Landport by a matter of hours, so the goods must wait two weeks for the next departure. This consignment will be the first loaded aboard the ship and the last to be discharged. Not only must the goods wait fourteen days, but at Seahaven they will not be released until the end of the two days needed to empty the ship. Total transit time for this cargo is twenty-six days (fourteen days of waiting, ten days of steaming, and two days for discharge). Blue Seas Line's customers must be prepared to accept a maximum transit time of twenty-six days, but can obtain a minimum of ten days. If no objections are voiced by shippers, management would be correct in assuming that the service offered within these limits is adequate.

As cargo offerings improve, Blue Seas Line assigns a total of four ships to the route, making possible weekly departures from both termini. Maximum transit time is reduced to nineteen days (seven days of waiting, ten days of steaming, and two days for discharging) while the minimum transit time is maintained at ten days. Although each ship carries a near-capacity load, there is space available for additional cargo. Calls therefore are ordered at Harborside and Transitown, which lie on the direct route to Seahaven and require no increase in steaming time. At Harborside, a day and a half are used to handle the cargo, while at Transitown working the cargo takes two full days. The duration of the round trip has been lengthened to thirty-five days. To continue to provide weekly sailing, Blue Seas Line must place a fifth ship on the route.

The new schedule challenges management with two significant problems. The first is the complaint of the shippers that, although weekly departures are available, transit time has been increased by the calls at Harborside and Transitown. The minimum now is thirteen and a half days, compared to ten formerly, and maximum transit time has been extended from nineteen to twenty-four and a half days. For those exporters who are paid on delivery of their goods to the importers, the additional time represents a significant economic burden. Management concedes that the service offered by Blue Seas Line between Landport and Seahaven no longer meets the needs of the shippers.

The second problem is comparable in magnitude. The tonnage of cargo offered on the route did not increase despite the fact that to maintain weekly departures on the route by way of Harborside and Transitown, it was necessary to assign a fifth ship to what economically is a four-ship service. If freight rates were raised to the point where all ships earned a profit, the higher charges would force some shippers to withdraw from the market. If ship revenues remained unchanged, however, the company would be pushed into a money-losing operation.

The requirement originally presented by the shippers for a weekly service was justified by the additional cargo revenue that resulted. Attempting to enhance ship earning power by adding the calls at Harborside and Transitown undermined the adequacy of the service and imposed heavy financial burdens on the carrier. While it was technically possible to have the ships call at the two intermediate ports, the decision proved to be faulty because it did not adequately consider the impact of the longer transit time on the shippers.

The first step in making a schedule is to convert the broad statements of what is desired by the traffic department into the particulars of the number of tons of cargo that must be handled in terminal ports and in primary and secondary ports of call; the physical characteristics of the ports of call that affect the movements of ships into and out of their waters; the hours during which these ports provide cargo-working arrangements; and critical times of arrival of the ships at certain intermediate primary ports. As these details are assembled and appropriately related to the expressed desires of the traffic department, the outline of the schedule begins to emerge. Many suggestions will be put forward as the various versions of tentative schedules are examined. Of major importance to the operating department is which ports the traffic experts will designate as primary ports along the route, to be visited on every trip outbound and homebound, and which ports will be considered as secondary, to be served only when sufficient cargo is offered to justify the expense of the call.

Secondary ports present a problem to the liner service that is operated with little spare time in its schedules. If, for example, calls are made at three primary ports en route, and turnaround at the outbound terminus is to be accomplished in forty-eight hours, an occasional six-hour call at a secondary port can be troublesome. One solution lies in the operational and traffic histories of the line. If calls at one or more secondary ports have been included on every voyage, it is good management to provide sufficient time for those visits. This arrangement will eliminate the unavoidable disruption to schedules that must follow unprogrammed demands on ship time. Another solution is to develop the schedule at a cruising speed that can be increased as necessary to compensate for the time required to make the calls at the secondary ports. In either instance, the value of close coordination between the operating and traffic departments is evident.

Cargo ships are designed to operate at a certain speed, and barring unusual events beyond the control of the owner or the master, they will be run at that speed. No allowance is made for the possibility of unfavorable weather interfering with the completion of the appointed voyage, unless there are reliable data showing that at certain seasons of the year it is impossible to maintain maximum speed. This is especially true of the North Atlantic, where winter storms reach fantastic strength. In other regions, for example along the eastern coast of South Africa, winter storms make slow speeds necessary if major damage to vessels is to be avoided. In different areas, like the Caribbean Sea and the Gulf of Mexico, weather usually is excellent but the threat of hurricanes is known to all who voyage in those waters. These disturbances are unpredictable in every way: when they will occur, where they will reach dangerous dimensions, what courses they will follow, and how long they will menace the sea lanes. Operators sending ships into those regions have found over the decades that they can meet the problem best by alertness and flexibility at the time the storm approaches. If a hurricane delays a voyage for several days, this is an isolated phenomenon that does not justify altering schedules for the duration of the hurricane season.

A basic rule in making schedules, therefore, is that the ships will be operated at prescribed speeds, and from sea buoy at the port of departure to sea buoy at the port of arrival, the ship will perform to that standard.

Next in order of consideration and complicated by their variability are the type and tonnage of cargo to be transported over the entire length of the intended voyage. Not all items moving by sea can be handled with the same rapidity (computed in tons per hour): cotton bales are stowed aboard the ship at one speed, while agricultural machinery is placed in the hold at a markedly different pace. Similarly, elevators in New Orleans deliver grain to ships at a very great number of tons per hour, but in India the laborers shovel it out at an agonizingly slow tempo. The variety of commodities, the quantity of each, the skill and rapidity with which the stevedore performs, and the ability of a designated berth to handle the flow of breakbulk cargo are vital pieces of information on which to base the forecast of time needed in each port of call. The accurate determination of what will be carried and in what quantity is a factor in developing the schedule. A study of the current and past manifests of actual loads carried in the ships assigned to the route provides much of this essential information. Supplementing these data will be the traffic department's estimates of anticipated trends in the movement of cargo, by commodities and ports of loading and discharge and often by seasons of the year.

The transformation of this accumulation of information into a proposed sailing schedule is accomplished by combining the accrued experience and pragmatic wisdom of shipmasters, terminal superintendents, and stevedores who have worked with these goods, ships, and ports, and who know what can be accomplished at every port where the ship calls. The importance of accuracy in fixing the number of hours needed to unload the inbound cargo and to take aboard the outbound tonnage cannot be overestimated in the breakbulk trades, where performance of longshoremen varies greatly from port to port. Errors in the estimate of time needed to turn the ship around are cumulative and can disrupt the regularity that is the essence of liner service.

To establish a workable schedule that will ensure maximum performance for the big, fast, and very expensive containerships now operated on major trade routes between industrialized countries is at least as crucial to ultimate profitability of the shipping enterprise as it is in the breakbulk trades. The aggregate hourly costs of these huge carriers come to hundreds of dollars and delay, other than those occasionally and unpredictably arising from causes beyond human control, are intolerable.

Few, if any, of these vessels are what the trade calls "self-sustaining," meaning equipped with cranes to handle the containers in which their cargo is loaded. In setting up the port working schedule, the critical element is the availability of dockside cranes to lift the containers off and on the ships. This is especially true for those ships that transport the equivalent of 4,000 or more 20-foot boxes and require from two to five cranes for optimum dispatch.[1] To produce a schedule that brings two ships into a berthing area where there is space for only one, or where insufficient cranes are available, is an economically unacceptable practice.

Schedule makers for containerships are not concerned about the capability of individual gangs of longshoremen and the difficulties of stowing certain types of cargo in a breakbulk ship. Instead, they are responsible for ensuring that the complex operations of the container terminal make possible the most efficient use of the time the ship is in port. The terminal superintendent has to keep the schedule makers informed about those factors under his cognizance that have an impact on the schedule.

One aspect of scheduling that affects the operations of containerships is the current trend toward intermodal transportation.[2] In addition to the constraints encountered as a routine part of schedule making by other types of marine carriers, schedules for ships that carry hundreds of containers destined for intermodal connections in minilandbridge or landbridge services must be planned in conjunction with those of rail and motor carriers. This means that the containership schedule makers must communicate and develop relationships with their counterparts in the other modes of transportation. Scheduling by all concerned with transporting cargo on an intermodal movement is complicated manyfold by the requirement to coordinate arrivals and departures of each of the connecting modes. It also is predicated on the promise that all carriers will meet their obligations on time.

The structure and equipment of breakbulk carriers merit special consideration from the scheduling team. Few fleets in the merchant service consist of identical vessels; most are made up of a heterogeneous collection of ships built in different yards to different plans and often intended for trades different from those in which they now are employed. The individual characteristics of these ships can affect the rapidity with which longshoremen handle the cargo, whether they are loading or unloading.

For the fleet that was the basis for the hypothetical Blue Seas Line example, the common characteristic of the ships was their 20-knot speed. Two of the five ships assigned to sail between Landport and Seahaven had six hatches, each rigged with two sets of cargo booms and equipped with high-speed winches. The other three ships had seven hatches, five of which had individual fast-acting cranes, while the No. 1 and No. 7 hatches each had one conventional mast and boom assembly. At first glance it would appear that the rapidity with which cargo could be handled would differ significantly between the two types of ships. The actual experience was that all the ships worked cargo at about the same speed, greatly facilitating the development of the timetable for the fleet.

Despite the remarkable success of naval architects in giving greater balance in cargo-handling capability to all hatches in a breakbulk ship, the problem of the "limiting hatch" or "long hatch" has not been eliminated. To some extent, the difficulty of having more cargo in one hold than in any other is structural, and to some extent it is the result of the quantity or characteristics of the cargo stowed in a hatch. The Liberty ships of World War II had one disproportionately large hatch. If the whole load were to be taken off in one port, the working schedule for the ship had to be keyed to the big hatch, which determined the length of the ship's stay in port.

Timetables for containerships reflect the complexity of the terminal operations that support the ships. When a number of ports of call must be considered by the schedule maker, realistic evaluation of the experience of the ship fixes the most efficient employment of the vessels. Ideally, all terminal operations are standardized, with only minor deviation from approved activities. In practice, many departures from the ideal are encountered. Analysis of terminal operations at ports along the route is supplied as a matter of business routine to the schedule makers in order that adequate, but not excessive, time may be assigned to each port. Although it is economically imperative that the ship gets to sea as quickly as good management and proper care of the cargo will permit, it is equally important to control the movement of the containership to ensure that there will be a berth at the next port and that the terminal will be ready in every respect to service the ship on her arrival.

Calculating accurately the length of time the ship must spend in port to work her cargo (turnaround time) is a major challenge in making liner-service schedules. The ship earns no revenue for her owners while in port, and therefore much effort is devoted to finding ways to reduce this unproductive period. It sometimes happens that significant reductions in turnaround time will make possible more voyages per year, thereby increasing the profit-making potential of the ship.

The number of hours needed to work the cargo is fundamental in determining port turnaround time. The calculation is related directly to the productivity of longshoremen in each port of call. "Productivity" is measured in terms of the number of tons of cargo handled per worker per hour. From port to port, and even from terminal to terminal within a port, there are wide variations in the rate of productivity. Schedule workers not only must take this into account, but must also respect local labor customs and working hours in the different ports of call. Meal hours in some ports, for example, are inviolable; no work is carried on during this period. In other ports, work will be continued, but the laborers are paid at the overtime rate until a meal hour is granted. Certain holidays are observed by stopping all work throughout the port. Other considerations that schedule makers must take into account are related to ship movements within the harbor and pose questions such as these: Is a port (like London) made up of docks that are open only at high tides? May ships be moved after dark, either from one terminal to another, or out of the harbor to sea? When do harbor, channel, and docking pilots work?

Underlying the idea of liner service, whether by breakbulk or container-carrying ships, is regularity—the dependable arrival and departure of ships at the ports listed in the itinerary and the timetables. To ensure this regularity, many expedients are practiced. The amount of cargo accepted for a port may be limited to the quantity that can be handled in the time allotted for the call. For example, a breakbulk ship works cargo at the rate of 50 tons per hour and is scheduled to spend only fourteen hours in port. To maintain the schedule, therefore, a maximum of 700 tons will be booked into and out of the ship.

Certain assumptions must be made as the plan for liner service is converted into the reality of the schedule. These assumptions are predicated upon the experience of the shipowner in the operation of seagoing vessels and are intended to achieve the dependability that is implicit in liner service:

- The vessels in the schedule will be operated consistently at the assigned speeds. It is incumbent, therefore, that the shipowners maintain the ship to high standards.
- The cargo liner will be loaded with a representative variety of goods, stowed according to the line's approved stevedoring practices. This representative load is based upon analysis of cargo manifests of enough voyages to define trends in the movement of commodities.
- Ports of call, and the sequence in which they are visited, will not be changed during the projected life of the timetable. Working conditions in each of these ports are considered to be stable.
- Port operations will not be disrupted by strikes, riots, or civil commotion, and there will be no major breakdowns of the cargo-handling equipment in these ports.
- No allowance is made for unfavorable weather because of the unpredictability of storms and their intensity, or the effect they might have on cargo operations.

It is important to note that ship schedules reflect occurrences that affect the practicality of the ship's movements. Pertinent, therefore, is the analysis of harbor depths and the range of the tides. If a port of call can be navigated only at high tides, the schedule must be sufficiently flexible to accept the unavoidable variations in arrival and departure times. The flexibility may be ensured by including an adequate number of unprogrammed hours and authorizing the master to adjust speeds to schedule arrival at high tide. This same device may be used in connection with sailing times, depending upon the problem that may be confronted at the next port. If several ports of call are affected by the tides, failure to make appropriate allowance for the changes in the hours of high tide can destroy the schedule.

Some ports have strict rules about the hours when ships may move within the limits of the harbor. In Capetown, South Africa, for instance, pilotage from the sea buoy to the ship's berth is compulsory and is available only during daylight hours. Pilots take the ships from the sea buoy in strict observance of their times of arrival—first come, first served. In the hope of avoiding long delays, some shipowners plan ship arrivals at the pilot station well before dawn. If the ship is first in line, it means that cargo work will begin at an early hour, with resulting economy and efficient use of ship time.

Longshoremen observe different working hours from port to port. These idiosyncracies must be taken into account in preparing the schedule, so that adequate time will be available to handle the cargo. Some of these local peculiarities involve no night work, no work on Saturdays after five o'clock in the afternoon, lunch hours extending from eleven o'clock in the morning until one or two o'clock in the afternoon, and no work during certain religious holidays.

Holiday work, when local customs permit, presents some problems for ship operators. Much of the commercial activity of the port is suspended, consequently no cargo is delivered to the terminal or taken away. Supporting services (tugs, cranes, flatbed trailers) must be arranged for in advance and, because of the holiday, are very expensive. Many longshoremen, often the best workers, elect not to report for work, and overall efficiency is reduced. Schedule makers therefore seek to adjust timetables on an individual basis to avoid bringing ships into port over holidays.

Breakbulk cargo liner service, concerned as it is with handling thousands of tons of hundreds of commodities, requires somewhat flexible schedules. It is usual for a ship to be considered as "on time" if she arrives during working hours on the scheduled day, regardless of what time had been set in the schedule for her docking. This is accepted practice during those seasons of the year when the final two or three days of the voyage may be spent fighting storms that slow the ship. If these liner service vessels sail at intervals of two or three weeks, no serious difficulties result from these unavoidable delays. A realistic schedule will include an allowance of time to ensure departure at approximately the advertised hour. Shorter intervals and less slack in the schedule require managerial attention to prevent overlapping arrivals of ships of the company's fleet.

Delays may not be especially serious in themselves, particularly when they are only of two or three hours duration. In their cumulative effect on fleet operations, however, they may cause numerous difficulties, not least of which is the overlapping of schedules. This overlapping, known as "bunching," is the obvious and cumulative result of a number of delays (or "slips") along the route. Ships of a single fleet that have bunched up in a port overtax the facilities available to the operator. As a result, at least one ship might miss her next outward sailing from the home port.

To prevent bunching is one of the major objectives of the schedule makers. Depending upon the relative importance to the carrier of the outbound and homeward trades and the cargo commitments made, it may be possible to compensate for lost time by omitting ports on one leg of the voyage. Speeding up cargo operations is practical only to a certain extent, especially if port time already has been figured at approximately the maximum capability of ship and port. It is worth noting, also, that it is not always possible to transship cargo to avoid calling at smaller ports.

Throughout this discussion of schedule making, there has been no mention of the effect on the schedule of the operational necessity to make repairs and to put ships into drydock at periodic intervals. Routine voyage repairs are accomplished while the ship is in port on her regular schedule. The proper performance of this work within the allotted port time is supervised by the staff of the superintendents of the deck, engineering, and catering/hotel departments. Drydocking for normal hull inspection and repainting is set months in advance, and adjustments are made to permit the ship to be withdrawn from what otherwise would be normal port activity for the relatively short period required in drydock. As the vessel gets older and the magnitude of repairs increases, it may become mandatory to set aside several successive days for the required work. This presents no insurmountable problem so long as it can be foreseen and appropriately scheduled. Emergency repairs are effected on an emergency basis, and any changes brought about as a result are made in the most satisfactory manner possible.

Schedules for voyages of tramp ships in the dry-cargo trades are predicated upon the same considerations that govern schedule making for cargo liners. The major difference is that for vessels on single-voyage charters, no subsequent trips have to be taken into account. Time-chartered vessels, if employed on the same route for the duration of the charter, are integrated into the charterer's schedule of liner service. If, during the life of the charter, the time-chartered ship is assigned to different voyages, the planning would be the same as that for vessels chartered for single voyages.

Tanker schedules follow much the same patterns as those of cargo liners, except that often the ship does not repeat a voyage immediately. The schedule may be made for a number of voyages over a period of several months. Since tanker cargoes are liquid and are pumped rather than handled by longshoremen, that aspect of scheduling is eliminated. In its stead are substituted several problems peculiar to tankers: the location of the shoreside tanks into which the cargo is to be pumped (i.e., the distance and gradient of the pipeline through which the oil must be pumped by the force of the ship's equipment); the diameter of the pipes (i.e., the quantity of oil that can be moved in a given period); the season of the year, because heat or cold affects the speed with which the liquid flows through the pipes. Port time for tankers always is set in terms of hours, and much effort is expended to turn the ships around within the allotted time.

When one considers the extent of the sea routes, the variations in winds and currents, the almost complete lack of uniformity in the methods of handling ships in different areas of the world, and the amazing amount of detail that must be taken into account in making up the schedule, it is remarkable—and a credit to the schedule makers—that the ships come in to port and depart as near to the predicted hour as they do.

CHAPTER FOURTEEN

Terminal Management and Operations

A marine terminal exists for the purpose of effecting the efficient transfer of cargo between a ship and other modes of transportation. It is a service facility with its management and operating structure designed and organized to be flexible and responsive to the needs of the shippers. Its operations are planned and carried out to ensure that cargoes are handled safely at the lowest cost and in the least possible time. Specifically, terminal management operates on the following principles:

1. Personnel must be protected from injury while in the terminal area.
2. The ship must be unloaded, reloaded, and made ready for sea in the least possible time.
3. Cargo must be handled efficiently and economically between the ship and a variety of inland transportation modes using standardized procedures.
4. Cargo must be protected from loss or damage while on the terminal.
5. Paperwork necessary for the movement of cargo must be completed quickly and done accurately.
6. Terminals are not long-term storage areas and every effort should be made to move cargo through the terminal as rapidly as possible.

Achieving these objectives is a day-to-day concern of the terminal management team, which must provide for economical and efficient operation.

Terminal management must follow generally accepted management functions to accomplish expeditiously the many activities on the terminal. The management structure of the marine terminal, although differing somewhat from terminal to terminal, is always structured so that the principles of operation as well as the terminal's objectives are met.

In charge of the whole operation is the terminal manager, who is responsible for coordinating and controlling the day-to-day activities of the terminal. The principal assistants to the terminal manager are the chief receiving clerk, who supervises all routines relating to cargo brought to the terminal to be loaded on board outbound vessels; the chief delivery clerk, who performs the same duties for cargo from inbound vessels being turned over to consignees; the security chief, who is responsible for the physical safety of the facility and its contents; the timekeeper, who keeps detailed records of the employment of every laborer hired on an hourly basis; and the stevedore or vessel superintendent, who directs vessel loading and unloading operations. Often the superintendent is employed by the stevedore contractor rather than the terminal, but serves as a member of the terminal manager's staff and advises on all matters directly connected with the labor force and actual handling of cargo into and out of ships.

The security chief is responsible to the terminal manager for the physical safety and security of the terminal and its contents. Guards are directed by the chief of security and have a number of important duties: to control access to the terminal area, to visit all parts of the terminal during periodic rounds but at irregularly scheduled intervals, to prevent theft, and to detect fire or other problems on the terminal. The security force is also responsible for these ancillary functions:

1. Connecting and disconnecting refrigerated containers, as required, when they arrive at and depart from the storage areas.
2. Inspecting refrigerated container cooling units to ensure that their machinery is operating and the proper temperatures are being maintained.
3. Observing the operations of tying up or letting go the mooring lines of a ship to prevent smuggling and stowaway activities.
4. Operating an intraterminal personnel bus service to minimize or even eliminate pedestrian traffic.
5. Controlling the maintenance and porter units to ensure that hazards to safety resulting from damage or accumulation of waste are removed quickly and efficiently.
6. Establishing contingency plans for emergencies such as fire, severe weather, earthquakes, hazardous material spills, and serious injury to personnel.

The logic behind these additional assignments is that security guards constantly patrol the transit sheds, storage yards, container marshaling yards, refrigerated container storage, and the piers and wharves. They must be alert to any deviations from safe and accepted practices that endanger the physical safety of the plant or cargo, and they must take appropriate actions to have any observed problems corrected.

A modern, well-designed terminal built on a wharf. Wide aprons, numerous doors, and skylights enhance efficiency. Photograph by Sutton, courtesy The Port of New Orleans.

None of the ancillary functions, however, should suggest that the primary mission of the security chief is other than the safety and security of the terminal premises and the cargo stored therein. Continuous vigilance and resourcefulness are needed.

To ensure cargo security, one proven technique is for security to study the movement of vehicles, cargo, and paperwork within the terminal. The greatest security risks are at those areas—known as "danger zones"—where vehicles stop or paperwork is processed. The procedures at each stop in these danger zones therefore should be scrutinized:

1. *Gate.* The driver shows documents to the gate guard, who verifies that the truck and cargo are expected and issues a gate pass.
2. *Gatehouse.* The driver surrenders all documents to the receiving clerk, who starts the terminal paperwork and directs the driver to the drop point on the terminal.
3. *Inspection area.* For breakbulk shipments, the truck stops to pick up a checker who will supervise the unloading and note, on the *dock receipt,* the condition of the cargo at the moment it is accepted by the terminal. For containerized shipments, the checker inspects the

box for evidence of actual or potential damage to the contents. The condition and number of the seal on the container doors are observed and recorded by the checker on an *equipment interchange receipt* (EIR).

4. *Unloading area.* Breakbulk cargo is examined and tallied by the checker, who initials the dock receipt. The exact location in the transit shed is identified, so that plans can be made for the most efficient use of time and equipment to load the cargo aboard a ship. Containers brought to the terminal for outward loading in ships are trucked to the designated slots to await transfer to the ship. Once the container is released from the truck-tractor, the driver returns to the gatehouse.

5. *Gatehouse.* The driver presents all papers to the gatekeeper, who separates the finished papers, gives a copy of the dock receipt to the driver, and inspects the truck (if it carried breakbulk cargo) before releasing the vehicle.

6. *Gate.* The driver then returns the gate pass to the guard at the gate and departs the terminal.

Other measures that the security chief takes to protect the cargo include liaison with police units and contact with major shippers to learn if the protection system devised imposes undue delay or expense or is in any way objectionable to these customers.

The timekeeper is another important member of the terminal manager's staff. Detailed records must be kept of the employment of every laborer hired on an hourly basis. Longshoremen work in gangs hired for four-hour shifts; their names must be inscribed individually on the time sheets at the beginning of each shift. If they handle obnoxious commodities ("penalty cargo") and are entitled to additional compensation for such work, the timekeeper is to note the actual time during which the extra money is payable. Workers employed to do the many tasks around the terminal, but not members of longshoremen's gangs, are listed under the heading of "dock labor" or "extra labor" and are paid according to the number of hours they work. It is essential that the timekeeper periodically determine that the records show exactly who is working, and that the pay accounts are consistent with the labor actually performed.

Underlying every consideration of good terminal management is the awareness of the need for safety. Not only is safety important for the good morale of employees, but it is vital if the goodwill of shippers and consignees of goods is to be retained. Working practices that endanger the lives of the laborers are intolerable both morally and financially. Equally intolerable are habits of handling cargo that result in damage or loss of customers' goods.

Enforcing safety rules and preventing accidents among longshoremen and other terminal workers are major responsibilities of terminal management. Three areas of concern require constant scrutiny on the part of supervisors: personnel and vehicular traffic patterns, physical safety (i.e., structural and plant condition), and operation of equipment and vehicles.

On many pieces of cargo-handling machinery, the driver has very limited vision when actually working cargo. By designating specific pedestrian walkways or eliminating pedestrian traffic completely in areas where cargo is being worked, exposure to accidents can be reduced. Due to the size of the loads that terminal equipment carries nowadays, accidents between machine and pedestrian can have major consequences.

Terminal management is equally concerned with the possibility of accidents between cargo-handling machines. To minimize the risk, it is prudent to set specific traffic patterns in transit sheds as well as in the marshaling or container yards. In addition, these precautions are important: enforce safe speed limits, properly train equipment operators, require pre-start safety inspections of the equipment, eliminate cross traffic at intersections, and install mirrors at all blind corners. Preventing accidents protects personnel, cargo, and machinery.

The physical structure of the terminal itself has a significant impact on safety and efficiency. If the terminal is dirty or improperly lighted, ventilated, or heated, or if the deck surface is in poor condition, there is risk to personnel and cargo. Everyone working on a marine terminal shares in the responsibility of ensuring that the condition of the physical structure and plant is in good order. The terminal manager, of course, has final responsibility for seeing that all is safe.

The provision of good, well-lighted, and spacious toilet and washroom facilities for terminal employees reflects excellent management. In this regard, it is good practice to have proper shelter for the laborers somewhere in the terminal, so that in times of bad weather they may be protected from the elements. Not only is this humane, it is also efficient, because it keeps the labor force together and permits immediate resumption of work when conditions are favorable. It also eliminates having a large number of workers wandering aimlessly through the transit shed with the possibility of being injured. A further advantage in providing a shelter is that smoking can be controlled, and the chance of a fire being started by a carelessly discarded cigar or cigarette is reduced.

Although speed is essential in all processes of receiving, stevedoring, sorting, and delivery of the cargo, the ideal terminal manager never ac-

Spools of barbed wire, stacked on wooden pallets, are transported by a crane truck. Lifting bridles and spreaders and the design of the pallet are clearly visible.

cepts the report that work was accomplished at "maximum speed." Managers are always under pressure to find ways to reduce turnaround time, for when vessels cost $2,000 or more per hour to keep in commission, few operators can afford the luxury of idle ships at the terminal. Everyone must be aware that ships earn money only when they are actually transporting goods from one port to another. The shorter the port time, the more voyages a ship can make in a year and the greater her earnings.

In the United States, modern breakbulk terminal operation is predicated upon two facts: manpower is very expensive, and machines can do more work than people. Many types of mechanical equipment are available for use in handling cargo, but determining how many pieces of machinery will be purchased and operated and establishing the ratio of workers to machines is the responsibility of the terminal manager. In the ceaseless efforts to reduce turnaround time and cargo-handling costs, it is imperative that the managers are alert to the possibility of replacing obsolete machinery with more suitable equipment. At the same time, the division of costs between investment in equipment, expense of equipment operation, and the wages of laborers must be taken into account.

Necessarily, every decision as to replacement of equipment has to be based on the determination that more work will be done at lower cost if more efficient machines are procured.

Increasingly, all terminal managers are being faced with new challenges that they must address. These include such things as how to dispose of dredged spoil recovered in the ongoing task of providing sufficient depth of water at their docks to accommodate the larger ships; how to manage the hazardous materials passing through the terminals each day; how to keep current on all the constantly changing regulations governing hazardous materials; how to maintain the delicate balance between the protection of the environment and the needs of the shippers (to move their goods) and the shipowner (to get ships out in a minimum of time); and how to address adequately the needs of labor as they relate to terminal efficiency.

The proper management of a marine terminal is an exciting and demanding challenge for anyone. The person who fills the position of terminal manager must have good written and oral communications skills, good interpersonal skills, an eye for detail, and an analytical mind. The person must be an innovator and must be calm, patient, and willing to work long hours when needed. In short, the person must have general management knowledge and skill as well as specific maritime knowledge about ships, terminals, and labor.

TYPES OF MARINE TERMINALS

In general, terminals are designed and built for some specific purpose without much input from the people who will ultimately manage them. Once the terminal is built, the manager must make the operation work with existing resources.

Some factors that affect the design and operating characteristics of a marine terminal are the following: the size and type of vessels that will call at the terminal; the types of cargo that will be expected at the terminal; the volume of cargo anticipated; the mechanical cargo-handling equipment to be used; the space available for use as a terminal; the availability and access of land transportation; the degree and type of federal, regional, and local regulations; and the impact that the terminal will have on the environment.

While the principle of good terminal management remains the same no matter what kind of terminal is being operated, there are seven distinct types of terminals, and each has its own unique management challenges:

1. *Breakbulk* or *general cargo* terminals are designed to accommodate several kinds of ships and a variety of cargoes packaged by the

shipper. This type of terminal has large transit sheds located close to the face of the dock and large open areas adjacent to the transit sheds to collect cargoes that are not weather sensitive. These terminals can be both capital-intensive and labor-intensive.

The manager of a breakbulk terminal is concerned that the limited terminal space is used wisely, that cargo is being received and delivered on time, that the proper mix of labor and machinery is maintained, and that the different types of equipment are all maintained properly.

2. *Bulk product* terminals are designed to accommodate cargo that is not packaged. There are two kinds of bulk terminals: dry bulk, which consists of cargoes such as grains, ores, and wood chips; and liquid bulk, which consists of cargoes such as petroleum products, vegetable oil products, and any other liquid product shipped in bulk form. Bulk terminals are designed to accommodate tankers and dry-bulk ships. They have fixed cargo-handling systems (pipelines, conveyors, etc.) that run from the berth to large storage facilities ashore. The storage facilities are always located well inland because of the very dense nature of the cargo worked. Due to the deeper drafts of bulk carriers the berths are generally extended further into the waterways. These terminals are generally very capital-intensive but not very labor-intensive.

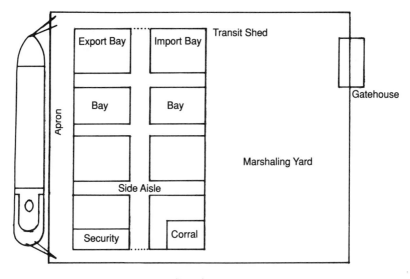

Typical breakbulk terminal configuration.

Bulk wheat is delivered by the supply pipe and spread through the ship's hold. Courtesy the Port of Sacramento, California.

   The manager of a bulk product terminal is concerned that the
quality of the cargo being received or delivered is that which is
specified, that the fixed cargo-handling systems are properly maintained, and that the storage facilities are ready to meet the requirements of the customer.

3. *Neobulk* terminals are designed to accommodate homogeneous cargoes that cannot be loaded or discharged using fixed cargo-handling
   systems. Some examples of neobulk cargoes are logs, scrap steel, or
   automobiles. Neobulk terminals are designed to accommodate specialty carriers such as car carriers, bulk carriers (i.e., scrap steel),
   and breakbulk carriers (i.e., logs). They have no transit sheds and
   very large open areas. These terminals are less capital-intensive
   than a bulk terminal, but are more labor-intensive.

   The manager of a neobulk terminal is concerned that there is
ample yard space for the cargo, that the specialized cargo-handling
equipment is properly maintained, and that there is a sufficient
number of laborers available to take care of the work (especially for
car carriers, when the terminal may need more than one hundred
drivers to work the ship).

4. *Container* terminals are designed to accommodate cargo that has
   been loaded into containers for transportation in containerships.
   They have very large open areas known as container yards (CY),
   specialized container-handling equipment, and no transit sheds. The
   terminal may contain a container freight station (CFS), which looks
   like a transit shed and serves many of the same functions as a transit

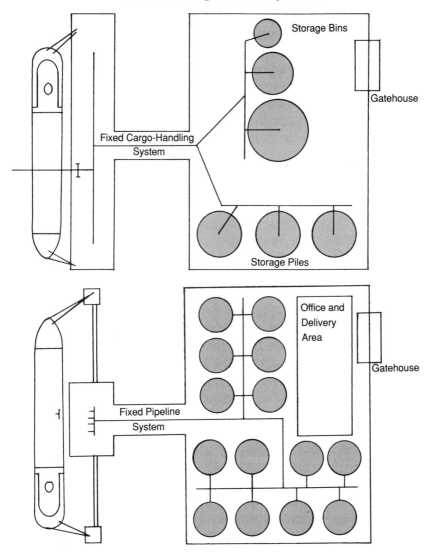

Top: Typical dry-bulk terminal configuration. Note: Storage area must support very heavy weights and is usually on solid land for this reason. *Bottom:* Typical liquid-bulk terminal configuration. Note: Storage tanks must support very heavy weights and are usually on solid land for this reason.

shed. The major difference is that the CFS is not located near the face of the terminal. This type of terminal operation is very capital-intensive and requires a work force that is highly trained.

The manager of a container terminal is concerned that the large number of transactions that take place on the terminal and the detailed paperwork associated with each transaction are recorded

The shipboard gantry crane can be fitted with different specialized cargo-handling devices to expedite loading and unloading. Courtesy Munck International.

accurately, that the computer is operating properly, that the container yard is laid out properly, and that the highly specialized container-handling equipment (cranes and straddle carriers) is properly maintained.[1]

5. *Passenger* terminals are designed to accommodate human "cargo." They are built to accommodate passenger ships and have large, often double-decked buildings. There are no open areas. These terminals feature large and well-lighted waiting rooms designed for the comfort of the passengers with rest rooms, baggage areas, ample communications equipment, and easy access to land transportation.

   The manager of a passenger terminal must ensure that passengers can be processed by passenger traffic department personnel quickly and efficiently. Embarkation is facilitated by the availability of sufficient numbers of porters and baggage handlers. When passengers are disembarking, provision must be made for customs and immigration inspection, and adequate numbers of baggage handlers

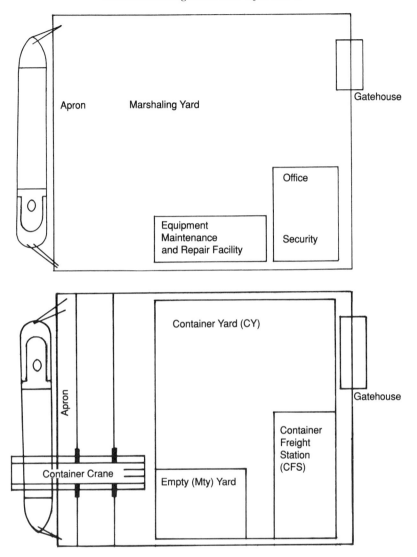

Top: Typical neobulk terminal configuration. *Bottom:* Typical container terminal configuration.

must be on duty. Loading areas for land transportation must be clean, neat, and under constant surveillance by the security force. A manager would do well to remember that the passenger terminal is the first and the last thing seen by the passenger on a sea voyage. The experience in the terminal can set the tone for the voyage and can leave a lasting impression (good or bad) in the mind of the pas-

The enormous size of container-handling cranes may be gauged by comparing the 4-meter (13-foot) high trucks and trailers with the towering cranes. Courtesy Ray Soto, Port of Houston Authority.

Crane operator's view of a container ready to be hoisted aboard ship. Courtesy North Carolina State Ports Authority.

senger. Obviously, the passenger ship operator has a great interest in the proper operation of the terminals where its ships call.

6. *Combination* terminals are designed to accommodate cargoes of various types (i.e., bulk, general cargo, containers, passenger). The terminal must be designed to accommodate all types of ships; it must have ample transit shed space of high quality as well as

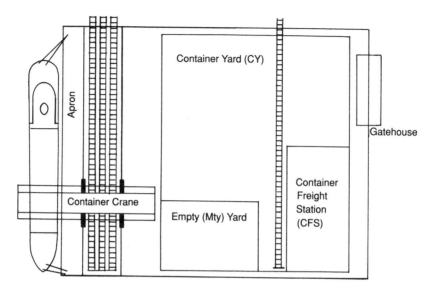

Typical intermodal terminal configuration.

sufficient open space to handle a variety of cargoes. This is perhaps the most challenging type of terminal to operate.

The manager of a combination terminal must be notified as to the type of ships using the facility. If a passenger ship, a breakbulk ship, and a bulk carrier are at the terminal at the same time, it will be necessary to segregate operations and to ensure that the shippers and passengers are served efficiently. Problems relating to cleanliness of the terminal and arrangements for processing passengers will absorb the attention of the manager and key staff members. All equipment must be maintained and in readiness to work.

7. *Intermodal* terminals are designed to accommodate cargo that is involved in a "through container movement." The terminals are built to accommodate containerships and have very large open areas, specialized cargo-handling equipment, and convenient access to land transportation (primarily rail). Many of these terminals have provided rail access to handle double-stack railcars and these terminals are referred to as intermodal container transfer facilities (ICTF).

The manager of an intermodal terminal is concerned with speed and proper land use. It is imperative to coordinate the cargo moving from one mode to another in time to make the connecting mode's schedule. This requires a skilled labor pool and a well designed mix of labor and machinery.

TERMINAL OPERATIONS

As previously stated, a major concern of management is that the ship sail on time, and the entire working schedule of the terminal is adjusted toward that end. Terminal operation depends upon the availability of a large force of workers whose skills and productivity set the level of efficiency. These workers are proud of their craft and are steadfastly loyal to their unions. Few terminals in the world today can be operated without due appreciation of the role of the labor unions and their members.

Of the seven types of terminals, the breakbulk terminal is probably the most complicated operation. For that reason, the operations of a typical breakbulk terminal will be examined in detail.

The terminal manager is the director of cargo operations for the shipping company and is responsible for the efficiency and economy of all terminal activities. The manager is expected to keep the ships on schedule insofar as port working time is concerned. The actual supervision of loading and unloading vessels is delegated to the chief stevedore with other key tasks being delegated to the security chief, the chief receiving clerk, the chief delivery clerk, and the timekeeper. The manager, however, is called upon to make decisions on specialized aspects of cargo handling, the types and number of cargo-handling equipment, the number and skills of laborers needed to perform an unusual job, and the procedures to be followed by clerks, checkers, longshoremen, watchmen, and other personnel in the performance of their assigned duties.

The proper use of cargo-handling machines is of major concern to the terminal manager, who is guided by these basic principles of materials handling:

1. *Safety of personnel is of first importance.* Every piece of machinery and every work technique must be analyzed to determine if danger exists for the operators assigned to the job. If danger is detected, the machine must be altered or the technique corrected to eliminate, insofar as is humanly possible, the threat to the worker. Experience has shown that these analyses are worthwhile because safe work practices permit faster and better performance by employees. Along with safe equipment and safe work practices goes proper training of operating personnel, including checking equipment for safety, safe equipment operation, and standardized work practices.
2. *Cargo must be handled safely.* Maximum effort must be made to ensure that the cargo is stowed and segregated properly, inspected diligently, and protected from theft or damage.

Mechanized cargo handling. *Left:* Rolls of newsprint are hoisted aboard ship with vacuum-cup grips, while a forklift truck uses clamps. *Upper right:* a short-masted, propane-fueled, solid-tired forklift truck of 8,000 pounds capacity stuffs cargo into a seagoing container. *Lower right:* A high-masted forklift truck, equipped with a spreader, removes bagged rice from a truck. Courtesy Port of Sacramento, California.

3. *Operations must be balanced between men and machines.* To take maximum advantage of the capabilities of a machine, one or more workers must be assigned to work with it. The judicious determination of the exact number of workers required to produce maximum efficiency from a machine is a major responsibility of the terminal manager. The manager must guard against the possibility that too many—or too few—people are put on a job at the expense of efficiency. It often happens that, even with the will to work, too many people in a gang will interfere with each other, and the result of their collective labors is not as good as it would have been if fewer workers had been assigned.

4. *Work practices must be standardized.* To calculate costs in terms of money, manpower, time, and machinery, it is necessary that standard work practices be followed throughout the terminal. There will be minor variations depending upon the personality and experience of the individual supervisor, but the pattern of activity in handling a particular commodity should be reasonably close to identical in all parts of the terminal. The manager must guard against complacency and be

Sacks of rice contained in large bags are lifted by a "bagged rice spreader" for stowage in a ship's cargo hold. Each unitized lift of fourteen bags retains its lifting cables, expediting discharge. Courtesy Port of Sacramento, California.

alert to suggestions for improvements in the techniques employed. Until a new procedure is approved, however, all subordinate leaders are required to perform their tasks in the accepted manner. It is common practice for the majority of longshoremen to work at a different terminal each day or every few days. Therefore, practices for the same task must also be standardized between terminals in order to maximize the efficiency of labor. The purpose of this standardization is to assist management in controlling output and expense.

5. *The proper type of equipment must be assigned to the job.* It is generally accepted that it is inefficient to use heavy equipment for light work or light equipment for heavy work. Management selects the machinery to be employed by the longshoremen and dictates the specific equipment to be used for designated types of work.

6. *Movement must be direct.* Circuitous routes are longer and require more time, both for operator and machine, than direct routes. From management's viewpoint, the routes followed by wheeled materials-handling equipment should be the shortest possible so that minimum time is involved in transporting loads. Lengthening the distance

As an economy measure, this pier was built with just sufficient width to serve vessels with a small cargo-working area. The pier extends from shore to a depth needed to berth the ship. Bow and stern are not secured to the cargo pier. Courtesy Stolt-Nielsen Inc.

     inevitably increases machine time and hence requires additional equipment if the same rate of tonnage movement is to be continued.

7. *Handle cargo as few times as possible.* Each time cargo is handled there is potential for damage due to rough handling.
8. *Cycle cargo where possible.* Ideally, materials-handling equipment moves payloads in both directions (known as "cycling"), but the average marine general cargo terminal affords little opportunity for such efficiency. Consideration should be given to the possibility of back-hauls when routes are laid out. In all cases, the goal of the routing must be to move the greatest tonnage per machine-hour.

     Labor relations are an important management skill because terminal operation is affected by the fact that longshore labor is almost universally unionized, and union customs and working agreements must be taken into account in planning how the cargoes are to be handled. A few examples from the port of San Francisco will make this clear.

     By long-standing agreement between employers and union, longshoremen working a breakbulk ship are hired in units of eight people. These units (gangs) are worked intact and may not be divided. Any gang, however, may be augmented by individually hiring additional people for the job as may be required by the contract.

The period of work for longshoremen also is governed by union agreement. These workers are hired for a minimum of eight hours, except in carefully defined circumstances. If a ship is not expected to berth until nine o'clock in the morning and work is to commence immediately, the gangs must be hired and paid from eight o'clock. During the waiting time, the gangs may be used for any work the terminal may assign, such as piling cargo, shifting equipment, or sweeping the decks of the transit shed.

Except for berthing a ship, handling the mail, or handling an emergency, no work of any sort will be performed on Labor Day, and no work is done after five o'clock on Saturday afternoons except to "complete" a ship. To complete means to finish a job if it can be accomplished in a maximum of four hours.

The other laborers on the terminal belong to a group collectively known as "dock labor," hired from the ranks of union members as individuals rather than as a gang. Varied skills such as those of the carpenter, cooper, wire splicer, and cargo checker are found in the dock labor force. When it is determined that four carpenters, two wire splicers, three equipment operators, and six checkers are needed for the day's work, these fifteen people are hired individually. Their wages, hours, and conditions of working are set forth in detail in the union agreements.

Many terminals, especially in the larger ports, have sufficient activity to keep a nucleus of longshoremen and dock laborers regularly employed. These workers (known as "steady men") come to the terminal each day, and although unionized and subject to the working agreement, they are not compelled to apply each morning and afternoon for work at the union hall. The very nature of terminal operation, however, makes it necessary to hire additional people of those grades and skills that meet the particular needs of the different ships. These supernumeraries are hired for periods of eight hours and may be released at the end of any shift. In most American ports, it is customary for supernumeraries to be obtained through some sort of hiring hall. The normal routine calls for notifying the center (which may be operated by the union as in San Francisco or by a governmental agency as in the Port of New York) of the needs for the next day. The center, in turn, has its own arrangements for making contact with gang foremen and individual craftsmen. At the appointed hour, the desired contingent of longshoremen and craftsmen reports to the terminal for assignment.

The individual gang members look to the foreman (or gang boss) for practically everything: the place and time of the next job, the rotation of work within the gang, promotion to less arduous and more responsible work, the acceptability of excuses for absences, and recommendations for retention in or dismissal from the gang. The privileged position of foreman is earned by showing superior ability to perform the work of each person in the gang and by demonstrating the ability to enforce discipline. The foreman has only supervisory duties when the gang is working and is usually on deck where all that transpires can be observed. Ordinarily, the foreman oversees the work of the hatchtender, who directs the exact spot where a draft of cargo is to be placed and who makes certain that the workers understand where and how they are to stow the individual packages of cargo. If a difficult parcel is being handled, the foreman may be in the hold to coordinate the work efforts. As the need arises for dunnage, separation paper, and other supplies, the gang foreman notifies the walking boss, the senior-ranking longshore worker on the job.

The hatchtender is the signalman who directs the winch operators and serves as the means of communication between them and the hold or the apron, using a code of hand signals to transmit orders to the winch driver. Excellent depth perception is required since the work station is on the uppermost deck of the ship and it is necessary to judge accurately when a draft of cargo is approaching the last inches above the landing point perhaps fifty feet below. The hatchtender should be of a placid temperament, not easily excited, and able to give undivided attention to the movement of a single cargo draft. The safety of fellow workers and that of the cargo depends on the hatchtender's decisions and hand signals.

Winch operators are chosen from members of the gang on the basis of their ability to work with the hatchtender. They control the motors turning the drums that wind the cables connected to the cargo hook. Perfect timing and teamwork are mandatory when two operators are employed. In any event, undeviating attention to the travel of the hook and the signals of the hatchtender is absolutely mandatory.

Dockmen are those members of the gang designated by the foreman to work alongside the ship. The dockmen make up the drafts of cargo and hook them to the crane for loading aboard the ship. If the ship is discharging, they guide drafts to the platform, unhook the gear, and distribute the packages to appropriate piles. Holdmen perform the same duties, except that they work in the ship's cargo spaces. Comparatively, the hold work is more arduous and requires more skill, but since the gang members are rotated from pier to hold at the discretion of the foreman, there is no difference in wages.

A guiding principle in determining the financial advantage of using labor in overtime periods is derived from accurate knowledge of the true

Skilled longshoremen complete securing a heavy locomotive against the perils of sea passage. Courtesy Delta Line.

cost of a ship's time. This is a complex subject involving not only the tangible, out-of-pocket costs of ownership, such as wages, insurance, and fuel oil, but also the intangible "earning potential" of the vessel on her assigned trade route. To fix the earning potential, it is necessary to compute the actual demand for the services of the ship (represented by the number of tons of cargo offered at each port of call) as well as to estimate the number of voyages that could actually be made in the time saved by working after normal hours. Unless it can be shown that the shipowner derives a measurable gain, good management dictates that the vessel lie idle rather than pay laborers at the overtime rate.

Complete mechanization of the handling process—similar to that found in a soft-drink bottling plant—has not yet come to the breakbulk terminal, nor does it appear to be economically feasible to attempt to develop such systems because of the nature of general cargoes. Since packages are not uniform in size or in weight, they cannot be handled as are the bottles and cases in a bottling plant. In addition, stowage of vessels must be planned to give adequate stability and proper trim when the ship is at sea. The vessel's load changes from voyage to voyage. Only rarely is weight distributed the same way for two consecutive sailings. Additionally, packages must be stowed compactly belowdecks so that they will not be damaged when the ship rolls or pitches in a heavy sea. A major problem is to keep commodities that could cause damage to each other, such as marble and redwood, from coming into contact. Finally, lots of cargo must be segregated by ports and consignees to prevent misdelivery. So far, no mechanical installation with adequate flexibility, ruggedness, and economy has been devised to solve all these problems of cargo stowage.

Today, material handling of breakbulk cargo on the waterfront depends almost entirely on the cargo pallet. This invaluable piece of equipment is a light, double-faced platform of wood, usually 4 feet long by 40 inches wide. It is inexpensive considering the number of times it is reused. As cargo is received at the terminal, it is general practice to place the goods on pallets to build up a "handling unit" weighing one or two tons. This "palletized" unit must be moved by machine and is not broken up until the individual containers are removed for stowage in the ship.

The principle underlying the use of pallets is simple: it provides a more economical method of employing the resources of the terminal (space, manpower, and money). The greatest expense in terminal operations lies in the requirement to handle literally thousands of packages (bales, boxes, bags, crates, and loose items such as automobile tires) each day. By combining many packages into a single large handling unit at the time they are received by the terminal, then using a machine operated by one person to perform all movement within the terminal, obvious economies are effected. Concurrently, increased efficiency is obtained by the use of terminal shed space, always critically short of requirements, and better service can be rendered the shippers by reducing the time needed for either loading or unloading cargo.

Many ocean carriers have been able to convince shippers that this palletization and later the containerization of their cargoes should be accomplished at the warehouse or factory where the shipment originates. The shipper builds up and straps the load into a single unit that remains unbroken until the consignee receives it at the destination. There are notable benefits from this practice.

1. Individual packages are not subject to handling at the terminal, and therefore breakage and other types of damage are reduced, if not eliminated completely.
2. The opportunities for pilferage and loss of individual packages are minimized, especially if the entire shipping unit is enclosed in a protective cover. A sheet of heavy plastic serves the purpose very well.
3. Cargo checking by all parties is simpler, more rapid, and more accurate because fewer units have to be counted.
4. Economies of time can be effected at every transfer point.

Where pallets are used extensively in the terminal, a number of important determinations must be made by the manager. Roadways and passages for the forklift trucks are basic requirements, and space for them must be allocated first in the general layout of the shed. Then the load-bearing capacity of the shed's deck must be ascertained, and rules promulgated as to the number of tiers of pallets that may be permissible. The tiers will vary with the weight of the commodity piled on the pallet, and therefore guidance must be given to the labor force if structural damage is to be avoided. The nature of the packages in each pallet also will influence the number of tiers because the bottom pallets must be protected from crushing. If cargo is palletized by the terminal, then adequate quantities of pallets (often numbering in the thousands) must be kept on hand. Provisions for storing, repairing, and issuing or receiving pallets becomes part of the routine of cargo operations.

After completing these arrangements, it is necessary to select the sizes, types, and capacities of materials-handling equipment to be used in moving pallets economically and efficiently around the terminal. This machinery is expensive and only those units required should be procured, along with spares to ensure good maintenance.

Cargo on a breakbulk terminal is worked by hand with some mechanical assistance. The principal types of machines used in terminal operations in U. S. ports today are the forklift truck (sometimes referred to on the waterfront as the "hi-lo"), the mobile crane, and the tractor-trailer train. Of these, the forklift truck is the most versatile and most widely used. Traditionally, forklifts have been powered by either a gasoline or a diesel engine, but increasingly they are found with battery-operated electric motors to reduce environmental pollution and to enhance safety from fires or from carbon monoxide poisoning. The versatility of the forklift truck is amazing, and a competent operator can accomplish near miracles with it. It is able to lift its burden high in the air to stack it for storage, or it may deposit it on the ground.

The forklift most favored by terminal operators has a capacity of 2 to 5 tons and can lift as high as 7 feet. Alternate models also are available with lift capacity of 15 or more tons and a stacking height in excess of 16 feet.

The tractor-trailer train provides an excellent means of moving cargo over a considerable distance. It consists of a power unit or tractor (commonly known as a "jitney") that tows a train of two or more trailers loaded with either palletized or loose packages or sacks. Although it can be used to advantage in any terminal where hauling distances are rather great, it is most efficient where wide aprons extend beyond the sidewalls of the transit shed and trailers can be brought directly under the ship's cargo hook. Most authorities agree that the optimum benefit from this type of equipment is obtained where the design of the terminal includes both wide aprons and long travel distances. The train also is useful in moving cargo from the truck dock to a place of rest in the shed, then from that place to the ship's side. A forklift truck usually is needed to handle the pallets. Trailers at the ship's side are loaded or emptied by means of the ship's cargo gear.

Trailers are comparatively inexpensive, and large numbers are found in terminals utilizing the tractor-trailer system. The tractor, an expensive unit with a highly paid driver, should be kept moving as much of the time as possible. Ideally, a train of loaded trailers is delivered under the ship's hook and uncoupled from the tractor. The tractor then is moved to a point where it hooks on a train of empty trailers and tows them to the loading point, where another exchange is made between "empties" and "loads."

Pneumatic tires are favored for most materials-handling equipment, which is generally designed to provide maximum simplicity of operation combined with safety and comfort for the driver. Experience has shown that employee morale and efficiency decrease in direct ratio to operator fatigue.

A major problem in terminal operation is truck traffic. If large motor vehicles are permitted to enter the transit shed, roadways and turnaround spaces must be provided. Some terminal managers exclude trucks completely and receive and deliver cargo at the headhouse. By excluding trucks, maximum deck area is reserved for cargo. The forklift trucks and other motorized equipment of the terminal require only narrow alleys and can move more rapidly when they do not have to watch for moving trucks. If trucks are unloaded at the headhouse, maximum benefit is obtained from the labor of the people assigned to this job because they spend their working time on the truck line, handling cargo as fast as trucks can be put into position. Cargo is discharged from trucks to pallet boards or cargo nets and is taken directly to the ship for loading or is transported to the place where it is to rest until loading time. Goods are delivered to the trucks of the

Railroad passenger cars are unloaded at a gantry-crane-equipped open pier. The ship's whirley cranes and exceptionally large hatches are noteworthy. Courtesy F. J. Duffy.

consignees after being sorted in the transit shed and placed on pallets or in nets. Appropriate equipment is used to transfer cargo to and from the truck loading platform.

This same pattern of traffic control can be followed on the wharf. Instead of bringing trucks to the headhouse, they are driven to the loading platform that parallels, on the land side, the ship's berth. The shed is reserved exclusively for materials-handling equipment and cargo. An advantage the wharf enjoys over the typical finger pier is that trucks may be directed to the loading platform most nearly opposite the ship's hatch where the cargo is being worked. The movement of cargo is limited to the short distance across the wharf. This plan is especially successful where a wide, sheltered platform is provided at truck-bed height.

In ports where railroad lines extend to the waterfront, it is usual for the tracks to parallel the ship's berth. This arrangement permits railroad cars to be placed under the ship's hooks and their contents to be transferred directly into the hold of the vessel. Conversely, the goods carried in the ship may be discharged into waiting railroad cars. Terminal management techniques for operations of this sort are the same as for lighters bringing cargoes to the offshore side of the ship. Delivery of cargo by railcars to be "spotted" at the ship's side must be scheduled to conform to switching schedules of the railroad. Many terminals have their own means of moving cars after they are spotted on the tracks. Where no method of moving cars is provided by the terminal, the railroad company must be requested to make a switch locomotive available.

Whether thinking in terms of people or machines, the terminal manager has to remember that working cargo is the sole reason for the organization. Ideally, the terminal manager or a skilled representative takes part in forming the plans for receiving cargo, whether it is unloaded from ships or brought to the terminal for movement overseas. The assignment of precise locations for designated lots of outgoing cargo usually is a function of the stevedore superintendent, who recommends to the terminal manager certain patterns for laying out the transit shed. This layout is planned to ensure sufficient space in the shed for those goods to be discharged from the ship and most likely held for several days before delivery. When the terminal handles cargo in only one direction, either outgoing or incoming, it may be possible to assign permanently certain spaces in the shed for cargo for each port of call. This arrangement is satisfactory where the quantity of cargo moving does not vary greatly from voyage to voyage, where there is not much pressure resulting from frequent arrivals or departures of ships, and where floor space so assigned and not used can be spared.

A more flexible plan usually is followed in sheds where two-way traffic must be processed. Outbound requirements are ascertained from a study of the cargo booking sheets to determine how much space is needed to accommodate consignments to each of the ports of call. Examination of the incoming ship's cargo stowage plan and manifest reveals approximately how many square feet must be allocated to each of the major blocks of her cargo. With this information, the available space in the terminal enclosure can be assigned for most effective use. It must be noted, in this connection, that the layout must be adapted to any congestion that may exist in the transit shed because consignees of cargo delivered by earlier arrivals have not picked up their goods.

The actual layout of the transit shed necessarily depends upon its design. If the shed is long, narrow, and cluttered with many stanchions, there will be a significant loss of working area because of these stanchions. Modern terminal design provides for wide sheds with stanchions placed as far apart as possible in order for the available floor space to be put to the most efficient use.

Interior of a well-designed and well-lighted transit shed. Courtesy the Port Authority of New York and New Jersey.

A wharf lies parallel to the shoreline and is easier to work than a finger pier. It has two advantages over the pier: there is accommodation for ships on the one side only, and traffic has access to the transit shed at each end as well as at intermediate points of the wharf structure. The finger pier, as the name suggests, projects into the waterway at an angle to the shore. Ships usually are berthed on both sides, and some long piers provide moorings for two or even three vessels in tandem. Cargo operations in such circumstances are impeded because all wheeled traffic must enter and leave through a single gateway at the land end. A major cause of lost floor space in this type of installation is the need to provide clear areas where trucks can turn around.

The rule of thumb for the amount of transit shed floor space needed to work a ship's cargo is 9 square feet per ton. Ideally the shed should have only one level in order to use modern terminal and materials-handling techniques at their highest levels of efficiency. Wheeled vehicles of any description are able to move anywhere, and traffic control is comparatively simple. Routine inspection and inventory procedures are made easy. An important but occasionally overlooked gain in the desirable illumination of the working area may be obtained through the installation of skylights in the roof.

Safety is not limited to personnel; it can have considerable economic force when applied to cargo entrusted to the carrier. The ship operator is obliged to handle a consignment so that the condition at the moment of delivery to the consignee is no different from what it was when presented by the shipper. Unless it can be shown that the damage or loss occurred as a result of a cause for which the law grants an exemption, the carrier is responsible and must pay the shipper or consignee the agreed value of the goods. Often the settlement of a single claim for one broken article can absorb the profit earned on the transportation of several hundred tons of other cargo. The terminal manager must strive constantly to ensure that cargo moving through the terminal receives the best possible treatment.

Care of the cargo requires two things: skillful and gentle handling of packages to prevent even superficial damage and thorough inspection of packages to verify the condition in which the cargo is presented by the shipper to the carrier. The terminal manager must assume that the longshoremen and their supervisors are competent to handle the individual packages properly, and periodic inspections are made to ensure that no one deviates from approved standards of performance. The inspection of goods, it must be emphasized, is a task of utmost importance since the carrier will base any defense against a claim for damage or loss on the completeness and accuracy of the examination of each package. It is mandatory that the

receiving clerk and the staff of checkers are instructed in desired procedures, that inspections are performed conscientiously and efficiently, and
that adequate records of the inspection are entered on the dock receipt. The
same significance attaches to the careful inspection of cargo removed from
the ship. The delivery clerk is responsible for this activity. At the time the
consignee accepts the shipment, the condition of each identifiable unit
must be noted and appropriately recorded.

Checkers are very important in terminal operation. Usually there is a
checker assigned to each gang of longshoremen, and thus employment opportunities for checkers vary with those of the longshoremen. In those terminals where a ship is on berth practically all the time, a fixed number of
longshoremen and checkers are certain of steady employment. These "reg-
ulars" (or steady men) can be instructed in the terminal's procedures of
checking, and their integrity and accuracy can be established in fact. In
U.S. ports, additional checkers are obtained by notifying the longshoremen's union hiring hall. Although these casual employees are competent
to inspect, measure, and weigh packages, the accuracy and completeness
of their records may not always be in accordance with established terminal
practice. Furthermore, there is no satisfactory system for determining the
personal integrity of these individuals before they begin their work. This
aspect of operation poses a serious, recurring, and nearly insoluble problem in the economy of terminal management.

Checking cargo in a typically busy, two-way breakbulk terminal is of
the utmost importance. The carrier must inspect the cargo as it is received
and record any defects noted. In terminal parlance, this is known as "taking exceptions" and refers to the phrase in the bill of lading that cargo is
accepted for shipment "in apparent good order and condition, except as
noted hereon." The exception is the carrier's defense against the charge
that the damage was inflicted after the package was turned over to him or
her. Ideally, the shipowner should refuse to accept any damaged cargo and
should insist that perfect packages be substituted for damaged ones, or else
the bill of lading should be corrected to show the number of perfect packages actually received. Practice is short of the ideal, and the carrier may
have to accept packages that have already been damaged somewhat before
coming into his custody. The carrier is responsible only for damage in excess of that noted at the time of receipt of the goods. Unfortunately for the
shipowners, it often transpires that the shipper or consignee blames them
for damage that was sustained prior to the cargo's receipt by the marine
terminal. The more complete the carrier's record of exceptions, the better
will be their legal position.

"Taking exception": A cargo checker examines steel pipe on arrival at a marine terminal. Courtesy North Carolina State Ports Authority.

Efficient terminal management requires that notations made by checkers be accurate, definite, and complete. It is not necessary to define further the word *accurate*. The term *definite* refers to the identification of the particular item, the exact description of the damage, and the reason therefor, if readily detectable. *Complete* means that when the checker turns in the notation, there will be no need to seek further information. A few examples follow:

A bag of coffee is noted to be only partially filled ("slack"). Further examination shows that the sack has been torn and resewn. There is no ready explanation of how the bag was torn or when it was resewn. The checker's entry should be "SACK No. 4, torn and resewn. Stamped weight, 110 lbs. Actual weight, 78 lbs."

A sack of flour is observed to have a large brown stain on the lower portion of the bag. It is not possible to determine what damage has been caused to the flour. The entry should be "SACK No. 22. Water-stained, lower half, front of bag."

An unboxed automobile is discharged, and one fender is found to be scratched and dented. The entry should be: "Ford Sedan No. 332. Right front fender, deep scratch, 9 inches long, beginning 14 inches from headlamp, running diagonally to bottom beading. Small dent, 3 inches in diameter, on top of fender 8 inches behind headlamp. Paint not broken."

Efficient operation of a breakbulk cargo terminal requires care in planning each stage of activity, and nowhere is this more true than in the layout of the transit shed(s). The booking clerk keeps the receiving clerk informed as cargo commitments are made, so that adequate space may be allotted to handle the consignments to the different ports. In the case of a company maintaining a service to a number of ports of call—for example, through the Mediterranean, to the southeast coast of Africa, or to the Pacific coast of South America—not only must there be an area reserved for each port, but there must be a plan for properly segregating the various types of cargo destined to each port. The following categories must be segregated within each port space so that they do not contaminate each other:

1. Wet cargo (liquids in barrels or drums) to be stowed in the bottom of the ship's holds.
2. Long steel, timber, or other pieces to be stowed on the bottom or in the wings of the cargo holds.
3. Odoriferous or obnoxious commodities requiring special stowage.
4. Hazardous articles (acids, gases, inflammables, and explosives) that must be stowed on deck or in special lockers aboard the ship.
5. Packages containing commodities like lamp black, flour, and cement, which sift out and may damage other cargo.
6. Refrigerated or other perishable cargo.
7. Fragile goods, such as glassware.
8. Valuable packages requiring security stowage (this sometimes is known as "mate's cargo").
9. Heavy-lift items. Port equipment or the ship's heavy-lift gear must be used to handle this type of cargo, and therefore careful scheduling of details incident to the use of this specialized equipment is essential to eliminate lost time.

Of equal importance to the terminal for planning purposes is information concerning cargo on incoming ships. The quantity, nature, and disposition of the load must be known since storage space has to be provided within the terminal enclosure. When a considerable portion of the inbound cargo is to be transshipped into barges or lighters working on the offshore side of the vessel, there is an immediate easing of the requirement for accommodation in the transit sheds. If the cargo must be brought into the shed for sorting and delivery to consignees, suitable space will be needed. These arrangements depend upon coordination of all the divisions of the terminal to achieve the desired goal of expeditious turnaround of the ship.

It is interesting to note that the terminal manager has little control over the types or amounts of cargo being booked to the ships calling at the terminal. These decisions are made by the shipping company and the terminal is merely informed what cargo to expect. The only area that the terminal manager can control is the actual movement of the cargo through the terminal. This control, and the subsequent efficiency of the movement, is a function of proper space allocation on the terminal and proper balance between labor and machinery as dictated by management prerogative and labor contracts.

The receiving clerk ensures that outgoing cargo is so marked that everything for one port will be easy to locate in the holds of the ship. Usually this is accomplished by means of "port marks" or symbols applied to every box, bag, crate, or other container received for shipment. For example, Genoa might be designated by a red circle, while Istanbul would be symbolized by a green square. There are no fixed rules for port marks, except that they should be simple in design, distinctive, and easy to see. They may be affixed at the convenience of the terminal, sometimes in the transit shed and sometimes after the cargo is stowed in the ship. Affixing the mark after stowage makes it certain that it will be visible during discharging operations. Regardless of where or when the mark is put on, it must not harm the container and must not rub or wash off. Unpackaged articles such as lumber or steel are marked with a quick-drying paint; some bagged or baled goods on which painted marks are not practical are tagged, using the same color scheme as for painted marks.

Cargo discharged by the ship is picked up by the consignee on notification by the carrier that it is available. Normal routine of delivery is in accordance with the following pattern.

The truck driver presents the shipping carrier's delivery order to the gatehouse delivery clerk, who verifies that the papers are in order. The process includes obtaining clearances from the customs officers on duty and also ascertaining that all freight, terminal, and demurrage charges have been paid. If everything is in order, the driver is dispatched to the slot where the cargo is located. A checker will count the packages to ensure that the number matches what is designated on the delivery order. Discrepancies are noted and reconciled if possible. When the truck is loaded, the driver returns to the gatehouse and acknowledges receipt of the cargo; the truck is sent on its way.

A cardinal principle of terminal operation is that transit sheds will not be converted into warehouses. One device widely employed to accomplish this is to charge those consignees who are slow in picking up their shipments a punitive storage fee, called *demurrage*. In the United States, the general rule is that the consignee has five working days after the ship completes discharge during which to take delivery of the goods. After the expiration of this "free time," demurrage is charged on an accelerating basis. After two days, for instance, the rate is doubled; after four days, it is tripled; after five days, it is quintupled. A necessary corollary of the demurrage plan is the efficient operation of an inventory system that will reveal daily what cargoes have been left on the terminal beyond the allowed free time, and what packages have been picked up. An incidental benefit to the terminal operator is that the systematic examination of cargo piles within the terminal enclosure often uncovers items discharged at the port by mistake. A box destined to Baltimore that is removed from the ship in New York will be "short delivered" in Baltimore, and a claim will be filed. Locating the box in New York removes the basis for the claim. Occasionally a box previously reported as missing or lost will be found to have been placed on the wrong pile in the transit shed. Only as deliveries are accomplished is the missing package discovered.

To control the flow of cargo effectively and to establish a system for locating a 50-pound package in the midst of 15,000 tons of assorted commodities, the terminal maintains a variety of records. The first of these, in order of compilation, is the receiving clerk's *list of cargo received,* on which are recorded, by dock receipt numbers, the various consignments of cargo delivered by truck. A separate list is opened for each ship to be worked and stays open while that vessel is in port. When loading is completed and the ship is ready to sail, the list is closed. In appearance, the list is very simple since it shows only the serial number of the dock receipts in one column and the cubic footage and weights of the shipment in adjacent columns. In normal circumstances, it is used only by the receiving clerk to keep informed on what consignments have been brought to the terminal. It has no circulation outside this office.

A similar list for cargo delivered by barge or lighter is maintained by the receiving clerk. It differs slightly from the truck record, because it is the permanent notation of when the lighter was delivered by the harbor carrier, when work was started, and when the lighter was released to its owner. There is a column in this *lighter record* to show where the cargo is stored in the terminal or stowed in the ship, as appropriate.

Each morning at eight o'clock, the receiving clerk compiles a report of cargo work completed during the preceding twenty-four hours. A separate report is submitted for each ship and contains these details: number of tons of cargo booked into the ship, tons of cargo actually delivered by shippers during the day, tons loaded, and the quantity still to be worked. The *daily cargo report* also shows hatches worked, number of laborers engaged, actual time they were employed, and commodities handled during the period.

The daily cargo report can be used for many purposes; it is the basis for forecasts of commodity-handling speeds and the comprehensive record of the actual gang-hours required to unload and reload the ship. If there has been any period of *detention* (time lost from the cargo-working period), the length of the detention and the reason for it are shown. The state of the weather also is set down, as well as any unusual incidents that might explain the rate at which cargo was handled. The report provides information on both discharging and loading operations. It is circulated to the vice-president, operations, the vice-president, traffic, the freight traffic managers, and any other persons concerned with the data contained in this document.

The *wharfage report* is the inventory of all cargo on which demurrage is payable because it has been left on the pier beyond the allowed free time. It is compiled for each ship by the delivery clerk and shows for every shipment the commodity, consignee, marks, bill of lading number, and the reason for nondelivery. The report is made initially at the expiration of allowed free time and periodically thereafter as each demurrage period ends until the cargo is removed from the terminal.

When a vessel's discharge has been completed, the terminal manager gathers into one report all data relating to irregularities—cargo for which no documents are on hand and which investigation shows should have been delivered to another port. These are known as "over-carried" or "short-delivered" cargo. There will be consignments in which shortages have been noted. Inevitably there will be some damage; claims from consignees for restitution of the loss will follow. These data are assembled into the *over, short, and damaged cargo report,* commonly referred to as the O. S. and D. report. This document is of great value in determining the actual efficiency of the terminal and the carrier's operations, for it helps to pinpoint actual damage; it puts losses, overs, and shorts into their proper perspective; and it serves as a convenient means of notifying all other ports on the company's route that certain cargo is either missing or on hand seeking an owner. The O. S. and D. report is disseminated to the master of the ship, the terminals in every port of call, the claims department, the vice-presidents for operations and traffic, and the terminal's receiving and delivery clerks.

Terminal efficiency is generally gauged by the number of tons of cargo handled in one hour by a gang of longshoremen or, alternatively, by the total annual throughput. This rating is not based upon individual performance, nor does it show how fast or how slowly particular commodities are loaded or discharged. It does, however, set up a reasonable standard by which to compare terminals in a port and is useful in evaluating relative efficiency in the different cities where a ship owning company may operate general cargo

Derrick (whirley) cranes hoist palletized, bagged cargo. Note the wide apron of the marine terminal. Courtesy Port of Sacramento.

terminals. To be valid, comparisons must take into account the use of machines by the gang. All too often, expensive tools become simply effort savers. In the Port of New York, for instance, at least one forklift truck is required to support a gang, but the number of tons of cargo handled per hour is not much greater than it was when manpower alone was used.

The terminal manager depends upon the superintendent to supervise the actual labor of handling cargo to and from ships, upon the security director to take care of cargo while it is in the transit shed or the area immediately adjacent, and upon the receiving and delivery clerks for accurate performance of their duties. Without these assistants, it would be impossible to operate the terminal.

As can be imagined, operating a marine terminal is a twenty-four-hour-a-day job. The level of detail required to discharge and load a ship successfully is incredible; each detail must be completed accurately and on time in order for the terminal's objectives to be met. A key element in the smooth operation of a terminal is that all terminal workers realize they are an integral part of a special team whose task is necessary for proper growth and operation of international trade. For the individual member of the terminal team, it is gratifying to watch a ship sail on schedule and know that the part played by that person helped make the sailing possible.

CHAPTER FIFTEEN

The Stevedore Contract

Among the documents describing the duties and responsibilities of ship-owners and shoreside specialists, none is of greater importance than the stevedore contract. In its basic form, the contract describes what equipment, documentation, and information concerning cargo and vessel scheduling the shipping company is required to provide the stevedore and what equipment, labor resources, documentation, and other tasks the stevedore is required to provide the shipping company. In addition, all the rates and charges agreed to by both of the contracting parties are listed and described.

Prior to entering into any contractual agreement, each of the contracting parties must describe in detail exactly what is to be done or what each one is willing to do. Of necessity, this description must be much more complete than the shipping company's simple statement that it wants its ship(s) unloaded (or loaded, or both) in a particular port and the stevedore company's basic declaration that it will unload the ship for a specified price.

To begin the bid and negotiation process that leads to a formal contract, the shipping company, for its part, provides the stevedore with the following information:

1. The type(s), size(s), and detailed description(s) of the vessel(s) to be worked.
2. The frequency that the vessel(s) will be calling at the port, along with approximate arrival dates and times.
3. The vessel(s) berthing requirements (i.e., will the shipping company make berthing arrangements or will that be a task for the stevedore).
4. The nature of the cargo (i.e., dry-bulk, liquid-bulk, breakbulk, passenger, or container) and the quantity of inbound and outbound cargo anticipated.
5. A detailed description of cargo to be loaded or discharged, together with pertinent special instructions or requirements.
6. A list of the types, if any, of ship's cargo gear available to the stevedore, along with a list of gear that the stevedore is expected to provide.

7. The turnaround time desired.
8. A list of the specific cargo and billing documentation to be provided by the stevedore.
9. Terminal receiving and delivery services to be furnished by each contracting party.
10. The requirement that the stevedore provide liaison with U.S. Customs or other government agencies concerning vessel and cargo operations.
11. The requirements for any extra labor services (i.e., arranging for tugs and pilots, loading or discharging ships stores, cleaning holds, etc.).

With this information in hand, the stevedore can calculate the anticipated costs for services requested. If the stevedore is to provide the cargo-handling equipment and all gear used in the operation, the bid must reflect the investment in that equipment. If, on the other hand, the shipowner is to supply the cargo machinery, slings, nets, and other items of equipment, the stevedore's bid should reflect this arrangement.

A number of relatively fixed cost factors must be taken into account by the stevedore as the computations are being made. For example, the size of the longshoremen's gang cannot be altered by an individual contract, since it has been fixed by negotiation between the union and all of the employers of longshoremen in the port. The wages to be paid and the working conditions under which the laborers perform their tasks have a significant effect upon the rates to be charged for the cargoes handled. The stevedore's bid will depend on his knowing the amount of cargo and the total hourly costs of labor (including fringe benefits paid by the employer as well as actual wages, insurance premiums, and related taxes), then estimating as accurately as possible the number of tons of the commodity or the number of container moves that the standard gang of longshoremen can load or unload in one hour.

Once the cost analysis has been completed, the stevedore will submit the bid for the contract to the shipowner and begin the negotiation process to produce a contract that meets the needs of each party and is financially agreeable to both.

While contract clauses for different types of cargo operations vary by necessity, some language is common in most stevedore contracts used in major U.S. ports. Typically, all stevedore contracts will contain the following general clauses:

1. Type of agreement (i.e., bulk cargo agreement, breakbulk cargo agreement, container cargo agreement, etc.).

2. Name and description of contracting parties and ships covered (in as much detail as necessary).[1]
3. Port(s) and/or terminal(s) where the stevedoring services are to be provided.
4. Contractor's general obligations.
5. Services provided (in minute detail to include which party is responsible for labor resources, specific equipment resources, documentation, etc.).
6. Applicable rates (including those set by current labor agreements, wages, benefits, additional charges for unique situations, equipment charges, etc.).
7. Safety and insurance requirements (including requirements for inspections, applicable safety organization, procedures governing injured workers, and liability and minimum insurance requirements).
8. Billing information (including rate adjustments and payment schedules).
9. Duration of contract.
10. Default circumstances and remedy procedures.
11. Miscellaneous clauses.

The following sections show clauses taken from standard stevedore contracts, setting forth similarities and differences in breakbulk and container cargo-working contracts.

SIMILARITIES IN BREAKBULK CARGO AND CONTAINER CARGO CONTRACTS

General Obligations. As part of the Contractor's general obligations, the Contractor agrees to provide the following:

a. A berth on a first-come, first-served basis for Company's vessels upon arrival.
b. Proper and safe mooring facilities such as mooring bitts, fenders, and bollards.
c. Adequate yard space for the purpose of receiving, delivering, and handling agreed-upon cargoes.
d. All necessary employees, labor, supervision, normal watching service; all necessary electrical power and all necessary equipment to perform the terminal services as described hereinafter.

Safety and Insurance. To reduce the risk of injury to persons and property during the Contractor's operations, and to ensure that each party may clearly understand its duties and responsibilities, it is agreed:

a. Company shall maintain and offer for inspection by Contractor prior to the commencement of cargo operations the valid cargo gear register and certificate, any amendments to the Safety and Health Regulations for Longshoring of OSHA, United States Department of Labor, or the Code of Federal Regulations. Both Company and Contractor shall be responsible for compliance with all other provisions of such safety and health regulations and any amendments thereto and with any other state or federal regulations which may be applicable.

b. Contractor, in accord with normal custom and practice, shall inspect and determine the safety of all work areas and of all gear and equipment to be used in its operation, whether supplied by Company, Contractor, or other person. Contractor shall not commence or shall immediately terminate its operations in the area involved until it has corrected any dangerous conditions and/or any unsafe gear and equipment which it has found to exist.

c. Contractors will supply Company with copies of all reports of accidents which occur during work on its vessels or which occur in the terminal and sheds, to the extent they relate to Company's vessel, cargo, equipment, or personnel.

d. Contractor agrees to maintain in full force and effect for its own account Worker's Compensation, Employer's Liability, and Longshore and Harbor Worker's Compensation Insurance in accordance with all applicable state and federal laws, Comprehensive Public Liability Insurance in the amount of one million dollars covering the Contractor's liability for bodily injury, including death, sustained by third parties, arising out of operations performed hereunder and five million dollars with respect to any one accident or occurrence, and Comprehensive Property Damage Liability insurance in the amount of five million dollars with respect to any one accident or occurrence.

Responsibility for Damage or Loss. The Contractor will be legally liable for damage to the ship and its equipment, and for damage to cargo, through its negligence. Contractor and Company shall each notify the other immediately after it should have become aware of any injury, loss or damage with respect to Contractor's operations so that each party can make a prompt investigation. In any event, notice of any claim for which a party may be liable to the other party shall be given to the other party in writing within thirty days of the injury, loss, or damage occurring, or if such time being uncertain, within thirty days of such loss or damage being discovered. With respect to claims for loss or damage to cargo and/or baggage, the liability of the Contractor shall be limited to physical damage caused by the negligence of the Contractor and to such claims that result from fraud on the part of employees of the Contractor engaged in the delivery, receiving, and watching of cargo.

Detentions. Whenever work is delayed or interrupted after starting and detentions of not over six minutes duration occurs, the Contractor will make no charge for reimbursement therefor. Should such detention time exceed six minutes' duration, the Contractor will charge for the full detention time at cost. When men are employed and unable to work through causes beyond the Contractor's control, or when men are to be paid for a minimum working period in accordance with the wage agreement, the cost of such waiting or idle time will be charged for by the Contractor at cost. Detention or standby time will be logged in six-minute increments.

Overtime. When overtime hours are worked, additional wages thereby incurred and paid to all labor and other stevedoring personnel so employed will be charged for by the Contractor at cost plus insurance.

Increase or Decrease in Wages. All rates specified are based on and subject to the employment of present longshore labor at the rate scale and working conditions existing in the port in the month of ___ 20___ under the local longshore contract, and prevailing port tariffs. In the event of an increase or decrease in such wage scale or change in the present longshore labor or working conditions, or changes in the port tariffs, the rates specified herein shall, as a consequence, be proportionately increased or decreased.

Billing. Company shall deliver to Contractor, within five working days of the vessel's departure, all documents which Contractor requires to bill for its services.

Payment. All payments owing hereunder by Company for services of Contractor shall be paid within thirty days of the invoice date. Any payments not received by Contractor within thirty days of their invoice date shall accrue interest from the thirty-first day at the rate of ___ per month. In the event that Company disputes an amount on an invoice issued by Contractor, Company shall give Contractor notice within ten days after receipt of the invoice by Company and shall pay the undisputed balance of such invoices in accordance with the payment terms of this agreement and shall negotiate with Contractor to settle such dispute.

Condition of Cargo. If the condition of the cargo or packages is other than in customary good order, thereby delaying prompt handling, special arrangements shall be agreed upon in lieu of the rates herein specified.

Acts of God, War, etc. No liability shall attach to either party to this agreement if the terms of this agreement cannot be performed due to acts of God, strikes, lockouts, slowdowns or other industrial disturbances, acts of public enemies, acts of a governmental authority, or any cause or event not reasonably within the control of such party who would otherwise be liable or in default.

BREAKBULK CARGO CONTRACT

Commodity Rate Inclusion.[2] As part of the foregoing specified rates,[3] the Contractor agrees to include in the commodity rate the following described services:

a. Transport Contractor's gear and equipment to and from the pier where the ship is berthed, excepting to locations that are inaccessible to motor trucks.

b. Provide all necessary stevedoring labor including winchmen, hatchtenders, tractor and dock crane operators; also foremen and such other stevedoring supervision as are needed for the proper and efficient conduct of the work.

c. Adjust rigging of booms and guys, etc., at hatches where work of discharging and/or loading will be conducted, and unrigging when completed; also removing and replacing beams and hatch covers.

d. Discharge cargo from or load cargo into vessels' holds, tween decks, on deck, shelter, or bridge spaces, deep tanks, cargo lockers and lazarettes, also temporary bunker spaces, but excluding fore and aft peaks and bilges.

e. Shift gangs as required between inshore and offshore, also from lower to upper floor (or vice versa) on double-deck piers. Shift lighters into working position after they have been placed alongside vessel, when this can be done without tugs.

f. Sort (by longshoremen) and stack cargo man-high on pier upon discharge of vessel or break down cargo from man-high upon loading of vessel.

g. Perform such long trucking as required within the limits of the pier where the vessel is berthed; limited to the section occupied by the vessel, should the pier have multiple sections.

h. Load and lay dunnage board (except freighted dunnage lumber) as required during loading for proper stowage of cargo.

i. Work two gangs simultaneously in hatches when required and when practical to do so, provided necessary additional booms, falls, and winches are supplied by vessel or from shore facilities.

j. Provide, at all times, attendance by an experienced stevedore superintendent.

Equipment. The ship is to supply booms and adequate winches, in good order and with sufficient steam or current for their efficient operation; blocks, topping lifts, guys; wire or rope falls of sufficient length and strength, hatch tents, lights for night work; tugs, derricks or cranes for such heavy lifts as exceed the capacity of the ship's gear, and cranes in the absence of ships' winches. The ship is also to supply dunnage, paper, and all material for shoring and lashing cargo as well as grain bags and separation cloths.

The Contractor is to supply all other cargo-handling gear and equipment, such as hooks, pendants, save-alls, nets, trays, bridle chains and slings (except slings for heavy lifts when hoisting by heavy-lift floating or shore derrick), also hand trucks, mechanical trucks or tractors, also dock tractor cranes as needed for efficient stevedoring work.

Receiving and Delivery Services. Contractor agrees to perform the following services on regular working weekdays, Monday through Friday, exclusive of holidays, covering the eight-hour shift, normally 0800 to 1700.

a. Receive and deliver cargo through the gates of the terminal to and from a point of rest in the transit shed or marshaling yard.

b. Inspect visually cargoes' condition at point of rest and report to the Company damage or defects, if any.

c. Sort cargo by port and/or consignee as required.

d. Mark cargo as required.

e. Plan layout of cargo at the terminal.

f. Handle all necessary security, sanitation, janitorial services, garbage collection and disposal service at the terminal.

g. Execute receiving and delivery documentation in accordance with the standard format used by Contractor, including:

    1. Cargo inventory report

    2. Dock receipt

    3. Undelivered cargo list

h. Provide liaison with the following organizations in order to obtain all required permits and receipts necessary for the delivery, storage, and movement of cargo while in possession of Contractor:

    1. U.S. Customs

    2. U.S. Department of Agriculture

    3. Motor carriers and railroad companies

Extra Labor Services. When required by the Company to supply extra labor, the Contractor will render its charges therefor at cost plus 10 percent and insurance for the following described services: (a) handling ships lines and gangways; (b) cleaning ships holds; (c) discharging excess dunnage or debris; (d) tiering cargo on pier above man-high upon discharge of vessel or breaking down cargo on pier to man-high upon loading of vessel; (e) loading or discharging ships stores, material or equipment, mail, baggage, specie, bullion, livestock, animals, live poultry and birds; (f) carpentry or coopering work of any nature; (g) handling and placing flooring or timbers for heavy lifts or for use by carpenters; (h) services of Harbormaster for the berthing and unberthing of lighters; (i) lashing and shoring cargo; (j) bolting and unbolting tank lids; (k) battening down hatches when called upon to do so upon completing of the vessel; (l) rigging and unrigging heavy-lift booms and hatch tents; (m) supplying extra labor for any other services when authorized.

CONTAINER CARGO CONTRACT

Throughput Rate Inclusion. In consideration of the throughput rate and subject to the terms, conditions, and rates as outlined, the following services will be provided by Contractor:

a. Longshoremen, crane operators, foremen and supercargo; their wage, insurance, and tax and man-hour assessment cost.

b. Stowage of containers on board vessels in accordance with the instructions of designated agent or representative of the Company, preparation of preliminary and final container stowage plans, including stability calculations and summaries prior to the vessel sailing. Accuracy of stability calculation to be the responsibility of the vessel.

c. Load and discharge ISO fitted containers to/from vessel holds, decks, and other usual spaces for containers and transport such containers to/from a point of rest in the terminal.

d. Rehandle containers to and from the same vessel as directed by the Company.

e. Visually check and tally containers moving on and off vessels.

f. Initial and final opening and closing of all ISO fitted hatches, including dogging and undogging within the capacity of gantry cranes, as required.

g. Lash and unlash containers using appropriately certified lashing equipment supplied by the Company.

h. Provide stevedoring documentation in standard format used by Contractor, including the following:

    1. Unloading and loading container report

    2. O. S. and D. reports

    3. EIR

    4. CLP supplied by customer and completed by trucker or shipper.

    5. Outbound vessel stowage plans

    6. Dangerous cargo manifest

    7. Reefer container manifest

    8. Container and chassis inventory reports

    9. Stowage plan

Equipment. The Contractor shall provide container gantry crane(s) suitable to handle ISO fitted containers and hatch covers of Company's vessels.

Receiving and Delivery Services. Contractor agrees to perform the following services on regular working weekdays, Monday through Friday, exclusive of holidays, covering the eight-hour shift, normally 0800 to 1700:

a. Receive and deliver containers and chassis through the gates of the terminal to and from a point of rest in the container yard; includes setting up containers onto chassis at time of delivery to inland carrier and decking containers on ground upon receiving containers from inland carrier.

b. Do visual inspections of condition of containers and chassis at the gate and report to the Company damage or defects, if any.

c. Plug and unplug refrigerated containers in container yard and read and record the temperatures of loaded refrigerated containers in the terminal in accordance with the Company's instruction; limited to three times per straight-time day.

d. Pretrip (inspect) and precool refrigerated containers per schedule.

e. Weigh export containers and report the results to the Company.

f. Check container security seals and reseal if necessary.

h. Plan layout of containers at the terminal.

i. Handle all necessary security, sanitation, janitorial services, garbage collection, and disposal services at the terminal.

j. Execute receiving and delivery documentation in accordance with the standard format used by Contractor, including the following:

    1. Container inventory report
    2. Equipment interchange receipt
    3. Undelivered container list

k. Act as liaison with the following organizations in order to obtain all required permits and receipts necessary for the delivery, storage, and movement of containers while in possession of Contractor:

    1. U.S. Customs
    2. U.S. Department of Agriculture
    3. Motor carriers and railroad companies

Extra Labor Services. When required by the Company to supply extra labor, the Contractor will render its charges therefor at cost plus 10 percent and insurance for the following described services: (a) handling ships lines and gangways; (b) cleaning ships holds; (c) loading and/or discharging containers requiring special handling; (d) loading or discharging ships stores; (e) discharging loose cargo resulting from container damage aboard vessel and loading or discharging breakbulk cargo work of any nature; (f) supplying extra labor for any other services when authorized.

Many companies have standard contract forms along with worksheets listing items to be included or excluded from the rates structure. The use of such forms, along with more detailed cost information available because of the advances and integration of computer technology, has simplified the contracting process and has allowed it to proceed at a faster pace.

In a highly competitive industry partially dominated by factors beyond the control of the contractor, the methodical determination of stevedore costs is of immense importance to both the shipowner and the contractor. The more each party to the contract understands the problems of the other, the more likely it is that the final agreement between the two will be fair and reasonable.

CHAPTER SIXTEEN

Containerization and Its Impact on Transportation

As technology advanced to the point where increasingly heavier loads could be handled easily and quickly, material handling "shifted" paradigms. An earlier chapter described the complex operation of a breakbulk marine terminal. Traditionally, packaged goods were received at the terminal by dockworkers who loaded the packages on hand trucks and trundled them to the place of rest to await moving to the ship's side. The actual process of hoisting cargo from a dockside platform to the ship's deck was no different from that used by the Phoenicians except that steam or electric power had been substituted for human muscles. The individual packages were stowed by hand in the appropriate spaces in the ship. The whole operation was infinitely laborious and consumed much time for which the ship was not paid, for a ship earns money only when at sea actually moving cargo from one point to another.

The great expense of this activity was always of major concern to senior executives, terminal managers, stevedore superintendents, and ships officers, and over the years many suggestions were offered to improve the traditional practices. There was, for instance, the logical proposal that cargo piled on pallet-boards should be strapped to permit each loaded pallet to be placed aboard ship as a single unit. Out of this concept of unitizing cargo developed the thought of placing certain types of cargo, especially fragile items, in large boxes that would be transported to the overseas destination without rehandling the contents.

The use of containers in the movement of goods dates as far back as 1911. Then, several commercial enterprises engaged in the packing, crating, and shipping of household goods began to stow these valuable items in heavy steel boxes for intercity movement by rail. Overseas shipment of household goods in these steel boxes was occasionally accomplished, but in each case shipment was a matter of a series of disconnected movements arranged for and supervised by the shipper. As for the carriers, the container was nothing more than an oversized and sometimes excessively heavy unit handled as any other package would be. The number of these shipments in containers was small and cannot be considered as anything more than a minor part of conventional breakbulk carriage.

About 1935, the forklift truck was introduced to the marine terminal. Its use required that packages be piled systematically on a pallet so that the truck could fit its forks under it and lift it before transporting the load to any designated point. So successful was this development that the hand truck disappeared from the waterfront within a few years, and a new technique of handling unitized lots was adopted.

Immediately following World War II, Great Lakes businessman Leathem D. Smith developed a steel "container" approximately 8 feet square and almost 8 feet high. Smith was concerned with the persistent problem of containers: the return voyage, usually without any cargo, involved substantial expense to the owner of the container. To reduce this back-haul cost, Smith's containers were intended to be folded so they would measure only 8 feet square by approximately 3 feet high. Unfortunately, the rough handling given to the boxes made the folding feature unworkable, and that idea was dropped.

However, the idea of stowing certain commodities in containers for transportation by ship began to spread widely. Great Britain, Denmark, Belgium, the Netherlands, Germany, and France were the western European nations where the practice received greatest attention; concurrently, there was some increase in the use of containers in the United States. The boxes varied in dimensions according to the notions and experience of the carriers who owned the equipment and made it available to shippers. Generally, the containers were small, ranging in capacity from about 4 to 10 cubic meters (5 to 15 cubic yards). Shippers who had sufficient goods to fill a container were sometimes given the option of having the container sent to their premises for loading, or delivering their cargo to the marine terminal where the carrier's personnel stuffed the container. By 1949, it was common for a ship to sail with the square of one or more hatches filled with these steel boxes. Because of where they were stowed, these containers were the last packages to be placed aboard ship and the first to be taken off, thereby shortening total transit time for the goods—an immediate advantage to shippers.

In the United States, the Alaska Steamship Company and the Bull Line, operating respectively out of Pacific northwest and Atlantic northeast ports to noncontiguous U.S. possessions, were among the leading advocates of containers to reduce ship turnaround time. Alaska Steamship used metal boxes in 1949, added what it called "collapsible cargo cribs" in 1952, and began carrying loaded trailers aboard its seagoing ships in 1953.

The cribs were developed from the standard wooden pallet and consisted of a base with lattice sides and a plywood top; capacity was 1.68 cubic meters. Cribs were made available on request to shippers who could pack and strap them. If they were received by the terminal in this condition, they were delivered to the consignee in that same condition.

The Bull Line commenced its experiment with containers about the same time as Alaska Steamship. Because shippers to Caribbean destinations often used packaging for their goods that was too light to withstand the rough handling involved in movement by ship, the carrier was interested in finding methods to reduce the inevitable damage. Large steel boxes in which the fragile cartons could be stowed appeared to be one solution. In time, the company developed a box of 19 cubic meters capacity. Later, a larger unit was devised that was 4.6 meters long, 2.4 meters wide, and approximately 2.4 meters high. These dimensions were suggested by the need to fit two boxes on a standard flatbed truck-trailer, which was 9.75 meters long. These containers, which Bull Line called "vans," were stowed in the holds of conventional breakbulk ships. Their handling below decks was simplified by casters permanently fitted at the corners and by rugged frames that permitted lifting by forklift trucks.[1]

The stowing practices noted in the preceding pages were the results of efforts to improve the techniques of marine terminal operations and by that to reduce the time required to discharge and reload a conventional breakbulk vessel. Concurrent with this objective was the desire to reduce cargo loss and damage in order to cut down on costly claims by shippers for lost and damaged goods. The containers used by shipowners at this time rarely, if ever, left the terminal premises. Shippers apparently preferred to send their offerings to the terminal where, at the discretion of the superintendent, they might be stowed in a container or they might be put aboard ship as individual packages. An essential component in the structure of the unitization evolution was the introduction of the integrated transportation system.

THE INTEGRATED TRANSPORTATION CONCEPT

April 26, 1956, was a rainy, cold day in Port Newark, New Jersey, not unlike many other spring days in the New York area. The departure for Houston, Texas, of the partially converted World War II vintage T-2 tanker *Ideal X* was very much a routine affair except for one thing. That one thing was destined to change transportation practice around the world, but at the time it was not recognized as being of any real significance.

As Malcom P. McLean waved farewell to his ship, he could not have been aware that he was initiating a revolution in transportation that would have as great an impact upon that business as did the coming of steam propulsion. McLean was watching the first movement of cargo in which carriage by truck and ship was purposefully combined to form an integrated transportation system. The achievement of McLean lay not in the mechanics of the operation but in the wholly new approach to relating diverse modes of transportation to each other and to the shipper. What had been a series of disconnected haulings by rail, highway, and waterborne equipment was converted into a coordinated and mutually supporting procedure that made the most efficient and economical use of the potentials and capabilities of the different modes.

Very briefly described, McLean's new approach modified the standard 35-foot-long highway trailer used by trucking firms in the United States to permit the cargo-containing box (which almost immediately came to be called simply the "container") to be separated from the chassis. Most important to the whole scheme was the fact that a single contract of affreightment covered the entire movement from the shipper's loading dock to the consignee's warehouse.

The "container revolution," as the McLean conception of an integrated transportation system was named, originated in the mind of a man who had spent more than twenty years in the intercity trucking business, building up his enterprise until his big trucks linked many cities in coastal states between New York and Florida.[2] He was well aware that a large portion of what was hauled in his vehicles came from shippers who filled trailers with goods consigned to single addresses. Systematic analysis of this one-shipper-to-one-consignee business revealed that there was a substantial proportion moving between those cities along the Atlantic and Gulf coasts that had good facilities for handling oceangoing ships. Furthermore, it was learned that a considerable quantity of other cargo came to or went from points some distance inland from these port cities. It was clear, therefore, that if the means were developed to carry the trucks by ship along the coasts and simultaneously to simplify the paperwork involved in a multimodal system of transportation, at least some of the complexities that bedeviled the interstate movement of merchandise by truck might be alleviated.

As a possible answer to the dilemma, McLean remembered earlier proposals to put trailers aboard ships built expressly for the purpose. The ships themselves resembled in many details a single-deck garage. Once loaded, the relatively high-speed ships were to proceed to major coastwise

ports where truck-tractors would be waiting to haul the trailers to their
destinations. Preliminary considerations of these schemes intrigued the
veteran trucker, who directed his staff to make detailed studies of the proposals, including careful financial analyses. A consulting naval architect
was commissioned to draw preliminary plans for the "floating garage"
ship and to discover its performance capabilities.

The economic analyses revealed some startling facts that dampened
the enthusiasm of the champions of the garage ships. Although the trailers
could be rolled on and off the vessels in a very short time and port turnaround therefore was at the optimum, too much of the available space in
the ship was absorbed by the nonrevenue-producing chassis of the trailers.
After all, only the goods *inside* the container were charged for transportation. Identifying the problem suggested the solution. The containers must
be separated from the chassis and loaded aboard ship in no more time than
the roll-on process required.

McLean redirected the energies of his staff to devise the means to accomplish the goal envisioned by the economic analysis. The first move
was to initiate technical discussions with the trailer manufacturer, who was
asked to create a new type of highway trailer. This new unit was to consist
of a flat-bottomed box strengthened vertically to withstand stacking, reinforced longitudinally so that it could be lifted by a crane when fully
loaded, and capable of being quickly separated from, or connected to, the
chassis. The next step was to put aside the proposal for a garage ship and to
concentrate upon the design of a ship to accommodate the specially constructed container.

It became obvious at this point that a full-scale test had to be conducted to determine the reaction of the shipping public to the innovation.
This meant acquiring ships to transport the containers. Because they would
be operated in the coastwise trade, certificates of public convenience and
necessity from the Interstate Commerce Commission were essential.[3] To
design and build container-carrying ships was a multiyear project, entail-
ing a very large investment while the process of obtaining original certificates from the commission was a tedious and protracted undertaking. With
what proved to be characteristic boldness, McLean solved the problem by
purchasing the seven-ship fleet of the Pan-Atlantic Steamship Company, a
subsidiary of the Waterman Steamship Corporation of Mobile, Alabama,
which held valid certificates for operation in both the coastwise and the
intercoastal trades.[4]

The conventional breakbulk cargo carriers obtained in his bold move
were not adapted to McLean's new idea. Rather than delaying the test until

A container is lowered to its cell in the *Gateway City*. Courtesy Port Authority of New York and New Jersey.

the ships could be converted, four standard T-2 tankers built during World War II had spar decks installed above their main decks. The containers were secured to the spar deck for the ocean voyage between New Jersey and Texas. McLean and his technical staff thus capitalized upon a wartime expedient devised to transport fighter aircraft to the European theater of combat—a steel skeleton deck had been built above the tanker's main deck so the aircraft could be lashed to this structure. The only difference between the two conceptions was that the McLean spar deck was solid, with sockets inserted at appropriate locations to accept the legs of the containers and to lock the boxes to the deck by means of devices built into the socket-leg combinations. The payload of each ship's "suit" of 58 containers was about 1,160 tons.[5]

The two potential obstacles to the development of this idea having been removed by the acquisition of the certificates of convenience and necessity and by the purchase and modification of the four tankers, McLean was free to devote his energies to working out the details of moving the containers to and from shippers and consignees. Getting the container to the ship for loading was simple enough; it was more of a problem to ensure that there would be a chassis and a truck-tractor awaiting each container when it was lifted off the ship by the dockside crane. By a series of contracts with truckers, these details were brought completely under McLean's control. At last, he could solicit business based on a single bill of lading that applied to the entire movement from the point of origin to the final destination of the goods no matter the number or type of participating carriers.

To Malcom McLean, therefore, must go full credit for conceiving and developing the integrated transportation system. An examiner on the staff of the Interstate Commerce Commission included this comment in his recommended decision submitted to the full commission on November 27, 1956:

> Malcom McLean is pioneering in the integration of sea-land transportation and in the application of the latest technological developments. A man of vision, determination, and considerable executive talent, he is making a valuable contribution.[6]

Anticipating at this point the development that came about later, it is appropriate to observe that, in time, a more complex interchange was arranged. The container was stuffed and sealed by the shipper who directed the drayman to haul the trailer to the railroad yard. There the container was transferred to a flatcar on which it moved from the inland city to the seaboard. When the flatcar reached the seaport, the container was shifted to a chassis and towed by a truck-tractor to the ship's side. In this manner, the most efficient use of three distinct methods of transportation was made without costly and time-consuming rehandling of the goods. This combination of complementary modes of transportation eventually was designated as "intermodal transportation."

Traditionally, the over-the-road trailers would have been unloaded in the transit shed of the terminal, and the separate packages would then have been moved to a consolidation point before being taken to the side of the ship to be hoisted aboard and stowed in the appointed cargo space. McLean's procedures bypassed this time-honored routine by bringing the container directly under the crane and hoisting the entire box, unopened, aboard ship. In five minutes, some 40,000 pounds of revenue cargo would have been shifted from a highway vehicle to a seagoing vessel. To the farseeing observer, the implications were tremendous.

To appreciate fully the loftiness of this stroke of commercial genius, it is necessary to sketch, in a highly oversimplified manner, the whole procedure involved in what was known technically as "breakbulk carriage" and what later was called "conventional" handling of seaborne goods. For convenience, a single crate of electronic equipment will be followed as it moved from Grand Rapids, Michigan, to the inland city of Tours, France, about 100 kilometers from Paris. The same pattern of activity was followed for a thousand packages, whatever their contents, if each package could be identified.

The shipper crated the electronic equipment with great care to ensure its safe delivery despite the many handlings that lay ahead. The first movement was by truck from the warehouse to the railroad yard in Grand Rapids, where the crate was transferred to a boxcar for the trip to New York. On arrival at that point, the crate was removed from the boxcar and placed in a truck to be carried to the marine terminal. The truck was unloaded at the ship operator's transit shed, and the crate was shifted to a place of rest where it waited until time to be loaded in the ship. At the designated moment, the crate was picked up by a forklift truck and brought to the ship's side. It was hoisted aboard the vessel and lowered into the hold. Dockworkers set it securely in its predesignated place where it remained until the unloading process began at the port of Le Havre. What happened until the crate was delivered to the consignee in Tours was the reciprocal of what had occurred between Grand Rapids and New York. At least eleven handlings were needed from the moment the crate was placed in the shipper's truck until it was taken into the consignee's warehouse. It is unnecessary here to expand upon the expenditure of time and money and the possible damage to the crate and its contents that this multiple handling entailed.

McLean saw a means of simplifying the process. When the shipper loaded the container and then sealed it, a bill of lading was filled out, certifying to the carriers concerned that certain items, and only those items, were within the box. So long as the seals were not broken, McLean reasoned, the shipper's declarations were binding, and no verification was needed. All documentation required by the ship operator therefore could be in terms of the big box, considered as a single package. Instead of four inspections of each individual package, there would be one when the container was received at the marine terminal and one when it was released to the consignee's drayman. Labor, money, and, above all, precious ship's time would be saved.

Shippers responded with enthusiasm to McLean's new development and provided the empirical proof of what would be required for further

Package Handling Process

Breakbulk operation

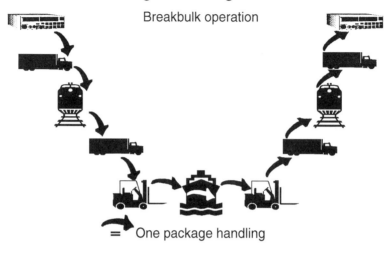

= One package handling

Container operation

growth and evolution to occur. To be profitable, however, at least two hundred loaded containers had to be transported on each trip. This was beyond the capabilities of the spar deck tankers. New construction was deemed unwise at this stage of the fledgling shipping company's existence, and therefore conversion of existing ships was the only alternative.

George G. Sharp, an American naval architect, planned the conversion of the ships acquired from Waterman. At a cost of approximately $3.5 million each, the ships underwent a major reconstruction. All interior bulkheads and decks were removed, and weather deck hatch openings were enlarged to a uniform length to accommodate the 35-foot-long containers. The cargo spaces were fitted with an elaborate steel framework to form cells into which the containers were lowered and stacked one atop another to a depth of five units. Two additional tiers of containers could be carried on deck. By installing a 30-ton gantry crane forward of the midships house and another abaft this structure, the ships were made self-sustaining and could be sent to any port that had a dockside apron wide enough to permit a truck-tractor to maneuver a chassis on which to place the container. Powered by diesel-driven generators, the cranes traveled up and down on tracks laid on sponsons built on each side of the hull for a total additional width of 9 feet. Each crane had arms that, in port, projected about 20 feet over the side of the ship; when the vessel was ready to sail, the arms were folded down to touch the hull.[7]

When the ships were initially placed in service in the coastwise run from New York to Houston, Texas, they astounded observers by the rapidity with which a full cargo of inbound containers could be removed and replaced by a complete set of outbound boxes. In 1958, a newspaper report noted that only fourteen hours of ship time were needed for this procedure, and together 42 dockworkers were hired, compared with about 126 for a breakbulk vessel.[8] Admittedly, the ship operator could economize on cargo-handlers' wages, but the more important saving was in ship time. The hours a ship spends in port working cargo are not revenue-producers. By reducing cargo-handling time from the eighty-four hours needed for breakbulk operation to the fourteen used to handle the containers, the number of ships required to maintain a specified frequency of service on a given route was reduced significantly.[9]

With experience, the McLean management team learned that equipping each ship with gantry cranes, while it made possible calls at ports that lacked the facilities needed to handle containers, resulted in more drawbacks than advantages. The cranes were idle while the ship was at sea; they were very heavy and therefore reduced the tonnage of cargo that could be carried; they added greatly to the cost of shipbuilding; their presence aboard ship restricted the load of containers to two tiers on deck; and the maintenance of the cranes was an expensive aspect of ship operating cost. On the other hand, dockside cranes were larger, faster, and easier to maintain, and they could be used continuously, serving one ship after another. Although the land-based cranes were purchased and installed by the operators of the ports (usually public bodies like the Port Authority), their great cost—the first ones were acquired for one million dollars each, and later versions were priced at least four or five times higher—was reflected in the dockage fees charged to ships for the berthing spaces they occupied. These increased charges, however, were less than the investment required to provide cranes aboard every ship. All of McLean's later ships, both conversions and new construction, were designed to depend upon dockside cranes. Worldwide, containership operators have followed this precedent almost without exception.[10]

As an inducement to shippers to use the new method of transportation of goods by sea, McLean made the specially designed containers available

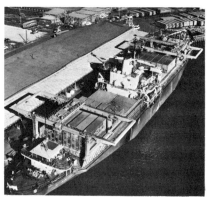

Top left: A container goes aboard the *Ideal X*. Note the "feet" to fit into securing sockets. *Top right:* Spar deck of the *Ideal X*. *Bottom left:* Containers are secured to the spar deck. Note sockets for securing containers' "feet." *Bottom right:* The *Gateway City* was the first ship converted to carry containers in cellularized spaces. Her gantry cranes made her independent of port facilities. Courtesy Port Authority of New York and New Jersey.

to his customers. This expense was required by the fact that the standard over-the-road trailer used by American trucking fleets did not have a detachable box, nor was it built with the reinforced corners required for stacking the boxes aboard ship. McLean vessels, therefore, loaded and carried only McLean-owned containers. This was the reason why the containership operators initially assumed full responsibility for procurement, maintenance, and control of containers, and only those boxes that belonged to, or were leased by, a particular shipping company were transported by that company. The financial burden imposed upon the shipowner may be gauged by the fact that when McLean sold his interest in the shipping company in 1969, the inventory listed 27,000 containers that cost about $3,500 each—an investment conservatively estimated at nearly 100 million dollars.

It was not long after the maiden voyage of the *Gateway City* (the first ship converted to carry containers) that other operators began cautiously to explore the new methods. This excessively careful attitude was based in part on a number of factors: consideration of the capital investment required, changes in terminal operating practices and the resultant conflict with the longshoremen's unions over reduced employment opportunities, and possible legal problems connected with extending the carrier's liabilities beyond the marine terminal. It also reflected the conservatism characteristic of much of the ship-owning fraternity, which accepted change only after proof that what was proposed was both practical and necessary.

In fairness to operators in the international overseas trades, it must be conceded that conditions encountered on these routes were very different from those prevailing in the coastwise service between two U.S. ports. If the overseas area was well developed with internal highway and railroad networks, and the ports were equipped to handle the big boxes (which might weigh 25 tons or more), adopting the new method of integrated transportation was feasible. If, however, the overseas nation was still in the process of internal development, it would be a major error in judgment to convert to containers. Some operators were quick to perceive the long-range benefits of an integrated system. They ventured into the new era by modifying one or more hatchways so the ship could accommodate some containers while still retaining the capability to handle large amounts of breakbulk cargo.[11]

THE ECONOMICS OF CONTAINERIZATION

To understand the attitudes toward the novel system, it is appropriate to examine the following aspects of the economics of containerization:

1. The process of unitizing merchandise in the container was a logical step by carriers in their search for more efficient and more economical ways to handle cargo. This technique had several advantages: (a) pilfering the individual package was more difficult; (b) the time required to check the condition of individual cartons was reduced; (c) stowage in, and breakout from, the ship's hold was more expeditious and efficient; (d) the goods themselves were less susceptible to loss and damage; (e) the cargo operations could be carried out in almost any weather; and (f) individual packaging costs were less.

This load of the multimeasurement containers aboard the containership *Cape Hatteras* demonstrates how variable lengths of containers may be stowed. Courtesy Columbia Shipmanagement Ltd.

2. With containerization, the task of stuffing and stripping the container was transferred from the carrier to the shipper and consignee, thereby reducing significantly the shipowner's cost to check the condition of cargo when received and delivered. Additional benefits in which all parties shared were the allocation to the shipper of responsibility for proper stowage of the goods in the container, a marked reduction in the total transit time from warehouse to warehouse,[12] and the elimination of many rehandlings of the merchandise. When the container was turned over to the ocean carrier, all that was required was to inspect the exterior for evidence of possible damage and to establish that the original seal attached by the shipper was intact.

3. Handling individual packages of merchandise in the marine terminal before placement aboard ship and after removal from the vessel represented a major portion of terminal expense. By transferring this process and its associated costs back to the shipper and consignee of the goods, the ocean freight rate could be restated to reflect more accurately the actual cost of port-to-port transportation.

4. Containerization saved time by having cargo brought to the ship's side in boxes that could be loaded directly into the vessel. The benefits to the shipowner of the shortened stay in port have already been delineated. To the shipper, the reduction of the time needed to deliver the goods to the ultimate consignee meant receiving payment with less delay.

5. Marine terminals were made much more productive and efficient when they were operated around the clock, whatever the weather, whenever a ship was at the berth. This shortened the ship's turnaround time and by that effected savings for the ship operator.

6. The operation of a modern, well-outfitted container terminal required fewer dockworkers, checkers, and equipment, but remained a major item of shipowners' cost because of the large number of expensive machines needed to handle the containers. Straddle carriers, very-high-capacity forklift trucks, mobile cranes, and similar equipment were indispensable. Their operators, being especially skilled, commanded premium wages.

CONTAINER TYPES AND SIZES

Once the feasibility of the container movement had been proven in the U.S. coastwise trade, shipowners in the international services began to

A partial view of the enormous area of Port Elizabeth's containerized cargo terminal. Courtesy Port Authority of New York and New Jersey.

look with interest on the new method. For many reasons, including the entirely pragmatic one that there was a shortage of the proper containers, it was not until early 1966 that any regular transportation of containerized cargo was offered to shippers on the busy North Atlantic route.

From this 1966 beginning, the conversion to full use of containers for international shipping on the main trade routes was rapid and dramatic. The worldwide yardstick for determining the capacity of containerships as well as expressing the statistics of container traffic is the "twenty-foot equivalent unit," universally abbreviated to TEU. Containers loaded with dry cargo and engaged in international trade increased in numbers from a total of 2.1 million TEUs in 1970 to 27.6 million TEUs in 1990, with compound annual growth averaging 15 percent over the period. Further, projections for the year 2000 are for an annual volume of 40 million TEUs.[13]

To satisfy shippers' needs, carrier-owned and lessor-owned containers totaled approximately 9.2 million TEUs at mid-1995, an increase of 10.3 percent from mid-1994. Carriers owned 48.6 percent of the containers but their annual rate of increase is less than that of the lessors. The total world fleet of containers grew at a rate of 7 percent per year between 1995 and 2000, when the size of the container fleet was around 13.5 million TEUs.

A major growing pain of the container age has been the conflict over the size of the containers. When Malcom McLean began his operation with the sailing of the *Ideal X,* he modified, for shipboard stowage, the standard 35-foot trailer used by the U.S. trucking industry. As other steamship owners cautiously entered the new phase of seaborne commerce, they designed containers that seemed most appropriate for the trades they served. Before many years had passed, but well before the almost complete conversion of liner-service shipping to container transportation, there was a profusion of containers. All were 8 feet wide and approximately 8 feet high, but in length they ranged from 10 to 40 feet, although not in uniform increments. Boxes were 20, 24, 27, 28, 35, and 40 feet long. Each was excellent for a particular route, but as shippers began to accept the new method and to demand that their goods be moved in the big boxes on many trade routes, shipowners faced the gigantic problem of making containers interchangeable so that, as with railroad cars in the United States, Canada, and Mexico, cargo could be moved across international boundary lines without mechanical hindrance. Also, having uniform container sizes that were compatible with land-based transportation modes made more inland routes available to shippers.

In 1961, the International Organization for Standardization (ISO) strongly recommended that containers be designed and built to "standard" specifications. Many carriers adopted the idea. The basic ISO module was 10 feet; approved containers therefore were 10, 20, and 40 feet long and 8 feet wide by 8 feet high. Over the intervening years, the battle of size appears to have been won by the proponents of 20- and 40-foot units, and most of the containerships built today are designed to accommodate either or both sizes. The mid-1995 survey of the container fleet revealed this distribution of container lengths: 20-foot containers, 58.0 percent; 40-foot containers, 39.5 percent; 45-foot containers, 0.8 percent; 48/53-foot containers, 1.1 percent; and all other lengths, 0.6 percent.[14]

The latest trend in container sizes is to build them longer and higher, with correspondingly greater capacities. Containers are still being built with the same ISO strength specifications as for any container intended for marine use.[15] However, they are now being made as long as 53 feet, as high as 9 feet 6 inches (called "high-cube"), and as wide as 8 feet 6 inches (102 inches). The new high-cube 48-foot and 53-foot containers meet North American domestic specifications and are intended to compete more

A container is attached to the lifting frame of the massive shoreside crane. Courtesy North Carolina State Ports Authority.

efficiently in the domestic market. They are not seen on ships although they are built to ISO sea container standards.

To aid in the identification of containers, each container has a unique alphanumeric number. The name of the owner is encoded in a four-letter system preceding the number. The codes are generated by the Paris-based organization Bureau International des Containers and are known as *BIC codes*. In the case of American President Line, its containers are labeled APLU—the U stands for unit. The BIC is followed by a seven-digit number.

Below this unique alphanumeric number is a two-letter code signifying the country where the owning company is registered and, on ISO-standard boxes, a numeric four-digit code that signifies the size and type of container.[16]

Besides being built in various sizes, containers are designed to accommodate a variety of cargoes. There are dry-freight containers for the conventional cargo, dry-bulk containers for grains and other similar cargo, tank containers for liquid-bulk cargo, refrigerated/insulated containers for perishable cargo, flat-rack and open-top containers for odd-sized cargo or cargo that needs special handling, garment containers, livestock containers, automobile containers, and chemical-tank containers for specialty chemical cargo.

The question of making containers universally interchangeable between steamship lines and between ships and other modes of transportation (an essential element of intermodalism) has resisted rapid settlement. Pioneer containership owners had to buy their own boxes and make them available to shippers. Inevitably, they tended to load their ships only with goods packed in these company-provided containers. In overseas and foreign trades, the dispersion of containers to destinations quite remote from the ports at which the ships called quickly became a major problem. Significant losses of boxes were sustained by some operators, and elaborate measures had to be devised for tracing them. Some were discovered to be serving as warehouses for consignees, who explained that it was cheaper to take the goods out of the containers only as their counters needed replenishment than to empty the big boxes into warehouses and then shift the goods to shelves and sales racks. Other owners learned that the containers were used not only as warehouses but as the stores themselves. Often, in the more impoverished regions of the world, containers were converted into houses by cutting windows and doors into them and placing them on hard stands.

From these findings, complex and expensive systems for retaining control of containers were developed, but the high cost of buying, maintaining, and tracing the boxes has encouraged the formation and growth of companies with no interest except to buy containers and lease them to shipowners. The emergence of these entities has brought closer to fruition the dream of interchangeability, and attention now is directed toward forming "neutral pools" of containers. The term is a shorthand reference to those boxes owned by leasing companies which are used for one-way movements and then turned over to an agent. This functionary places the containers in a central collecting point where they form a pool from which individual units can be drawn to meet the needs of shippers within a geographical range of that central point. Because they are specialists in the procurement and management of containers used in world-wide trade, the leasing companies have devised elaborate, computer-based systems by which they can keep informed of the location of every one of their containers and chassis at any time.

There are three compelling reasons why shipowners, as their invest-ments in containers are amortized, will withdraw from owning the boxes and will depend entirely upon leasing organizations except perhaps for some very specialized containers that some customers may require. First, the new containerships are so expensive that little capital is left to the shipowner with which to purchase the required thousands of containers. Second, the need for interchange is growing day by day, and the folly of attempting to force shippers to use only carrier-owned containers is in-creasingly evident. Third, the requirement for tracking and balancing equipment is very expensive in terms of both labor and computer equip-ment. By using leased containers the burden of tracking and balancing is shifted to the leasing company.

One major user of containers complained that "empties" had to be re-turned to the shipowner within a fixed number of hours, but there would be a delay of a day or longer for the same shipowner to bring a container in which to pack the next outbound consignment. Said this traffic manager, "Sometimes my returning 'empty' passes the incoming container, which also is empty. It is a very wasteful and extravagant way of doing business."

Both shipping lines and shippers obtain their boxes from the pools maintained by companies specializing in owning and renting containers. Each container is acquired by the carrier for a definite, individual move-ment, and when the contents have been delivered to the ultimate consignee, the container is returned to the control of the pool. This is accomplished by the consignee notifying the representative that the container is empty and re-questing instructions as to the disposition of the box. If the consignee needs a container for an outgoing shipment and the just-emptied unit is satisfac-tory for the contemplated load, it is assigned immediately for that purpose. This eliminates the present wasteful procedure of returning the empty box to the marine terminal.

The neutral pool eliminates the need for miniature pools set up by two or more operators who agree to interchange their equipment. These smaller pools have limited resources and encounter problems in tracing, cleaning, repairing, and positioning the boxes. Operators of the neutral pools are experts in these areas and have the organization needed to handle them effectively and economically.

Neutral pools supply standardized equipment that is interchangeable among all ships and all modal carriers. Procedures for handling containers could be uniform in all parts of the world, to the benefit of shippers and receivers of goods. Local shortages could be eliminated; should there be an unforeseen demand for boxes, the neutral pool would have its huge resources on which to draw.

GLOBAL ALLIANCES

The financial burden that was suddenly thrown upon shipowners by the technological advance of containerization was immense and ultimately led to the formation of global alliances. New containerships not only cost much more to build than did the breakbulk vessels they were displacing, but they were capable of higher speeds and had significantly greater capacity. The duration of sea voyages was shortened and port turnaround time was reduced radically, contributing to the heightened performance of these big ships. In theory, one modern cellularized container carrier with a speed of about 26 knots and a deadweight of approximately 29,000 tons, carrying close to 2,000 20-foot containers, could transport the same quantity of cargo in a year that five or six conventional breakbulk ships could handle. Had it been possible to effect a simple reduction of ship numbers according to that ratio, it would have resulted in a reasonably satisfactory solution to many problems spawned by containerization. However, shippers had become accustomed to a certain frequency of service, such as one sailing a week by a favored operator, and looked askance upon any suggestion to change this to one sailing every third or fourth week. To harassed shipowners, this intractable attitude might have seemed most unfriendly, but in the end they acknowledged that, as always, the requirements of the shipper determined the nature of the trade. It was a case of satisfying the customer or going out of business.

To provide that satisfaction, shipowners were forced to accept the idea of building and operating whatever number of large, fast, high-performance, and extremely expensive carriers might be needed to give the service demanded by their customers. It worked out, in practice as opposed to theory, that the new fleet of very-large-capacity vessels would replace the older, low-capacity vessels in the ratio of one to three. Because the new ships were so much larger and faster than the older ships they replaced, the carrying capacity available to shippers increased significantly. In terms of potential revenue tonnage, there was only one interpretation of this fact: there was a great deal more capability (or cargo space) than there was cargo.

The obvious solution was the one adopted by many operators. They joined forces with one or more of the other carriers on the same trade route to form a sort of composite management of that number of ships that would be justified economically while still meeting the demands of shippers and consignees. For example, four owners could band together and each supply one ship to the association that was first called the consortium and later termed global alliance. Every week there would be a sailing, by that satisfying the shipping public while simultaneously ensuring revenue cargo adequate to pay the expenses of the voyage. Before any operators participating in the foreign commerce of the United States could become active in such an association, prior approval by the Federal Maritime Commission was required. As the relative cost of container shipping fell, individual lines started to pursue their own goals, except where necessary in specific trade routes.

An example of an early consortium was the formation in 1967 of the Atlantic Container Line. Three Swedish firms (Swedish American Line, Wallenius Shipping Company, and Transatlantic Steamship Lines), the Holland America Line (a Netherlands organization), the Compagnie Generale Transatlantique (a subsidiary of the French Compagnie Generale Maritime), and the Cunard Steamship Company (part of Trafalgar House, an English conglomerate) each contributed one or two ships of approximately the same size, speed, and characteristics to a new company in which the six operators had equal holdings. Denominated the Atlantic Container Line, this organization operated between European and British Isles ports and United States Atlantic Coast cities from Boston, Massachusetts, to Norfolk, Virginia. The first sailings were made in the fall of 1967, but it was not until some months later that the planned ten ships were placed on a 21-day cycle. Not all ships called at all ports, but dependable schedules for the different routes were set and maintained. A computer-oriented system controlling the loading and discharging of containers ensured that consignees could obtain their boxes with a minimum of delay. Full containers for a single consignee were ready for pickup not later than thirty hours after the ship arrived, while cargo shipped as part of a containerload and requiring more attention was available to the consignee less than seventy-two hours after the ship was berthed.

The new generation of containerships and the increased level of service demanded on the important east-west routes between the Far East, Europe, and North America require massive investments by the shipowners. The current growth of new alliances has resulted from major carriers trying to consolidate their position by reducing their cost per container without changing the level of service their customers demand. In 1996, there were three new Pacific alliances that captured 38.7 percent of the total container slots. They were (1) Maersk and Sealand with 13.4 percent; (2) Nippon Yusen Kaisha (NYK) Line, P & O Containers, Hapag-Lloyd, and Neptune Orient (NOL) with 13.5 percent; and (3) Nedlloyd Lines, APL, Mitsui OSK Lines, and OOCL with 11.8 percent.[17]

The essence of the consortium or global alliance is to substitute cooperation for competition, forming a long-term partnership in which the predominant principle is the good of each participant, replacing the frantic scramble by individuals for the greatest possible share of the available business. An association of this sort can be successful, however, only if the members provide equipment of substantially the same capability, and a single management handles the enterprise. Carriers are disposed favorably toward this idea in view of the enormous cost of setting up a complete container service (ships, containers, acquisition of appropriate terminal facilities, and the necessary supporting network of agents), to say nothing of the problems inherent in the training and oversight of qualified salespersons, office personnel, and supervisors at every level.

Success crowned the idea of the global alliance, if one is to judge by results. It proved highly practical on trade routes having a sound economic base and a reasonable balance between incoming and outgoing cargoes. Not every prospective alliance, it must be noted, can achieve its goals. Some associations were proposed but died aborning; others were put together with every prospect seemingly favoring the scheme but had to be dissolved in the face of insurmountable obstacles, many of which were not of the carriers' making. Still others began their existence with many operators but in short order were narrowed down to as few as two partners.

An alternate method used by shipowners to help control costs is the current practice of chartering space on containerships owned by other companies on the same trade route. This practice allows the shipowner to maintain its company identity and by that the recognition by customers of that company. At the same time it allows capacity to be increased without acquiring additional ships. The reciprocal of this practice also applies. Excess capacity on its ships is chartered out to other carriers seeking shipping space.

Global alliances and space chartering are important business strategies used by carriers to cope in a demanding and competitive market. These strategies are as dynamic as the business itself and in all likelihood will continue to change in the years to come.

CONTAINERSHIPS

Since the sailing of the *Ideal X* with her fifty-eight containers, ships de-signed to carry containers have changed significantly. In the late 1960s, the early purpose-designed containerships were built to carry between 1,200 and 1,300 TEUs. The ships were usually steam propelled and designed with cell guides in each hold for the easy loading and securing of the containers, hatch covers to protect the containers below decks from the weather and seas, and the capability to stack containers on deck on top of the hatch cov-ers. The containers on deck had to be secured with lashing chains, wires, or rods. These ships were designed with no cargo gear of their own.

By the early 1970s the demand for container slots on ships had in-creased to the point where carriers began to look for larger ships to take advantage of economies of scale. A new generation of containership was built that could carry 3,000 TEUs. These new ships were deployed in the Europe–Far East run. Because of the oil crisis in the early 1970s, steam propulsion became uneconomical and new construction was being fitted with diesel engines. Vessels that carried 3,000 to 3,500 TEUs effectively were Panamax size (50,000 tons) because of their length and particularly their breadth.

In 1988, American President Lines made a bold move and introduced the post-Panamax container vessel when it took delivery of a series of five 4,500-TEU ships built by HDW and Bremer Vulkan in Germany. Too large to pass through the Panama Canal, these vessels were limited in their abil-ity to enter different trade routes. Many companies had to decide whether to follow the lead of APL or stay with the smaller vessels. The answer came quickly; the post-Panamax size vessel became the standard for main haul routes.

By the mid-1990s, containership size had gone to 5,000 TEUs, and in 1996, Maersk Lines took delivery of the *Regina Maersk,* the first 6,000-TEU ship. At the time this ship entered service, designs were being drawn for a 15,000-TEU ship. While the technology is available to construct such a ship, major port problems are beginning to become apparent as these large ships are brought into service. The greatest problem will be port conges-tion.[18] These very large ships converge on load centers with infrastructures incapable of handling the tremendous numbers of containers brought into and out of the terminals in a very short time. The port authorities of these load centers, in the belief that there will be a steady increase in the demand for containerized cargo, are seeking techniques to deal with the problem. Until this is achieved, the capacity of containerships is restricted.

Besides the trend toward larger ships, there are two other noteworthy trends. The first is a rather significant design change—constructing containerships without hatch covers. This allows for faster discharge and loading, and it allows some added flexibility in the sequence with which containers are worked. The first ship without hatch covers was developed by Nedlloyd Lines and used in a series of 3,100-TEU ships and more recently in two 4,100-TEU post-Panamax vessels.[19] While safety regulators concede that these vessels are safe to operate at sea, cargo insurance underwriters are cautious in their outlook.[20]

The second trend is the construction of smaller sized feeder vessels with cargo cranes to work their own cargo. These more versatile container vessels will bring cargo from the smaller "outports" to the major load centers. This will allow the larger line-haul vessels to travel only between the major load centers where all cargo will be assembled.

THE BENEFITS OF CONTAINERIZATION

When international traffic of containerized cargo was introduced in 1966, there were many statements about the great benefits that would redound to the shipper. There also were predictions of new prosperity for shipowners. That these anticipations were voiced in sincere optimism and hope cannot be denied, but in the light of subsequent events, it must be admitted that the reality fell short of the dream. In fact, many lessons have been learned in the years since 1966. Among the most important are these:

1. Container services are of maximum benefit to exporters and importers when there is a two-way movement of goods. Only when the greater proportion of boxes are filled in each direction may the promised advantages of containerization be enjoyed. A corollary of this principle is that the benefits of container service accrue only on trade routes joining areas ready and able to receive and ship goods in the big boxes.
2. Maximum efficiency and therefore greatest economy in transporting containers can be attained only by employing ships built and operated for that purpose.
3. Containers used in intermodal movements must be of uniform, standardized design and sizes that can be interchanged worldwide as the flow of commerce dictates.
4. Essential to realizing the potential of containerization is the growth of neutral pools.

5. Computerized control of the entire container transportation system is mandatory. As the neutral pools become more common and use of their equipment grows more general, the need stands out for carriers to have not only the kind of data the computer can provide, but also to interchange information concerning the location, condition, and employment of individual containers. Thus EDI and AEI must be developed and accepted.

6. Contributing to the effectiveness of this computer-based system are the elements of the infrastructure supporting container services: third parties, container depots, maintenance and repair units to keep the containers in good condition, and the other associated activities.

7. Intermodal transportation is demanded by importers and exporters who seek the fastest and least expensive means of getting their goods across the oceans. They want not only the convenience and the rapidity of the landbridge, but they also seek a standardized contract of carriage enunciating the responsibilities of both shipper and carrier at every stage of transportation.

In summary, it may be said that the idea underlying the use of the container in the transportation of goods over the world's sea routes has spread because it met a need and facilitated international commerce. At the same time, it must be acknowledged that it created many new and unforeseen challenges, not the least of which was the enormous financial cost of the transformation of ships, ports, and techniques of business. The change has been as profound as that resulting from the development of efficient and economical steam engines for ships. Equally undeniable is that the concepts of handling cargo movements and patterns of sea-trade have been altered irreversibly, and in every sense a new era has dawned for all who use the sea as an avenue of commerce.

CHAPTER SEVENTEEN

The Intermodal Transportation Concept

As the complexities and tremendous potential of containerization became understood, there was a concurrent movement within the industry to capitalize on the inherent advantages of other modes of transportation to create an economical and effective system. This movement was given the name of "intermodal transportation."

Intermodal transportation is defined as a systems approach to transportation in which goods are moved in a continuous through-movement between origin and destination using two or more modes of transportation in the most efficient manner.[1] Intermodal includes the interchange of cargo between any mode of transportation no matter the state of the cargo (i.e., containerized, packaged, bulk, etc.). However, current emphasis is on the container as the package of choice due to its convenient interchangeability.

The purpose of intermodal transportation is to give shippers those routings that will result in the fastest and least costly carriage of their goods. A typical case might require the services of an intercity trucker to haul the container to a feeder-barge collection point, transit by feeder barge to the ship selected to take the container to a foreign port, then a railroad trip to an inland point where a trucker would accept the container for transportation to the ultimate consignee. There are no technical or mechanical difficulties associated with the process of shifting the container from one form of transportation to another as long as the container will fit into the designated cell aboard a ship, but initially, there was a legal problem.

The differences between deep sea and inland transportation were substantial enough to preclude immediate adoption of a truly uniform contract of carriage applicable to all parties involved in the intermodal movement. A uniform contract required the originating carrier to furnish the shipper its bill of lading, which placed upon that carrier full responsibility for any loss or damage sustained during the entire transit. By separate agreements negotiated between the carriers, the liabilities of inland carriers for loss or damage were established, and appropriate remedies were set forth to protect the shipowner in cases where the inland carrier might be found at fault.

Containers filled by the shipper ordinarily are not subjected to inspection when the carrier accepts custody. The description of the goods provided by the shipper must be accurate under a penalty of legal action. Unless the container is received in a condition that shows that some damage probably has been sustained, the carrier and the shipper agree that they will be bound by the contractual stipulation that the "package," i.e., the container, is "in good order and condition." The consignee is obligated to set forth in detail any damage discovered when the container is opened and may be invited by the shipper to prove that this damage was not the result of faulty stuffing.

Participants in an intermodal movement that crosses one or more national boundary lines must take notice of the rules and regulations applicable to their business. The shipowner and the parties responsible to the shipper must be well informed on these points; of necessity, the shipper depends upon the inland carriers for notification of any changes affecting the intermodal arrangements.

The shipper is interested only in three details: the party to whom claims should be presented for loss or damage during transit, the rapidity with which the container is moved from origin to destination, and the total cost of transportation. Intercarrier relationships are of no concern to the shipper, which helps to explain the pressure for a single, comprehensive bill of lading.

One obstacle to developing an intermodal contract of carriage acceptable to all participating carriers is the question of financial responsibility for loss or damage to the goods. Participants in the intermodal movement understandably are reluctant to become involved in claims actions when there is no evidence of their culpability. Added to this reluctance is the fact that in most circumstances the container is not opened while it is in transit, so the true condition of the contents at any given time is unknown to any of the carriers.

The following description of a hypothetical intermodal shipment of a container loaded by the manufacturer of high-grade porcelain tableware will illustrate the problem.

A consignment of 106 cartons of the finest quality tableware, valued together at approximately $200,000 and with some cartons worth as much as $5,240 each, was loaded by the manufacturer into a new and carefully inspected container supplied by direction of a shipping line operating from Oakland, California, to Honolulu, Hawaii. The purchaser demanded that the goods be sent by the fastest possible surface means. Pursuant to this instruction, the shipper's traffic manager decided to move the container by intercity trucking service from Trenton, New Jersey, to the railroad yards in Newark and thence overland to Oakland, where the transfer to a fast containership would be effected. Transportation was accomplished accordingly, with no external evidence that the container had been subjected to any forces that might cause damage or that it had been the victim of pilferage. Inspection of the exterior of the container confirmed the original statement by the initiating carrier that the container was in good condition, the seal unbroken, and the contents in apparent good order and condition.

When the container was delivered to the consignee in Honolulu, it was discovered that one carton, worth $1,000, was missing; a void space near the door of the container gave undeniable evidence that the cargo had been loaded. Two other cartons, each with a declared value of $5,240, had been crushed into rubble. These were loaded at the forward end of the container, and even if the doors had been opened by a carrier for an inspection, their condition would not have been detected. The total claim by the consignee amounted to $11,480, a sum sufficiently large to make it important for those not involved to prove their lack of responsibility for the loss and damage.

Inquiries were initiated by the shipping line as the delivering carrier. In the order of their contact with the shipment, these facts were assembled by the claims agent:

1. The manufacturer in Trenton stated in an affidavit that everything listed in the manifest had been placed in the container, that expert packers handled the stowage, that no careless or rough treatment was accorded to any of the cartons, and that the container had been sealed after a final inspection to ensure that all was in good order within the container.

2. The intercity trucker declared, also under oath, that delivery had been effected to the railroad yard in Newark without incident. The driver of the truck was identified by name and license number, and his record for safe driving was confirmed by the state police. Furthermore, the driver testified that he personally had examined the seal at the time custody was transferred to the railroad, and the seal had not been damaged in any way.

3. The railroad set forth in its notarized comment that the container had been lifted off its chassis by a skilled and dependable operator of a mechanically perfect crane, and there was no record of improper handling at the time of loading or unloading of the railroad flatcar. Examination of the train crews' reports did not lead to any conclusions that those cars making up that particular train had encountered any abnormal circumstances or had been treated in an unusual manner.

    4. The ship operator had its own records of the container from the time it was brought by the trucker who accepted it from the railroad until it was turned over to the consignee's drayman and he was cleared for departure from the Honolulu container yard. The external appearance of the container was satisfactory, and the condition of the seal corroborated the drayman's statement; there had been no basis for questioning the accuracy or veracity of the shippers description of the contents, and therefore the container had not been opened for inspection.

The determination of who was responsible for the loss and damage clearly posed a problem. Because of the high value of the claim and the unusually complete data relating to the transfers, placing responsibility on any one carrier was impossible. Negotiations among all the participants were conducted by the ocean carrier's claim department, and it was agreed that the consignee would be reimbursed by assessing each carrier an amount that was in direct proportion to the freight money earned.

The illustration has been simplified deliberately by keeping the entire transaction under U.S. jurisdiction, which permitted one of two solutions: (a) to initiate legal action in a U.S. court, pursuant to laws and regulations known to and binding upon all participants; or (b) to permit negotiations within the framework of the pertinent regulations. It takes only a little imagination to comprehend the practical difficulties resulting from an intermodal shipment in which, for instance, an American railroad was the initiating carrier, a Dutch ship provided the ocean transportation, a German barge service moved the container inland and turned it over to a Swiss trucker for delivery to the consignee.

True intermodal transportation as described is still in the process of evolution. A major step toward realization of the ultimate goal of intermodal transportation—the most efficient use of the available means of transportation without the requirement for special intercarrier contracts—has been taken. The single bill of lading is a reality. The ocean carrier is willing to issue the bill of lading because that carrier controls the inland movement. That is to say, the shipowner has already contracted for use of the inland carriers and knows exactly what the relationships are with them. Drawing up the bill of lading for shipments involving inland carriers is, therefore, a comparatively simple legal exercise.

The essence of the intermodal contract is an agreement among carriers of different types, such as barge lines, railroads, and trucking firms, to perform certain carefully described and defined services for agreed rates of compensation. Ideally, the ocean carrier offering intermodal service should be free to negotiate the most favorable rates, terms, and conditions for the type of service required. The resultant intermodal rate is the total of what must be paid to connecting carriers plus the shipowner's compensation. There are persuasive reasons why the carriers in the same trade (for example, Japan to the U.S. Pacific coast) would find it advantageous to negotiate with the intermodal operators to establish the charges for inland transportation. Although this may be a logical element in the conception of intermodal transportation, the Shipping Act of 1984 bars any association of ocean carriers domiciled in the United States from negotiating "on any matter relating to rates or services provided to ocean carriers within the United States by those non-ocean carriers." Ocean carrier groups, however, are permitted to set "joint through rates" for cargo destined to inland points. From the text of the law, it would appear that the intent is to permit the individual ocean carrier to negotiate a rate for intermodal service and then to meet with the other carriers in the group to agree upon a combined sea and land rate that would be used by all members.

In reviewing the trends that support the growth of intermodalism (landbridge and neutral equipment pools), it must be noted that the ocean carrier has come to depend increasingly upon supporting activities and various third parties doing business in cities far inland. These important members of the import-export team provide rapid and accurate information on the progress of a shipment and make possible the effective intelligence network on which the structure of containerization has been built. Until recently, the value of these support operations in forecasting demand for shipping capacity, both in terms of containers and ship spaces, was not appreciated. Lacking a scientific basis for estimating their needs, shipowners in the early days of conversion from breakbulk operations depended entirely too much on the anticipated economies of scale and built more container-carrying ships than the facts of trade justified. This produced the crisis of overtonnaging that afflicted the major trade routes, especially the North Atlantic and the North Pacific. Inevitably, destructive freight rate wars occurred, and there were many allegations of unethical and illegal practices adopted in the scramble to find cargoes for the big, expensive, and unfortunately superfluous ships. As the crisis eased, everyone involved in the movement of containerized cargo became aware of the interdependence of all concerned with the new procedures, an interdependence essential to the improvement of the whole business of liner shipping.

Looking ahead, future growth and acceptance of the container as a means of packaging goods for transfer from point to point must depend upon the establishment of true intermodal systems. Before this can be achieved, all the different users and carriers who would be involved in the system must agree on the following points:

1. The standardization of container sizes.
2. Complete interchangeability of containers between carriers.
3. Establishment, maintenance, and control of container depots by an agency or agencies that would be neutral (unaffiliated with the carriers) and dedicated to working only with containers.
4. Drafting a uniform contract of carriage binding upon all participants. This is necessary to process claims and to simplify negotiations concerning clauses of the contract.
5. Reduction in the present number and complexity of documents required for cargo shipped in containers. The ultimate goal must be one document that will be accepted by commercial and governmental interests as meeting legal and other stipulations relating to origin, value, ownership, and routing instructions.
6. The introduction and widespread use of highly sophisticated computer systems to support the interchange program. This would include acceptance and use of electronic data interchange (EDI), which involves the electronic transfer of commercial transactions using an agreed standard by which to structure the transaction or message data.[2] This would also include the use of automatic equipment identification (AEI), which involves the electronic tagging of all equipment used in intermodal movements, making the tracking of the equipment easier.[3]
7. Efficient, economical collection and distribution of containers from and to the marine terminals monitored by all parties concerned. In the United States, this may not be possible without legislation exempting from existing antitrust law the cooperation inherent in the intermodal principle.
8. Uniform rules concerning responsibility for the condition of containers while in the custody of a given person.
9. Agreement on a uniform method of processing and adjudicating claims.

LANDBRIDGE SERVICE CAPABILITIES

Although containerization depends upon fast, efficient ships for the ocean passage, the growth of landbridge service is rooted in the land. The shipowner has no choice but to become involved in every phase of transportation if there is to be a smooth, uninterrupted flow of cargo to the ships.

As the use of containers for international shipping expanded, seeking ways to obtain even greater benefits was logical for both operators and shippers. A look at a map shows that from Tokyo to New York there are two routes: one through the Panama Canal, an all-water trip that might take up to thirty days, depending upon the speed of the ship, and the other to a port on the West Coast of the United States and overland to the eastern metropolis. With the goods already packed in a container, the time and risk factors involved in transferring from ship to railroad are reduced and between seven and ten days could be saved by using the second route.

The landbridge concept simply uses the land mass as a "bridge" in what otherwise could be an all-water routing. Landbridge services are of three types: landbridge, minilandbridge, and microlandbridge. Landbridge service is characterized by the use of a major land mass to connect two water routes. An example is the movement of cargo from Japan by ship to a port on the West Coast of the United States, then across the United States using a mode of land transportation (usually rail) followed by a ship movement from an East Coast port to its final destination in England. Minilandbridge service is characterized by the use of a major land mass to bridge an all-water route where the final destination is on the opposite coast, as in the movement of cargo from Japan by ship to a port on the West Coast of the United States, then across the United States using a mode of land transportation (usually rail) to its final destination at Boston on the East Coast. Microlandbridge service is a little different in that it is characterized by the use of a land mass to complete or begin a voyage that involves water. This is exemplified by the movement of cargo from Japan by ship to a port on the West Coast of the United States, then across the United States to Kansas City. There are no all-water alternatives in the microlandbridge service as there are in the landbridge or minilandbridge service. Properly developed, landbridge or minilandbridge services offer savings of time, money, and energy.

Sealand Lines generally is credited with being the initiator of the landbridge services, with the first shipments completed in 1972. The idea, however, was neither new nor original, but a revival of what had been a successful operation during the 1920s. Known informally as the "silk express," the service connected Yokohama and New York via Seattle, carrying bales of raw silk as primary and premium cargo. Express steamers loaded their valuable consignments in Japan, followed the great circle course to Seattle, and transferred the silk to waiting railroad baggage and express cars that were dispatched at high speed to the market in New York. This coordinated arrangement was offered to shippers whenever the need arose and therefore was not a regular feature of transpacific steamship operations. It was popular and lucrative and was ended only as economic conditions and international rivalries created circumstances inimical to its continued existence.[4]

The silk express was a coordinated operation of the ocean carriers and the transcontinental railroads. Two separate contracts of carriage were issued, one by the water carrier and one by the land carrier. The only reason for the service was to reduce transit time between Japan and the New York silk market. Each transporter functioned in its own area; there was mutual support without any attempt to establish single control. Both the shipowner and the railroad company benefitted, but besides adjusting schedules and assigning equipment so that there would be no delays in transshipment, the silk express was the result of two distinct activities.

What differentiated the Sealand scheme from the earlier arrangements was that the company assumed and retained full responsibility for all transportation and that it made subcontracts with the transcontinental railroads. The shipper dealt only with Sealand, which added to the attractiveness of the new method. As the number of containers booked to this service increased, Sealand arranged for "unit trains" to transport the boxes across the United States. A sixty-car train, loaded with two 20-foot containers on each car, was dispatched not more than forty-eight hours after the ship docked in a west coast port, then proceeded under special orders to Weehawken, New Jersey, the Atlantic coast container terminal maintained by Sealand.

In 1979, as part of its strategy to expand its hinterland, American President Lines initiated a "linertrain" service from Seattle to Chicago and New York. Compared with the all-water route, this saved seven days of transit time. Capitalizing on the success of this venture, the company in 1984 introduced its individually designed railroad double-stack cars that carried containers stacked two high. A contract was negotiated with the railroad to provide unit train service transporting a total of 200 40-foot containers, with two departures a week in each direction. So effective was this operation that two additional "linertrains" per week were scheduled from Los Angeles to Chicago and New York. A freight forwarding company, Trans-way International Corporation of New York, served as the company's representative in the Midwest and northeast.

As often occurs in business, a successful venture encourages others to emulate the pioneer. In the case of American President Lines, the port authorities in Seattle purchased sufficient double-stack flatcars to commence common carrier unit train operations from Seattle to Chicago and New York. This was available to any shipping company using the port of Seattle. By the middle of 1985, the Danish-owned Maersk Line had duplicated in every detail the pattern of service from Seattle by American President Lines. Orient Overseas Container Line announced in June 1985 that it was initiating liner-train service from the West Coast to Houston and New Orleans.

Any survey of the extension of landbridge service must include reference to the activities of the Russians in developing the trade between Germany and Japan, using the trans-Siberian railway as the link to the ships. In March 1971, the Russians sent a few containers from Moscow to Nakhodka, where Japanese flag ships were waiting to transport the boxes to Yokohama. A year later, the service was extended to Germany in what became known as the Trans-Siberian Container Service. This trade grew significantly, and not only was the port of Nakhodka modernized and enlarged, but a nearby harbor, Vostochny, was converted into a container terminal. Both Japanese and Russian ships handled the water phase of the movement. Despite problems inherent in moving containers through the extremely low temperatures of a Siberian winter, the saving of seven to ten days in transit time and a lower cost for freight was approved by the shipping public. The only difficulty of any significance resulted from the greater number of loaded containers moving toward Germany as compared with the traffic flow toward Japan.[5] Returning the containers to their respective owners has been a problem, however, since the dawn of the container age and promises to remain a matter of concern well into the future.

In the United States, landbridge operations have been the source of controversy. Atlantic and Gulf Coast ports that formerly handled cargo destined from the coastal states to the Far East complained that the new system was "diverting" business from regions that were "naturally tributary" to those ports (their hinterland). They contended that for decades before the coming of the container revolution, exporters domiciled within a certain radius of a port had sent their goods to that city's waterfront to be loaded into ships that then proceeded through the Panama Canal to ports of the Orient. With the introduction of containers and the adoption of the landbridge scheme by Sealand and other carriers, the containerized cargo was placed on railroad flatcars that went directly to Los Angeles or Oakland, California, or to Seattle, Washington, for transfer to the containerships. This disrupted the economy of these ports. The dispute was brought before the Federal Maritime Commission in 1973, and after prolonged hearings involving many facets of administrative law, a decision promulgated on August 8, 1978, held that landbridge service did not violate any laws.[6]

A basic principle of traffic management is to find the most economical routing for a consignment of goods. In this context "economical routing" always has had a twofold meaning, applied both to the cost of transportation and to the time the goods must spend in transit. If using landbridge service would speed up delivery to an overseas market by two or three days, it must be assumed that the faster method will be selected. This would be true especially if the shortened transit time cost no more than the longer, all-water route.

Another problem encountered early in the new era of containerization was the liability of the water carrier for the loss of a container or damage to its contents. Most containerships carry some of their boxes on deck and therefore subject them to the effects of storms and heavy seas, to say nothing of temperature changes on passages through different climatic zones. For many years, steamship practice held that the maximum amount for which the carrier would be liable in case of loss of a package was $500, unless a higher valuation had been declared at the time the bill of lading was issued. With the arrival of the container, however, the question arose, "What is a 'package'?"

The answer was provided in a 1978 court decision stating that, in those instances where goods stowed in the container had been packaged in cartons or wrappings that clearly separated each item or each quantity contained within the container from similar items or quantities held in other cartons or wrappings, liability of the carrier was $500 for each of the individual packages. If the goods were not segregated—as would be true for a container filled with steel pipe, lumber, or bulk grain—and therefore no separate mark or number might be ascribed to each unit being transported, the liability of the carrier would be fixed at $500 for the entire container, which the court considered as the "package." Chapter 19 provides a more detailed discussion.

LOAD CENTERS

Two developments have occurred since the initial long-distance movement of containers in international commerce. The first was the reassertion, as a practical precept of containership management, of the old ideal that an oceangoing ship is economically most efficient when operated between a single port of origin and a single port of destination—what quickly became known as "load centers." Also, the enormous daily cost of the big ships compelled reduction of port turnaround time. The costly and time-consuming practice of sending the ship after the cargo had to be abandoned, which led to the second development—the use of "feeder vessels" to assemble cargo at the load centers.

Operations acknowledged that containerships depended upon shore facilities for loading and unloading and consequently had to be routed to appropriately equipped ports. A complete cargo of containers therefore could be assembled in the marshalling area before the ship arrived. It was recognized, however, that all the containers needed to fill the ship might not be available at a single port. Quite often, several hundred boxes would be held at a marine terminal located within a comparatively short distance of the main port, while additional containers would be offered at outlying ports separated by at least a full day of steaming. The question to be answered, quite literally on a port-to-port basis, was this: "Is it cheaper and more efficient to pay trucking costs to bring the containers from port Y to the ship's berth at port X, or to send the ship to port Y?" Clearly, the number of containers and the ocean freight rates payable on their contents would have much to do with the answer, but generally it may be asserted that where the number of containers is small and the highway distance from Y to X is less than one hundred miles, it pays the owner to keep the ship at port X and to absorb the trucking costs. Where the quantity of containers is substantial and the road distance significant, as from Norfolk, Virginia, to Newark, New Jersey, or from Los Angeles to Oakland, California, the usual decision is to move the ship.

In shipping circles, the matter of "vessel cost" invariably is related to total performance, which means that the time required to make a coastwise voyage to deliver or pick up cargo often becomes the compelling factor, surpassing even the very measurable fuel and port fees. To send a ship from port A to port B may be approved because it involves only eight to ten hours of travel time. To get from port B to port C, however, twenty-eight to thirty hours of travel time is needed. The total cost in ship time must be determined because it affects the number of voyages completed in a year and also many other aspects of efficient management of the vessel and the fleet. Every operator must balance the advisability of moving the ship against the cost of assembling the cargo at a single port. Where assembling the cargo at a single port results in a net reduction of expense to the shipowner, the idea of naturally tributary cargo vanishes in the harsh glare of realistic cost analysis.

When it was proposed to take advantage of coastwise sea routes and inland waterways by using smaller craft (either barges or deep-sea vessels) to distribute and pick up cargo at outlying ports, the response was immediate and affirmative, as demonstrated by the actions of a towing company based in New York City. It set up a common carrier barge service linking New York with New Haven and Boston, departing every Tuesday from each terminus. Containers destined to these cities were transshipped to the barges, and a fixed fee was paid for their onward transportation. If no containers were offered to the feeder carrier, no payments were made. The success of these efforts was owed to the regularity of schedules. Shippers and consignees knew when their containers would be picked up or delivered, and the deep-sea carrier could determine in advance what the feeder service would cost.[7]

The question of distributing and picking up containers in the Western European area, including the United Kingdom and Ireland, demanded attention at the inauguration of service. "Was it feasible," asked the operators, "to send the ship from New York to Rotterdam only, and to bring to that port containers originating as far away as Bergen, Oslo, Stockholm, Glasgow, and Southampton?" The answer lay in the existence of a large fleet of "short-sea traders," smaller ships designed to run between Southampton and Dunkirk, for instance, or from Oslo to Bremen. Somewhat larger coastal vessels were also operated between Rotterdam, Le Havre, Marseilles, and points in the eastern Mediterranean. If these ships could be used and their schedules synchronized with the arrivals and departures of the oceangoing containerships, the objective of load centers might be attained while still providing container service to an extensive area of Europe.

While the existing short-sea traders and coastwise vessels could apparently be used, they lacked the capability to handle containers rapidly, efficiently, and economically. This deficiency was remedied in some cases by modifying the little ships for the trade. In other instances, bold entrepreneurs designed, built, and offered for charter vessels intended expressly to serve as feeders for the transoceanic carriers. In the years since 1966, more purpose-built feeder ships have been introduced into these waters and have accomplished two objectives: they have extended the network of container services over an enormous area without adding unreasonably to total transit time for import and export cargoes, and they have made possible the most efficient use of the big containerships, with resulting economies for all concerned.[8]

It was to be expected that the advantages of feeder service would be appreciated in other parts of the world, especially in the Orient. Because the ports in this area are separated by greater distances of open ocean (compared with either Europe or the United States), the feeder ships had to be significantly larger than the vessels employed in those two regions.

A case history is provided by American President Lines. This company selected Yokohama, Japan, and Kaohsiung, Taiwan, as principal ports for its mainline transpacific container service. It assigned six smaller but fully containerized ships to run from Japan and Taiwan to major collecting points at Hong Kong, Singapore, Colombo, and Fujaira (a United Arab Emirate). Containers destined to, or originating in, either of the major ports or their outports were handled by the vessels of the support fleet that consisted of chartered ships and also common carriers working under contract with American President Lines. Transfers between ships were accomplished at the major collecting points. When the company-owned containerships returned to Taiwan and Japan, the containers they had collected were loaded aboard the mainline ships for ultimate delivery to the United States. Although two transshipments were involved, the combination of rapid and dependable service, along with company insistence on meticulous care in the handling of the boxes resulted in customer satisfaction and an enlarged territory in which American President Lines could seek business.

Generally speaking, there are two reasons why the deep-sea carriers charter feeder vessels rather than purchase them. First, the investment in containerships is so great that little capital is available for acquiring the small craft. Second, by taking the feeder ships on time charter, the management of ships engaged in the highly specialized coastal trade is left in the hands of experts, with corresponding reduction in the responsibilities of the transoceanic carriers. No matter whether the feeder ships are owned or chartered, the shipper of goods receives a single bill of lading covering the entire movement from the moment the carrier accepts the container until it is delivered to the consignee.

Intermodal transportation is growing every year and water transportation is a key component in international intermodal movements. Although this transportation strategy is still evolving, there is sufficient anecdotal evidence to suggest that the business community is embracing the concept in its attempt to integrate and optimize all aspects of the supply chain.

CHAPTER EIGHTEEN

How Freight Rates Are Made

An amazing assortment of goods is moved over the world's ocean trade routes. Of necessity, the carriers charge for the service they render. These charges vary almost as widely as do the cargoes, for they mirror both the shipowners' costs and the special conditions prevailing on the trade routes traversed by the ships.

THE THEORY OF FREIGHT RATES

Ocean freight rates may be described as the prices charged for the services of water carriers. Each ship operator develops its own rates, usually without consultation with the shippers. The charges reflect the cost of providing the carriage, the value of this service to the owner of the goods, the ability of the merchandise to support the expense of transportation, and economic conditions in general.

No exact pricing formulas are applied uniformly to the various items moving in transoceanic commerce. The cost of ocean transportation offers little interference with the international movement of goods. To a noticeable extent, ocean freight rates truly reflect the working of the laws of supply and demand. In tramp shipping, particularly, it is possible to observe how these factors influence the rise or fall of freight rates from day to day and from cargo to cargo.

Tramp ships transport, in shipload (or *full cargo*) lots, commodities that can be moved in bulk, like coal, grain, ore, and phosphate rock. The fact that usually only one shipper and one commodity are involved simplifies the establishment of a freight rate for this particular movement. To the capital charges of ownership and the expense of administration and overhead must be added the costs of running the ship, handling the cargo, and paying port fees and harbor dues. Against this total is set the number of tons to be hauled, and the resultant figure is what the tramp must charge, per ton of cargo loaded, to break even on the contemplated voyage. If competitive conditions permit, a margin of profit will form part of the quoted rate. If, however, the prevailing economic climate is unfavorable, the owner has the privilege of retiring the ship to a quiet backwater, there to wait until the financial skies are brighter.

To illustrate this mathematically, recall that total cost is the mathematical sum of the fixed costs and the variable costs of doing business:

$$\text{Fixed costs (FC)} + \text{Variable costs (VC)} = \text{Total cost (TC)}$$

Further, the cost per ton to break even (B/E) is simply the total cost divided by the number of tons carried, expressed in whatever unit of tonnage is being used. (Note that this does not take into account any of the intangibles such as desirability of the cargo, desirability of the route, or market conditions).

$$\frac{\text{Total cost}}{\text{Tons carried}} = \text{Break-even (B/E) rate per ton}$$

Under favorable conditions, it is possible to include a profit in the formula as follows:

$$\frac{\text{Total cost} + \text{Profit}}{\text{Tons carried}} = \text{Quoted rate per ton}$$

The following calculations will demonstrate the theory. A producer of a bulk high-grade ore wishes to ship 75,000 tons from port A to port B. The owners of a vessel positioned in port A and suitable for this movement make an offer through their broker for this work: fixed costs for the entire voyage, estimated to take 30 days, total $135,000 (30 days × $4,500 per day); the variable costs for the voyage total $324,000 (30 days × $10,800); and a desired profit of $70,000. Therefore:

$$\text{Fixed costs (FC)} + \text{Variable costs (VC)} = \text{Total cost (TC)}$$

$$\$135,000 + \$324,000 = \$459,000$$

$$\frac{\text{Total cost}}{\text{Tons carried}} = \text{Break-even (B/E) rate per ton}$$

$$\frac{\$459,000}{75,000 \text{ Tons}} = \$6.12 \text{ per ton}$$

If economic conditions are favorable, the desired profit would be calculated:

$$\frac{\text{Total cost} + \text{Profit}}{\text{Tons carried}} = \text{Quoted rate per ton}$$

$$\frac{\$459,000 + \$70,000}{75,000 \text{ Tons}} = \$7.05 \text{ per ton}$$

The tramp operator does not depend upon the long-term goodwill of the shippers, but is free to accept those offers that appear profitable at the moment. When adversity threatens, those charters are accepted that minimize anticipated losses. If there is a choice, the cost of temporary layup is contrasted with the loss that continued operation might produce, and the less expensive alternative is selected in a bow to the inevitable, made with such grace as can be mustered.

Liner-service companies, on the other hand, depend for financial prosperity upon the accumulated goodwill of shippers who, through the years, come to rely upon the regular and continued operation of the company's fleet. Temporary withdrawal from service whenever economic conditions are less than favorable is unthinkable.

The liner will sail on her regular run, whether full or not. She will carry a wide variety of commodities, each with its own peculiarities, in quantities that can be estimated in advance more or less accurately but never with complete certainty. The ports of call are known far in advance of sailing, and the total expense of working the ship can be calculated with acceptable precision. However, since the exact distribution of tonnage, commodity by commodity, varies with every trip, it is not possible to establish a rate that reflects the cost of transporting a single ton of a particular commodity as closely as does the tramp owner's computation.

This is not to suggest that liner-service operators cannot compute to a nicety the cost of owning and operating their ships. They know to a fraction of a cent their daily costs for amortization and interest on borrowed capital as well as what administrative expenses they must charge to individual voyages. In the same manner that their counterparts in the tramping trade are able to fix individual rates, liner owners can determine what they should charge per ton to carry a single commodity when it is offered in lots sufficient to fill one of their ships. The difficulty arises when the liner operator is forced to compile a list of charges for transporting hundreds of different commodities not in the ship sailing tomorrow, but in ships departing at weekly intervals during the next year or even over a longer period.

Because the ship is committed to sail on a fixed date, there may be a tendency among some shipowners to say, "It makes little difference what I charge for individual commodities, as long as the aggregate revenue is adequate to cover my expenses." The contrary view is, "Unless I know that each ton of cargo will pay its full cost and earn a profit, I will not accept that item."

Between these contrasting outlooks there is an intermediate theory, which deserves thoughtful scrutiny.

From experience, liner-service operators know approximately what is going to move voyage after voyage, and they have a good idea of what tonnage to expect. They must estimate the overhead to be charged against each commodity and the out-of-pocket costs of handling them at ports of loading and discharge. An apportionment of revenue must be made to defray the administrative expense of vessel operation. Finally, a small profit should be added to compensate the owners for the risks they assume as well as for their skill and enterprise, for by providing timely transportation they enhance the value of the goods (*time utility* and *place utility*). They are justified in assigning reasonable value to these real, albeit intangible, contributions.

Underlying these general principles are certain factors that influence, in one way or another, the establishment of freight rates for individual commodities moving in liner-service vessels.

The first of these factors is that freight rates should be reasonable to both shippers and carriers. The shippers must be satisfied that the money they pay for transportation will not drive the price of their goods above the competitive level of the markets where they trade. If the exporters or importers are trying to compete with goods from sources closer at hand, they will consider that the cost of transportation, no matter how low, is nothing less than a barrier to trade.

In determining what is reasonable as a charge for transportation, the shipper's complete indifference to the financial condition of the carrier must be remembered. The sales appeal of a given article often is set by the price that necessarily includes the expense of transportation. Should the margin between the seller's total costs and the market price be too narrow to leave a profit, the seller attempts to convince the carrier to reduce the prevailing freight rates. The argument always is, "If you don't come down, you will lose all my business. If you will help me to keep my price at the competitive level, you will benefit by my continued patronage. After all, your ship is going to sail on this route anyhow, so why not make this concession?"

The second factor influencing the establishment of freight rates is competition. If a carrier sets rates higher than those of its rivals, patrons may be lost to shipowners whose services are available at lower prices. If, however, a figure that nets no profit is quoted, the outreach may be too successful, and the carrier may be overwhelmed by the volume in which this commodity is offered. Whereas a few tons could be handled on each voyage, this nonprofit item cannot be allowed to crowd out other commodities on which the rate is remunerative.

Another kind of competition is the rivalry between ports. In their search for cargoes to move through their facilities, the various ports of an area advertise their modern piers and wharves, their intraport systems of roadways and railroads, and the frequency of sailings to all parts of the world. Ports call attention to their location with reference to major overseas destinations and also to the excellent rail and highway networks feeding the port.

A good deal of cargo for overseas markets originates with shippers in inland cities who have the option of using one of several ports. The rail or truck routing that gives the lowest cost of transportation normally is preferred. A shipper may develop the habit of moving all goods from city X to seaport A because the inland freight rate is a few cents per hundred pounds cheaper than to seaport B. Rail or truck lines operating only between city X and seaport B must compete for the business by bringing their rates to the level of those applying to seaport A. This *port equalization rate* applies only on cargo with foreign destinations and actually represents a reduction in revenue on the part of the domestic carrier(s). Where the shipping line maintains service only from seaport B, it is possible that it may develop special *through rates* in conjunction with the inland carriers, under which each of the modes of transportation offers a reduction provided the business is routed through seaport B.

Some commodities are found naturally in widely separated geographic locations. The sellers of these commodities compete with each other on a worldwide basis. Buyers seek the lowest cost. If the combination of foreign price plus transportation produces a figure higher than the quotation from a rival area, the buying pattern may be changed to take advantage of the more favorable price. The following examples make this clear.

Tin originates in Bolivia, Malaysia, Indonesia, and Zaire. When exporters of Bolivian tin raise their prices, or the carriers of tin from Bolivia to the consuming market establish a new freight rate, the users of tin compare the new total with that of acquiring the mineral from the other sources and place their orders accordingly.

Copper is imported to the United States from Chile, Canada, and Central America. The difference of one cent a pound in the landed price in New York often determines whether the movement will be from one area or another.

No factor of competition is more difficult to assess in the analysis of freight rates than that which results from the struggle of different geographic areas for the same market. This emerges when the trade from two widely separated manufacturing nations comes into direct conflict in a consuming market thousands of miles from both producers. For instance, the United States and Japan both send large quantities of the same kinds of machinery to Chile. The Chilean buyers consequently are in the position of pitting Americans and Japanese against each other and taking advantage of whatever bargains they can obtain. While ocean carriers serving the two supplying nations are not faced directly with a demand to meet a freight rate established by the purchasers, they are aware that they are in competition. The pressures are felt from both suppliers and importers, and therefore the carriers must establish (or maintain) a rate acceptable to the consignees. That the freight rate may not be profitable to the ship operator is of no concern to the buyer, who is interested only in obtaining goods at the lowest possible total cost.

Competition is keen between the operators of the big containerships. The two most important trade routes—transpacific (linking the Orient to the West Coast of the United States and Canada) and transatlantic (connecting Western Europe and the United Kingdom with ports of Canada and the United States on the Atlantic and Gulf Coasts)—have become very attractive, and in mid-1993 there was an excess of capacity compared to the quantity of cargo moving. A factor contributing to the problem was the fluctuating value of the U.S. dollar relative to other currencies. This meant that imports from abroad sometimes were comparatively cheap, and good sales were made easily; at other times, exports from the United States were expensive (in terms of the foreign buyers' currencies) and therefore not in great demand. The imbalance of trade was reflected in the number of empty containers that had to be transported at minimal freight rates or free of charge from the United States back to the overseas areas. It was a logical step, therefore, for carriers to add whatever they could to the freight rates for cargo destined to the United States in the hope of defraying some of the expense of repositioning the empty boxes.

On the long routes such as the round-the-world service, where all the cargo is in containers, the carriers selected a limited number of ports serving productive hinterlands and restricted calls to those ports or load centers. Containers filled with goods for export were brought to and assembled at these centers by rail, truck, and barge. Inbound containers were distributed by the same means to destinations within a specified radius of each load center. The cost of pickup and delivery within this territory was included in the ocean freight rate.

Certain commodities essential for many purposes in the world economy are always in demand. Very rarely do these commodities move in shipload lots. To put them into the hands of their users, they must be dispatched by liner-service ships, but their value is so low that they cannot be charged the actual cost of transportation. Facing this dilemma, the rate maker has no choice but to set rates that permit their movement even though it means the carriage is performed at a financial loss to the shipowner. To offset this difficulty, the only solution is to set rates for items of high value that will absorb the loss incurred on the low value commodities.

"Charge what the traffic will bear" is a basic tenet of rate making, the significance of which may not be evident at first glance. A hypothetical example will make it clear. Imagine that electric washing machines were assessed $2.50 per cubic foot and bagged cement was charged $1.00 per cubic foot for transportation from San Francisco to Valparaiso, Chile. Based on the value of the two items, the cost of sea-carriage would add about 12 percent to the landed price of the washing machine, but it would double the price of the cement. The comparatively small markup in the price of the washing machine will not affect its sale. The increase in the price of cement is the limit to which cost can rise without driving it off the market. The shipowner knows that it cost $1.25 per cubic foot to operate the vessel. The revenue from the washing machine left a surplus from which the deficit incurred by the cement could be paid.

Illogical and superficially indefensible as this system may appear to be, it is the only workable method of providing the transportation for those commodities that must move but cannot afford to pay the cost of liner service. It follows (quite logically, in this case) that if cement is to move at all, it must be accompanied by a reasonable tonnage of washing machines, so that the total mix of cargo will produce a profitable load. Ideally, if there is an equal balance between the two commodities, there will be a profit of $1.00 per cubic foot. When this balance is destroyed, and twice as much cement as washing machines is stowed in the ship, the shipowner loses substantially.

The following calculation will demonstrate the theory:

Ideal Mix of Washing Machines and Cement		
40 cubic feet @ $2.50 per foot	$100.00	
40 cubic feet @ $1.00 per foot	40.00	
Ship's revenue		$140.00
Cost for 80 cubic feet @ $1.25 per cubic foot		100.00
Surplus		$ 40.00

Actual Mix of Washing Machines and Cement		
20 cubic feet @ $2.50 per foot	$ 50.00	
60 cubic feet @ $1.00 per foot	60.00	
Ship's revenue		$110.00
Cost for 80 cubic feet @ $1.25 per cubic foot		100.00
Surplus		$ 10.00

Because exploitation of the shipper seems to be implied in the understanding of "charging what the traffic will bear," it is preferable, given the economic conditions existing in the last decade of the twentieth century, to think in terms of the value of transportation in the interchange of goods. This interchange, or trade, takes place only when the object traded commands a higher price at the market than it does at the point of production. A corollary of this is that the market price is fixed by the competition of similar goods from different sources. If follows, therefore, that in modern commercial practice, transportation has become an integral part of the distribution process established by the manufacturer or exporter. An efficient process reflects cooperation and coordination in which every participant is aware of the impact of transportation upon the final demand for the object offered for sale.[1]

In recent years, as shipping capacity exceeded the requirements for cargo space, the ability of the carrier to assess rates on a unilateral basis was eroded. Shippers had more influence on associations of carriers and became more insistent that their abilities to pay freight rates should be considered. An example of the impact of shipper demand was furnished in June 1985 when the Transpacific Westbound Rate Agreement (TWRA) carriers announced that they would raise the rate by one hundred dollars on 40-foot containers moving from the Orient to the United States. This was to be effective on July 1; on September 1, the rate would be increased again by another two hundred dollars. At a meeting held in Hong Kong, shippers protested so vigorously that the carriers first postponed action until a later date and then canceled the proposal altogether.[2]

Shippers want their cargoes delivered in good condition and on time. They have indicated by action and in expressions of opinion that the price of transportation is of less significance than the quality of service. This was made known in a survey of several hundred shippers of high-value goods who evaluated these features of ocean transportation in this order of priority: (1) date of ship's sailing and scheduled arrival at port of discharge; (2) duration of the voyage from loading port to discharge port; (3) the reliance that shippers could place on the carriers' published schedules; (4) quality and availability of containers; (5) the reputation of the carrier, based on previous experience or history; and (6) the freight rate charged. Shippers of goods of low value understandably gave higher consideration to the freight rate but placed it second to the date of sailing and the date of arrival, which were considered most important in the selection of a carrier. In third place was the reputation of the carrier, followed by the reliance that the shipper could place on the ships' meeting published schedules. Transit time was in fifth place, and the availability of containers was given lowest priority.[3]

The shipowner is faced with the necessity of earning maximum profit from the goods offered on its trade route while interfering as little as possible in their flow. In theory, the ship operator seeks to carry a minimum of those cargoes that pay either noncompensatory or break-even rates and looks always for those items on which there is assurance of good profits. Even in theory, however, all the unprofitable commodities cannot be excluded. Frequently the low-grade raw materials are essential to the manufacture of goods that, in their turn, offer handsome profits when later transported across the seas. Since the carrier depends for much of its profit on continued trade in their manufactured articles, the unprofitable item must be lifted at whatever rate the shipper of that commodity will pay.

Carriage by water is still the cheapest form of transportation ever devised by man. In terms of the cost per pound of most commodities moved across the seas, the charges assessed by the liner operator are insignificant in proportion to the sales price at the overseas market. It is substantially correct that carriers would be happy if profits from freight rates averaged one and a half to two cents a pound. For those commodities moved in tramp ships, the return to the ship, in terms of cents per pound, is almost ludicrously low. A sampling of charter rates during a period of comparatively good business showed that it was possible to send a pound of sugar a quarter of the way around the world for less than half a cent. One authority computed that to raise tramp rates on grain by $1.50 a ton, which might be welcomed by many owners, would increase the cost of the flour in a one-pound loaf of bread by approximately one-sixteenth of a cent.

FACTORS IN OCEAN FREIGHT RATE MAKING

The ideal of the ocean carrier is to foster international trade and to build up the tonnage of cargo carried by the proprietary ships. Although more attention may appear to be given to the large-scale shippers of goods, the small businessman actually is not ignored because the rates quoted by liner companies are the same for all shippers, regardless of the quantity of cargo offered. In practice, the small-scale shipper benefits from the ability of the large-scale shipper to demand more favorable treatment—a demand that can be supported by the threat to transfer business to a competitor.

As indicated above, liner-service operators may increase the cost of sea-carriage only with extreme caution. Although they may need more revenue, shipowners cannot take the risk of raising rates to levels that might throttle trade or invite new competition by making profits so attractive. The usual method is for the carrier to increase rates gradually by increments of 5 to 10 percent and to be guided step-by-step by the reaction of the shipping public.

Inasmuch as the shipowners must have cargo in sufficient quantity to provide adequate loads for their vessels, any commodity that moves in substantial and regular volume from a given port is important to their economic well-being. It is reasonable, therefore, that the rate on that commodity is somewhat lower than on items moving only occasionally and in small lots. For example, cotton is a major export cargo from a port on the Gulf Coast of the United States. Month after month, the flow of the white staple can be depended upon to provide nearly half of each ship's load. The rate, therefore, may be lower per ton than on wool, which moves through this same port only occasionally and in much smaller quantities.

A very significant factor in making a freight rate is the amount of ship space needed to stow a ton of the commodity. In theory, all rates are based on a weight ton (either the long ton of 2,240 pounds, the metric ton of 2,204 pounds, or the short ton of 2,000 pounds) occupying 40 cubic feet of ship space. It is pertinent to note that, as the metric system gains worldwide acceptance, the metric ton and the cubic meter (rather than the hundredweight and the cubic foot) are becoming the standards for freight rates.

The amount of cargo space required for one long ton of a given commodity is known as the commodity's *stowage factor.* Cargo with a stowage factor of less than 40 (requiring less than 40 cubic feet for the stowage of a weight ton) is referred to as *deadweight cargo* and habitually is freighted by weight, usually at a certain charge per hundred pounds. Cargo with a stowage factor of greater than 40 (requiring more than 40 cubic feet for stowage of a weight ton) is known as *cubic cargo* and is freighted by volume, usually at a particular amount per cubic foot. Since packaging varies, the carrier in many instances will offer two rates, one per cubic foot and one per hundredweight, but reserves the right to charge "by weight or measurement, whichever yields the greater revenue."

A vessel loaded so that all cargo space is filled and the hull is immersed to the load line is said to be *full and down.* A ship with 400,000 cubic feet of cargo space and a deadweight of 6,000 tons might be "down to her marks" with 6,000 tons of a heavy (dense, or deadweight) commodity with a stowage factor of 17 and still have 298,000 cubic feet of unfilled space. If she carried cargo with a stowage factor of 40, only 240,000 feet of space would be used for a full load of 6,000 tons. If, however, the cargo had a stowage factor of 60, the revenue tonnage would be 6,667 with all space filled.

In making rates, the handling and stowage characteristics of a commodity are taken into account. For example, an unboxed automobile requires ship space in excess of the actual measurement of the vehicle. The rate therefore includes a charge for this empty space. Fragile cargo must be protected; to do so may take cubic footage beyond the measurement of the package. Steel beams need little care and occupy a small amount of space in comparison to their weight. They may be used to offset electric light bulbs, which are exceedingly bulky and very fragile. The rates for these items are adjusted in accordance with their varying characteristics.

The perishability, fragility, bulkiness, odor, or dangerous nature of a commodity and the resulting responsibility for its protection and care significantly influence freight rates. Since certain commodities are damaged easily or may be especially attractive to pilferers, the losses sustained from these causes must be made good when the claim is settled. Freight rates on items of this sort consequently include an allowance to cover the anticipated loss.

Some commodities can be loaded only at special berths to which the ship may have to be moved at considerable expense. For example, explosives normally are loaded in a remote area of a harbor, and the ship must be taken to this isolated spot before any of its cargo can be worked. No other cargo is available at the explosives loading facilities. The very high rate for this commodity reflects these restrictions.

Another vital factor in making rates is the actual cost of handling cargo at the ports of origin and destination. The charges for stowing the commodity in the ship and the expenses of receiving, checking, watching, coopering, shifting around the terminals, and delivering vary with the items. Refrigerated cargo, for example, is expensive because of the extra compensation demanded by the longshoremen who work in subfreezing temperatures. Coal and grain are loaded and unloaded mechanically, and therefore the charge per ton is low. No uniform fee for handling can be assessed against all cargo moving through a particular terminal because the cost varies with the individual commodity.

In general, it is true that the possibility of obtaining return cargo influences freight rates. If the ship always returns to her home port in ballast, the revenue from the outbound passage has to be sufficient to defray all cost of the round voyage. By way of contrast, where cargoes are available in both directions, the average rate per ton probably will be lower than in the trade that offers business only in one direction.

Exceptionally heavy packages, defined in the breakbulk services as those weighing more than 3 tons, traditionally have been charged freight at the regular rate for the particular commodity, with a scale of surcharges based on the actual weight. This practice reflected the fact that, until relatively recently, ship's cargo gear had a safe working load of only 3 tons, and to hoist anything heavier required that the heavy-lift, or *jumbo* boom, be used. Depending upon how the ship was rigged, working the jumbo might entail using the winches for four booms. This would idle one or more gangs of longshoremen for whatever time the jumbo might be in service. An alternative to rigging the heavy-lift boom was to hire a truck-mounted or barge-mounted crane of very great capacity. This saved much work and time on the part of the longshoremen but added noticeably to the cost of handling the overweight parcel. Unavoidably, the expense so incurred had to be charged to the shipper. Even where modern ships have cranes or booms handling up to 10 or more tons without rerigging, there still is much arduous, time-consuming labor involved in stowage of a heavy piece of cargo, and compensation to the ship is justifiable. Extra-long pieces (timbers or steel beams, for instance) cannot be handled quickly and often interfere with the process of stowing other cargo. While there is no uniformity in the actual basis on which the charge is computed, many carriers have set a size limit of 35 feet as the maximum to be accepted without assessing additional fees. It should be understood that the operator rarely derives a profit from handling these overweight or over-length items; usually the added charge offsets the out-of-pocket expenses incurred.

An important expense of a voyage is the premium paid for insurance of the vessel. Many considerations affect the underwriters' computations, not least of which is the geographical area in which the ship is to be operated. Some regions present greater dangers to ships than do others; seasons of the year also have a bearing. Insurance coverage will not be valid, except at a higher premium rate, if the ship is sent to regions not included in the description and limitations of risk. War risk and perils of navigation in ice-clogged waters are not part of normal coverage. When a carrier is offered a consignment of cargo that will require the ship to depart from the insured area to effect delivery or will take the ship into a war zone, it is appropriate that the shipper pay the higher insurance fee. Sometimes this is accomplished by adding a surcharge (usually a fixed percentage) to the freight rate. In other cases, where the "off-limits" ports are visited only occasionally, the carrier will impose an arbitrary charge. From this procedure the shipping industry refers to these addenda as *arbitraries.*

Arbitraries also may be assessed against cargo destined to ports where facilities are antiquated, primitive, or nonexistent, and where the ship will face the risk of delays in handling the cargo. Regardless of the words used to describe the extra charge, it is standard practice for carriers to compute, as an integral part of the rate, the expense of putting into ports that do not ensure a quick turnaround. An interesting variant on this was the imposition of a 25 percent surcharge on cargo carried by the transatlantic superliners. The explanation was the heavy expense of working cargo at the passenger ship terminal in Southampton.

Freight rates in international trade have to be quoted in the currency of some country. For many years, the U.S. dollar served this purpose. When the dollar lost its stability, shipowners were troubled because their freight tariffs were more rigid than the international money market. To protect carriers who accepted payments in a foreign currency and then converted to the national funds at a loss, a *currency adjustment factor* was adopted. This could be modified as often as needed to keep ship revenues approximately in balance with the prevailing rate of exchange.

Only after the foregoing items have been taken into account in setting freight rates does the ship's rate maker consider cost of vessel operation. When fuel oil prices were increased drastically in 1973, shipowners had to devise a means by which to adjust their revenues quickly with the least possible impact on existing trading patterns. Two possibilities existed. One was to establish new rates whenever the cost of fuel oil escalated beyond an agreed level. This was rejected because of the extreme volatility of oil prices and the resultant instability of freight tariffs predicated upon these prices. The alternative was to continue existing tariffs and to impose a *fuel oil surcharge* on every revenue ton of cargo. This surcharge could be varied upward or downward as oil prices fluctuated. Shippers agreed that as a temporary measure this scheme was probably the most nearly satisfactory arrangement that could be found.

Fuel oil prices, however, never returned to the pre-1973 level, and a new system that reflected the changed conditions had to be generated by the carriers. Rather than continuing the surcharges, freight rates were recomputed to encompass fuel oil costs on a given day, designated as a "base date." As fuel prices fluctuated from the level prevailing on the base date, increases or decreases (in the form of percentage figures) were included in the carriers' bills. The merit of this plan was that the recomputed freight tariffs had some stability, and changes were made only after appropriate notice.

Other costs of ship operation do not exert so great an influence in making freight rates. Supplies, spare parts, repairs, maintenance, crew wages, and vessel time need to be calculated in addition to the dues exacted in ports of call, canal tolls, pilot fees, and other miscellaneous expenses of the voyage.

While these are not negligible, it is not practicable to prorate them against individual commodities because liner-service operators cannot predict infallibly what the composition of a ship's load will be on any single voyage.

A ship carrying 20,000 manifest tons of cargo on each fifteen-day leg of a round voyage lasting thirty days might have direct operating expenses, other than fuel, of $10,000 a day. Assessed against the total lift, this would mean that each ton of cargo should contribute $0.50 a day, or $7.50 per leg. Divided by 40 cubic feet, this would equal $0.1875 per foot; divided by 20 hundredweight, the charge would be $0.3750 per unit. Given the size of this contribution, it is understandable that direct operating expense is the least significant of the criteria for setting freight rates.

TYPES OF OCEAN FREIGHT RATES

Ocean freight rates are divided into two categories, *class rates* and *commodity rates*. In general, the class rate may be described as the rate assigned to a large number of unrelated commodities that have been studied individually and found to require the same revenue for their transportation. The commodity rate is a charge for carrying a specified article such as, for example, granulated sugar in bags.

Class rates vary in number, but many water carriers establish from six to nine classes, depending upon the variety needed in the rate structure. The most expensive is class D, assigned to dangerous cargo (explosives and corrosive acids). The next most expensive is class 1, and the least expensive is class 8. The higher the number of the class, the lower the rate—a standard pattern followed by liner service tariffs. There is no mathematical relationship between classes.

Examples of the classification of cargo are shown:

Article	Class
Flowers, artificial	1
Formaldehyde	2
Fuses, hazardous	D
Glass, sheets, frosted	7
Grilles, iron or steel	4
Graphite, not otherwise specified	3
Graphite, in bulk, in bags or barrels	6
Gypsum	8
Heaters, coal burning	5

The corresponding rates are these:

	D	1	2	3	4	5	6	7	8
Per 100 lbs.	$4.45	$3.50	$2.90	$2.25	$2.20	$1.78	$1.65	$1.56	$1.35
Per cu. ft.	2.50	1.95	1.65	1.25	1.12	1.00	.92	.88	.75

Commodity rates are fixed by water carriers usually as a result of pressure from shippers who find it competitively impossible to pay the freight rate of the class to which the commodity otherwise would be assigned. In many cases, the difference between one class and the next lower class represents a reduction in freight revenue that is greater than the carrier is willing to grant. In that event, to avoid establishing a new class, a special rate will be assigned to the item. For example, frosted glass in sheets is placed in class 7 and the rate is $0.88 per cubic foot, or $1.56 per hundred pounds. The carrier, in response to a request for special consideration, decides that an acceptable rate for frosted glass in sheets could be $0.80 per cubic foot or $1.45 per hundred pounds. This is a compromise between two classes. On the one hand, the shippers are convinced that they cannot pay the higher rate; on the other hand, the carriers are unwilling to come down to the next lower class rate. The result is a commodity rate that is mutually acceptable.

Commodity rates take precedence over class rates, so that if the same item were listed in both parts of the tariff, the commodity rate would be applied. There is no necessary relationship between commodity rates since they are made after special consideration of each item. The description of every listing is very definite:

Commodities	*Freighted Per*
Citrus fruit, fresh, viz: oranges, lemons, limes, tangelos, tangerines, and grapefruit, under refrigeration, in cartons or boxes not exceeding 42 lbs. each	Carton
Nails, iron or steel, plain, galvanized, or cement coated (except shoe or horseshoe)	100 lbs.
Paper, wrapping, not corrugated, other than cellulose film (cellophane), cloth-line, glassine, gummed, laminated, oil, parchment, tissue, transparent, or waxed	100 lbs.

Regardless of how an item is freighted, the carrier always incurs some expense in processing the papers related to the shipment. It is customary, therefore, for shipowners to require a minimum payment on every bill of lading issued.

Through rates are charged for shipments originating with one ocean carrier but transferred to connecting carriers at intermediate ports. By way of illustration, a consignment is sent from Hamburg, Germany, to Antofagasta, Chile. It goes in a German vessel from Hamburg to New York and there is transshipped to a Chilean flag steamer for the voyage to South America. The combined operation is handled under one bill of lading and therefore is known as a "through route." The freight rate for cargo moving in this manner is designated as a "through rate." Usually the originating carrier issues the bill of lading, collects all charges, and subsequently divides the revenue with the other carrier(s) in the proportions established by the through rate agreement.

In many cases, the through rate is lower than the combination of rates of each of the participating carriers. For example, a ton of coffee may be sent from Buenaventura, Colombia, to New York in a Colombian flag ship for $22.00. The freight rate for coffee carried from New York to Livorno, Italy, by an Italian flag vessel is $36.80. The through rate from Buenaventura to Livorno, by agreement between the carriers, is $54.00. Each carrier has reduced its rate by $2.40 in order to meet the competition of a Greek operator whose ships sail directly from Colombia to Italy and whose charge for the service is $54.50.

Not all through rates represent concessions in the rates charged by participating carriers. In some cases, two ship lines will offer the benefits of through service, but each will charge the full tariff rate for its portion of the total transit. This situation eventuates either from lack of direct sailings between countries of origin and destination or from significantly less desirable schedules by the only carrier linking the two ports. Some shippers will use the through service even though it is more expensive because they consider the shorter time in transit to be worth the difference financially. There are other cases where no direct link exists between the exporting and importing countries. Lacking the pressure of competition, the through rate is the total of the connecting carriers' charges plus any accessorial fees. For example, if no line sailed directly between Australia and Chile, an Australian importer wishing to bring Chilean wine to Melbourne would have had it carried to San Francisco and there transshipped to a transpacific operator for the onward movement to Australia. The through rate would be constructed in this manner: from Valparaiso to San Francisco the rate would be $32.00 per ton; transfer costs in San Francisco from one marine terminal to the other, $11.00 per ton; and the freight charge from San Francisco to Melbourne, $40.00, bringing the through rate to $83.00 per ton.

FREIGHT RATES FOR CARGO IN CONTAINERS

Although vast changes in shipping have been occasioned by the container revolution, there is no difference between the principles by which freight rates are made for cargo carried in containers and those by which rates are established for breakbulk cargo.

Certain facts must be accepted. Containers are of uniform size and are loaded and unloaded by mechanized and almost completely automated methods. Regardless of their contents, these big boxes are handled at the same speed, using the same number of longshoremen and the same equipment. To position and secure an empty container requires the same care as it does to stow a box filled with delicate precision instruments of high value. Certainly not to be overlooked is the fact that most containers are stuffed by the shippers, who thereby become responsible for the efficient and economical use of shipping space.

Among the factors influencing breakbulk freight rates is the demand for high levels of stevedoring skills in handling and stowing various commodities and products. The susceptibility to damage and pilferage is another basis for computing cost. The amount of ship's space necessary to accommodate a revenue ton also is taken into account. However, when goods are received at ship's side in huge weatherproof boxes that are stowed in the vessel with exactly the same care regardless of their contents, the applicability of these justifications for a freight rate becomes questionable. If it costs no more to put a filled container into its shipboard cell than it does to deposit an empty container in the adjoining cell, how can the shipowner defend a rate structure built on theories and practices displaced by technological developments?

The first argument in support of the existing system is that the possibility of sustaining a major loss is much greater in the container age than it was in the days of breakbulk shipping. A container loaded with washing machines might be swept overboard during a storm, and the claim would amount to many thousands of dollars. Loss of a single washing machine would cost the carrier a few hundred dollars. There is a modicum of truth in this argument; many containers have been carried off by boarding seas. However, the freight rate, which has been assessed against all the washing machines in the container, includes an allowance to cover this contingency. The argument loses much of its force in the face of fact.

The second point advanced in defense of existing freight rates is that the introduction of the container did not end the need to transport those low-value commodities that move in small quantities and therefore are dependent upon liner service. Some method is required to continue the subsidy of these commodities, but nothing better than the breakbulk principle has been brought forth. One school of thought advocates the adoption of a single rate for all containers, regardless of the commodities inside. This may be logical in view of the technology of container shipping, but it poses as many problems as it solves. If the rate favors the movement of cement, the revenue to the ship will be inadequate. If the rate is predicated on washing machines, this will stop the movement of cement. It also will reduce correspondingly the tonnage of cargo offered to the ship.[4]

Some years ago, an operator in the transatlantic trade instituted a *container rate* and illustrated the method by which it would freight cargo. A shipper of microwave ovens would be charged a gross figure of $1,500 for the container. Other merchandise could be mingled with the ovens so long as it had approximately the same value and was subject to the same freight rate. The shipper, of course, was responsible for stowing the packages within the container.

In this case, the ship operator substituted for the traditional commodity rate schedule a new listing for containers loaded at the shipper's option with one or more types of cargos that were "compatible" and therefore were charged the same freight rate. The shipper furnished the carrier with an accurate manifest showing exactly what had been placed in the container. Regardless of how much of the container's interior space was used by the shipper, the rate for the container remained the same.

A variant on the foregoing system was adopted by a carrier plying between New York and South Africa, charging the same rate for all containers without regard to what might be in the boxes. This *freight all kinds* rate was set arbitrarily by the carrier: initially it was $4,150 for a 20-foot box and $3,700 for a 40-foot container.

Shipping line rate makers for years have been searching for a logical and simple system by which freight rates can be applied to cargo moving in preloaded containers. No entirely satisfactory substitute has been found for the existing (and frequently criticized) rate structure, which produces adequate revenue without unduly antagonizing shippers.

Several tentative suggestions have been propounded by both carriers and shippers as bases for discussion. Rates for containers would be established for designated groupings of goods. High-value merchandise, typified by the washing machines mentioned earlier in this chapter, would be charged a fixed fee for a container load. Less highly valued merchandise would be assigned appropriately lower rates. The problem commodities typified by cement, which cannot pay fully compensatory liner rates, would be identified and a minimum charge fixed for their transportation.

Once the system became effective, shippers would be charged a single fee for the use of a container from origin to ultimate destinations. The fee would be predicated upon the shipper's declaration of value of the goods in the container. To illustrate, a hypothetical shipping line running between New York and Rotterdam would set charges for completely filled containers according to this scale:

Valuation under $200 per metric ton or cubic meter	$500
Valuation of $201 to $500 per metric ton or cubic meter	$800
Valuation of $501 to $750 per metric ton or cubic meter	$1,050
Valuation exceeding $751 per metric ton or cubic meter	$1,400

The shipper would be free to load any number and variety of commodities in the container, so long as the value did not exceed that stipulated when the reservation was made with the carrier.

To protect against abuses, the carriers would have the right to open and examine containers and would enforce these rules:

1. Only one shipper is permitted to use a container.
2. A single bill of lading is issued to each container.
3. If the valuation of any of the merchandise loaded in the container exceeds the agreed dollar limitation, the rate for the whole container will be that which applies to the goods with the highest value.
4. All containers are considered as fully loaded; there is no prorating for less-than-container lots.

PROJECT RATES

From time to time, a major contractor will be engaged in an overseas project involving the movement of thousands of tons of many kinds of equipment and supplies. Rather than calculating each shipment by the tariff, the contractor and the carrier(s) on the route will negotiate a special freight all kinds rate per agreed ton. In this case, an "agreed ton" means that everything will be freighted uniformly by one method (i.e., exclusively by weight, or exclusively by measurement). This project rate applies only to those shipments by the contractor that are part of the construction project, and it expires automatically when the job is completed.

During the life of the project, shipments will be incremental, sometimes filling a ship and sometimes amounting to only a few hundred tons, and will be as varied as these sample listings: pressure vessels, tanks, catalytic cracking towers, and reactors for oil refineries; boilers, generators, transformers, and turbines for electric generating plants; kilns, plant components, machinery, and furnaces for mining operations. In one instance, an ammonia plant had individual lifts that ranged up to 420 tons, and some were more than 40 feet long. The total movement for the project came to 20,863 tons.

The study of the development of ocean freight rates and the application of those rates to the movement of cargo is of major concern to those who are involved in either shipping goods or transporting those goods. As the use of computers becomes more and more widespread, it is predictable that shippers and carriers will engage in probing analyses and searching comparisons of different freight rates as a normal part of their business.

For a transoceanic transportation system to benefit both shippers and carriers, freight rates must be sufficiently lucrative to furnish the economic incentive to carriers to offer the needed or desired means of transportation, while still being low enough for shippers to profit financially by sending their goods to overseas markets. It is abundantly clear to users and providers of deep-sea shipping that there is—and very probably always will be—as much art as science involved in finding these nearly magic points.

CHAPTER NINETEEN

The Ocean Bill of Lading

It is much to be regretted
That your goods are slightly wetted
But our lack of liability is plain,
    For our latest Bill of Lading,
    Which is proof against evading,
Bears exceptions for sea water, rust and rain.
    Also sweat, contamination,
    Fire and all depreciation
That we've ever seen or heard of on a ship.
    And our due examination
    Which we made at destination
Shows your cargo much improved by the trip.
    . . . .
    It really is a crime
    That you're wasting all your time,
For our Bill of Lading clauses make it plain
    That from ullage, rust or seepage,
    Water, sweat or just plain leakage,
Act of God, restraint of princes, theft or war,
    Loss, damage, or detention,
    Lock out, strike or circumvention,
Blockade, interdict or loss twixt ship and shore,
    Quarantine or heavy weather,
    Fog and rain or both together,
We're protected from all these and many more,
    And it's very plain to see
    That our liability
    As regards your claim is absolutely nil,
    So try your underwriter,
    He's a friendly sort of blighter,
    And is pretty sure to grin and foot the bill.[*]

---

[*] From "Them Damaged Cargo Blues," by James A. Quinby, as quoted by Daniel A. Tadros in "COGSA Section 4(5)'s 'Fair Opportunity' Requirement: U.S. Circuit Court Conflict and Lack of International Uniformity; Will the United States Supreme Court Ever Provide Guidance?" *Tulane Maritime Law Journal*, 17, no. 1 (fall 1992): 17–18. Reprinted by permission of *Tulane Maritime Law Journal*.

Evolving slowly through the centuries from a simple receipt for goods loaded aboard a ship into a document serving several important functions in international seaborne commerce, the bill of lading is a carrier's standard contract setting forth the terms and conditions under which goods are accepted for transportation.

Not all oceangoing carriers issue bills of lading. Vessels filled with the cargo of a single shipper and designated as private carriers are operated under contracts specifically applicable to the business in hand and therefore issue only receipts for cargo loaded. Vessel owners who carry the property of any who offer it, in quantities less than a full shipload, are classed as common carriers. Dealing with many different parties, the common carrier uses a standardized contract applicable to all clients.

The differences between these two carriers and the role of the bill of lading are significant and require some explanation.

THE PRIVATE CARRIER

As the name implies, the private carrier transports the goods of a single person and is employed exclusively for the benefit of that person. It is neither ready nor willing to accept cargo from the general public. Some private carriers are owned by the entity using the transportation so provided; others operate under some form of charter. A bulk carrier chartered to a steel manufacturer and transporting iron ore to be used by that company in fabricating its metal products is a private carrier. A refrigerated cargo carrier owned and operated for the sole purpose of transporting perishable fruit and other produce for that owner is a private carrier. A fleet owned by a publicly-held corporation and carrying only the goods of its owner is a private carrier. The legal test is that the entire cargo-carrying capability of the vessel is used by only one shipper.

The private carrier is not protected by the provisions of the laws of various maritime nations affecting the carriage of goods by sea. It is answerable to the shipper only for that damage or loss attributable directly to the fault of the vessel owner or operator. The carrier's liability for loss or damage is established by proof that when the cargo was accepted by the carrier it was in good condition, but when delivered to the consignee it had sustained damage or loss. The private carrier is obligated to furnish a vessel that is seaworthy at the outset of the voyage and must be able to show that due diligence to make the vessel seaworthy has been exercised by the owner. If the ship is owned outright by the shipper of the goods, this obligation would be a matter of good management rather than legal responsibility.[1] If the shipment is consigned to the owner of the goods, the bill of lading is no more than a receipt for cargo loaded. The actual contract of carriage is found in the relationship between the vessel owner and the shipper. The protections extended to the shipowner by the maritime laws do not apply to the private carrier.

THE COMMON CARRIER

A common carrier is one that holds itself out to the general public as ready, willing, and able to transport, for a reasonable price, the goods of any person.[2] In addition,

1. The common carrier is required to serve all shippers alike; it may not choose its shippers and it must accept, within the limits of the facilities and capabilities of its vessel, the legitimate business of any and all such applicants.
2. The common carrier may limit its business to a certain type of goods to be transported: for instance, refrigerated cargo in a refrigerated ship.
3. The common carrier normally operates over a definite route in repetitious service between stated termini.

The Shipping Act of 1984, as approved by the president of the United States, defines a common carrier as "a person holding itself out to the general public to provide transportation of passengers or cargo between the United States and a foreign country for compensation that (a) assumes responsibility for the transportation from the port or point of receipt to the port or point of destination, and (b) utilizes, for all or part of that transportation, a vessel operating on the high seas or the Great Lakes between a port in the United States and a port in a foreign country."

Prior to the enactment by the Congress of the United States of the Harter Act in 1893 and the Carriage of Goods by Sea Act of 1936, the common carrier was required to deliver the cargo at the stipulated destination in the same good condition in which it was received from the shipper unless the carrier could show that the damage or loss resulted from one of five exceptions: (a) the act of God (lightning, floods, storms); (b) the acts of public enemies (a bombing attack upon a ship by an enemy during a period of hostilities); (c) the acts of public authorities (the confiscation of tainted food by the health authorities of a nation); (d) the inherent nature of the goods (the perishability of fruit like grapes or bananas); and (e) the acts of the shipper (faulty packaging or improper marking of the shipment).

Even with these exceptions, which ordinarily would relieve the carrier of responsibility for loss or damage traceable to these causes, the carrier had to show that no negligence on its part had contributed directly to the loss or damage. The general rule was that when the customary stowage resulted in damage to the cargo, the cargo interests had to demonstrate conclusively that the stowage and care given by the carrier were inadequate.

It is noteworthy that the courts, in determining the liability of carriers for damage to or loss of cargo, have extended maximum consideration under the law to the welfare of shippers. For example, when cargo was damaged in a storm, the carrier was held responsible because the worst of the disturbance could have been avoided by a reasonable deviation from the ship's initial course. In a similar ruling, the court decided that the failure of a master to take adequate precautions to meet a weather emergency constituted negligence within the meaning of the statute. The carrier consequently was held liable for the loss sustained by the cargo. Under laws enacted in England in 1855 and in the United States in 1893 and 1936, more specific rules were established as will be described in these pages.

HISTORICAL DEVELOPMENT OF THE BILL OF LADING

As a device of transoceanic commerce, the formal, detailed bill of lading is of comparatively recent origin. As early as 1063, however, the "Ordannance Maritime de Trani" (a town in Italy) refers to the requirement that every shipmaster must have on board a clerk who records the goods loaded aboard ship. A document from Spain, dated 1255 and entitled "El Fuero Real," includes a note that owners of ships should "cause to be enrolled in the register all the articles put on board ships, giving their nature and quantity." A fourteenth-century manuscript, believed to have been drawn up in Barcelona and called "Customs of the Sea," mentions that the ship's clerk had to keep a "register book." This same document states that merchants traveling with their goods should make known to the clerk as soon as the ship sets sail any goods not in the record, because the shipowner was responsible only for that which had been recorded in the ship's register.

About 1600, the bill of lading had come into common usage and was defined in *Le Guidon de la Mer* as the "acknowledgment which the master of the ship makes of the number and quality of the goods on board." The bill is distinguished from the charter party by the specific statement that three copies were to be made and that "one of them being accomplished, the other shall be void"—a phrase that has persisted to the present day in the phraseology of the bill of lading.

These precursors of the modern bill of lading, however, were appendages to the charter party and in fact were no more than acknowledgment that cargo had been placed aboard ship in the quantity and character set forth by the shipper or owner of the goods. For instance, a charter party from the sixteenth century records the following terms: (1) the owner of the vessel, either directly or through the ship's master, had leased the ship and promised to prepare it, by a fixed date, to take in the goods provided by the charterer; (2) the ship would sail with the first convenient wind to the stipulated port; (3) in accordance with a receipt or bill of lading, the ship would deliver the cargo in good condition to the designated person; and (4) the ship would remain at that port for a fixed period to take in the goods offered by the person named in the charter party, and the ship then would return to the port of origin, there to deliver the second cargo in good condition.

In 1629, G. Malynes published a pamphlet entitled *Consuetudo vel Lex Mercatoria 97,* which makes it clear that shipping practice in England had integrated bills of lading and charter parties. This author approved a bill of lading that set forth the name of the vessel and the date of sailing, the cargo loaded aboard, the conditions governing payment of the freight owed by the shippers ("laders"), and the owner's disclaimers of responsibility for nonperformance and assurances that the goods would be delivered to the merchant or its assign. Malynes further stipulated that three copies of the bill of lading were required:

> Of these bills of lading, there are commonly three bills of one tenor made of the whole ship's lading, or of many particular parcels of goods, if there be many laders; and the mark of the goods must therein be expressed, and of whom received, and to whom to be delivered. These bills of lading are commonly to be had in print in all places and several languages. One of them is enclosed in the letters written by the same ship, another bill is sent overland to the factor or party to whom the goods are consigned, the third remaineth with the merchant, for his testimony against the master, if there were any occasion for loose dealing; but especially it is kept for to serve in case of loss, to recover the value of the goods of the assurors that have undertaken to bear the adventure with you.[3]

The ocean bill of lading was separated from the charter party when shippers stopped accompanying their wares to overseas destinations and relied upon the ocean carrier to make safe delivery to the named consignee. Jacques Savary, a leading commentator on European commercial laws of the seventeenth century, offered this explanation:

> The charter party is the document made between the merchant and the . . . owner of the ship to make a voyage . . . . The bill of lading is a document that the master of the vessel gives to the merchant-shipper in which he acknowledges having received on board a number of packages or cases containing the quantity or quality of merchandise to be consigned or delivered to a person in the place where the ship must go.[4]

Savary emphasized that the charter party did not in itself attest to the ownership of the goods, since the charterer was a lessor of the space, and not (by the terms of the charter party) the shipper of the goods. To prove ownership, the shipper needed a document issued by a trustworthy person who was in control of the cargo space and had knowledge of who had shipped what goods. This trustworthy person was the master of the carrying vessel, and his document attested to both the existence of the consignment and its ownership.

Requiring that the name of the shipper be shown in the bill of lading was justified by Savary in these words:

> One must absolutely state the name of the person for whose account the merchandise is loaded; otherwise it is a fraud . . . . [I]f the shipper's name were not stated, the master would be able to take the merchandise on board for the account of a merchant who is a citizen or subject of an enemy state [and this] merchandise [could be] subject to confiscation. It is the law of the usages and customs of the sea of all the European nations, and it conforms to the Maritime Ordinance of August 1681.[5]

This bill of lading, issued in 1713, reflects the foregoing statements:

> SHIPPED by the Grace of God in good Order, and well conditioned by ____ in and upon the good Ship called the ____. Hereof is Master under God for this present Voyage ____ and now riding at Anchor in the ____ and by God's Grace bound for ____ to say Four hh [hogsheads] of rum. Being on the proper acco.t & risk of M.r Benj.n Bronsdon merchant in Boston being marked and numbered as in the Margent, and are to be delivered in the like good order and

well conditioned, at the aforesaid Port of ____ (the Danger of the
Seas only excepted) unto ____ or to ____ assigns, he or they paying
Freight for the said Goods ____ with Primage and Average accus-
tomed. In Witness whereof the Master or Purser of the said Ship
hath affirmed to three Bills of Lading, all of this tenor & date, the
one of which three Bills being accomplished, the other two to stand
void. And so God send the good Ship to her desired Port in Safety.
Amen.
Dated in ____
(Insides and Contents unknown.)
(Signature.)[6]

The stipulation in this bill that the shipowner was not responsible for
damage or loss sustained by the cargo as a result of "the Danger of the
Seas" is an early example of the effort to avoid liability for loss of or damage to the cargo. Later contracts contained additional statements exonerating the shipowner for losses sustained as a result of an undefined "act of
God," or caused by the "inherent vice" of the goods. Whenever the decision of a court of law imposed burdensome responsibilities upon the carriers, their legal counselors inserted exculpatory clauses into their contracts
of affreightment in their effort to make the terms and conditions as favorable to themselves as possible.

LAWS APPLICABLE TO CONTRACTS OF CARRIAGE

A significant deficiency in these early bills of lading was that they did not
permit transfer to third parties of the contract of carriage (or of affreightment) with all its rights and liabilities. Under English common law, when
title to the goods was passed to a consignee by the shipper, the original contract was not simultaneously transferred by the shipper. To rectify this situation, the Bills of Lading Act was adopted in 1855. The full text of this
important law follows:

Whereas, by the custom of merchants, a bill of lading of goods being transferable by indorsement, the property in the goods may
thereby pass to the indorsee, but nevertheless all rights in respect of
the contract contained in the bill of lading continue in the original
shipper or owner; and it is expedient that such rights should pass
with the property: And whereas it frequently happens that the goods
in respect of which bills of lading purport to be signed have not

been laden on board, and it is proper that such bills of lading in the hand of a *bona fide* holder for value should not be questioned by the master or other person signing the same on the ground of the goods not having been laden as aforesaid:

(1) Every consignee of goods named in a bill of lading, and every indorsee of a bill of lading to whom property in the goods therein mentioned shall pass, upon or by reason of such consignment or indorsement shall have transferred to and vested in him all rights of suit and be subject to the same liabilities in respect of such goods as if the contract contained in the bill of lading had been made with himself.

(2) Nothing herein contained shall prejudice or affect any right of stoppage *in transitu,* or any right to claim freight against the original shipper or owner, or any liability of the consignee or indorsee by reason or in consequence of his being such consignee or indorsee, or of his receipt of the goods by reason or in consequence of such consignment or indorsement.

(3) Every bill of lading in the hands of a consignee or indorsee for valuable consideration, representing goods to have been shipped, shall be conclusive evidence of such shipment as against the master or other person signing the same, notwithstanding that such goods or some part thereof may not have been so shipped, unless such holder of the bill of lading shall have had actual notice at the time of receiving the same that the goods had not in fact been laden on board: *Provided,* that the master or other person so signing may exonerate himself in respect of such misrepresentation by showing that it was caused without any default on his part, and wholly by the fraud of the shipper, or of the holder, or some person under whom the holder claims.

This act remained in force until 1992, when it was succeeded by a new law regulating carriage of goods by sea. The new law deals extensively with the transfer of rights under the contract of affreightment.

Until 1893, American carriers and shippers were governed by the general maritime law that made the ocean carrier the insurer of the goods while in its custody, except for damage caused by an act of God, the acts of the public enemy, the fault of the shipper, or a cause specifically disclaimed in the contract of affreightment. As their British counterparts did, the American shipowners inserted into their contracts more and more clauses exonerating themselves from liability for loss or damage. Among the many losses for which carriers refused to accept liabilities were those resulting from thievery, heat, frost, seawater, rust, collisions, and even for unseaworthiness of the vessel if the owner had exercised due diligence to render the vessel seaworthy.[7] One bill of lading, for instance, cited more than thirty possible causes of loss or damage for which the carrier assumed no responsibility.[8] The effect of these exemptions was to place upon the shipper the almost overwhelming burden of proving that the carrier was at fault.

Reflecting the dissatisfaction of American shippers with the exemptions from liability claimed by the carriers, legislation was introduced in the Congress and approved in 1893. The new law, known as the Harter Act, distinguished between faults in the navigation and management of the vessel and faults (or deficiencies) in the care and custody of the cargo. Declared void were any clauses in the bill of lading that were intended to relieve the carrier of the consequences of its negligence in the "proper loading, stowage, custody, care, or proper delivery" of the goods. By terms of a succeeding section of the law, the owner was obligated "to exercise due diligence [to] properly equip, man, provision, and outfit said vessel, and to make said vessel seaworthy and capable of performing her intended voyage . . . [and] to carefully handle and stow her cargo and to care for and properly deliver same." For the first time in United States history, there was the legal directive that the bill of lading set forth the identification marks and the number of packages or quantity of cargo. The bill of lading also had to show whether the weight was provided by the shipper or by the carrier.

From the viewpoint of the American shipowner, the law's directive that the bills of lading indicate the apparent order or condition of the cargo gave protection from allegations by the shipper that the cargo had been delivered to the carrier in perfect condition and had been damaged while in the custody of the vessel operator. Notations on the bill of lading such as "shipper's load and count," or "shipper's description," or the words, "said to contain," transferred to the shipper, at least in part, the burden of proof of damage.

The carriers were freed from responsibility for damage to cargo caused by errors in navigation or management of the vessel, perils of the sea, act of God or public enemies, inherent defect or insufficiency of packaging, seizure under legal process, saving or attempting to save life or property at sea, or fault of the shipper.[9]

THE HARTER ACT AND THE CARRIAGE OF GOODS BY SEA ACT

The Harter Act continues in effect today. It applies to both the foreign and the domestic commerce of the United States and is binding upon "the manager, agent, master, or owner of any vessel transporting merchandise between ports of the United States." The provisions of the law cover the movement of cargo from the beginning of the voyage (defined by court decisions as the moment when the anchor breaks ground or the last line is let go) until the goods are delivered to the consignee, when the carrier-shipper relationship is dissolved.

No changes were made in the law for over a quarter-century. In 1921, representatives met to discuss the possibility of establishing uniform rules to be included in all bills of lading. In 1924, the results of these deliberations, known as the Hague Rules, were offered to the maritime nations for approval. The United States ratified them in 1925. To bring American law substantially into harmony with this convention, the Carriage of Goods by Sea Act (COGSA) was passed by the Congress in 1936.

The new law did not fully supplant nor did it repeal the Harter Act. If the carrier does not elect the coverage of COGSA, the older law applies to the American coastwise and inland waterways trades; it also applies to the period during which the carrier, in both foreign and domestic trades, has custody of the goods before they are loaded on the ship and after they are unloaded from the ship until they are delivered to the consignee at the named port of discharge. COGSA applies to all shipments in the foreign trade of the United States, but only from the time the ship's cargo hook takes hold of the goods until the discharge at the end of the ship's tackle in the port of destination ("hook to hook" coverage). Domestic operators in the coastwise service may place themselves under the protection of COGSA by stipulation to that effect in their bills of lading.

Other limitations to the liability of the carrier normally are included in the bill of lading by reference to the appropriate statutes. Principal restrictions state that there is no responsibility for damage by fire (unless caused by the design or neglect of the carrier), and the liability of the shipowner is limited to the value of his interest in the ships plus pending freight. There is also the provision that if the owner's interest is sufficient to meet all losses, the shippers will accept a proportionate settlement. It is significant that the operator of a vessel under bareboat charter is given all the rights and privileges of a shipowner.

Both the Harter Act and COGSA hold the carrier responsible for loss or damage resulting from negligence in proper loading, stowage, custody, keeping, care, and delivery of the goods if they have been packed adequately. Rough handling causing damage is a fault of the carrier. Poor stowage that allows the cargo to shift or to come in contact with other commodities that produce taint or odor is considered the shipowner's responsibility. Failure to deliver the stipulated quantity of cargo for which receipt was given becomes the basis of a collectible claim against the carrier.

Neither the carrier nor the ship may be held blameworthy for loss or damage from the following causes:

1. Act, neglect, or default of the master, mariner, pilot, or the servants of the carrier in the navigation or in the management of the ship.
2. Fire, unless caused by the actual fault or privity of the carrier.
3. Perils, dangers, and accidents of the sea or other navigable waters.
4. Acts of God.
5. Acts of war.
6. Acts of public enemies.
7. Arrest or restraint of princes, rulers, or people, or seizure under legal process.
8. Quarantine restrictions.
9. Act or omission of the shipper or owner of the goods, his agent, or representative.
10. Strikes or lockouts or stoppage or restraint of labor from whatever cause, whether partial or general; provided that nothing herein contained shall be construed to relieve a carrier from responsibility for the carrier's own acts.
11. Riots and civil commotions.
12. Saving or attempting to save life or property at sea.
13. Wastage in bulk or weight or any other loss or damage arising from inherent defect, quality, or vice of the goods.
14. Insufficiency of packing.
15. Insufficiency or inadequacy of marks.
16. Latent defect not discoverable by due diligence.
17. Any other cause arising without the actual fault and privity of the carrier and without the fault or neglect of the agents or servants of the carrier, but the burden of proof shall be on the person claiming the benefit of this exception to show that neither the actual fault or privity of the carrier nor the fault of the agents or servants of the carrier contributed to the loss or damage.

Liner-service companies fill their vessels with miscellaneous cargo and often find it advantageous to send ships into ports not on their advertised routes. COGSA permits a "reasonable" deviation to save human life or property at sea. The shipowner, however, must be able to prove that his change of routing for the purpose of loading or delivering cargo or passengers is not "unreasonable." For example, if a vessel were loaded partially at Norfolk and then called at Baltimore for additional cargo without having included Baltimore in its advertised schedule, the delay of a day or two probably would be construed as reasonable. In one actual case, a ship advertised to sail directly from Calcutta to North Atlantic ports called at an Indian outport to take on a cargo of castor beans. The loading of the beans required two weeks, thereby delaying by that length of time the ship's arrival in the United States. The court held this to be an unreasonable deviation.

COGSA fixes the shipowner's limitation of liability for goods as the value of the vessel plus pending freight, regardless of the value of the cargo lost or damaged. Should the vessel be lost, liability is limited to the amount of the freight earnings. If it can be shown that the loss or damage occurred with the shipowner's knowledge of factors leading to that loss or damage, the carrier's petition to limit liability will not be granted by any court.

COGSA stipulates, in Section 1303 (b), that the bill of lading shall show the "number of packages or pieces, or the quantity or weight, as the case may be, as furnished in writing by the shipper."

The carrier's dock receipt and tally sheet are its permanent records of the number and weight of packages accepted for transportation. The use of large containers on all the world's trade routes, however, made it impractical for the carrier to verify numbers and weights of individual packages. The alternative was to weigh the container when it was delivered to the carrier. If the carrier did not have access to a scale, the shipper's statements as to quantity and weight would not be challenged. To protect themselves from fraudulent claims, many carriers added qualifying clauses to the bills of lading, such as "shippers weight, load, and count."

In 1982, a United States circuit court ruled that the carrier's acceptance of the shipper's statement concerning the weight of the container acknowledged that there was no reasonable ground for questioning that statement. The carrier had access to a scale and could have weighed the container, but did not, absent any reason to do so. This ruling was confirmed in 1994 by the same circuit court, which decided that the carrier is under no obligation to weigh a container at the port of discharge prior to delivery to the consignee. If proof of cargo loss was required, it was the duty of the consignee to weigh the container before the seal was broken.[10]

Pursuant to the provisions of the 1936 Act, the carrier is responsible for the value of the individual package or other customary shipping unit up to a maximum of $500,[11] unless a higher valuation has been declared in the bill of lading and a correspondingly higher freight rate has been paid by the shipper.[12] The claimant must be able to prove that the damage or loss occurred while the package was in the custody of the carrier. If the packages were shipped in apparent good order and condition and the contents were found to be broken or damaged upon opening the containers at destination, the claimant must prove that the goods were in sound condition when they were delivered to the carrier. If the carrier can show that the damage was not due to his negligence, he may be absolved of liability. Explosive and flammable cargo may be destroyed or landed short of destination without the carrier incurring any liability if, in the opinion of the master, this action was necessary to ensure the safety of the ship.

COGSA prohibits shipowners from phrasing their bills of lading to reduce liability under that act. The shipowner may not limit responsibility for the negligence of the ship's personnel with regard to loading, stowage, custody, care, or delivery of the cargo. A list of exonerations from liability, however, is included in both COGSA and the Harter Act, and these exonerations have been sustained in the United States. The net effect has been to change the status of the common carrier in American waterborne commerce. No longer is that carrier the absolute insurer of the goods, subject to certain specified exemptions set forth in the general maritime law. Instead, the carrier has been placed in the category of one who sells only careful transportation governed by special and very definite laws of sea-carriage.

THE BILL OF LADING AS A CONTRACT OF CARRIAGE

As a contract of carriage, the bill of lading sets forth the terms of the agreement between carrier and shipper under which certain goods, in exchange for a financial consideration, are accepted for transportation between named ports in a designated ship with a stipulated sailing date. The contract becomes effective when it has been signed by the master (or an authorized deputy) and accepted by the shipper.

Pursuant to the provisions of both the Harter Act and COGSA, the carrier is required to issue a bill of lading as a receipt for the goods, and the bill constitutes prima facie evidence of such receipt. The bill must contain information as to the marks and numbers of the packages, the quantity of packages or the weight or measurement of bulk cargo, and any exception to the basic statement that the goods were received "in apparent good order and condition." On demand of the shipper, the carrier must provide a "shipped" or an "on board" bill of lading (meaning that the cargo has been stowed aboard ship on or prior to the date of the bill of lading).

In promulgating the terms of the contract, the carrier often includes many provisions not covered by existing statutes but recognized as valid contractual conditions. For example, in a clause describing how goods may be stowed in the vessel, the term "underdeck stowage" is extended to cover the use of poop, forecastle, deckhouse, shelter deck, or other covered space. Cargo will be given ordinary stowage unless the bill of lading stipulates that it be refrigerated or heated; failure of the shipper to demand this care exempts the carrier from liability for resultant damage.

The master is granted authority to discharge cargo short of the agreed port of destination when, in that professional's judgment, there is a reasonable apprehension of danger to the ship or the cargo. This apprehension cannot be based on rumors or imagined dangers; it must be founded on actual or substantial peril. Once cargo is discharged under this provision of the contract, the shipowner has no further responsibility. The shipper or consignee must accept delivery and assume any expense that may be incurred as a result of this delivery short of destination.

Another example of the clauses included in the contract is the reservation to the carrier of the right to effect transshipment to other carriers of cargo destined to ports not on the ship's route; this "on carriage" is to be executed pursuant to the terms of the connecting carrier's bill of lading, regardless of whether those terms are easier or more onerous than those of the originating carrier's contract.

Each carrier, within the limits set by the Harter Act and COGSA, is free to draw up its own contract of carriage, inserting whatever clauses it deems necessary, appropriate, or desirable. One American steamship company specified its liberties and the shipper's responsibilities as follows:

- *Clause 4* placed on the shipper the burden of proving the carrier's negligence in caring for the goods after discharge from the vessel.
- *Clause 8* disclaimed any liability for damage to deck cargo.
- *Clause 11* imposed liability for extra freight if the connecting carrier increased its freight rate.
- *Clause 20* relieved the carrier of the duty to perform if navigation were closed or threatened with closure. The clause further imposed upon the shipper the liability for additional freight if the voyage were prolonged because canals or other waters were closed.[13]

Only a few of the clauses included in a bill of lading have been singled out for comment. They are sufficient to indicate the nature of the contract. While each carrier will write its own contract, there will be similarity in the basic provisions of bills issued to shippers in the foreign commerce of the United States.[14]

It is important to observe that the information statements contained in the bill of lading are accepted in three particulars:

1. The accuracy (truth) of the loading tally; the statement that the cargo has been "shipped" in a named vessel; or the declaration that the cargo is "on board" a particular ship. There is no allowance for shortages. A deficiency (shortage) in one lot may not be made up by a surplus (overage) in another lot of identical goods. The quantity of goods delivered to the consignee must correspond to the tally stated in the bill of lading.
2. The truth of the statement that, unless otherwise attested by the carrier's notation on the bill of lading, the cargo gives the external appearance of being in good order and condition.
3. The truth of the date of loading. A "shipped" or "on board" bill of lading issued by the carrier states that on the date of the bill of lading, the cargo actually was stowed aboard the vessel. This may be significant in proving that the seller complied with the terms of the contract of sale, which often stipulate that shipment must be made by a certain date.

THE BILL OF LADING AS A RECEIPT

Current shipping practice in the United States provides that, when a shipper delivers the goods to a terminal for loading aboard a vessel, a certificate known as a "dock receipt" (in some trades this is called a "mate's receipt" or a "boat note") must be furnished acknowledging that the cargo has been received and is in the custody of the carrier. This receipt is presented to the shipper after the individual packages making up the consignment have been examined by one of the carrier's inspectors (checkers) to detect external or superficial damage or shortages or any other exceptions to the statement of "apparent good order and condition." The shipper must supply the description of the goods, the numbers of packages, and the weights. On the reverse side of the receipt, the checker inserts the measurements of the packages and the "exceptions" that have been disclosed. At the bottom of this sheet, authenticating the memoranda, are the initials of the checker. The document then passes to the designated official, usually the receiving clerk, for signature and return of the original to the shipper. The dock receipt is the carrier's permanent record of the exact quantity and condition of the shipment at the time it came into its custody. The document serves as a temporary receipt until the freighted and signed bill of lading is obtained from the carrier; at that time, the shipper surrenders the original dock receipt, which is filed with the other papers relating to the shipment.

The bill of lading is completed by the shipper on forms supplied by the carrier. COGSA requires that the shipper furnish in writing certain data concerning its goods, and current practice dictates that the shipper insert these specifications in that section of the bill of lading headed "Particulars Supplied by the Shipper of Goods:"

1. The exact name of the commodity, i.e., granulated sugar, dried kidney beans, industrial refrigerator cabinets, etc.
2. The details of the shipment, showing the types of packages (bags, bales, boxes, crates, or whatever is appropriate), including the number and identification marks of the packages.
3. The gross weight of the goods.

The shipper "shall be deemed to have guaranteed to the carrier the accuracy at the time of shipment of the marks, number, quantity, and weight, as furnished by him; and the shipper shall indemnify the carrier against all loss, damages, and expenses arising or resulting from inaccuracies in such particulars" (COGSA, Section 3 [5]).

Normally, the contents of each package are not examined by the carrier; the shipper is obligated by law to provide an accurate description. Most carriers, however, reserve the right to open the packages for verification should there be any suspicion that the contents are not as declared in the bill of lading. In accepting the goods in apparent good order and condition, the carrier is bound to describe the external appearance of the cargo.[15] Where bulk cargo weight is ascertained neither by the carrier nor by the shipper (as in the case of bulk grain loaded at a public grain elevator), the master may insert that fact in the bill of lading and so be freed of the obligation to discharge the exact weight stated in the bill of lading.

The shipper guarantees to the carrier the accuracy of the marks, number, quantity, and weight of the goods. If there should be a claim for nondelivery of a part of the shipment, the shipper must be able to prove among other details that the quantity stated on the bill of lading actually was delivered to the carrier in good condition. One of the defenses open to the carrier is to show that the packages were delivered in the same quantity and condition as they were at the time they had been received, and that there was no negligence on the carrier's part in the loading, handling, stowage, carriage, care, and discharge of the goods. Under COGSA, the statute of limitation is fixed at one year; notice of loss or damage must be given not later than three days after the cargo has been delivered to the consignee, and suit for recovery of damages must be filed by the claimant within one year after delivery of the goods.

THE BILL OF LADING AS EVIDENCE OF OWNERSHIP

In medieval and early modern times, when the merchant accompanied his goods, he always could assert his ownership. As this arrangement yielded to a less direct contact with the cargo, some method of transferring title had to be devised. The simplest means of accomplishing this was to send the consignee a copy of the bill of lading that had been issued by the ship to the merchant. This might be done in a special envelope entrusted to the master, or it might be dispatched by a faster vessel so that the consignee would be awaiting the arrival of the ship with the goods. If there were some desire to protect the goods against the possibility of an impecunious purchaser taking possession, the merchant's agent in the port might be the addressee of the bill of lading. The carrier agreed to transport the goods from port A to port B and there to deliver them to the shipper, or to the agent of the shipper, or to the person designated by the shipper to receive them, or the order of the consignee.

The bill of lading in this manner came to represent the goods in respect to which it had been issued. The possessor of the bill of lading could pass authority to accept delivery to a third party by a statement written on the bill that he transferred his interest to that party. Endorsements and transfer by the owner of the bill of lading actually transferred legal ownership and the bill of lading became a document of title to the goods.

THE NEGOTIABLE OR ORDER BILL OF LADING

In seaborne trade between nations, the predominant characteristic of the bills of lading issued by the carrier is that they permit the legal transfer of title to the goods described in these bills to persons other than the named consignee. This is accomplished by adding the words "or order" after the name of the consignee, which means that the carrier will deliver the goods to whoever presents the bill of lading properly endorsed to the new owner. The legal effect of adding "or order" to the bill is to convert it from a receipt for the goods and a contract of carriage to a fully transferable (or negotiable) document of title. The law governing "order" bills states expressly in Section 3:

> A bill in which it is stated that the goods are consigned or destined to the order of any person named in such a bill is an order bill.

Lykes Bros. Steamship Co., Inc.

has been informed that one or all of San Fran-cisco Bills of Lading SFR. 1, SFR. 2, SFR. 3 issued in Mombasa for the S.S. Leslie Lykes, Voyage 94, have been stolen, and further it has been reported that attempts have been made to sell these negotiable documents in the Nairobi area. The public is hereby advised that the above indicated Bills of Lading stand null and void and therefore of no value.

Advertisement in *New York Journal of Commerce,* September 30, 1985, 1-B.

Any provision in such a bill, or any notice, contract, rule, reg-ulation, or tariff that is nonnegotiable shall be null and void and shall not affect its negotiability within the meaning of this Act un-less upon its face and in writing agreed to by the shipper.

The legal ownership (the property interest in the goods described in the bill of lading) can be transferred from the consignee named in the bill to any other persons and by them to still other persons without any of them seeing the goods or having physical possession thereof. This transfer of possession is accomplished initially by the consignee signing the bill of lading, thereby converting the bill into a "bearer" document. A refinement of this is for the consignee to direct that the goods are delivered to a partic-ular person and then to sign the endorsement.

The bill of lading thus becomes in practice a negotiable instrument. The endorsers and holders of the bill are entitled legally to rely upon the tally and upon the statements in the bill of "apparent good order and condition." In the eyes of United States courts, the bill has been fully negotiable since 1916 when the Federal Bills of Lading Act (the Pomerene Act) was passed.

There are advantages to the seller who uses the order bill of lading. For instance, the merchant who ships his property under a negotiable bill of lading can insist on payment for the goods before endorsing and turning over the bill of lading to the purchaser. Similarly, by retaining possession of the bill, a bank that advanced money against goods represented by the order bill has security for its financial interest so long as it retains posses-sion of the bill. Order bills of lading should be canceled or repossessed by the carrier at the time of delivery to avoid claims by those who might have purchased the bill of lading in good faith from an unscrupulous person.

THE STRAIGHT (NONNEGOTIABLE) BILL OF LADING

Markedly in contrast with the order bill of lading is the "straight" or nonnego-tiable bill, under which the carrier accepts cargo for delivery to the named consignee only. Transfer of title to the property cannot be affected. Possession of the goods can be obtained only by the named consignee on presentation of a copy of the bill together with satisfactory identification of the claimant. Good business management practice favors delivery against the original bill.

Except for the fact that the words "or order" following the name of the con-signee are deleted, the physical appearance and the text of the two bills of lading are identical. Some carriers use a paper stock of different color for ready separa-tion of the straight from the order bills. Frequently, a conspicuous heading on the straight bills will be imprinted to prevent confusion on the part of the user.

Because of the limitations on the use of the straight bill of lading, normally it is employed by shippers who likewise are the consignees (e.g., a manufacturing company sending components to its assembly plant overseas, or consignments dispatched to purchasers who have paid in advance for the goods).

THE BILL OF LADING IN FOREIGN TRADE FINANCING

Payment for goods shipped in export trade is more complicated than in do-mestic commercial arrangements and often requires the services of a financial agent like a bank. Without attempting to describe the intricacies of payment for goods moving in international commerce, the following sketch will indi-cate the role of the negotiable bill of lading in financing such transactions.

Assume that a consignment of ten computers, worth $2,000 each in New York, is sold to a purchaser in Lima, Peru. Shipping cost comes to $1,225, and the insurance premium on the transaction is $275. The amount of money involved is $21,500. To ensure prompt payment in United States currency to the seller, the buyer arranges with its bank to issue a letter of credit in favor of the seller for $21,500. (The letter of credit is a certificate confirming that the amount of money stipulated therein has been allocated to meet the seller's charges.)

To collect from the buyer, the seller assembles the documents re-quired by the bank handling the finances. These are (1) three original

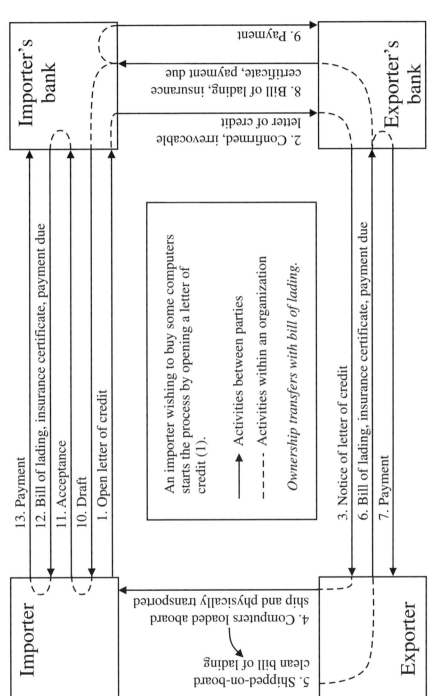

Importer's bank

9. Payment

8. Bill of lading, insurance certificate, payment due

2. Confirmed, irrevocable letter of credit

Exporter's bank

An importer wishing to buy some computers starts the process by opening a letter of credit (1).

→ Activities between parties

- - - Activities within an organization

Ownership transfers with bill of lading.

13. Payment

12. Bill of lading, insurance certificate, payment due

11. Acceptance

10. Draft

1. Open letter of credit

3. Notice of letter of credit

6. Bill of lading, insurance certificate, payment due

7. Payment

Importer

4. Computers loaded aboard ship and physically transported

5. Shipped-on-board clean bill of lading

Exporter

The bill of lading is an invaluable tool used in the movement of cargo.

freighted and signed bills of lading, to the order of the seller; (2) the bill of sale, itemizing all charges; (3) the certificate of insurance; and (4) the draft against the buyer, supported by the letter of credit.

To simplify the process of collection for the seller and also to safeguard the ownership of the goods, the order bill of lading would be made out so that the name of the seller would appear on the lines for both shipper and the person to whose order the shipment is consigned; the actual purchaser's name would appear on the line designating the person to be notified when the ship arrives at the destination port.

The seller is required to endorse the three original bills of lading to the order of the bank and thus transfers title to that financial institution. All the supporting documents also are surrendered to the bank. The seller, having received full payment, drops out of the transaction and the bank assumes temporarily the role of owner of the goods.

The seller's bank in New York, in possession of the collection of documents, endorses the bills of lading to the order of the buyer's bank in Lima. All the papers are now sent to Peru, and the Lima bank assumes the role of temporary owner of the goods. As a matter of routine explaining the existence of three original, signed bills of lading, one copy is sent by airmail on one day, followed by a second copy the next day. One copy is retained in the sender's file for use in the event that the two forwarded copies are lost in transit.

When the documents reach Lima, the bank informs (instructs) the purchaser to come to the office to receive the bills of lading, now endorsed to its order. The Lima bank, having fulfilled its function, drops out of the picture, and the buyer proceeds to the carrier's office where the original bill of lading is exchanged for a delivery order. The marine terminal will release the shipment when the delivery order is presented.

The carrier must demand that the original bill of lading be surrendered at the time the goods are turned over to the consignee. The bill should be canceled and filed along with the executed delivery order as proof that the contract of carriage has been fulfilled by delivery. The outstanding original bills automatically are voided by delivery of the goods.

The bill of lading is an invaluable tool used in the movement of cargo. This multipurpose document permits cargo to move between owners, carriers, and countries with relative ease. Although changes undoubtedly will be made to the laws governing this document, it is unlikely that it will ever disappear from the shipping scene. What is more likely to happen is that an electronic version of the bill of lading will be developed. Whatever form this document ultimately takes, it will remain one of the fundamental documents used in the movement of goods.

CHAPTER TWENTY

The Traffic Study

Among the responsibilities of the executives charged with developing sources of revenue for a shipping company, none is more exacting than preparing the *traffic study.* This is a systematic compilation of data concerning one or more of the many problems related to selling the service the ships offer to the public. It may involve an aspect of traffic management, such as commencing service on a new trade route; it may be limited to a simple matter of determining the most attractive color to be used in redecorating a public room used by the passengers. In either case, the traffic study is a methodical procedure by which to reach a decision affecting the earning capability of the ships.

The traffic study is a forecast of future trade trends in the business of the carrier—which may be in the tramping trade, regular liner service, or the transportation of coal, ore, and grain—based upon present practices and past experience. It may be directed toward a new field of sea carriage, such as a general purpose dry-cargo tramp operator contemplating the possibilities of the refrigerated fruit trade. Necessarily the study depends upon the records of the shipping company or on the best available data from reliable sources. Equally important is the personal knowledge and expert opinion of those persons participating in the study.

Two traffic studies conducted by American shipowners typify the possible outcome of these efforts. The first shows how even the most careful examination of all aspects of a new idea may be upset by the failure of the executive involved in the study to understand and to evaluate a single feature. The second demonstrates how success is achieved when all participants share the vision of what is desired.

The first study was conducted before the practicality of handling cargo in large containers had been proven worldwide. At the time the study was initiated, the project was of unusual complexity because it dealt with the new and labor-saving practice of delivering cargo encased in a sealed box which, without being opened by dockside laborers, was placed directly on a waiting truck or trailer. Only enough longshoremen were needed to hook the hoisting gear to the box and to release it.

Among the many elements that had to be taken into account were the best size for the boxes, the feasibility of obtaining return cargoes that could be stowed in the boxes, the problem of recovering the boxes from inland points remote from the ports, the desirability of making the ship self-sustaining through the installation of very expensive gantry cranes rather than developing special facilities to handle the containers at each port, the potential savings in stevedore costs that might offset the expense of starting the program, and the reactions of waterfront labor groups to the new technique.

One of the critical items in the study was the size of the containers, which was linked to the capabilities of trucking contractors in the destination countries. After it was established that these contractors could and would support the new service, the condition of the highways came under intensive scrutiny, especially the arc of the road curves. The recommended solution was quite ingenious, and it took into account the trucking industries of all the different nations involved. Three of the proposed boxes could be fitted on an American trailer, two could be loaded aboard a foreign trailer, or one box could be carried on the bed of a medium performance truck in any area of the ship's proposed operation.

Each of the problems was studied systematically, and the traffic study was completed except for the labor aspect. Trouble was encountered in measuring the extent and strength of the reaction from foreign longshoremen. As it turned out, the best available advice from experts in the evaluation of labor attitudes appeared to be conservative and realistic, but it was colored by some misinterpretation of labor's demands and by a certain amount of unwarranted optimism. In the light of the available data and pursuant to the recommendations of the study group, the costly project was approved, and millions of dollars were spent. Two ships were converted, containers were purchased, and much publicity was given to the new system.

No difficulties were experienced with the longshoremen's union when the ship was loaded in the American port. At the first foreign port, however, the longshoremen refused to work the ship except under terms and conditions that destroyed the whole idea. Although the possibility of such a reaction had been given some consideration by the study group, the militancy of the work force in that foreign port was neither adequately appreciated nor anticipated. In the discussions following the boycott, no compromise position was reached beyond an agreement to discharge the cargo from the ship. The project had to be abandoned, and both ships were laid up.

The second illustrative example of a traffic study deals with the replacement of a fleet of obsolescent cargo ships. Major changes in cargo packaging procedures had occurred in the five-year period before the study was initiated. In addition, a substantial movement of refrigerated produce from and to the United States had developed. Of immediate and critical importance was the fact that the competing carriers were introducing ships capable of much higher speed. It was imperative, therefore, that the proposed vessels embody the best and newest conceptions in ship design.

First, consideration was given to speed. A canvass of both the sales staff and representative shippers proved that there was a strong demand for drastic reduction in transit time. Intensive study of port working schedules led to the finding that, given the cargo-handling techniques of the time, only a few hours could be saved by improving production on the part of the stevedores. To meet the competition and to give the shippers the shortened voyages, sustained sea speeds would have to be increased to 20 knots as compared to the existing fleet's normal service speed of 15 knots. Engineering computations by the naval architect indicated that it was operationally and economically feasible to build the new ships with that greater capability.

The next step in the process was to examine those characteristics of the ship that affected the rapidity, ease, and economy of emptying and refilling the cargo spaces. Ships' officers, stevedores, terminal superintendents, and operating executives were directed to carry out this aspect of the study. Exhaustive consideration resulted in the recommendation that the new ship have three hatches abreast over each hold, in effect opening the entire below-deck area. Coupled with this improved access to stowage space was the need for flexible, high-speed cranes rather than the conventional booms. Insulated spaces for the transportation of perishable produce were to provide cooling down to 0° Fahrenheit.

The naval architect took the result of these elaborate studies by the composite group of traffic specialists, cargo-handling experts, stevedores, ships' officers, cargo-gear riggers, and specialists in handling perishable foodstuffs and converted them into plans for a fleet of large, high-speed, versatile, and economical ships that proved to be outstanding in their responsiveness to the requirements of the trade.

In this instance, the future of this shipping company depended upon modernization of its fleet. The financial investment was so great that those in charge had good reason to use every resource available and to devote uncounted hours to examining every detail with painstaking thoroughness. The traffic study was correctly employed as a methodical device to achieve the desired result.

The traffic study is a tool of management. It systematizes thinking related to problems of every type of shipping traffic. It requires much imagination and complete freedom from preconceived notions on the part of those who direct the study. Finally, it places the responsibility for each step and each recommendation squarely on the shoulders of the individual participants.

To illustrate, imagine the action of a traffic manager who has received many complaints that the ocean freight rate on stainless steel kitchen sinks is so high that American exporters of these items are priced out of the overseas markets to which the ships are sent. To assess the general economic situation relating to stainless steel sinks in these countries, the traffic manager requests information from the appropriate government agencies. The records of the outbound manifest section are scanned to ascertain the ship-by-ship movement of steel sinks during the past two years. The terminal manager will supply data on the costs of loading and discharging as well as any special problems that influence the cost of handling. From the shippers will be obtained data relating to the sinks sold in overseas markets in direct competition with their merchandise. When all the material has been assembled and is available for study, the traffic manager is in a position to review the entire matter intelligently and systematically and to decide whether a reduction in the ocean freight rate is in order. Furthermore, he or she will be able to determine if the reduction will help the exporters to sell more sinks in the foreign markets, with the obvious benefit to the ocean carrier of obtaining more cargo.

As a normal routine of traffic management, it is customary for periodic analyses to be made of cargo manifests. These analyses often disclose changes in tonnage and revenue which suggest that a traffic study be undertaken to fund answers to questions such as these:

What are the most important commodities, in terms of tonnage and ship revenues, moving this year, and what changes are noted when compared to last year's cargo lift? What are the current freight rates? What were the freight rates a year ago? Have shippers made any formal applications for adjustments in freight rates, and if so, what disposition was made of those applications? Are there any obstacles to the movement of these important commodities that exist today but that did not exist a year ago? Have any barriers been removed?

What is the cost of stevedoring for each of the major commodities? What is the total per-ton cost to the company to transport each of these commodities? What is the frequency of claims? How does the cost of claims settlement compare with freight revenues from each item? What is the true margin of profit? Are these items carried more as a convenience to shippers than as contributors to company profits? If there has been a loss of business this year as compared to last year, in the light of the information provided as answers to the foregoing questions, is it worthwhile to make an effort to regain this tonnage?

Earlier in this chapter, the story was recounted of a shipping company's successful fleet replacement program. With imagination, it is possible to visualize how complex and critically important a study might be.

The board of directors assigned the vice president, traffic, to be coordinator of the study and directed all departments to provide information and assistance when requested. When the detailed study was concluded, the coordinator was to submit to the board of directors the specific recommendations as to the character of service needed, the special features deemed essential in the design of the ships, and the maximum acceptable cost of the vessels.

The first step in the traffic study, therefore, was to determine what characteristics of the new ship would be most desirable. This involved not only determination of size, speed, capacity, and special features of the ships, but also the ports to be served, the approximate schedule each ship would have to follow to meet the demands of shippers, and the types and tonnage of cargo to be carried.

The coordinator ordered the managers of the inbound and outbound freight traffic divisions to compile statistics showing the fluctuations in the amount of business during the previous decade. The operating department furnished the data on the facilities and limitations of the ports along the route, the comparative cost of operating newer and larger ships at substantially increased speeds, and the number of tons of cargo handled in an hour by longshoremen in each port visited. The accounting department supplied information concerning the average revenue from each of the various items carried as well as the approximate net profit from a typical voyage.

As these data came to the desk of the coordinator, they were collated with statements from shippers and consignees setting forth their ideas, desires, and anticipated needs for marine transportation during the next decade. Various governmental agencies meanwhile supplied more elaborate and extensive information, statistical and otherwise, than company records could provide. Forecasts and predictions as to the economic growth of the region where the ships would operate also were solicited from international banking houses and foreign commerce associations.

When the accumulations of facts, figures, records, and statistics had been completed, the coordinator was able to determine with considerable accuracy what they signified in terms of ship speed, schedules, capacities, earnings, and the other details supporting his final recommendations for a certain number of ships of a particular design to operate on a set frequency of sailings. The needs of the service, the peculiarities of the cargoes, and the economic justification of the improved design were all recorded in systematic and convenient fashion. The completed traffic study filled hundreds of pages and represented a huge investment in the form of executives' time, clerical labor, and other costs.

There are no fixed limits to the subject matter of a traffic study. It is precisely what the words imply: a tool of management. It has only one purpose, and that is to provide a systematic method of analyzing a problem and giving to management the best possible resolution. In form, therefore, the study can be extremely varied. Depending upon its nature, it may take the shape of a learned researcher's written report, or it may be only an oral statement. It could take months of work on the part of practically the entire organization, or it might require only eight or ten hours of one person's time. Since it often contains many secrets of the company's operations, it never is released to the public, but its substance often is revealed in statements to government agencies, applications for route franchises, or announcements of new developments by the company.

The very nature of the traffic study requires that the person directing it have a wide knowledge of company operations. The more varied the experience and the more comprehensive the understanding of company activities and problems, the more likely it is that the conclusion can be accepted. By the same token, the responsibilities placed upon the person who must make the final recommendations in the traffic study are tremendous. Almost any other duty in the traffic department becomes, by comparison, less significant. A traffic manager whose predictions have proved to be correct most of the time is of incalculable importance to the success of any shipping organization.

CHAPTER TWENTY-ONE

Planning for a New Ship

Truly monumental in its impact upon the fortunes of a ship owning organization is the decision to build one or more ships. The mobilization of the fullest resources of the corporation is justified by the magnitude of the investment and the requirement that the ship produce sufficient revenue from constantly changing and often unpredictable markets. An axiom in maritime circles is that the best ship for a service is one built expressly to meet the demands of that service. To determine with exactitude not only the present demands but also those that will be encountered in the future is a project of formidable dimensions involving foresight, extensive research, and imagination.

If the ideal ship is built expressly for the trade she serves, the basic requirement must be to determine what the trade demands for a successful ship. Among the questions that arise immediately are these:

a. What special features are essential to meet existing and anticipated competition on the trade route?
b. Does the trade route offer sufficient stability to justify designing a ship for that service and no other?
c. Alternatively, will a ship built for possible assignment to several trade routes, but actually employed permanently in only one service, be an efficient, profitable unit in the fleet?
d. Is it in the long-range interest of the owner to build a ship that cannot transit the Panama Canal?
e. In what ways do technical advances in naval architecture and marine engineering affect the economic viability of the proposed ship?

Questions such as these lead naturally into a systematic examination of the basic proposal to build a new ship. The following list indicates the areas of concern and the depth of inquiry necessary to ensure that, if the decision is made to acquire the new ship, she will be a valuable addition.

Basic data

1. Anticipated years of operational life of the ship.
2. Ports of call, length in miles and duration in days of each voyage, and number of voyages projected for each year.
3. Estimated average tons of cargo to be lifted on outbound and homeward passages of each voyage.
4. Cubic capacity and deadweight tonnage required to accommodate anticipated cargo liftings. If specialized cargo (e.g., refrigerated produce, liquid-bulk commodities, oversize or overweight items) is to be transported, the quantity of such cargo must be stipulated, together with the equipment needed to handle each type.
5. Provision for transportation of dry-bulk cargo, especially the arrangements to load and discharge this type of cargo.
6. Cubic capacity and location of special cargo lockers, together with any special features needed for such lockers.
7. Recognizing that some cargo may be packaged in containers, does the proposed design of the ship accommodate the number, sizes, and types of boxes that may be offered?
8. If wheeled vehicles represent a significant proportion of cargo liftings, what provisions will be made for handling them, especially in the areas of square footage required, by decks? Will vehicles have access to stowage spaces? How will vehicles be secured? How will areas be ventilated?

Operations

9. Location of bunkering ports on the trade route(s) to which the ship will be assigned. What will be the capacity of fuel oil tanks (i.e., quantity of fuel oil to be carried)?
10. Propulsion equipment: slow- or medium-speed diesels, diesel electric, gas turbines, single screw or twin screw.
11. Cargoes requiring special capabilities from the engineering department: additional refrigeration equipment, ventilation of cargo spaces, electricity outlets for refrigerated containers, power for cranes and derricks.
12. Harbor restrictions: depth of the channel at low tides in the port with the least depth of water, tide ranges, turning basins, clearances under bridges.
13. Port restrictions: berthing arrangements, depth of water at the berth, canal locks, dimensions of lock chambers, dock entrance widths, depth of water on the sills.

Port cargo-handling facilities

14. Equipment in ports of call: number, type, and location within the port of fixed dockside equipment to unload and load bulk cargoes; number, capacity, and availability of dockside cranes to work breakbulk cargo; container-handling facilities; type, capacity, and availability of heavy-lift equipment.
15. Supporting facilities: provision for storage of dry- and liquid-bulk cargoes; access to ship's side of highway and railroad vehicles.

Regulatory agency requirements

16. Government regulations affecting ship construction (e.g., United States requirements that tankers trading to the United States and either ordered or built after 1990 must have double hulls).
17. Classification society requirements, load-line rules, accessibility of hull spaces for inspection and survey, tonnage admeasurement.
18. Requirements under international agreements for safety of life at sea.[1]

Data assembled from the foregoing examination provide the basis for determining the approximate size, speed, and outfit of the proposed ship. It can be prohibitively expensive for an individual owner to design, test, and build a single ship. The alternative is to negotiate with a building yard that has designed and built one or more ships embodying many of the desired characteristics of length, beam, draft, deadweight tonnage, and speed, and from these models develop the specific plans for the proposed vessel. Not only does this procedure reduce significantly the cost of the design phase; the owner can concentrate on those features that are necessary to fulfill the purposes for which the ship is intended.

This practical alternative is made possible by the fact that progressive shipyards often develop, on their own initiative and at their expense, designs for various types of ships that incorporate the latest trends in naval architecture and marine engineering. One yard, for example, announced it had designed a hull for a ship of 14,000 tons deadweight that could be built as a products tanker, a self-unloading bulk carrier, or a dry-bulk cargo ship. In 1967, British shipbuilder Austin and Pickersgill launched the first ship of its S.D. 14 (Shelter Decker, 14,000 tons deadweight) class. Over the next twenty-one years, 211 of these standardized units were delivered. Owners, particularly those operating in multicargo trades, found that the ship could be adapted readily to meet their individual needs.[2] More recently, Newport News Shipbuilding and Drydock Company of Newport News, Virginia, designed a 46,500 tons deadweight, double-hulled tanker which it named

Double Eagle. Nine orders were received shortly after the design was publicized in 1995.

The study outlined earlier in this chapter provides the basis for considering the cost of the ship, her potential earning capacity, and the freight
rate necessary to pay for the ship. A simplified example of this financial
analysis is offered below. It concerns a tanker carrying one grade of oil
from Texas to New Jersey for a full twelve months.[3]

Operations	
Days per year	350
Length of round voyage, in days	10.1
Number of voyages to be completed in one year	34.7
Cargo delivered in one year, tons	948,840
Costs	
Crew wages for 26 persons, per year	$1,470,000
Subsistence of crew	50,000
Stores, supplies, and equipment	95,000
Maintenance and repair	350,000
Insurance premiums	190,000
Fuel costs	1,980,000
Capital cost (construction amortized over 20 years;	
interest payable at 16% per year)	4,980,000
Total annual costs	$9,832,000

To meet these costs, the required freight rate is $10.04 per ton of cargo
carried. It is important to note that in a liner service, the "mix" of cargoes
changes from voyage to voyage and freight revenues fluctuate with the mix.
Adding to the complexity of predicting revenue is the nature of liner-service
freight rates, which are predicated upon long-standing practice epitomized
by these examples:

- A packaged washing machine is charged a higher rate than a simi-
  lar-sized carton of paper napkins and paper tablecloths.
- A container of refrigerated fresh fruits and vegetables is assessed a
  higher freight rate than a container of identical size loaded with
  canned goods.

How the ship is to pay for herself and ideally produce a profit for her
owner may be found in the answers to questions such as these: is the ship's
speed competitive? Will the ship's earnings pay the cost of the higher speed

demanded by the shippers? Will the shorter voyages attract more "high-rated" cargo (i.e., cargo paying high freight rates)? Is the ship's container-carrying capability sufficiently flexible to handle the anticipated traffic? Are container spaces adequately equipped to accommodate refrigerated boxes or other special requirements?

Notwithstanding the mass of statistical, mathematical, and economic information generated in the decision-making process, there is no substitute for the experience and accumulated wisdom of the senior executives who must make the final decisions. The traffic vice president draws upon experiences with the vagaries and uncertainties of the trade, its peaks and valleys, and the nature and intensity of competition to determine if the proposed ship will meet the requirements of the service during her lifetime. The chief financial officer evaluates the costs, the earnings forecasts, and the estimated profit. The operations vice president must ensure that the ship embodies the latest developments in naval architecture, ship operation, and marine engineering, and that the predictions of efficient and economic operation are within reason.

When the decision is made to build the ship, the naval architect draws up tentative plans and specifications, and these are subjected to critical examination. Ideally, this examination is not restricted to the executive level, but includes personnel who will work with and in the ship: deck and engineer officers, stevedores, and shoreside maintenance contractors. The experience of these "hands-on" people often leads to a probing study of details in the design that can be troublesome and expensive if not corrected. In a remarkable illustration of this fact, the chief engineer of a new cruise ship was appointed from another, older ship in the owners' fleet. His first contact with the ship occurred when he made a careful inspection of his department. He commented that the space between the two propulsion engines was about a half meter (18 inches) too narrow for convenient servicing of the engines. This mistake could have been avoided had the prospective chief engineer been invited to examine the plans before construction began.

It is appropriate at this point to look briefly at ships built for the dry-cargo trades during the approximately fifty years that ended in 1970. Throughout this period, breakbulk ships were quite similar in design, varying primarily in size. Speeds increased gradually from an average of 10 knots to a fleetwide figure of 14 to 15 knots. Welding replaced riveting in the fabrication of hulls, and diesel engines supplanted steam engines. Ships were improved to accommodate new developments in the patterns of trade, but no drastic changes were made in the techniques of cargo handling.

From 1919 to the middle 1960s, dry-bulk cargo was transported, with rare exceptions, in ships carrying about 15,000 tons of the particular commodity. During the decade of the 1960s, there was an unanticipated increase in the size of these carriers, as ships of 40,000 to 50,000 tons deadweight were introduced. This growth was continued until the present, primarily in the tramp fleets. Vessels exceeding 150,000 tons deadweight now number in the hundreds.[4]

Breakbulk ships in liner service during this same period increased in size to about 20,000 DWT and in speed to approximately 20 knots. Methods of cargo handling, however, underwent only minor changes.

In 1956, a genuine revolution in shipping practice began when containerships were introduced into United States coastwise service. Ten years later, the new system of cargo carriage was in operation on transoceanic routes. The demand for the containerized transportation of goods was met by construction of fleets of containerships, each generation larger and faster than the last. By 1997, a number of containerships of 100,000 DWT, which could sustain sea speeds of 25 knots, were in service. The prototype of this class was the *Regina Maersk* (built in 1996), which had a nominal capacity of 6,000 TEUs. The arrangements of the container cells permitted her to accept boxes that were 20, 40, 45, and 48 feet long.[5]

In the dry-cargo trades, ships are employed in one of two modes: tramp or liner service. Tramp ships in nonspecialized operation ("general traders") transport almost any cargo offered. Owners retain their traditional freedom to make evolutionary improvements in design, rather than radical changes. The ships still are intended to enter almost any commercial port and are restricted in their design mainly by the fact that the least well-equipped port with the shallowest draft determines the size and outfit of the ship.

Liner service implies repeated voyages over the same sea route with calls at specified ports of known capability. As the nature of cargo movements on the route changes over the years, the design of replacement ships reflects these changes. It is, however, rather unusual for the new ships to be fundamentally different from their predecessors. Significant alternations in the type of cargo moving on the route, however, will affect the design of the proposed liner.

Sealand Service commenced transatlantic operations in 1966 with fully equipped (self-sustaining) ships. It soon proved to be more efficient and profitable to construct dockside cranes and to use ships with no cargo-handling capability. Necessarily, the ships sailed only between the ports that provided these facilities. In 1980, however, Sealand opened a new containerized service to Middle Eastern ports that had no cranes at dock-

The 160-ton-capacity centerline cargo ramp of the *Hellenic Innovator* can be positioned to port or starboard to work cargo. Photograph by Jeff Blinn, courtesy Moran Towing Co.

side. To meet without delay the demands of the shippers for the new mode of transportation, the company equipped four ships with gantry cranes. The cost in money and in time of installing and maintaining the shipboard cranes was less than procuring shoreside equipment.

The characteristics of the cargo moving on a specific trade route determine, to a large extent, the major features of a cargo ship assigned to that service. There is so much variety in the normal load of a ship that emphasis must be placed primarily on the ease and efficiency with which cargo can be worked. This was pointed out in a treatise on naval architecture:

It is well to agree on the fact that what constitutes an efficient layout from the point of view of cargo carrying and cargo handling is greatly dependent upon the special requirements of each trade. It is obvious that if a great preponderance of the cargo moving in a given trade route consists of long rails, piling, pipes, etc., the optimum ship for that trade should have extra long and deep holds, long hatches, centerline pillars, special rig to facilitate handling extra long drafts of cargo in and out of the holds, etc. Extra long holds result in very large bale cubic per cargo gear; extra long hatches result in a smaller number of hatches, and a smaller amount of cargo handling gear, per ship. A ship designed with the object of being optimum for handling and stowing long pieces of cargo would not be an optimum ship to carry general cargoes. The ability of the ship to survive damage involving flooding [also] may be lessened.

A shipping company which wants to move general cargoes in and out of a large number of ports, on the other hand, has no interest in extra long holds and hatches. It will prefer to have as many hatches, and cargo handling gears, as can be installed satisfactorily in the ship, in order to facilitate reaching and moving the cargo to be handled in each port, with a minimum of interference. The requirements of the majority of long trade routes will average somewhere between these extremes.[6]

Containerships, despite their superficial similarity, are tailored to suit the requirements of their assigned routes. This is apparent in the provision of outlets (or plugs) for electrical power for refrigerated containers, the length of containers accommodated in the cells, the number of containers that can be stacked below and above decks, the location of the deckhouse or other protective structures near the bow, and the methods of securing containers in their cells. These features were seen very clearly in the *Jervis Bay*, a 22.5-knot vessel with cells for 20- and 40-foot boxes. Her capacity was 4,032 TEUs.[7] By way of contrast, the *Cape Hatteras* could carry 923 TEUs that might vary in size from 20 to 49 feet.[8]

If speed is crucial to successful competition, its cost must be determined to the nearest dollar. Speed is not attained just by adding horsepower to the engines; it entails many refinements in hull design that affect significantly (and often adversely) the cargo stowage capabilities of a ship. The plodding Liberty ship of World War II had one enormous advantage: her hull was almost rectangular, which made efficient use of all the space in the holds. In noticeable contrast was a postwar breakbulk cargoliner with twice the Liberty's speed. Her hull lines were so fine that the forward end of No. 1 hold was almost useless for cargo stowage. The full effect of increased speed must be determined before any decision is reached; failure to consider the less obvious aspects can be economically disastrous.

The versatility of a roll-on/roll-off ship was proven by this walk-on/walk-off cargo. Courtesy Atlantic Container Line.

Whereas in 1945 an aspiring shipowner could choose between reciprocating steam engines, geared turbines using high-pressure steam, and moderately powered diesel engines, the choice by 1990 had been modified to a range including steam, diesels, and gas turbines. There still was variety in the types of power plant available: medium- or slow-speed engines; single or multiple engine systems; direct, geared, or diesel-electric drive; and output of 30,000 to 90,000 horsepower.

Liner service worldwide has turned increasingly to the use of containers, evidenced by the introduction on many trade routes of fleets of large, fast, and extremely costly carriers. As noted earlier in this volume, one of these ships can do the work of three to five breakbulk vessels by reason of greater size, higher speed, and minimal port turnaround time. Owners, however, are on the alert to obtain greater productivity from their ships, both to meet competition from other carriers and to satisfy the demands of the shippers. Sea speed is a function of design, and not much can be done to increase it once the ship is in service. Cutting down the hours spent in port therefore commanded increasing attention in recent years. A radical approach to reducing transit time was seen in three ships.

Energy Independence was the first seagoing coal-burning steamship built in the United States since 1921. She loaded her first cargo, 32,366 long tons of coal, at Hampton Roads on August 8, 1983. Courtesy General Dynamics.

On December 10, 1991, the *Nedlloyd Asia* aroused interest when she sailed from Kobe, Japan, for Singapore. A containership built to carry 3,562 TEUs, she had no hatch covers to protect the holds from invading seas, and the cell guides extended the height of four containers above the weather deck. By careful design of the cells, clearance between tiers of containers was reduced to a minimum, so that an almost unbroken surface was presented to the elements. Unusually large-capacity bilge pumps were installed to cope with the volume of water predicted to enter during the worst storms at sea as well as during the heaviest tropical rainfall. By building the cell guides above the weather deck, containers were secured without the need of special lashing devices, saving time both in loading and unloading. Eliminating hatch covers permitted continuous stacking without interruptions to close the hatch, thereby reducing the time devoted to handling containers.[9]

Container sizes vary noticeably for any number of reasons. Shipowners seeking to increase their loads have grappled with the problem of transporting boxes of assorted sizes but have met with only moderate success. The *Cape Hatteras* represented a new approach. Movable guides were fitted to the cells and could be adjusted to accommodate containers between 20 and 49 feet in length.[10]

The *Atlantic Lady*, a 1,643-TEU containership owned by Oost Atlantic Lijn of Rotterdam did not have hatch covers either. As was true of the *Nedlloyd Asia*, the clearance between vertical tiers of containers was minimal, and the possibility of boarding seas was mitigated by placing the house at the forward end of the ship. In a winter crossing of the North Atlantic, she cruised at 18 knots into headwinds of near gale force, and "nothing ever [came] except rainwater," according to one reporter. In port, the absence of hatch covers cut the turnaround time in half when compared to a ship of similar size equipped with hatch covers. When this ship entered service, it was said that she was the "most advanced containership available for charter."[11]

Regardless of the types of ships involved, ship management must take into account many factors that influence decisions including the following:

1. *Trading pattern.* Does the design meet the needs of the established pattern of operation, including the ability of the ship to serve all the ports on the route(s), to carry the quantity and variety of cargo offered (or anticipated for the future), and to provide rapidity of transit satisfactory to the shippers?

2. *Speed of the ship.* Does the ship have sufficient speed to equal or surpass the competition on the route(s)? Is the proposed speed economically sustainable, given existing freight rates and predicted prices for fuel?

3. *Dimensions of the ship.* Is the proposed size correct for the ports the ship is to enter and the type and quantity of cargo she is to carry?

4. *Hull form and displacement.* Does the design incorporate the best hydrodynamic qualities possible within the limitations imposed by the requirements of the intended employment of the ship? Do the hull lines produce cargo stowage spaces that are acceptable and economical to work?

5. *General arrangement of the ship.* Does the interior design of the ship result in efficient and safe loading and discharge of cargo? Are cargo-handling devices correctly assigned to meet the requirements of the ship's employment?

6. *Cubic measurements within the hull.* Are the capacities of the cargo holds distributed appropriately with due appreciation of the need to balance working times for each compartment? Is cargo handling facilitated by the internal arrangements of space?

The 22-knot "lighter aboard ship" (LASH) *Benjamin Harrison* was built in 1980 to carry 80 lighters and 119 containers. Courtesy McAllister Bros.

7. *Choice of machinery.* Was the most effective and reliable system of propulsion selected in view of the projected employment of the ship? Is the recommended installation the most economical in terms of sustained performance in circumstances of maximum strain as well as in ideal situations? Does the problem of using fuel that barely meets the engine builders' specifications receive adequate attention?

8. *Outfit of the ship.* Are the weight and cost of different types of cargo gear and supporting equipment proportionate to the capabilities of the ship? What is the difference in cost between the optimum installation and one that meets minimum capabilities and specifications? What effects can be predicted from the decision to accept less than the optimum outfit?

Only by careful examination of every suggestion or proposal, not only for its immediate applicability and practicality but also for the "second order" effect of these ideas, are these questions answered. For instance, if the containership is to be built, the proposal to install gantry cranes to make the vessel independent of port facilities must be analyzed to establish "first order" effects like increased costs of building, reduced cargo tonnage, and more expensive ship maintenance. At the same time, second order effects like greater flexibility in scheduling ports of call and

The 500-ton-capacity traveling gantry crane of a LASH ship is prepared to hoist a lighter aboard the *Bilderdyk*. Courtesy LASH Systems, Inc.

elimination of the expense of hiring dockside cranes must be given due consideration. Systematic evaluation of both first and second order effects is required for correct decisions; the utility of the computer in this evaluation is self-evident.

By coincidence, the computer became a tool of ship management at approximately the same time that major changes in transoceanic transportation were taking place. The astounding rapidity with which containerization was accepted by shippers of many types of goods was perhaps the most conspicuous change, but it was not the only significant departure from traditional shipping practice. The old procedure of enhancing the capabilities of ships without any radical departures from prevailing customs was no longer satisfactory. Ship capacities and cruising speeds were increased by large measures, and many improved cargo-handling systems were devised and adopted. By linking the computer and the ship manager's need for better foundations for decisions, it became possible to project the profit-making potential of a ship over an extended period of time. That previously elusive but essential figure, the freight rate (or charter hire) required to break even, was given appropriate stature.

CHAPTER TWENTY-TWO

New Technology for the Maritime Industry

Throughout maritime history, technological changes came about quite slowly and, as often as not, were accepted reluctantly by the operators of ships and terminals. The most profound changes took place within the last two hundred years, including a number of major transitions: from wooden hulls to iron, from sail propulsion to mechanical, from the magnetic compass to the mechanical, from celestial navigation to electronic, and from the loud hailer to electronic communication. When Malcom McLean introduced the container-carrying ship, that change reverberated worldwide and still is being felt. Terminal operations evolved from labor-intensive breakbulk operations to container- and bulk-terminal operations, replacing much of the manual labor with technological improvements. Other changes have not been so dramatic nor so extensive, but all have combined to produce significant evolution of modern maritime commercial practices. Whatever the origin of the change—be it naval architect or engine designer, shipowner or terminal operator, communications genius or computer scientist, the force for change has been, and continues to be, irresistible.

This chapter will survey current technology in four interrelated areas of the maritime industry: ship design and vessel propulsion systems, navigation systems and watchkeeping practices, communication systems, and marine terminal operations and equipment. These are complementary to each other and collectively make possible the creation of an efficient system of water transportation.

SHIP DESIGN AND VESSEL PROPULSION SYSTEMS

As designers strive to create more efficient ships with better propulsion systems they must consider many factors: the type of cargo that will be carried, the state in which that cargo will be carried (bulk, container, roll-on/roll-off, etc.), the long-range effect of equipping ships to be self-sustaining, the operating environment, the demand for speed, the progress in diesel engine design, the availability of various fuels, the manning requirements, and the regulations. Generally speaking, vessels designed today for the major trades take advantage of economies of scale through their larger size and the use of high-powered and efficient slow-speed diesel engines that use heavy fuel oil. Incorporated into the design are such technological improvements as bridge controlled engines and automated, unmanned engine rooms. Each new ship is equipped with the latest satellite navigation system that interconnects to the vessel's satellite communication system, automatic steering system (autopilot), and radar (used for collision avoidance and navigation at sea). The combined use of these technological advances allows large, fast vessels to be legally certified to operate with as few as eight crewmembers. This is in marked contrast to ships built as recently as 1960, which depended on the old technology and had crews of thirty to thirty-five members.

In 1995, a new design for containerships was introduced to the trade. To understand the nature of the change, it is necessary to sketch briefly the standard containership. This vessel has "cells" created by rigid steel guides in the holds; these keep the containers in place. The guides rise from the lower hold to the weather deck. Access to these guides is through hatches, which at the weather deck level are closed to the sea and elements by heavy steel covers. Several additional tiers of containers are loaded on top of the covers. Generally, there are no permanent guides for the containers stowed on the hatch covers. They must be secured by one of several different types of securing devices, which may include interbox connectors (IBC) and/or steel cables.

The new design, known as "hatchcoverless," did away with the hatch covers and extended the guides to the top tier of containers. Containers are locked within the guides and therefore require no further securing. Considerable time therefore is saved in handling containers. The spacing between stacks of containers is reduced to the minimum to prevent water from working its way down into the hold. Large pumps are installed to free the ship of any rain or seawater that might be taken aboard. To the surprise of some observers, the hatchcoverless ships performed admirably, taking on no more water then conventional containerships.

By eliminating the need to secure the containers, certain positive benefits are accrued. Port turnaround time is reduced by 15 to 25 percent compared with standard containerships of equal capacity. Stevedoring costs are cut noticeably, dockage fees are less because the ship is alongside for a shorter time, and container cranes are used more efficiently.

The negative side of hatchcoverless ships is conspicuous. Building costs are about 10 percent higher than for the standard containership.

Container cranes must lift all containers over the taller rigid guides, by that slowing the cycle somewhat. The fixed guides also limit flexibility in mixing 20- and 40-foot containers. According to the 1969 Tonnage Convention, measurement tonnage was increased in some ports of call, which could mean an increase in port costs.

Although the nearly twenty hatchcoverless ships in service in 1997 earned the approval of their owners and operators, there was no widespread support for this design. This lack of support may be explained by the fact that several conventional containerships were delivered by their builders at about the same time the prototype hatchcoverless design made its appearance.

A completely new concept in containership design is the FastShip. The conceptual design of this vessel describes a vessel able to carry 1,416 TEUs at a sustained speed of 40 knots. Jet engines power the water-jet propulsion system. The cargo decks are designed to be discharged and loaded in six hours using a train-like carrier riding on an air cushion.[1] It is predicted that this ship, the fastest commercial cargo ship in the world, will cost more to operate than conventional vessels, but company officials believe shippers will pay the inevitably higher freight rates for cargo that is time sensitive. It is expected that the initial fleet of vessels will be in service sometime after 2000.[2]

The current trend in U.S. tanker design is the double-hull vessel with inert gas and vapor recovery systems. The purpose of these three design features is to improve safety and to reduce the risk of pollution of the environment.

Legislative mandates imposed by the Oil Pollution Act of 1990 require that tankers traveling to United States ports be constructed with double hulls. This design specifies that the ship have two hulls with a void space between them. A double-hulled vessel is more expensive to build and maintain; compared with a single-hull tanker of the same dimensions, it has a smaller carrying capacity. The purpose of the double hull is to reduce the risk of oil polluting the water should the vessel run aground and breach the outer hull. The space between the two hulls may be used as a void space or as a ballast tank.

Detailed descriptions of the inert gas system and the vapor recovery system may be found in chapter 9. These systems are designed to reduce air pollution or improve operating safety. The design features mentioned here have added to the safety of tanker operation and reduced the risk of pollution but at an increased operating cost.

The traditional breakbulk cargo ship that handles a mixed cargo of containers and palletized goods is also undergoing technological changes. Some European companies have developed the automatic seaborne pallet handling (ASPH) system, designed to handle palletized cargo automatically using the ship's own gear. The vessel has no hatches. Containers are loaded on deck, and the pallets are moved through side ports, thus allowing the two different cargo operations to take place simultaneously and additionally providing weather protection for the palletized cargo. In each hold is an automatic pallet shelving system similar to that seen in many automated warehouses. The racks are served by stacker cranes and both the cranes and the racks can handle pallets of different sizes and weights up to one ton. Once a pallet is placed on the ship's crane lift, it is loaded, stowed, and ultimately discharged without direct human intervention. The ASPH is designed to work in fully refrigerated spaces. A noteworthy advantage is that damage to cargo is reduced because neither stevedoring labor nor forklifts are required onboard.[3]

Many new breakbulk, container, RO/RO, passenger, and bulk carriers are being designed with bow thrusters and sometimes even stern thrusters. These thrusters are propellers whose axis of rotation is fore-and-aft instead of athwartships. At the bow or stern, they are placed in tunnels that are at right angles to the keel. When they are in operation, the propellers provide thrust to move the vessel's bow or stern to the port or starboard. A major advantage of these thrusters is that they reduce significantly the need for tugs during docking and undocking operations. The vessel operator gains greater operational flexibility.

It is also worthwhile to look at the changes that are taking place in tug designs. The tugs of twenty years ago were primarily single-screw (one-propeller) tugs powered by a 1,500 horsepower engine. As ships got larger, more maneuverable tugs with higher power were required, and the twin-screw (two-propeller) tug was developed. With two engines, these tugs had twice the horsepower of the single-screw vessels, and the two propellers gave them much better maneuverability. As ship sizes continued to increase, so did the demand for more powerful and more maneuverable tugs. One answer was the *tractor tug,* which is diesel powered and uses one of several special types of propulsion systems available (cycloidal, z-drive, azimuthal, etc.). Tractor tugs are unique in their power (up to 11,000 hp) and their unparalleled maneuvering characteristics.[4] Their hull and propulsion design is such that they can work in any direction with almost equal efficiency. This ability makes them highly desirable for use in tanker escort operations and close quarter docking and undocking of large vessels where strong wind or sea conditions prevail.

For ship propulsion, the current trend in all large vessels is toward slow-speed diesel engines capable of burning the low-grade heavy fuels. Even some

LNG carriers, which traditionally have used steam turbine propulsion systems—partly so that they could use the boil-off gas for propulsion—are now being built with diesel engines. The largest engine in service in 1999 was 89,570 bhp,[5] but as ships continue to get larger so will engine size.

An advantage of the diesel engine is that it is well adapted to operating control from the bridge. In fact, a diesel ship can be easily automated to the point where all engine monitoring functions are done remotely and the vessel is certified to operate with an unmanned engine room. Engineers are still carried but there are fewer of them, and they are all day-workers who maintain the plant in proper operating status.

For trades that require high speeds (relatively short ferry routes), the diesel engine with a fixed pitch propeller is not efficient. The new, fast vessels in use or under development are incorporating gas turbine and jet engine technology to drive water jets. The water jets are more efficient at the higher speeds, and no rudder (which creates drag and loss of efficiency) is required. This type of propulsion is expensive to operate and maintain, but it is necessary for those trades that carry time-sensitive cargo.

One of the most innovative propulsion systems, which is still very much in the experimental stage, is electromagnetic propulsion. The prototype Japanese vessel, which weighs 185 tons and is 90 feet long, was conceived in 1985 and put through sea trials in 1991. The concept of superconducting electromagnetic propulsion thrusters is based on the principle that when a magnetic field is created in seawater by use of magnets aboard a vessel, an electric current applied in a direction at right angles to the magnetic field will propel water through longitudinal ducts. The vessel is therefore propelled either forward or backward at great speed without moving parts and with no noise or vibration. While this is exciting technology, it is still years away from commercial application because superconductor technology still requires a sophisticated cryogenic system.

NAVIGATION SYSTEMS AND WATCHKEEPING PRACTICES

As recently as twenty-five years ago the sextant, chronometer, and paper chart were the primary tools used by the navigator to determine the position of the vessel at sea. While laboriously working out the vessel's position using the stars and other celestial bodies as guides, the navigator was normally assisted on watch by two able-bodied seamen and one ordinary seaman. It was the responsibility of the three seamen on watch to make sure that the ship was being steered on the ordered course and to alert the licensed deck officer if they saw another vessel. That was the bridge team of the day.

Recent technological advances have had a tremendous impact on navigation systems and practices. Gone is the navigator's reliance on the stars as guides and the sextant as the primary tool for determining position. Today, navigators depend on man-made satellites orbiting the earth. Gone is the chronometer as the sole means of determining time; today, navigators get very accurate time from the satellites. Gone is the total reliance on paper charts, many of which were made from surveys done in the nineteenth century; today, navigators are beginning to rely on electronic charts. Gone is the bridge watch consisting of four people; today only one person may be on the bridge. Navigation has become more precise and advances in technology have made practical the safe operation of ships with small crews.

The position of a ship at sea is determined by finding latitude and longitude. To establish longitude requires very precise information about time. This essential factor was not available until the chronometer was developed during the eighteenth century by John Harrison.[6] Once the time problem was solved, determining a vessel's position using celestial navigation was not difficult.

Today, time and position information (including three-dimensional positioning) is available through satellite technology. The current satellite system is known as the global positioning system (GPS). This system consists of a constellation of twenty-four satellites locked into orbits 11,000 miles above Earth. Each satellite has a clock accurate to within one second every 300,000 years. Each satellite continuously broadcasts its time and position to receivers on the surface of Earth. The onboard GPS unit measures the time interval between the transmission and the reception of signals from three or more satellites simultaneously, then calculates the distance between the user and each satellite, giving the user continuous latitude, longitude, course, and speed information. The error on GPS systems may be as much as 100 meters.

When near the coast, it is possible to minimize the error by using a differential correction that is locally broadcast to GPS receivers. This system is known as differential global positioning system or DGPS. It is accurate to less than one meter and portable enough to be used by all modes of transportation. This space-age technology is signaling the end of the older radiowave navigation systems such as Omega, Decca, loran, and RDF.[7]

All oceangoing vessels required to comply with IMO's Safety of Life at Sea convention must keep properly corrected paper charts on the bridge for use in navigation. Paper charts have been used for more than two hundred years and are the basic navigation tools of the mariner. With the introduction of electronic chart technology, some mariners (and many hydrographers) argue that the traditional paper charts have little place on the sophisticated bridge of modern vessels. That is where agreement ends and debate begins.

The International Hydrographic Organization, which is responsible for harmonizing national hydrographic practices and advising IMO, is divided about which of the two competing electronic chart systems to use. The two systems are the raster chart display system (RCDS) and the electronic chart display and information system (ECDIS). The RCDS is favored by the United States, Britain, and the Netherlands and consists of electronic charts produced by scanning existing paper nautical charts. These are called "dumb" charts because they are merely reproductions of paper charts displayed on a computer screen. The ECDIS, or "smart" chart system, consists of layers of vector data that the mariner can interrogate and customize as needs required. The two competing sides are trying to get the electronic chart system that they favor approved by IMO and accordingly granted full legal status. Once this happens, ships will no longer be required to duplicate their navigation work by having both the paper chart and the electronic charts.[8] Paper charts will then become a relic of the past.

The introduction of the powerful and versatile personal computer has changed the way the mariner operates the bridge of a ship. Computer programs are now available that allow the deck officer to do many things once done by tedious calculations. For example, software calculates tide and current information easily and quickly; takes information received from weather satellites and calculates the best routes for ships to follow to avoid storms, improve speed, or increase fuel efficiency (known as weather routing software); calculates quickly and accurately voyage planning information based on basic information provided by the navigator; and allows the log books and other record keeping and administration functions to be done in word-processing and accounting type packages.

The use of computer technology has also allowed integrated navigation systems to be developed. These systems link together navigation and ship-control functions. One example of this type of linking has the GPS navigation system tied into the ship's automatic steering system. The position information is provided continuously to the steering control system, which already has the vessel's route information; when integrated through software, the auto pilot directs the ship to move from one port to another without further human intervention. It is also possible to integrate collision avoidance information from the radar to electronic charts that have already been provided with GPS input. All these innovations in technology and its usage give the mariner access to more timely and better information and permit the vessel owner to operate the vessel with a smaller crew.

It is possible to operate a large, deep-draft vessel safely at high speeds because of the very accurate navigation information that is available on a continuous basis and the integration of navigation and ship-control functions. As these ships operate in more congested areas, there is an increased risk of collision with another vessel. Although there are sophisticated radar systems on the market, the problem develops when high-speed vessels approach one another on reciprocal courses. For example, assume that two large, 25-knot containerships are approaching each other on reciprocal courses. The relative speed of approach is 50 knots (57.5 mph). If the current radars can pick up the other vessel at 18 miles, which (depending on aspect) is not likely, the ships have only twenty-two minutes to react before a collision. If only one person is on the automated bridge, this watchkeeper might be doing something else and not notice the ship for several minutes. The potential risk is obvious, and as ship speeds increase, the reaction time will decrease even further.[9]

How can an accident be prevented then? Vessel transponders may be one answer. The transponder is a device that can be installed on a ship to send out an identifying signal in response to an incoming radar signal. The transponder's response includes vessel identification information, position, course, and speed. The use of transponders permits earlier detection and more positive identification of vessels. This technology is currently being used on only a few fast ferries, but it will eventually be adopted by all commercial vessels.

The use of radar and advanced transponder technology will help find and identify large commercial vessels, thereby avoiding collisions. However, it is much more difficult for a large commercial vessel to find, identify, and avoid small vessels. This is especially true in poor weather or sea conditions. Technology has found a way to help vessels solve this problem through the use of a thermal imaging camera. This type of camera is a thermal or infrared camera that senses differences in the heat emitted by objects and uses this input to generate a real-time, black-and-white video picture of the scene. The imaging camera may be used day or night in any weather condition.[10]

The use of computers has coincided with vessels becoming larger and more complicated. As cargoes get bigger, stability and stress and strain concerns become more important. One of the requirements of the vessel owner, and among the responsibilities of the deck officer, is to ensure that the vessel is always maintained in a seaworthy condition, with ample positive stability. Stability—the vessel's ability to return to an upright position after being inclined by an external force[11]—can be calculated, but these calculations involve a very tedious and time-consuming process. To help in these calculations, U.S. vessels use a trim and stability booklet approved by the U.S. Coast Guard. This book enables operating personnel to determine the vessel's stability as well as stress and strain numbers for various locations around the vessel.

In the past, vessels stayed in port long enough for the ship's officer to calculate, by hand, stability and stress and strain before sailing. With the shorter turnaround times in port, the ship's officers rely more on computers with their sophisticated stability software programs to do the long and tedious number crunching required. Typically, the officer merely supplies the needed data to the computer, which is programmed to calculate stability, stress and strain, trim, and draft. These programs make it possible to monitor the condition of the vessel during loading and discharging operations. Stress-monitoring gauges are fitted to ships to measure the effects during cargo-loading operations or to measure the effect of dynamic loading at sea, thereby keeping the ship from being overworked and consequently damaged. These programs can save the company the expense of repairing damage caused by insufficient stability or excessive stress and can assist the deck officer or the marine terminal's vessel planner to stow and work the vessel properly.

Another watchkeeping technology innovation has been receiving considerable discussion by mariners—the voyage data recorder (VDR). This device will be similar to the flight recorder that has been used for many years in the aircraft industry. The VDR will record a wide range of vessel data including conversations which, in case of collision, sinking, or other catastrophe, will be used by investigators to piece together exactly what happened prior to the incident. The specific standards for what data will be captured is not yet institutionalized, but IMO is working to standardize the data captured as well as format, length of recording, fire standards, etc. Eventually, a VDR will be required on all commercial vessels.[12]

COMMUNICATION SYSTEMS

Vessel owners demand to know where their vessels are at any given time as well as when they will be arriving at—or departing from—their assigned ports. It is not enough to know the calendar day; owners need to know the exact hour because their intermodal partners also have schedules to keep. With intermodal transportation becoming more important, the need is critical for each mode in the supply chain to be on time, every time.

Shippers and other transportation customers are insisting on more detailed information concerning the location and disposition of their cargoes.

Terminals are requiring more detailed information on the cargo that will be moving through their facilities, and intermodal partners want more detailed information on the movement of goods. The best way to satisfy all of these demands is through communications, and today, some significant technological changes in communications are helping everyone in the supply chain stay informed.

Shippers need information concerning the location and expected delivery time of their cargo. That, as well as other operational information, comes from the carrier who must be in constant touch with the ship. To accomplish this, ships communicate with each other and with shore facilities quickly and efficiently using satellite communication technology. In 1979 the International Maritime Satellite Organization (INMARSAT), a joint venture of sixty-four nations, was created to provide global communications via satellite for the maritime industry.[13] The INMARSAT satellite system allows ships to communicate clearly and efficiently twenty-four hours per day in any weather by telephone, telex, data transmission, e-mail, or video transmission.

There are several types of INMARSAT services available to ships. The INMARSAT-A system provides analog communications: telephone, data, and telex. It can be upgraded to provide compressed video, high-speed data, slow-scan video and more. INMARSAT-B service is the new standard and does everything that INMARSAT-A does, but it uses digital technology rather than analog. It will replace INMARSAT-A by 2003. INMARSAT-C is an inexpensive store-and-forward data messaging service for the transmission of things like weather reports and automated mutual assistance vessel rescue system (AMVER) messages, or for the remote monitoring of vessel functions. INMARSAT-M provides digitized voice, fax, and data capabilities through a smaller, less-expensive terminal than the INMARSAT-A. INMARSAT-M does not meet IMO requirements for global maritime distress and safety system (GMDSS) as do INMARSAT-A and -C.

Vessel safety is an important part of vessel management and has been improved by the technological advances in communication. GMDSS, described by IMO as "the biggest change to radio communication at sea since the introduction of radio at the beginning of the century,"[14] is an automated ship-to-shore distress alerting and safety system that relies on satellite and advanced terrestrial communication links. All passenger vessels and all ships over 300 gross registered tons were required to be in full compliance with GMDSS regulations by February 1, 1999. Current requirements are that each system be capable of transmitting or receiving distress alerts and safety information using multiple frequencies and systems (i.e., INMARSAT-A and -C, VHF radio, single-sideband radios, search-and-rescue transponders, and emergency position indicating radio beacons [EPIRBs]). This technology for effecting general as well as safety-related communication has ended the need for the traditional radio operator on merchant ships. Today, one of the deck officers maintains and operates this sophisticated equipment.[15]

The need for all parties involved to have access to information about a movement of cargo by sea is increasing. Pilots and port authorities must be informed when a vessel will arrive or depart; agents and customs officials need to know the requirements of the ship and what cargo is being brought into or taken out of a port. Safety officials insist on declarations of any hazardous material carried by the ship. Shippers and consignees need to know where their cargo is, when it will arrive, and when it will be available to them. With these increased requirements for information, many parties look to technology to make this information available in a seamless, electronic environment. The first step toward electronic data interchange (EDI) was for transportation partners to develop their proprietary protocol for transmitting information among themselves. The problem with this approach is that if a carrier deals with many different partners, familiarity with many protocols and programs will be required.

In 1993, a group of government and industry officials from over forty nations met in Geneva and set up the United Nations–sponsored Electronic Data Interchange for Administration, Commerce, and Transportation, known as Edifact. The objective of Edifact is to establish essential global standards to be used in developing the necessary EDI codes and rules to ease international trade procedures. Besides accelerating the development of EDI, Edifact officials are placing high priority on producing guidelines, directories, and codes, and translating and publishing them in many languages. With its impact on EDI transmission of commercial data, Edifact is seen as a tool for companies to use to improve competitiveness, enhance service, and ultimately boost profit.[16]

EDI is still developing and growing as a means of connecting various trading partners. At the same time, other means of transmitting information efficiently and cost-effectively are coming into use, including electronic mail (e-mail) and sites on the World Wide Web. Whether the correct answer to the need for information comes through EDI, e-mail, the World Wide Web, or a combination of all three, the use of these communication technologies will allow all parties interested in the cargo movement to be adequately informed.[17]

TERMINAL EQUIPMENT AND OPERATIONS

A key component in any transportation system is the interchange point—that point where cargo is transferred from one mode to another. No discussion of technological advancement would be complete without looking at changes taking place on marine terminals.[18] Until about forty years ago, marine terminals were very labor-intensive; they did not possess much technology besides the forklift truck to improve productivity. Since the introduction of containerization in the late 1950s and specifically since the 1980s, methods of handling cargo at marine terminals have been improved technologically.

In 1989, a Dutch terminal operator introduced the first automated guided vehicle (AGV) prototype and the first automated stacking cranes (ASC) for marine terminal use—two examples of robotics at its current best. What started in Europe as an experiment has subsequently spread to Singapore and Japanese ports. Each AGV consists of a remotely controlled, self-contained, unmanned vehicle capable of moving containers around a terminal. The average speed of the AGV is just 10 kilometers per hour (6 miles per hour) and each vehicle has sensors and bumpers to protect it from accidents. The AGV is equipped with an integrated navigation system that provides position and load information to an operation control center. The process control system that directs the movements of these vehicles then issues directions to both the ASCs and AGVs by remote digital data. The combination of these two robotic systems directs the movement of containers around the terminal and the stowing of cargo in specific locations.

Because of the equipment's mechanical reliability, the two most important benefits of AGVs and ASCs are the reductions of terminal labor costs and equipment idle time. Experience at the Europe Combined Terminals in Rotterdam proved these facts: (1) the AGV-ASC equipment is rugged and reliable; (2) each unit is very expensive (in 1995, a single AGV cost about U.S.$240,000); (3) greatest efficiency from the equipment is obtained when the operating area is sealed from workers, and all movements are directed by the control center; and (4) the labor force has been reduced significantly. Automation of ship-to-shore and shore-to-ship cargo movement has not proved feasible so far and port turnaround time for the ships has not been improved. The potential of this technologically advanced system is great, but it has not been realized up to now.[19]

Although robotics improves efficiency, other technologies are required for container identification, location, or assignment activities. In container yards with thousands of containers, losing track of one container is not difficult. In an intermodal movement particularly, this can have devastating consequences for both the carrier and the shipper. One solution combines an automatic equipment identification system (AEI) and the differential global positioning system (DGPS). These equipment identification systems use radio-frequency identification (RF) technology. RF tags are installed on equipment (containers, chassis, railcars, etc.), and readers are positioned in strategic locations throughout the terminal, such as at a gate, on cranes, or in mobile vehicles. AEI readers scan the tags that pass by them and record the transmitted information, which consists of data such as equipment identification number, size, weight, time, date, owner, and location. This information is used by terminals to trace equipment to ensure accuracy of inventory and to improve scheduling.[20]

AEI equipment tags are passive in their operation and depend on communications using a technology called "modulated backscatter." The tag on the equipment acts as a field disturbance device, sending the information to the reader by modulating and reflecting a constant carrier-wave signal transmitted by the reader. This allows the tag the capability to be frequency agile; it has shown an accuracy of better than 99.95 percent. The ability to operate at multiple frequencies is very important in international operations because every country where the equipment may be operated has its own regulations governing radio frequencies and power levels. A single tag with compatibility for all frequencies and power levels therefore has obvious advantages to equipment owners.

The next step is to assign, establish, and remember the location of each piece of equipment. This is accomplished by means of the differential global positioning system and computers that can save the acquired information. The DGPS is the same navigation system used for ships to determine their position accurately.

Necessary to the efficient real-time operations of these technologies are rapid, two-directional communications between the central processing or control station and the stationary and moving vehicles throughout the terminal. The low-power, wireless area network may be used to transmit DGPS corrections to all operating equipment or to relay bidirectional messages between the readers in the facility and the control station or between the control station and the operating vehicles, be they robots or manned.[21]

All of this technology is designed to permit a greater throughput at container terminals. These terminals therefore will be servicing larger ships. As the ships get longer and wider, acquiring the next generation of container crane is necessary for terminals. These cranes can work ships that have twenty-two containers abreast on deck.[22] The size is impressive, but these cranes are still operated by people, and people have difficulty with depth perception in positioning containers with such big cranes.

Several innovations are helping to solve some problems associated with large container cranes. One problem—that associated with positioning the container precisely over the chassis to ensure proper mating of the container and the chassis—can be solved by using a new, patented system called the container chassis positioning system (CCPS). The currently used positioning technique relies on people to guide hustler drivers by hand and voice signals. This is a difficult and time-consuming process. The CCPS system uses a set of video cameras arranged to provide continuous viewing of the chassis in the loading area, a machine vision processor with special chassis-tracking software, and a set of signal lights for the cab operator. Guided by these signals, the hustler driver can consistently place the chassis in the correct position for loading on the first attempt.[23]

A second problem, also associated with large container cranes, is that the load being moved continues to swing on the cables once the trolley has stopped. The load therefore cannot be lowered into the cell guides or onto the chassis until the swing has stopped. Some new cranes are equipped with a computerized electrical antiswing control system that allows high-speed trolley operation and faster hoisting and lowering times. The antiswing system uses a special camera that scans and detects the container's swing angle, whether it is caused by traveling, hoisting, or wind action. By tracking the swing angle signals and controlling the travel motors to obtain the optimum angle, the antiswing system achieves a swing of less than four inches only five seconds after stopping the trolley.[24] These two innovations can save the terminal a considerable amount of time.

Besides larger and more efficient cranes, many terminals are developing on-dock rail facilities to speed up the removal of containers that are part of landbridge services. On-dock rail facilities require terminal operators to use railcar-loading equipment. Most of it has been on container terminals for years. Having railcars on a terminal also requires a very close working relationship with railroad dispatchers when switching is required.

The emphasis here has been on container terminals. Other types of terminals are also changing, but at a slower pace. Oil terminals, for example, are being retrofitted with vapor recovery systems to reduce air pollution and improve safety while tankers are working cargo alongside. Dry-bulk terminals are building larger, automated cargo-handling systems with state-of-the-art dust-control equipment. The dust-control measures are designed to reduce air pollution.

Technological improvements for the maritime industry are evolving at a fantastic rate, fueled by the desire to improve efficiency and reduce the cost of transporting goods. While these changes are impressive, technology alone will not be sufficient to reach these goals. Training of personnel must be addressed in a proactive manner. After all, it is the people operating the new equipment who will ultimately determine its efficiency.

CHAPTER TWENTY-THREE

The Business of Shipping

In the preceding presentation of the intricate story of the management of a modern shipping company, some of the fascination and the deeply personal aspects of the business of shipping have received little attention. That fascination does exist, however much it has been covered over with operational detail. The rewards of the enterprise are understood by some, appreciated by others, and shared by those fortunate ones of all ranks who lift their eyes above their desks and seek the far horizons beyond which the ships sail.

To show how the many activities and responsibilities of management actually can be combined in one individual's experience, the career of an imaginary shipping company president is outlined here, together with this fictional executive's reactions to the challenges, changes, and rewards of shipping as a career. No single individual is the subject of the sketch; the career described is typical of that of many shipping company executives. The philosophical musings are based more on memories of comments by friends and associates than on imagination.

It is a fall evening in a large seaport city. Outside the building, the city lights are coming on one by one. Inside the big office, the jangle of telephones has subsided, and the clatter of business machines has been stilled. A few men and women linger at their desks, each finishing some small task before leaving for the day.

In the president's office, a man sits at the desk beside a window commanding a view of the harbor. He looks down at the unending activity on the water, and his eyes dwell upon the shape of a ship standing out to sea. The president reflects over the efforts that have gone into the ship's sailing, and his reflections take him back over a lifetime of service involved with the transportation of goods and people across the oceans.

He looks around his office. There, in a special place of sentiment and honor, is his certificate of graduation from a maritime academy. He had been well trained there; he had come to know something of the difficult yet fascinating career he had chosen for himself when only a boy. He also had the veil of management and its challenges lifted just a bit. It had been a good experience, learning to be a seaman and finding out why things were done in certain ways, some of which were ingrained in the traditions of the sea.

Just above the diploma was another framed document, this one written in an engraver's script and ornamented with pictures of two ships. This was a license authorizing the person named thereon to command any size U.S. flag ship on any ocean. His master mariner's "ticket!" What years of work and aspiration had preceded the wonderful day when he had been presented with that precious proof of qualification for that post of distinction and almost immeasurable responsibility! A year as an able-bodied seaman, four months as a quartermaster, a year as junior mate, and two years in tramp steamers plodding all over the world with cargoes of coal, grain, ore, fertilizer, and lumber—all had given him a firm knowledge of the changeability of the seaman's life and a competence in his chosen profession that no amount of theoretical study could have produced. He had a good time on the tramp; the ports were both familiar and exotic. The hazards of navigating with pilots who spoke no English and seemed to understand no sign language had added a grey hair or two. He made some good friends, too, real seamen who had no other ambition than to command ships sailing in international commerce.

Tramping was all right, but promotion required a variety of experience. So he transferred to a liner company, even though it meant starting over again as a third mate. He learned at first hand about precise schedules, difficult loadings of odd cargoes, round-the-clock operations in one port after another, endless paperwork, and always the need to keep the agents informed systematically of progress so that tugs, pilots, line-handlers, and supply people could be scheduled properly to avoid delays to the ship. It had been good duty. Promotions were swift, and soon he was chief mate.

Chief mate! Memories of the never-ending demands upon his time, skill, and knowledge crowded in on the president. Responsibility for the safety of the ship's cargo, the proper loading of the ship to ensure seaworthiness, and the efficient supervision of longshoremen, seamen, cadets, and shoreside workers who swarmed over the ship—all this had been his. He met senior company executives who came down to the ship; he learned to be everywhere at once, to carry a hundred details in his head without becoming confused or excited. He concentrated upon his daily duties, and he took real pleasure in knowing that each job had been done well.

Three years sped by for the chief mate, and after a total of only six years with that company he was transferred ashore to be a cargo superintendent in a small foreign port. The high-sounding title covered a hundred routine chores from arranging for line-handlers to tie up the ship when she arrived to explaining to unresponsive longshoremen for the hundredth time how to sling up certain types of cargo. Six months of that and he was moved to a major foreign port as assistant terminal superintendent. That had been a challenging job! He had his first contact with the financial aspects of shipping and began to relate ship time to money, efficiency on board to coordinated and systematic support from the shore staff, and the flow of cargo to economical employment of resources of the cargo terminal. This experience was intimidating, initially overwhelming, and finally appreciated.

Two years ashore, although crowded with interest and real accomplishment, still had not brought him to the pinnacle of his youthful ambition. He requested and received a return to sea duty and rejoiced once again to feel a ship's deck underfoot. Six months as chief mate preceded that wonderful day when the vice-president, operations, had informed him that the company had decided to recognize his outstanding performance by giving him a command of his own. How thrilling it had been to walk aboard *his* ship and to realize that he had the final responsibility for the safety of the ship and the lives of the people on board. He also knew that much pressure would be placed upon him to hold to schedules in spite of fog and storm, and how little understanding his problems would receive from landlubbers who thought of ships only as money producers.

He enjoyed his responsibility as master and watched the results of his efforts as he slowly shaped the ship to his own ideals of a well-run vessel. To his pleasant surprise, he received a letter—there it was, yellowed and creased, hanging alongside his license—from the company's board of directors expressing appreciation for his unceasing and exemplary devotion to duty. That letter was precious, citing some of his achievements: rescuing a dozen men from a foundering fishing boat in a frightful North Atlantic storm, winning the annual award for the safest ship in the fleet two years running, earning commendations for having the finest and cleanest ship in the company's service. He always had a good crew, and they had worked together with pride and a sense of purpose.

The president's eyes moved on and stopped for a moment in front of the naval reserve commission. What a change active duty had been, as he moved from master of his own ship to lieutenant and navigator in a destroyer! Responsibility sought him out, however, and before many months he had been promoted, assigned first as executive officer of a large ship and then commander of a small cargo ship. From that job he had moved up to the command of a large transport and then to a major shore station. In those years of naval service he had come to understand the reasons why merchant shipping was a vital component of a nation's seapower. He never forgot those lessons; they influenced his thinking and his life when he returned to civilian pursuits.

When he returned to civilian status, he found that significant changes in management ashore had come about. More emphasis now was placed on the art of management, and financial considerations loomed larger than ever before. To bring himself up to date and to meet the evolving standards of ship owning and management, the president attended graduate school, qualifying for the degree of master of business administration. Equipped with this testimonial to his intellectual acuity, the president found employment as chief mate with the company he now headed.

Two trips as mate were followed by assignment to a command of his own. The policy of the company was changing, and more attention was being given to capitalizing on sea experience. As an experimental move, he was brought ashore as a member of the sales staff in the outbound cargo department. *That* had been a change! "Pound the pavements; ring doorbells; work up a good sales promotion talk; never be downhearted"—these were the maxims he learned to follow. He enjoyed those contacts with the shippers. For years, he had served them impersonally when he was loading and transporting their goods, but now he was meeting them face to face. It gave a new dimension to his work at sea. He understood what the formerly anonymous "shippers" thought, and he was better able to meet their requirements. From sales representative, he was transferred to the manifesting department for a few weeks, more for the experience than for the value of his contribution to that type of work. That wasn't his "cup of tea," since he had been an active seaman. He disliked the routine of checking figures and cargo descriptions all day long, but he realized how important it was that he know this part of the business, even though it lacked glamour. A transfer soon came to the inbound traffic department, where he met the consignees, the men and women who were waiting for the goods his ships were bringing to the port. He came to know many people, including government officials, and he learned much about the business of keeping customers happy. He enjoyed this human contact, and he liked the idea of helping to generate patronage for the line by giving good service.

A new world was opened to him when he was promoted to general freight agent. He became intimately familiar with the manner in which freight rates were made. He spent uncounted hours in sessions with executives of other companies, both carriers and shippers, discussing and making policies and seeking solutions to problems. He attended those all-important meetings of the Conferences (he always spelled the word with a capital, to distinguish those meetings with associations of carriers on the trade routes from the routine face-to-face talks with his colleagues). He was very happy when the chairman, acting on behalf of the membership of the Conference, presented him with a letter expressing appreciation for his substantial contributions to the work of the Conference, based on his extensive seafaring experience.

It was during those months when he was general freight agent that he found himself an active participant in the greatest change in shipping practice since the initiation of liner service in 1817. Suddenly, it seemed that the skills acquired in handling breakbulk shipments had been made superfluous, as huge boxes were placed aboard a ship by enormous machines. Appearances, however, masked the fact that knowledge and care still were demanded in placing containers in the ship, ensuring safe delivery, preventing accidents to personnel and containers, and making certain that terminal areas were secure from theft. He drew upon his years of sea experience, and he found that he was the more competent executive because of his background.

Traffic and all it entailed were fine and had provided a wonderful education, but operating ships was the president's real love, for he was a seaman first and last. He welcomed, therefore, the assignment overseas as operations manager. It was good to get back to having direct contact with the ships and the seamen as well as the terminal personnel and the faithful watchmen, coopers, and tradesmen and women who worked so well and so anonymously! Long hours were spent at his desk and even longer hours in the terminal and around the ships, but they were rewarding, instructive, constructive, and, above all, companionable hours.

Those happy two years passed all too quickly. Then came the cable summoning him back to the home office to take over the duties of vice-president, operations. What a tremendous thrill that was, and how proud he felt! From cadet to vice-president in charge of all the ships! It had been quite a climb, and he had enjoyed every step of the way. He recalled those discussions of company policy that he had with the former president regarding the proper operation of the fleet, the positions he had taken and for which he'd fought vigorously because he believed them to be right even though they had not been popular.

Although the president had spent his shipboard years as a deck officer and ship master and had been a successful terminal operator, he had schooled himself in marine engineering practice. He followed with intelligent and informed interest the rapid replacement of steam turbines by diesel engines of previously undreamed of horsepower and astonishing reliability and economy. His company, always a leader in technology, had adopted a fleet replacement program that made great demands upon the engineering staffs afloat and ashore, equivalent to the changes in freight traffic management and cargo handling impelled by the container revolution.

After two years as vice-president, the directors called him into their meeting room. Everyone rose as he entered. The chairman greeted him and escorted him to the only empty chair in the room. As he walked toward the table, he noted that a handsome card beautifully lettered with the word "President," had been affixed to that chair. It didn't seem possible, but he was led to that chair, and when the directors burst into applause, he came out of the daze.

The president's gaze shifted to a frame that held two items—a photograph of himself in the uniform of a quartermaster standing beside the master of his first ship, and that red-lined page from an old desk calendar with the notation in pencil, "I was elected president today."

Thirty-odd years of his life were shown on the walls of his office, mused the president as he scanned the room quickly: cadet, seaman, quartermaster, mate, lieutenant, captain, master, pier superintendent, sales representative, general freight agent, operations manager, vice-president, and president. It had been a good life.

As the president reached for his hat, he glanced out of the window again. Another ship was standing out to sea, and her light shone brightly in the gloom. He walked out of his office and noted, from force of habit, the board showing locations of all the company ships—*his* ships, their next ports of call, and their dates of arrival and departure. He looked at that board every evening as he left the office; he liked to identify himself with the ships and the men and women on board. He remained a seaman—was proud to call himself by that term—and he loved the ships.

Outside the building, he walked briskly to the ferry landing and boarded the ferry. He went swiftly to his usual place forward, where he could see the ships and their lights. Another big ship was standing in from the sea. In his mind, he envisioned the preparations being made even at that hour to receive the ship. The hoarse whistle of an outbound ship turned his thoughts to the people who had toiled over manifests and crew lists, cargo plans and repair specifications, stores lists and bills of lading, and to the men and women who stowed the boxes and bales and assorted commodities and secured the huge containers in their appointed places in the ship.

The big vessel slipped down the harbor and was lost in the dark. She was outward bound, and she carried with her not only the work of hundreds of men and women but the fortunes of dozens and dozens of shippers and consignees, the dreams of countless people who would use the great piles of goods that she carried, and the lives of the fortunate men and women who were taking her to sea.

As he watched the moving ships he could not help but reflect that just as he had grown and changed, so had the maritime industry. It was, and would continue to be, a dynamic and energetic industry. What was once a world fleet of small breakbulk vessels was now a fleet of very large specialty carriers augmented by a much smaller fleet of traditional breakbulk ships. On certain routes around the world, tramp vessels had given way to large, fast, liner-service vessels. Through the years, technology changed virtually every aspect of the industry including ship design, satellite navigation equipment, electronic charts, electronic tagging of equipment, and the omnipresent computers. Government regulations became more comprehensive with new attitudes toward supervision of the industry and concern for the environment. The industry progressed from the basic operation of ships to the integration of services into intermodal transportation systems with the long-sought single bills of lading. Most conspicuous was the change in the nature of the work force. Today, it is much more diverse ethnically and in gender than it had been when he started his career. It is no longer surprising to go aboard ships or walk around terminals and find women working alongside men as equals in their jobs. Workers possess improved skills in interpersonal relationships, communications, and computers. Where will it end? One thing is certain—the dynamism of shipping will carry it forward.

The echo of the big ship's whistle sounded through the night. It was lonely, brave, challenging, competent, cheerful. The president looked down the harbor and said to himself, "It has been a wonderful career. I wouldn't exchange a minute of it for all the wealth of the Indies. It has been rewarding, exacting, exciting, dynamic, important, and, above all, necessary. What an honor to be able to say, 'My business is shipping!'"

Notes

Chapter 1. The Significance of Maritime Transportation

1. John Dalton, (U.S. Secretary of the Navy), "Law of the Sea," *Journal of Commerce,* July 17, 1998, A6.

2. Robert A. Kilmarx, ed., *America's Maritime Legacy: A History of the U.S. Merchant Marine and Shipbuilding Industry Since Colonial Times* (Boulder, Colorado: Westview Press, 1979).

3. Navigation Act of 1817.

4. Passenger Service Act of 1886.

5. Seaman's Act of 1915.

6. SOLAS Conventions.

7. Merchant Marine Act of 1920, Section 27, commonly referred to as the Jones Act.

8. "Cargo preference" legislation, Military Transportation Act of 1904.

9. Electronic transportation is considered a legitimate mode because it encompasses all of the factors common to the traditional transportation modes. Electronic transportation has a sender who initiates the movement, a consignee or receiver with a discrete address, a carrier who provides the transportation service, various regulators in both domestic and international movements, third parties available to facilitate the movement, and rates for the movement. The primary difference between electronic transportation and other modes of transportation is that the carrier does not assume responsibility for delays or lost cargo.

Chapter 2. Regulatory Involvement in Maritime Transportation

1. There are currently 153 member states plus two associate member states.

2. Following the sinking of the Titanic in 1912, the first international conference on safety at sea was convened by the major maritime nations in 1913. The purpose was to promote safety of life at sea by establishing a common agreement based on uniform principles and rules. A convention, known as the Safety of Life at Sea Convention (SOLAS 1913), was drafted but never adopted because of the outbreak of the First World War. It was not until 1928 that the maritime nations met again and finally adopted SOLAS 1929. Since then there have been a number of new SOLAS conventions.

3. COLREGS is the acronym for the IMO Convention on the International Regulations for Preventing Collisions at Sea. This convention took effect on July 15, 1977, and all vessels flying the flags of states that ratified the convention are required to abide by the Rules. In the United States, Congress adopted them as the International Navigational Rules Act of 1977, and they were codified in 33 CFR.

4. STCW, the acronym for the IMO Standards of Training, Certification and Watch-keeping, was originally adopted in 1978 and subsequently revised in 1995. The 1995 revision became effective on February 1, 1997, and will be fully implemented by 2002. With its latest revision, this convention recognizes the increased use of multinational crews and modern technologies. It addresses crew age, requirements for minimum training, medical fitness for duty, examination criteria, and sea service. "New Regulations Set Training Standards," *Lloyd's Ship Manager,* August 1995, 9.

5. MARPOL, the acronym for the IMO Convention for the Prevention of Pollution from Ships, was established in 1973 and contains measures designed to prevent marine pollution caused both accidentally and in the course of routine operations. The convention consists of five annexes: I. Pollution by Oil; II. Noxious liquid substances in bulk; III. Harmful substances carried in packaged forms; IV. Sewage; and V. Garbage.

6. ISM Code (IMO's International Management Code for the Safe Operation of Ships and for Pollution Prevention) is mandatory as of June 1998 for certain vessels and as late as 2002 for others. One requirement of the code is that every company develop, implement, and maintain a safety management system consisting of a safety and environmental protection policy, instructions and procedures to ensure safe operation of ships and protection of the environment, defined levels of authority and lines of communications, accident reporting procedures, emergency procedures, and procedures for internal audits and management reviews.

7. Mary Bond,"Ballast Water Management," *Seatrade Review,* September 1998, 41.

8. Bob Jaques, "IMO Explained," *Seatrade Review,* March 1996, 39–40.

9. Association membership includes ship management companies and crew management companies. All members must commit themselves to gain the ISMA certificate of compliance with the Code of Shipmanagement Standards (CSS), which was introduced in 1990. This quality assurance code consists of three parts: a general section with which all companies must comply, a manning section with which both ship management companies and crew management companies must comply, and a technical section with which ship management companies must comply. The requirements of ISO 9002 and the IMO ISM Code are in the process of being incorporated into the Code of Shipmanagement Standards.

10. The International Organization for Standardization (ISO) is a nongovernmental, worldwide federation of national standards bodies organized in 1947. "The mission of the ISO is to promote the development of standardization and related activities in the world with a view to facilitating the international exchange of goods and services and to developing cooperation in the spheres of intellectual, scientific, technological and economic activities." The office of the Central Secretariat is located in Geneva, Switzerland. "Introduction to ISO," http://www.iso.ch, December 15, 1996.

11. Det Norske Veritas (DNV), the Norwegian classification society, is an independent, autonomous foundation established in 1864 to safeguard life, property, and the environment. DNV establishes rules for the construction of ships and mobile offshore platforms and carries out in-service inspections of ships and mobile offshore units. DNV Web site, "About Det Norske Veritas," http://www.dnv.no, December 17, 1996.

12. For a table comparing the ISMA Code, the ISO 9002 Code, the ISO ISM Code, and the DNV SEPS Code, see a supplement to *Lloyd's Ship Manager,* October 1995, 11.

13. For a time table for the implementation of the ISM Code, see "ISM Code Explained," *Seatrade Review,* June 1994, 37.

14. "Landmarks in ITU History," http://www.itu.ch/itudoc/about/itu/history/landmarks _e_5517.txt, January 1997, 1.

15. The specific dates for implementation vary by ship type. Full implementation by all ships is February 1, 1999. Information on specific dates can be found in 47 CFR (Tele-communications) parts 80 to end.

16. One type of regulation merely specifies the amounts of emissions permitted to be discharged into the air, while another type requires that a ship's propulsion system actually be shut down during the period of time that the ship is in port. This second type of regulation is commonly known as "cold iron" law.

17. Barbara Hayden, "National Ballast Water Symposium," http://webtwo.rsnz.govt. nz/ballast/ballast.htm1#hayden1, June 27–9, 1995.

18. In the early 1990s, MARAD selected 56 countries as a basis for a study of the nature and kind of national preferences in domestic maritime matters. Countries were selected if they had an oceangoing fleet of at least 50 national flag vessels over 1,000 DWT, had coastal shores connecting to international waters, or had an established government without a major armed conflict which maintains diplomatic relations with the U.S.; 53 countries responded, of which 43, or 81%, indicated that they had strong cabotage restrictions. United States Government, Maritime Administration, *By the Capes Around the World: A Summary of World Cabotage Practices,* May 22, 1991.

19. Maritime Administration, *By the Capes: A Primer on U.S. Coastwise Laws,* 1986.

20. The United Nations Convention on the Law of the Sea contains international regulations relating to the exclusive economic zone in Part V—Articles 55–60. The law says that this zone shall not extend beyond 200 nautical miles from the baselines from which the breadth of the territorial sea is measured and most nations claim the full 200 miles.

21. Kilmarx, *America's Maritime Legacy,* 28.

22. Maritime Administration, "MARAD Annual Report," chapter 6, September 30, 1995.

23. United States Government, *United States Coast Guard* (Washington, D.C.: U.S. Government, 1994), 460–2.

24. United States Government, *National Transportation Safety Board* (Washington, D.C.: U.S. Government, 1994), 687–9.

25. As of 1970, the act provides for the maintenance of a capital construction fund. U.S. citizens meeting specific criteria may establish such a fund. The purpose of this fund is to provide replacement, additional, or reconstructed vessels built and documented in the U.S. for operation in the U.S. domestic, foreign, noncontiguous or Great Lakes trade, or in the fishing industry of the U.S. A specified maximum amount of the taxable income attributable to the vessel's operation may be placed in the fund each year. There are certain tax advantages to placing money in the fund. Davis Bess, *Marine Transportation* (Danville, Ill.: Interstate Printers and Publishers, Inc., 1976), 85.

26. United States Government, *Maritime Administration* (Washington, D.C.: U.S. Government, 1994), 476–7.

27. "Legislation Through the Looking Glass," *Lloyd's Ship Manager,* November, 1966, 21.

28. United States Government, *Federal Communications Commission* (Washington, D.C.: U.S. Government, 1994), 576–9.

29. "Non-Indigenous Aquatic Nuisance Prevention and Control Act of 1990," http://www.nfrcg.gov/nas/control.htm#HDRQ, November 18, 1996.

30. Military Sealift Command Web site, http://www.msc.navy.mil, January 1997.

Chapter 3. Tramp Shipping: Its Management and Operations

1. In descending order of magnitude, the cargoes carried by the dry-bulk ships in 1992 consisted of iron ore, steam coal, grain, coking coal, bauxite/alumina, and phosphate rock. (*The Motor Ship,* June 1993, 70) "Minor bulk" cargoes were agricultural products, forest products, fertilizer materials, ores and minerals, ferrous scrap and steel products, and manufactured products such as cement, petroleum coke, and "other cargo." In 1990, the aggregate of these minor bulks was 597,200,000 tons.

2. Grain exports in the crop year 1990–1991, by country of origin, were the following: Argentina, 9,800,000 tons; Australia, 14,700,000 tons; European Economic Community, 26,600,000 tons; Canada 25,800,000 tons; and United States, 79,400,000 tons. Drewry Shipping Consultants, *Dry Bulk Carrier Trading Prospects* (London, 1992), 19.

3. Tonnage was moved in 1998. The Baltic Exchange.

4. "Bulkers and Tankers Have Same Concerns," *Fairplay,* April 22, 1993, 17; also Drewy Shipping Consultants, *Shipping Statistics and Economics,* March 1993.

Dry Bulk Carrier Fleet (10,000 tons deadweight and larger)

Size	Number	Total Tonnage
10,000–30,000	2,099	46,773,000 tons deadweight
30,000–50,000	1,496	56,849,000
50,000–80,000	787	50,133,000
80,000–100,000	41	3,531,000
100,000–150,000	221	28,734,000
150,000 and over	142	26,561,000
	4,786	212,581,000 tons deadweight

5. In the days preceding World War I, a typical English tramp steamer had a triple expansion reciprocating engine, with or without a Bauer-Wach exhaust turbine. Three single-ended Scotch boilers, each with three (occasionally four) furnaces and possibly a superheater, generated steam at 180 to 220 pounds per square inch pressure. Such a vessel cruised at about 9 knots and burned 18 tons of fuel per day when loaded with 5,000 tons of cargo. There were three firemen and one trimmer per watch and three watches per day. Firing the boilers was a manual job.

Coal was stowed in cross bunkers and in the tween decks adjacent to the bunkers. It was brought to the firemen in wheelbarrow loads by the trimmers.

Using best Welsh coal, fires under the boilers had to be cleaned and the ashes and clinkers removed once a day. If coal of inferior quality was burned, this process might have to be repeated every eight to twelve hours. The fires were cleaned regularly in rotation. The routine was to allow the fires to cool somewhat, then to rake out the ashes and clinkers to the stokehold floor and to quench this hot mass with water. The ash then was shoveled into jute bags that were hoisted to the deck and spilled into the sea. The jute bags were not expendable. E. L. Green, "My Recollections of Coal-Burning Ships," *Seabreezes,* September 1994, 685 ff.

6. The Liberty ship hull was 134.12 meters (441.5 feet) long, 17.37 meters (57 feet) in the beam, and had a summer load-line draft of 8.45 meters (27.75 feet). There were five

hatches, each served by one set of cargo booms. Two oil-fired boilers generated steam at 220 pounds per square inch to actuate a 3-cylinder triple-expansion steam engine of 2,500 indicated horsepower. In calm seas, the ship had a cruising speed of 10.5 knots.

7. The "S.D. 14" was 140.87 meters (462.5 feet) long, 20.42 meters (67 feet) in the beam, and on a draft of 8.84 meters (29 feet) had a deadweight of 14,910 tons. Five hatches and five holds were served by cargo derricks of five tons capacity. The grain cubic capacity was 22,920 cubic meters (764,200 cubic feet). Speed in service under average fair weather conditions was 14.9 knots. The 5-cylinder diesel engine, nominally rated at 7,500 brake horsepower, used only 6,750 horsepower at cruising speed. The main engine consumed about 25.5 tons of heavy oil per day. In 1968, the price of the ship was £900,000. Ships of this type were built as late as 1983, with the last delivery in 1988. "The Austin & Pickersgill 'S.D.14' Liberty Ship Replacement," special supplement to *The Motor Ship*, May 1967.

8. *Berge Stahl*—Built in Japan, 1980; length overall 343.0 meters (1,125.7 feet), beam 63.5 meters (208.5 feet), draft 23.0 meters (75.5 feet); 175,720 gross tons, 364,767 tons deadweight; speed 13.5 knots; diesel power 24,858 bhp.

9. "Cunard's Growing Bulk Carrier Fleet: Two Further Ships Named in Seville," *The Motor Ship*, October 1973, 320.

10. The Baltic and International Maritime Council was organized in 1905 under the name of Baltic and White Sea Conference. Its original purpose was to end the fierce rate war in these two areas, and for that purpose shipowners from the United Kingdom, Denmark, France, Germany, the Netherlands, Belgium, Spain, Norway, Sweden, Finland, and Russia assembled in Copenhagen. At the first meeting in November 1905, 102 owners from ten countries, controlling 1,056 ships, were present. Sailing ship owners were admitted in 1917; four years later, 157 owners of 450 wind-driven ships belonged to the Conference.

Growth continued and in 1927, owners from 20 countries and their fleets represented almost 14 percent of the world merchant fleet. In that year, the name was changed to Baltic and International Maritime Conference.

The organization held its first meeting outside of Europe in 1985. At this convocation in San Francisco, the name was changed once again to Baltic and International Maritime Council to avoid confusion with the somewhat better-known steamship conferences. At the end of 1992, more than 950 owners controlling about 11,800 ships of over 365 million gross registered tons belonged to the council. In addition to the owner members, 1,600 brokers and 60 persons from marine insurance and other ancillary maritime enterprises belonged to BIMCO.

A fundamental activity of BIMCO is the development of charter parties, bills of lading, individual clauses, and several other documents related to shipping. The council also provides its members with up-to-date information on port conditions, tariffs and charges, cargo regulations, labor situations, working hours, and samples of cost. Seasonal ice conditions are reported as circumstances warrant. BIMCO Supplement to *Fairplay*, March 25, 1993, 7.

11. Roland Hobhouse Thornton, *British Shipping* (Cambridge: Cambridge University Press, 1939), 139–40. A brief history of the origins of the Baltic Exchange is included in these pages.

12. In rounding out this sketch of how tramp shipping is managed, it is fitting to include a number of case histories of ships that operated under time and voyage charters. The examples illustrate many of the principles discussed in the text.

Western Australia to Antwerp/Hamburg Range.
Motorship *Scotspark,* 25,000 metric tons, $21.50;
3,000 tons discharge free, barley. April 13–25.

This extremely brief report of an uncomplicated voyage charter is an example of the shorthand used in trade journals. The details of the ship's employment, derived from other sources, make an interesting story.

The motorship *Scotspark* was a bulk carrier of 27,175 tons deadweight with a below-decks capacity for grain of 42,000 cubic meters (1,400,000 cubic feet). A service speed of 15 knots required daily consumption of 40 tons of heavy oil and 2 tons of diesel fuel. With tanks holding 2,152 tons of oil, the *Scotspark* could make a 51-day voyage without refueling.

In the grain trade from Australia to Europe, it is customary for charterers and owners to agree that the cargo will be loaded at the expense of the ship at a minimum rate of 1,000 to 1,500 tons per weather working day. The cost of discharging in Europe is to be borne by the charterers, unless specific contractual provision is made to a different effect. In the case of the *Scotspark,* the shipowners undertook to defray to the expense of unloading 3,000 tons of the barley cargo.

Barley is one of the lighter grains and has a stowage factor of 1.68 cubic meters (56 cubic feet) to the long ton. The entire cargo space of the *Scotspark* would be filled when 25,000 tons had been taken aboard. To determine the tonnage available for fuel, the following computation was made:

Deadweight capacity at summer load line	27,175 tons
Barley cargo loaded	25,000 tons
Available for fuel, water, stores, etc.	2,175 tons
Estimated weight of water, stores, etc.	500 tons
Net tonnage available for fuel	1,675 tons

The record of this voyage shows that the ship arrived in Esperance Bay, Australia, on April 12, tendered at the earliest permissible date, April 13, and departed on April 14, arriving in Fremantle two days later. Cargo operations were finished and the *Scotspark* cleared for Antwerp via Table Bay (Capetown, South Africa) on April 20. Arrival in Antwerp was reported on May 31 after a 41-day voyage on which the average speed was 11 knots on a daily consumption of 30 tons of fuel. The owners ordered the ship to cruise at the most economical speed to reduce the cost of fuel and also to eliminate the purchase of fuel at Capetown.

On completion of discharge, the *Scotspark* was time-chartered to Continental Lines for a voyage from Antwerp to the United States south of Cape Hatteras.

Vancouver to Antwerp/Hamburg Range. Motorship *Regina Oldendorff,* 37,150 tons deadweight cargo capacity, 1,620,000 cubic feet (45,880 cubic meters) grain space. Lump sum $330,000, basis one discharging port, with option for two discharging ports $10,500 extra. Free in and out and trimmed. Eleven weather working days all purposes, Sundays and holidays excepted. Grain/seeds. April/May.

The *Regina Oldendorff* was a diesel-powered bulker of 37,150 tons deadweight on the summer load line. The charterer expected to transport any kind of grain or a cargo of oil-seeds, or a mixture of both, from Vancouver, British Columbia (Canada), to a port on the western European coast between Antwerp and Hamburg. From the fixture report, it is clear that when the ship was chartered the precise nature of the cargo was not known, and therefore the owner demanded that the charterer pay a fixed sum of $330,000, which would be owed regardless of how much grain or oil-seeds might be put aboard. To meet possible requirements to deliver the cargo in two ports, the charter party stipulated that this could be done for an additional $10,500. With these arrangements, the owner of the *Regina Olden-dorff* was guaranteed a satisfactory revenue regardless of what kind of grain or seeds, or both, might be loaded.

The *Regina Oldendorff* arrived in Vancouver on May 1 and sailed on May 9. Transit of the Panama Canal was effected on May 21, and on June 5 the vessel arrived in Rotterdam where the entire cargo was discharged. The charterer waived the privilege to have the vessel call at a second port. Loading and discharging consumed a total of 17 calendar days, including Sundays and holidays, which were not counted as part of the "all-purpose" allowance of 11 days. The charter party also provided that only weather working days would be debited against cargo-working time. The available data do not indicate whether adverse weather hindered cargo operations, so it is impossible to determine if demurrage was incurred.

The ship's cargo was wheat ("heavy grain"), which stowed at 1.32 cubic meters (45 cubic feet) per long ton. The below-decks cargo space of 48,600 cubic meters (1,620, 000 cubic feet) would be filled completely by 36,000 tons of grain. The record shows that the vessel actually loaded 35,370 tons, a figure derived from these facts:

Deadweight at summer load line		37,150 tons
Fuel (27 days @ 40 tons/day, plus safety reserve		
equal to 5 days' consumption)	1,280	
Water and stores	500	
Tonnage for ship's needs		1,780 tons
Quantity of wheat to be loaded		35,370 tons

River Plate to U.K./Gibraltar-Hamburg Range/Mediterranean not east of the Adriatic. Motorship *North Emperor,* 46,427 tons deadweight and 1,893,000 cubic feet grain space; 15 knots on 43 tons fuel oil, plus 2 tons diesel oil; $3,100 per day plus $127,500 ballast bonus. Trip, delivery River Plate, redelivery dropping pilot U.K., Gibraltar-Hamburg range, or Mediterranean not east of the Adriatic. Charterer: Continental Grain Corporation. April.

To put the ship in position to carry out this time charter, it was necessary for the owner to send the *North Emperor* in ballast from Koper, near Trieste, Yugoslavia, where the previous charter had terminated, to Argentina. The full cost of the voyage was for the owner's account, but the circumstances of the charter were somewhat unusual. From the statement in the fixture report that a payment of $127,500 would be made to the owner for the ballast voyage, it may be deduced that the market for ships at the time of the fixture was very competitive, and only a few vessels were available. To meet its own corporate commitments, Continental Grain Corporation was willing to assume part of the expense of the transatlantic voyage. The agreed charter hire of $3,100 per day was not to be paid until the ship had passed Recalada lightship (off Montevideo, Uruguay) on the way to Rosario, 191 miles up the Rio de la Plata (River Plate) from Buenos Aires.

The ship was time-chartered for that period required to make the trip from the loading port on the River Plate to a port in the United Kingdom, or in continental Europe between Gibraltar and the eastern shore of the Adriatic Sea. As is customary in time charters, the charterer was to pay not only the daily hire of $3,100 but also the cost of fuel consumed, which the owner warranted would not exceed 43 tons of intermediate grade fuel oil (1,000 seconds Redwood) plus two tons of diesel fuel for each 24 hours underway. The dead-weight (on summer load line) was stipulated to be 46,427 tons, and 56,790 cubic meters (1,893,000 cubic feet) of space below decks was guaranteed for a grain cargo.

To establish the precise moment when the ship would go "off hire," the charter party contained the provision that when the pilot was dropped as the ship was commencing her outbound voyage from the destination port, payments under the charter would cease.

The record of this voyage shows that the *North Emperor* departed from Koper on March 24, called at St. Vincent for bunkers on April 4, and arrived in Rosario on April 16. The port was congested, and departure was delayed until April 23. On arrival in Buenos Aires, the same type of difficulty was experienced, and there was delay in finding a berth until May 5. Topping-off operations were finished in time for the ship to sail for a port in Italy on May 7. The delays incurred in connection with loading were charged against the time charterer, whose responsibility according to the terms of the charter party commenced when the ship passed Recalada lightship and continued until she was redelivered at the end of the voyage in Italy

13. "BIFFEX Gets New Index," *Fairplay,* December 24–31, 1998, 47.

14. "BFI and BIFFEX Explained," *Seatrade Review,* December 1994, 31–3.

15. "Multipurpose Ships Fading Away," *American Shipper,* December 1995, 76.

Chapter 4. Chartering

1. Charles L. Trowbridge, "The History, Development, and Characteristics of the Charter Concept," *Tulane Law Review* 49, no. 4 (May 1975): 743 ff.

2. Michael F. Sturley, ed., *Benedict on Admiralty,* 7th ed. (New York: Bender, 1994), vol. 2-A, 3-1 and 3-2; Anthony N. Zock, "Charter Parties in Relation to Cargo," *Tulane Law Review* 45, no. 4 (June 1971): 737.

3. John C. Koster, ed., *Benedict on Admiralty,* 7th ed., vol. 2-B (New York: Bender, 1994), 3-2 and 3-3.

4. This charter is an updating of the well-known New York Produce Exchange Time Charter of 1946.

5. *Benedict on Admiralty,* vol. 2-A, 7-1 and 7-2; vol. 2-B, 1-25 to 1-27.

6. Braden Vandeventer, "Analysis of Basic Provisions of Voyage and Time Charter Parties," *Tulane Law Review* 49, no. 4 (May 1975): 836–7; *Benedict on Admiralty,* vol. 2-A, 7-15.

7. Michael Wilford, Terence Coghlin, and John D. Kimball, *Time Charters,* 3d ed. (London: Lloyd's of London Press, 1989), 167–8.; *Benedict on Admiralty,* vol. 2-A, 7-3.

8. Vanderventer, "Analysis of Basic Provisions," 838.

9. The term "demurrage" is derived from the old sense of the verb "to demur," when it means "to tarry." The root of the word is the French *demeurer,* to stay, stop, or remain.

10. *Benedict on Admiralty,* vol. 2-B, 1-30 to 1-32; "Master's Role at Loading," *Seatrade Week Newsfront,* August 6–12, 1993, 13.

11. Wilford, *Time Charters,* 248, 256–60.

12. The term is used in both instances, as shown in the text; the appropriate meaning is derived from the context in which it appears.

13. Raymond J. Burke, "Voyage Charters—Special Problems," *Tulane Law Review* 49 (May 1975): 950.

14. Johannes Trappe, "Recent Developments in Laytime Cases," *Lloyd's Maritime and Commercial Law Quarterly,* Part III, August 1990, 389.

15. Ibid., 388; Burke, "Voyage Charters," 842–5; Cromwell A. Anderson, "Time and Voyage Charters: Proceeding to Loading Port, Loading, and Related Problems," *Tulane Law Review* 49, no. 4 (May 1975): 881–3.

16. Wilford, *Time Charters,* 86.

17. Ibid., 87.

18. Ibid., 82–5, 97–8.; *Benedict on Admiralty,* vol. 2-G, 1-14 to 1-22.

19. Tim Howard and Brian Davenport, "English Maritime Law Update, 1992," *Journal of Maritime Law and Commerce* 24, no. 3 (July 1993): 440–2; Nicholas J. Healy, Jr., "Termination of Charter Parties," *Tulane Law Review* 49, no. 4 (May 1975): 845–56.

20. Trowbridge, "History of the Charter Concept," 752.

21. "Wear and tear" has been defined as "deterioration or depreciation in value by ordinary and reasonable use of the subject matter."

22. Trowbridge, "History of the Charter Concept"; Sheldon A. Gebb, "The Demise Charter: A Conceptual and Practical Analysis," *Tulane Law Review* 49, no. 4 (May 1975): 766–75.

Chapter 6. The Conference System

1. In discussing the need to amend the Shipping Act of 1916, the comments of the Senate Committee on Commerce are pertinent:

"Your committee has been constantly aware of the fact that further unilateral attempts by this Government to regulate the details of commercial transactions of shippers and carriers which take place and are documented abroad, are likely to have major deleterious effects and negligible counterbalancing benefits. First, they are likely the create further resentment among our foreign friends and, as a consequence, to cause reactions ranging from passive loss of confidence to active retaliation in foreign ports. In the process, they might well force foreign lines out of conferences, thereby destroying conferences and placing the high-cost American operation, even if subsidized, at a serious if not impossible competitive disadvantage. Second, and perhaps equally serious, to the extent such extraterritorial regulation cannot be as effectively enforced against their competitors, our Americans lines, we would be working at serious cross purposes with fundamental precepts of national maritime policy." U.S. Congress, *Senate Report No. 860,* "Steamship Conferences and Dual Rate Contracts," 87th Congress, 1st session, August 31, 1961, 3, hereafter cited as *Engel Report.*

2. An excellent short history of the origin of the conference system is contained in Inter-American Maritime Conference, *Report of Delegates of the United States* (Washington, D.C.: Government Printing Office, 1941) 159–63.

3. "Because of the peculiar mobility of ships, it is entirely possible for a shipowner to place his vessel in a particular service on relatively short notice and without hindrance from

any law or regulation of any nations. As a result, the only method that has proved practical to assure continuity of service on a particular route with a degree of stability of rates, in view of the very large investment required in the establishment of a regular service, is by providing specific inducements to shippers to utilize the services of the particular line or lines regularly serving that route. The conference system, with an appropriate tying device, has proven to be the most effective method, both from the point of view of the carrier and the shipper." U.S. Congress, *House of Representatives Report No. 498,* "Providing for the Operation of Steamship Conferences," 87th Congress, 1st session, June 8, 1961, 12 (hereafter cited as *Bonner Report.*

4. John A. Hobson, *The Evolution of Modern Capitalism,* rev. ed. (London: Allen & Unwin, 1926), 175–6.

5. American Maritime Council, *Foreign Trade and Shipping* (New York: McGraw-Hill, 1945), 25–6.

6. Ibid., 26–7; Daniel Marx, Jr., *International Shipping Cartels: A Study of Industrial Self-Regulation by Shipping Conferences* (Princeton, N.J.: Princeton University Press, 1953), 50–67, hereafter cited as Marx.

7. A flagrant example occurred in 1908. German passenger ship operators reacted to competition for immigrant passengers on the Hamburg–New York run by using fighting ships to destroy this rivalry. Suitable steamers were chosen from the conference members' fleets and were sailed on the same days and between the same ports as the independents' ships. Fares were reduced enough to attract most of the passengers to the fighting ship. When more passengers bought tickets than the fighting ship could accommodate, they were transferred to the conference members' ships at the same low fares. Losses resulting from this activity were prorated among the conference members in proportion to the number of their ships. The committee summarized the situation in these words:

It was thus a case of all the lines, united in conference, opposing every sailing of a single opposition line. By distributing the loss over the several members of the conference, each constituent line would suffer proportionately much less than the one line which was fighting the entire group, and which would inevitably soon exhaust its resources in the conflict with the combined power of the large lines with their superior speed and better third class accommodations.

This type of predatory competition also existed in cargo service, as the committee took pains to illustrate. The case in point was that of a German "fighting corporation" formed in 1905 by six cargo-liner companies. This corporation had as its sole purpose the destruction of rivals on its members' routes. Four ships were owned and others were chartered. These vessels sought the bulk cargoes normally transported by the independents at freight rates which were intended to bankrupt the independent carriers.

8. *Bonner Report,* 5.

9. Gunnar K. Sletmo and Ernest W. Williams, Jr., *Liner Conferences in the Container Age* (New York: Macmillan, 1981), 200.

10. *Federal Maritime Board v Isbrandtsen Co., Inc.* (354 U.S. 481, 1958). For a commentary on this case, see Allen R. Ferguson, et al., *The Economic Value of the United States Merchant Marine* (Evanston, Ill.: The Transportation Center of Northwestern University, 1961), 389–96.

The Shipping Board was in existence from 1916 until 1936, when it was superseded by the United States Maritime Commission. In 1950, the regulatory functions which had been performed by the commission were assigned to the newly established Federal Maritime Board. The chairman of the board was also the chairman of the Maritime Commission. President Kennedy proposed, and the Congress approved in 1961, a plan by which the Federal Maritime Commission was set up as an independent agency with sole responsibility for regulating maritime commercial activities.

11. Engel Report, 5–6.

12. Roy Pearson, *Containerline Performance and Service Quality* (Liverpool: University of Liverpool, Marine Transport Centre, 1981), 23.

13. Engel Report, 7–8.

14. Sletmo, *Liner Conferences,* 306–7.

15. "Australian Wool Exporters Continue Rate-Cut Efforts," *New York Journal of Commerce,* October 8, 1983, 24B.

16. See Sletmo, *Liner Conferences,* 278–86, for a comprehensive critique of the Australian experience.

17. Great Britain, Committee on Inquiry into Shipping (Chairman, The Viscount Rochdale): *Report* (London: Her Majesty's Stationery Office, Cmmd. 4337, 1970), 132, par. 468–69, quoted in Sletmo, xxxi.

18. Marx, *International Shipping Cartels,* 240.

19. Personal interview, L.C. Kendall and Sylvester J. Maddock, vice president, traffic, Seas Shipping Company, 1947. An excellent account of the rate war is contained in Robert Greenhalgh Albion, *Seaports South of Sahara* (New York: Appleton-Century-Crofts, 1959), 120–7.

20. An insight into the actions and reactions involved in a freight rate war was granted by the extensive hearings conducted by the Federal Maritime Commission into the friction between the American flag Grace Line and the foreign flag Viking Line during 1960 and 1961. The commission's findings were not made public until November 1962. The following excerpt is revealing:

When Conference rates were opened, it was the policy of Grace not merely to meet Viking's rate, but to go down immediately to the minimum rate which Grace considered it could charge. Thus when rates were opened, Grace's rates were not decreased by stages but generally in one big cut.

The Conference rate, effective on and after December 14, 1955, on agricultural implements, was $27 per ton. It was opened March 7, 1960, and Grace made its rate $12 on that date. Viking's rate prior to the rate war was $24 except for one shipment of $20.25 early in 1960. On household washing machines, the normal Conference rate of $20 was opened with a minimum of $15, effective February 22, 1960, which was the rate Grace made effective on that date. The Conference opened the rate without any minimum effective March 7, 1960, and Grace's rate on that date became $11. Viking's rate prior to that date was $18. On toys, with a value of less that $350 a freight ton, Viking normally charged $31.50 and the Conference charged $35. During August 1960, both Viking and Grace charged $13.50. Grace intended to go as low as Viking's break-even point in setting its rates, but even such low rates were met, and Grace went to even lower rates. On individual rates, both Grace and Viking undoubtedly reached noncompensatory levels.

When the rate war ended, although many rates went up to normal, others, while raised, did not rise to their previous levels. Commitments to shippers kept some rates from returning all the way up to their normal levels. Viking's policy during the rate war was to cut its rates, so long as it obtained enough revenue to cover loading, discharging, and commissions, plus "something for the ship," such as $1 or $2 a ton (Congressional Information Bureau, November 15, 1962).

The rate war lasted throughout 1960, in which year there was a major decline in trade with Venezuela. The war gradually ended early in 1961, and all rates slowly increased during that year.

21. The Japan Shippers Council and the European Shippers Council are beginning to work with U.S. shippers' associations to foster international understanding through communication. One specific project is to standardize electronic data interchange (EDI) formats. For additional information see Bob James, "NITL's Worldwide Focus: East Meets West as Shippers Unite on Issues," *Traffic World,* November 18, 1996, 36.

22. The Global Shippers Association (GSA) is believed to be the largest U.S. shippers association with such companies as Xerox, General Electric, PPG Industries, and Montgomery Ward as members. In October of 1996 they requested bid proposals for a 25,000-container contract covering all Atlantic and most Pacific cargo. This signifies the start of global contracts instead of the traditional contracts that cover only one trade lane. The National Industrial Transportation League (NITL) is another large U.S. shippers association.

23. "Ocean Reform Act Cleared," *Fairplay,* October 8, 1998, 8.

24. Terry Brennan, "Conference Changes, New Alliances Ahead in Wake of Maritime Deregulation," *Traffic World,* January 1, 1996, 19.

25. "Hyundai, NYK Come Together in Space-Charter Agreement," *Journal of Commerce,* December 9, 1996, 1B.

26. Bill Mongelluzzo, "Setting Course for Twenty-first Century," *Journal of Commerce,* August 9, 1996, 1A.

27. Janet Porter, "Merger Casts Doubt on Consortia's Future; Analysts Expect Grand, Global Alliances to Collapse Despite Carriers' Assurances," *Journal of Commerce,* September 12, 1996, 1A.

28. Tom Baldwin, "TACA, Stable and Unified, Prepares to Chart the Future," *Journal of Commerce,* September 23, 1996, 1C.

Chapter 7. Passenger Vessel Operations

1. "Cruising on a Luxury Liner Offers a Smorgasbord of Pleasure, " *Journal of Commerce,* April 7, 1995; "Cruise Industry," *Worldwide Shipping,* April 1993, 30; "A Taste for the Totally Tropical," *Cruise and Ferry Review,* supplement to *Lloyd's Ship Manager,* September 1993, 11–7.

2. Fairplay, March 11, 1993.

3. John Malcolm Brinin, *The Sway of the Grand Saloon* (New York: Delacorte Press, 1971), 495–502.

4. "Holiday in the Sun," *Via Port of New York,* December 1959.

At least two ships were built for and operated in year-round cruise service before World War I. The Hamburg-America Line introduced the *Princessin Victoria Luisa* in 1900. She had the sharp hull lines of a yacht, but carried 400 passengers, all of whom slept in brass beds. This handsome ship was assigned exclusively to cruise service. She was wrecked off Jamaica in December 1906. William H. Miller, Jr., *The First Great Ocean Liners in Photographs, 1897–1927* (New York: Dover Publications, 1984), 42.

The *Vectis* was built by the P&O Line in 1904 and was employed in full-time cruises from England to the Baltic Sea, the Mediterranean, and the Canary Islands. Thornton, *British Shipping* 209.

5. *Journal of Commerce,* October 23, 1973, 5.

6. "Kloster Cruises Sees Sales as a 'New Chapter,'" *Journal of Commerce,* December 16, 1995.

7. The "block coefficient" of a rectangle is 1.0. As the lines of the rectangle are modified to shape the ship's hull, the value of the block coefficient is diminished. Thus the fast (28.5-knot) *Queen Elizabeth 2* has a block coefficient of 0.56, whereas the 20-knot *Statendam's* is 0.70. It is worth noting that Carnival's 90,000 gross ton *Carnival Destiny* has a block coefficient of 0.73.

8. "The Return of the True Liner?" *The Naval Architect,* September 1994, 452–7.

9. "Cruise Lines Look Beyond Panamax," *Marine Log,* February 1995, 31.

The primary saving is in the deck and engine departments; obviously, hotel service is proportioned to the number of passengers embarked.

10. "Eagle Gets a Name," *Fairplay,* July, 1998, 4.

11. A sampling of builders' prices for ships ordered for 1996–1999 delivery revealed the following: Carnival Cruise's *Destiny* (2,600 passengers) cost $400 million (1996). P&O's 104,000-ton ship *Grand Princess* (2,600 passengers) had a reported price of $385 million (1997). Disney's *Disney Magic* and *Disney Wonder* (1,760 passengers) each had a reported price of $380 million (1998 delivery). Carnival Cruise's *Triumph* (2,642 passengers) had a reported cost of $400 million (1999 delivery). "Cruising: A Vibrant and Growing Niche," *Lloyd's Shipping Economist,* October, 1996, 5–9.

12. Specifications of the *Costa Allegra* are length, 183 meters (615 feet); beam, 25.36 meters (84.5 feet); cruising speed, 22 knots; gross tonnage, 30,000; crew and staff, 450.

13. *Marine Log,* "Cruise Lines Look Beyond Panamax."

14. "RCCL's Vision Produces Three Different Designs," *Nor-Shipping 1995,* supplement to *Lloyd's Ship Manager,* June 1995.

15. *Marine Log,* "Cruise Lines Look Beyond Panamax."

16. A recent round-the-world cruise had segments typified by a 16-day trip from Hong Kong to Bombay via Bangkok, Singapore, and Cochin (India). Another ship had a 14-day unit from Rio de Janeiro to Argentina, the Falkland Islands, Straits of Magellan, and Callao, Peru.

17. In 1992, trade sources reported that between 80 and 85% of all tickets sold had been discounted.

18. "Costa Paquet Right on Course," *Cruise and Ferry Review,* supplement to *Lloyd's Ship Manager,* September 1994, 6.

19. An operational commentary on the occasional hazards of cruise service was the fact that the Manseatic ran aground in Arctic waters, and passengers had to be airlifted home when the ship could not be refloated (August 1996).

20. The Russian icebreaker *Yamal* was built in 1992. She was 150 meters (492.3 feet) long overall and had an extreme width of 30 meters (98.5 feet) and a draft of 11.08 meters

(36.4 feet). She had three propellers powered by two thermonuclear reactors, each weighing 160 tons.

21. *"'France'* into *'Norway'* by Hapag-Lloyd," *The Motor Ship,* July 1980, 87.

22. *Seabourn Pride* and *Seabourn Spirit* were built in 1988 and 1989 at a reported cost of $34 million each. Each is 130.65 meters (439 feet) long, 18.75 meters (63 feet) in the beam, and has a gross tonnage of 10,000. A crew of 140 serves a maximum passenger load of 204 travelers.

The Royal Viking Line introduced the 212-passenger *Royal Viking Queen* in direct competition with the *Seabourn* and *Sea Goddess* ships. This vessel is said to have cost $80 million.

23. "Why Go Ashore when the Ship's So Nice?" *Wall Street Journal,* August 11, 1995; "New Cruise Ships Become Floating Cities," *Wall Street Journal,* January 5, 1996.

24. "With the Wind: Caribbean Sailing on a Clipper Ship," *San Francisco Chronicle and Examiner,* April 24, 1993, T3.

25. For a comment on the activity of a company specializing in the technical management of cruise ships, see *Cruise and Ferry Review,* supplement to *Lloyd's Ship Manager,* August/September 1994, 16–17.

26. "Cayman Islands: Limits Set for Cruise Calls," *Cayman Islands,* supplement to *Lloyd's Ship Manager,* February 1995, 12.

27. Medov S/A is a cruise service organization that is established in 57 ports and major cities of Italy. In 1992, it handled 450 cruise calls and 15,000 passengers. It is the exclusive agent for seven major cruise operators. Additionally, this organization has a catering service and a personnel manning branch.

28. "Charm is Part of the Job," *Los Angeles Times,* part VII, June 24, 1984, 23.

Chapter 8. Industrial and Special Carriers

1. Offshore supply vessels are those vessels, usually between 200 and 300 feet long, that carry supplies and equipment between offshore oil platforms and shore.

2. Anchor-handling vessels are those vessels, usually between 200 and 300 feet long, that stream and recover anchors for semisubmersible drill rigs. Their aft deck is designed specifically for that purpose. They may be used to carry supplies as well.

3. Cable-laying vessels are designed to lay regular and fiber-optic cable along the ocean bottom. They are also capable of recovering the cable to do any necessary repair or maintenance.

4. In October of 1998, there were 105 LNG carriers worldwide. "LNG Market," *Fairplay,* January 7, 1999, 34.

5. "World's Largest Cement Carriers from ASEA's Sestao Yard," *The Motor Ship,* December 1980, 103–4.

6. "Maintaining Market Equilibrium," *Lloyd's Ship Manager,* August 1992, 67.

7. "Chiquita Benefits from Danish Project Ship," *Lloyd's Ship Manager,* November 1991, 61–9; "Reefers," *Shipping World & Shipbuilder,* October 1992, 14.

8. "60 Year Anniversary of the First 'Reefer,'" *Lauritzen News,* no. 139, September 1995, 3. "Danyard Delivers World's Largest Reefer," *Lloyd's Ship Manager,* October 1990, 17–22.

9. "World's Largest Reefer Can Be Run by Crew of Six," *The Motor Ship,* September 1990, 38–9.

10. "Raising Reefer Ship Safety and Efficiency," *Lloyd's Ship Manager,* June 1995, 35. "Albemarle Island: Reviving Ammonia for Reefer Ships," *The Naval Architect,* September 1993, E382–7.

11. "Reefers Reviewed," *Lloyd's Ship Manager,* November 1994, 14; "Classification Changes for Reefers," *Shipping World & Shipbuilding,* October 1992, 20; "Running into Difficulties," *Seatrade Review,* July 1993, 43.

12. "Dealing with a Full Deck," *Cargoware International,* February 1993, 45.

13. The *Comet* was built at Chester, Pennsylvania, in 1958 as a vehicle carrier. She was 138.3 meters (465 feet) long, 23.3 meters (78 feet) wide, and had a draft of 8 meters (27 feet).

14. The total RO/RO fleet in October 1998 consisted of 1,850 ships of 26,397,836 gross tons. "RO/RO Market," *Fairplay,* January 7, 1999, 36.

15. "Car Carriers Can Also Cope with Mixed Cargoes," *The Motor Ship,* June 1992, 63–6.

Chapter 9. Tanker Management, Operations, and Chartering

1. The first bulk oil carriers were the products of the remarkable Norwegian team of shipowner Gustav Conrad Hansen and shipmaster Even Tollefsen, who converted the sailing ships *Jan Mayn* (258 registered tons), *Stadt* (377 registered tons), and *Lindesnaes* (674 registered tons) to carry petroleum in bulk. The conversion was done at Tømsberg in 1877–1878. See Ragnar Schjøttelvig, "Norwegian Sailing Tankers," *Proceedings,* United States Naval Institute, February 1958, 106–8. This brief article includes a reproduction of a picture of the *Lindesnaes* and the line drawing of her hull as converted.

2. "Of Shoes and Ships," *Fairplay,* March 19, 1970, 14. A photograph of the *Glückauf* is included in this sketch.

3. The motor-tanker *C. O. Stillman* was launched for the Panama Transport Company at the Bremer-Vulkan yard, Bremen, in 1928. She was 565.7 feet long overall, 75.6 feet in the beam, had a draft of 32.5 feet, and a gross registered tonnage of 16,436. The French tanker *Scheherazade* was contemporaneous with the *C. O. Stillman;* she was 167 meters (561 feet) long, and her beam was 21.95 meters (73.6 feet). She was reported to have had a capacity of 200,000 barrels.

4. The T-2 tanker was 159.56 meters (536.1 feet) long overall, with a deadweight of 16,750 tons on a draft of 9.16 meters (34.78 feet). About 140,000 barrels of gasoline could be carried. At a sustained sea speed of 14.5 knots, the ship consumed 385 barrels of high viscosity fuel oil per day. Because of the shortage of gear-making facilities during World War II, all these ships were powered with turboelectric propulsion units. After the war, the T-2 was used by many commercial operations. A number were enlarged in the late 1950s and early 1960s, and their power plants were overhauled to permit them to serve effectively until at least 1981.

5. Between 1946 and 1995, the world's tanker fleet grew from 1,947 ships with an average deadweight of 12,183 tons to 3,200 ships with an average deadweight of 86,675 tons. The average deadweight tonnage of ships, by decades, was as follows: 1946—12,183 tons; 1956—16,930 tons; 1966—32,122 tons; 1976—88,209 tons; 1986—83,846 tons; 1995—86,675 tons. Jacobs & Partners, Ltd., *World Tanker Fleet Review,* July–December 1995, 41. As of April 18, 1996, large tankers on order included six ships of more than 302,000 tons deadweight, 12 of 300,000 to 301,999 tons deadweight, 14 of 252,000 to

299,000 tons deadweight, and 21 of 150,000 to 155,000 tons deadweight. "New Buildings," *Fairplay,* April 18, 1996, 31–2.

The largest tanker in the world in 1993 was the *Jahre Viking* (ex *Happy Giant,* ex *Seawise Giant*), which was launched in Japan in 1975 but not completed until 1979. She was 458.45 meters (1,540.4 feet) long overall, 68.86 meters (231.37 feet) wide, and on a maximum draft of 24.61 meters (82.17 feet) had a deadweight of 569,783 tons. Her fuel tanks had a capacity of 13,138 tons. Steam turbines of 50,000 horsepower gave her a cruising speed of 13 knots.

The ship was almost destroyed by Iraqi warplanes during the Gulf War of 1990–1991. She underwent extensive repairs at the Keppel shipyard in Singapore. She was too large for the yards's drydock, and therefore all work was accomplished while the ship was afloat alongside a repair pier. She was owned in 1995 by Jergen Jahre Shipping A/S of Sandefjord, Norway.

6. Drewry Shipping Consultants, PLC, *Shipping Statistics and Economics,* vol. 26, no. 4 (April 1996).

7. Representative of this class of tanker was the *S/R Baytown,* built in 1989 by Avondale of New Orleans, Louisiana. She was 237.6 meters (779.5 feet) long, 32.25 meters (105.8 feet) in the beam, and on a draft of 14 meters (38.5 feet) had a deadweight of 59,588 tons. Her 17,000 brake horsepower diesel engine gave her a speed of 16 knots.

8. *The Motor Ship,* July 1995.

9. Texaco contracted with the Stena Group of Sweden to manage all its tankers under foreign registry. "Stena to Manage Tankers for Texaco," *Journal of Commerce,* December 21, 1994; "Oil Companies Shed Tankers to Reduce Liability Risks," *Journal of Commerce,* February 29, 1995.

10. In 1964, Erling Naess, an independent tanker owner and operator, ordered the first ship designed to carry full cargoes of oil or bulk commodities such as grain or iron ore. The theory was that relatively short voyages in ballast would bring the ship to a port where an alternative cargo would be loaded. The vessels were expensive to build and to maintain and never were granted great acceptance. In 1976, the peak was reached when 412 combination ("combi") ships were counted. The last ship of this type was built in 1994. "Combined Carriers: In Search for the Right Combination," *Lloyd's Shipping Economist,* April 1993, 16; "Builder of the Last Combi Carrier Touts Vessel's Flexibility," *Journal of Commerce,* April 21, 1994.

11. This does not mean 100% full as an allowance must be made for the expansion of the oil product as its temperature changes.

12. The four cargo pumps of the *Jahre Viking* had a combined capacity of 22,000 tons per hour. The *Berge Sigval*'s three pumps had a total capacity of 16,500 tons per hour.

13. The *Berge Sigval* was 1,085 feet long and had a beam of 190 feet and a draft of about 74 feet. Her diesel power plant of 35,000 brake horsepower gave her a speed of 16 knots.

The *Eleo Maersk* had 17 cargo tanks with an aggregate capacity of 2.14 million barrels of crude oil. The cargo tanks were protected by an inert gas system. A full cargo could be loaded under computer control in 18 hours; it could be discharged, with crude oil washdown, in 36 hours. If the COW system were bypassed, discharge time was reduced to less than 24 hours. The very efficient vacuum system of stripping the cargo tanks left a residue of only 55 barrels. "World's First Double-Hulled VLCC Built by Odense for Maersk Tankers," *Marine Engineers Review,* February 1994, 21; "Maersk Launches Green Fleet,"

Lloyd's Ship Manager, April 1995, 17; "A.P. Moller Bullish on Market as it Takes Delivery of Tankers," *Journal of Commerce,* May 12, 1993, 1-B.

14. Peter B. McGuiness, *Marine Cargo Vapor Control Systems.* (Vallejo: California Maritime Academy, 1995).

15. Bill Box, "Worldscale Fixtures," *Seatrade Review,* January 1994, 30–1.

16. The *Natalie O. Warren,* a dry-cargo ship built in 1944 at Wilmington, Delaware, was converted in 1947 by the Warren Petroleum Corporation of Tulsa, Oklahoma, to carry liquefied petroleum gas. She had 68 vertical cylindrical independent pressure tanks with a capacity of 1,300,000 gallons of liquid propane. Classed by American Bureau of Shipping as an oil carrier, the ship transported full cargoes of liquefied gas between Houston, Texas, and New Jersey. She was in service for a number of years, disappearing from the ABS *Record* in 1963. "New Ship Will Increase New York Gas Supply," *Marine Engineering and Shipping Review,* September 1947, 68.

17. "Sophisticated and Safe," *Lloyd's Ship Manager,* February 1993, 49–51.

18. Bruce E. Keer, "Liquefied Gas Carriers in Port Areas," *Seaways,* May 1993, 11–2.

19. *Fairplay,* "LNG Market," January 7, 1999, 36.

20. The Moss system uses aluminum cargo containment spheres that are two inches thick. Unstiffened tanks are connected at the equator to a single supporting skirt. The lower part of the skirt is welded to the ship's structure. Insulation is arranged over the tanks' outer surface and the upper part of the skirt. "First South Korean LNGC Delivered," *The Motor Ship,* October 1994, 42–7.

21. The membrane system is defined by Lloyd's Register as a "non-self-supporting tank consisting of a thin layer (the membrane) deriving support from the adjacent hull structure via the interconnecting insulating material." Membrane tanks are used primarily for LNG transport, and the two systems currently in service are those of Gaz Transport and Technigaz Mark I. The Technigaz tank system involves a double-hull structure with a flat upper deck. The tanks are constructed of stainless steel membranes and insulation panels made of glass reinforced polyurethane foam.

22. Two types of cargo containment systems are approved: integral and independent. An integral tank contributes to and forms part of the ship's strength. An independent tank is not part of the hull structure and does not share the dynamic loadings experienced by a ship in a seaway.

23. Keer, "Liquefied Gas Carriers," 11–2.

24. *The Motor Ship,* July 1992; *Marine Engineers Review,* April 1993.

25. *IMO News,* no. 2 (1995): 12.

26. Progressive refinements by Kvaerner and its licensees improved the Moss design and reduced the BOR from 0.25 percent to 0.01 percent of the cargo per day. "First South Korean LNGC Delivered," 42–7.

27. "Gas/diesel Could Take the Steam Out of LNG Ships," *Fairplay,* November, 1998, 15.

28. "Back in the Tank," *Hazardous Cargo Bulletin,* December 1996, 26.

29. "LNG Carriers Supply Far Eastern Energy Needs," *Hazardous Cargo Bulletin,* July 1992, 49–54.

30. The *Mubaraz* was 290 meters long overall, had a beam of 48.1 meters, and a deadweight of 72,950 tons on the summer draft of 11.8 meters. "Finland's First LNG Ship," *Hazardous Cargo Bulletin,* April 1996, 54–8.

31. In 1949, the *R.E. Wilson,* a T-2 tanker of 16,436 tons deadweight, was converted into a chemical carrier with 28 tanks. In 1955, the *Mayflower,* also a T-2 tanker, was converted into a 25-tank chemical carrier and renamed *Marine Chemical Transporter.* The *Esso Bangor* and the *Esso Huntington,* both owned by Esso Shipping Company, were fitted with 34 and 39 tanks respectively. "Shipping Chemicals via Parcel," *Surveyor,* February 1984, 23.

32. "Today's Parcel Chemical Tankers: A 25-Year Development," *Stolten* 9, no. 3 (December 1984): 30–3; "Stolt-Nielsen: Four Generations," *Stolten* 10, no. 1 (April 1985): 1–17.

33. Edward Crowley, "The Carriage of Chemicals in Bulk," *Fairplay,* July 30, 1970, 37–9.

34. "In Search of the Universal Cargo Tank Coating," *Stolten* 10, no 1 (April 1985): 18–9.

35. "Chemical Tankers Set Safety Standards," *The Naval Architect,* July/August 1995, E391.

36. "Stolt-Nielsen's Diesel-Electric Class: A New Generation of Chemical Tankers," *The Naval Architect,* November 1995, E614.

Chapter 10. Vessel Management Companies

1. Lloyd's Ship Manager publishes a "Guide to International Ship Registers and Ship Management Services," which is a listing of third-party ship managers and the services they provide. The listing is based on information supplied by the managers to *LSM.*

2. Adrian Bascombe, "The Changing Role," *Containerisation International,* July 1995, 103.

3. On January 1, 1996, ISMA membership stood at 42 companies of which 34 offer full ship management services, 20 members have received ISMA certification, and 4 companies were undergoing their audits.

4. In November of 1995, the International Maritime Organization (IMO) granted the ISMA consultative status. IMO comprises a total of 152 governmental and 60 nongovernmental organizations worldwide.

5. Bob Jaques, "Shipmanagers Here to Stay," *Seatrade Review,* August, 1996, 57–61.

6. For a detailed comparison and illustrative table of the four codes, refer to "Quality Standards Compared," supplement to *Lloyd's Ship Manager,* October 1995, 11.

7. Bob Jaques, "Ship Management & Crewing—Codes of Conduct," *Seatrade Review,* February, 1994, 88–9.

8. For estimates on the cost of becoming certified and maintaining the certification refer to the following two sources: "ISMA: United on Quality, Divided on the Future," supplement to *Lloyd's Ship Manager,* October 1995, 16; and "PCL Cadet Training Returns to the High Sea," *Lloyd's Ship Manager (Far East Quarterly Review),* October 1995, 34.

9. Jon Helmick and Nicholas Glaskowsky, Jr., "Regulatory Constraints on Innovative Manning Practices in the U.S. Flag Merchant Fleet," *Logistics and Transportation Review* 30, no. 3 (1996): 283.

10. Bob Jaques, "Shipmanagers Here to Stay," 61.

11. Most major maritime nations do have some restrictions as to nationality, training, certification of personnel, numbers and ratings of crewmembers required, hours of service, language, etc.

12. As reported in the published minutes of the ISMA annual general meeting by Marine Information Limited, e-mail: marine@dial.pipex.com, February 16, 1996.

13. *Lloyd's,* "New Regulations Set Training Standards," 9.

14. Terry Roomes, "Where's My Relief?" *Fairplay,* October 19, 1995, 14–5.

15. In a paper presented at the *Lloyd's Ship Manager* Philippine Manning and Training Conference in 1997, Harry Gilbert, Chief Executive of the Wallem Group, stated that there currently are no standard salary scales for Chinese seamen serving foreign owners and wages vary considerably, but that a master receives about U.S.$2,250/month and a rating U.S.$650/month with deductions of 10 to 25% to enable domestic employers to cover social benefits such as salary and insurance on leave and retirement benefits.

Chapter 11. Vessel Bunkering

1. Bunkers typically may approximate 40 to 60% of a ship's operating and voyage costs. Mary Bond, "Bunker Arguments Rumble On," *Seatrade Review,* April 1997, 20. Shipowners worldwide purchase about 140 million metric tons of fuel oil per year. "Bunker Prices at the Mercy of Wider Market Trends," *Lloyd's Ship Manager,* December 1996, 53. An average-size bulk carrier may consume 10,000 tons of residual (heavy) marine fuel oil and 1,200 tons of diesel fuel per year, at a total cost of U.S.$1.2 million. R. Viswewaren ("Dr. Vis"), "Light at the End of the Tunnel?" *World Bunkering,* February 1997, 60–3.

2. Ivar Tennesen, "Bunker Buying Techniques," *World Bunkering,* August 1996, 56.

3. The charge for delivery of bunker fuel in Philadelphia in January 1997 was $3,516.23 for a lot of 585 tons or less and $2.43 per metric ton for deliveries of 3,400 tons and over. A sliding scale was applied to deliveries within those two limits. "Industry Round-Up" *World Bunkering,* August 1996, 4. Singapore charged U.S.$1.00 per gross ton for a 24-hour bunkers-only call. *World Bunkering,* February 1997, 5.

4. Without attempting to trace the history of the load line agreements, suffice it to recall that in 1875, Samuel Plimsoll, a member of the British Parliament, led a successful campaign to require ships to bear markings on their sides showing the depth to which they could be loaded safely in various areas of the world and seasons of the year. These rules eventually became international conventions, and the world is now divided into zones designated by the self-explanatory terms of tropical, seasonal tropical, summer, and seasonal winter. A further marking allows for the difference in the buoyancy of fresh and salt water. These markings are determined to give greater freeboard to vessels facing the increasing hazards of the sea as the seasons change. Ships of not more than 100 meters (328 feet) in length are required to have an additional load line for voyages into the North Atlantic in winter. This line appears on the sides of these small vessels with the distinguishing letters WNA.

5. "Thumbs up for Bunkering Procedures," *Singapore's Maritime Industries,* supplement to *Lloyd's Ship Manager,* December 1992, 10–1; "PSA Raises Bunker Standard," *Far East Review,* supplement to *Lloyd's Ship Manager,* September 1994, 17.

6. "Safety, Standards, Quality," *Lloyd's Ship Manager,* August 1992, 64–6. "Bunkers Mixed to Measure: Blending Moves to Point of Supply," *Fairplay,* March 28, 1996, 41. Marine fuels for the modern, efficient, and economical diesel engine ideally should be of consistent quality. The quality of fuel available, however, has declined as fuels are formulated by blending a constantly multiplying variety of by-products of the refining processes used by the petroleum industry. "A Standardized Bunker Industry," *Lloyd's Ship Manager,* January 1993, 43.

Marine engine builders have responded to the challenges posed by inferior fuel by modifications in design and materials, together with recommendations for operating the engines on the available fuel. "Coping with Difficult Fuels on Board," *Lloyd's Ship Manager,* March 1993, 53. See also "Quality: An Ongoing Concern," *Guide to Worldwide Bunkering Services,* supplement to *Lloyd's Ship Manager,* 1994; and "Time to Be Realistic about Fuel Quality," *Marine Log,* April 1994, 24.

7. Bunkering vessels are of two types: towed barges and self-propelled craft, sometimes known as harbor tankers. A modern, self-propelled, well-equipped bunkering vessel, purpose-built in 1996, cost approximately U.S.$4 million to U.S.$7 million, depending upon size. In both barges and self-propelled vessels, the tanks must be segregated to reduce the possibility of contaminating the fuel oil. *Lloyd's,* "PSA Raises Bunker Standards," 17.

In 1996, a British operator put into service a new purpose-built self-propelled bunkering vessel of 2,750 metric tons capacity. This highly specialized ship was 75 meters (230 feet) long, had a speed of 11 knots, and was equipped with two main engines, two propellers, two rudders, a bow thruster, and double bottoms. She was operated in the port of Portsmouth.

BP Marine put the *Marine Partner* into service in 1994 and claimed that this was the world's largest purpose-built lubricating oil barge. The cargo pumps could deliver bulk oil, carried in tanks with a total capacity of 450 metric tons, at the rate of 45 cubic meters per hour. Space was provided for 1,500 drums of oil, and a lifting mechanism was available to handle this cargo. Ellen Clark, "Steady Demand, Competitive Supply," *Seatrade Review,* May 1994, 67.

8. Kohler, "Time to Be Realistic," 24–6; *Lloyd's,* "A Standardized Bunker Industry," 43; *Lloyd's,* "Safety, Standards, Quality," 64–6.

9. "Sampling Methods under Analysis," *Guide to Worldwide Bunkering Services,* supplement to *Lloyd's Ship Manager,* July 1994, 4.; *Seatrade Review,* "Bunker Arguments Rumble On," 19–21.

10. "Bunker Risk Management," *Seatrade Week Newsfront,* June 25–July 1, 1993, 13.

11. Det Norske Veritas Petroleum Services, the oldest and largest bunker testing laboratory in the world, reported that it had made over 300,000 tests of ships' bunker fuels, and found that about three percent of ship bunkers worldwide contained used lubricating oil in small concentrations. The laboratory had found no instance where that amount of waste oil had caused any damage. These findings were corroborated by a research project at Trondheim University. "DNVPS Sets Out the Facts," *The Motor Ship,* February 1997, 17.

12. For a brief but comprehensive commentary on these characteristics on bunker fuels, see *Fuel Oil Manual,* issued by Kittiwake Development Limited of Littlehampton, West Sussex, England, in 1996.

13. *Lloyd's,* "Quality: An Ongoing Concern," 3.

14. The ASTM has had standards for marine fuel oil in the United States since 1934 and for marine diesel fuel since 1978. The Congres Internationale des Machines a Combustion (CIMAC), representing engine manufacturers worldwide, wrote its own specifications for the whole spectrum of marine fuels. ISO issued its standards for marine fuels, which are recognized worldwide. "Efficient Use and Proper Handling Are Vital for Good Bunkering," *Directory of Worldwide Bunkering Services,* supplement to *Lloyd's Ship Manager,* July 1989, 5. "Fuel Standards Attempt to Prevent Bunker Disputes, but . . ." *Marine Engineers Review,* January 1997, 29; "ISO Fuel Standards—Beware the Loopholes," *Marine Engineers Review,* April 1994, 17–8.

15. *Lloyd's,* "Efficient Use and Proper Handling," 8.

16. *Lloyd's,* "Thumbs Up for Bunkering Procedure," 10–1; "PSA Raises Bunker Standards," 17.

17. Det Norske Veritas Petroleum Services was started in 1980 principally for Norwegian shipowners and in 1989 employed more than 50 staff members worldwide. Over $1.5 million has been invested in establishing dedicated testing laboratories in Norway, Singapore, Great Britain, and the United States. These proprietary laboratories provide complete standardization and control of the testing process. All ship, machinery, and present fuel oil and prior fuel oil sample data are maintained on a main frame computer at Sidcup, England. The services provided included fuel oil testing with the target of 24-hour turnaround time for samples, on-site investigations, fuel oil quality surveys, blending advice and calculations, and worldwide technical support. Lloyd's *Guide to Worldwide Bunkering Services,* 12.

18. The Fuel Oil Bunker Analysis Service (FOBAS) from Lloyd's Register started operations in 1982. In 1989, it had a full-time staff of 20. It provided these technical services: routine fuel evaluation through specialist laboratories in the United Kingdom and Singapore; staff inspectors to interpret laboratory results in terms of fuel quality and in the light of practical engineering practices; fuel investigations conducted whenever the provision of competent assistance is considered desirable to resolve suspected problems and to prepare for claims against the supplier of the fuel oil; FOBAS surveyors available to attend bunkering operations at the site in order to advise clients; fuel advisory service including seminars, training programs, and a monthly report on the grade of fuel oil distributed by suppliers in a list of ports. *Guide to Worldwide Bunkering Services,* 12.

19. ABS Worldwide Technical Services, Inc. from the American Bureau of Shipping offers routine fuel analysis of ship's bunkers, complete with a comparison of the results of that analysis with any set of standards that the ship operator wishes to monitor. Deviation from the standard's limitations are brought to the attention of the ship's staff, thereby permitting a check on the actual quality of the oil being delivered compared to that which was ordered. This permits the ship's staff to make any appropriate adjustments or modifications to operating machinery in order to attain maximum efficiency. *Lloyds' Guide to Worldwide Bunkering Services,* 13; "What is ABS Oil Testing Services?" *World Bunkering,* February 1997, 100–1.

20. Advertisement by Det Norske Veritas Petroleum Services in *Lloyd's List Maritime Asia,* March 1995; "DNV Petroleum Services," *Seatrade Review,* March 1994, 56.

21. "'Caveat Emptor' Is a Good Rule," *Directory of Worldwide Bunkering Services,* supplement to *Lloyd's Ship Manager,* July 1989, 10.

22. "Bunker Group Moves to Increase its Ranks," *Journal of Commerce,* January 28, 1994; "Industry Drive to Standardize Procedures," *Seatrade Review,* February 1993, 65–73; "The International Bunker Industry Association Ltd.," *World Bunkering,* August 1996, 31.

23. For a brief but comprehensive description of the functions of a ship's agent, see "Ship Agency," *Seatrade Review,* January 1996, 26–7.

24. ISO 8217 at paragraph 4.1 specifies: "Fuels shall be blends of hydrocarbons derived from petroleum refining. This shall not preclude the incorporation of small amounts of additives intended to improve some aspects of performance." A rider was attached to this statement when the standard was revised in 1996: "The fuel should not include any added substance or chemical waste which jeopardizes the safety of ships or adversely affects the performance of the machinery, or is harmful to personnel, or contributes overall to additional air pollution." Quoted in "The Oil That Fuels Argument," *Marine Engineers Review,* January 1997, 3.

25. Tennesen, "Bunker Buying Techniques," 57.

26. For a carefully worded reaction to the terms of FUELCON by members of the International Bunker Industry Association, see the commentary entitled "Documentary Working Group," *World Bunkering,* February 1997, 21.

27. Ibid., 2.

28. Doug Barrow, "What the Seafarer Should Know," *World Bunkering,* August 1996, 34–6.

29. Michael Grey, "The Unsung Heroes," *Lloyd's List Maritime Asia,* July 1996, 31; Ian Green, "Beware Surveys!" *World Bunkering,* August 1996, 44–7, explains the role of the bunker surveyor; "Complaints Lead to Code of Practice for Bunker Surveyors," *Far East Review,* supplement to *Lloyd's Ship Manager,* June 1996, 17; Rahul Chouduri, "Practical Procedures for the Transfer of Bunker Fuels to Ships: a Surveyor's View," Seventeenth International Bunkering Conference, Oslo, Norway, November 8, 1996.

Chapter 12. Ship Husbandry: Procurement of Vessel Stores, Supplies, and Services

1. Throughout this portion of the chapter, unless otherwise indicated, the presentation is concerned with the spare parts and supplies used by the operating departments. Supplies for the hotel services of the ships are treated separately.

2. As used in this chapter, the description "consumable stores" refers to items like flashlight batteries, cleaning materials, parts, and welding rods. Foodstuffs are among the topics covered in the section on hotel needs.

3. Ken Bloom, "Purchasing Power," *Stolten* 20, no. 1 (April 1995): 12–4.

4. The allowance list comprises the following items, and is maintained in the shipowner's home office:

    a. Engineering experience for the company fleet.

    b. Fleet and individual vessel experience for this class of ship.

    c. Recommendations from manufacturers and equipment suppliers.

    d. Shipbuilder's allowance list.

    e. Shipowner's records of reliability, performance, wear, and failures.

    f. Regulatory and classification society requirements.

    g. Loss of ship time incident to failure of a specific item of equipment.

    h. Availability of spare parts (i.e., lead time for procurement).

    i. Limits on the cost of individual spare parts and total inventory.

    j. The trade route(s) on which the ship will be employed (the possibility of acquiring needed parts at a port of call).

    k. Where the ship was built (i.e., availability of parts in other countries).

    l. The warranties by manufacturers of equipment installed aboard the ship.

5. In most cases, nongenuine parts are copied slavishly from genuine originals and will perform satisfactorily in the equipment for which intended. Because they are copies, rather than having been made from the engineering drawings, there always is the possibility that some clearances or cuts may be slightly different from the genuine part and could cause operational difficulties. The use of genuine parts is the ideal, because the buyer gets the correct design, proper material, and expert fabrication procedures. Furthermore, by using genuine parts, the purchaser is dealing with a source that maintains engineering and de-

sign departments, a quality assurance group, and an inspection team, all of which combine to give the buyer exactly what has been ordered. J. V. White, "How Cost Effective Are Pirate Spares?" *The Motor Ship,* March 1982, 39–42.

6. Shipbreaking as an industry has been moved to the less-developed nations. Dealers in used parts who served the owners of ships based in industrialized areas consequently have been largely cut off from their sources. The availability of used parts is, therefore, questionable as a resource.

7. "Supermarket of the Sea," *Surveyor,* August 1983, 16–20; "Increased Pressures Will Be Brought to Bear on the Ship Chandler," *Lloyd's Ship Manager,* July 1988, 22–8; "Ship Handling," *Seatrade Review,* October 1995, 35–7; Bloom, "Purchasing Power," 13.

8. One ship chandler held itself out to provide these services:

"We carry a full range of cabin, deck, engine, medical, and bond stores, dry stores and produce such as frozen meats, fish, fruit, and vegetables. In addition to locally produced supplies, we can supply oriental and other international products, being direct bulk importers. Our new premises allow for large stockhold, which assures availability of supplies and the quickest and most efficient service.

"Our multilingual representatives are on call 24 hours per day, seven days per week, to assist our customers. Deliveries from our warehouse to vessels are effected by our own fleet of trucks, which include refrigerated transport, allowing fresh and frozen supplies to remain cool under any conditions. Our headquarters are conveniently placed for off-port servicing of ships on passage, and in these cases, we deliver supplies to vessels by either launch or helicopter." (This advertisement appeared in *Lloyd's Ship Manager* for the first time in October 1995.)

9. This catalog is advertised in *Lloyd's Ship Manager,* November 1995.

10. "Survey Reveals Preference for Accredited Suppliers," *Lloyd's Ship Manager,* August 1995, 76–8.

11. "Ship's Pharmacy Survey Reveals Alarming Facts," *Lloyd's Ship Manager,* August 1995, 78–80.

12. For a comprehensive explanation of the duties and responsibilities of the ship's agent, see J. D. Eadie's articles entitled "Ships' Agency," which were published intermittently in *Fairplay* between September 23, 1982, and February 3, 1983. The series later was reprinted under the collective title of Ships Agency.

See also Box, "Ship Agency," 25–7; and Hans Hansen, "Service with a Smile," *Hazardous Cargo Bulletin*, May 1997, 30–2.

Chapter 13. The Logic of Ship Scheduling

1. The internationally accepted measurement for a container is that of a box 20 feet long. A container that is 40 feet long would be equivalent to two 20-foot units. From this developed the terminology of the "twenty-foot equivalent unit (TEU)." A modern ultra-large containership might be described as having a capacity of 6,000 TEUs, but would be loaded with 3,000 40-foot boxes.

2. "Intermodal" refers to the use of two or more different types of transportation to reach a certain destination. For example, a truck hauls the package 200 miles to the railroad, which carries the goods to the port. There it is placed aboard ship. At the overseas discharge point, the parcel is transshipped to a barge for ultimate delivery to the consignee. See the glossary for a specific definition.

Chapter 14. Terminal Management and Operation

1. An excellent comparison of the organizations of a container terminal and a breakbulk terminal is offered in Warren H. Atkins, *Modern Marine Terminal Operations and Management* (Oakland, California: The Port of Oakland, 1983), 24–6.

Chapter 15. The Stevedore Contract

1. In a stevedore contract, the two contracting parties are the stevedore company, referred to in the contract as the "Contractor," and the shipowner or shipping company, referred to in the contract as the "Company."

2. The commodity charges stipulated in the contract are the result of careful consideration of a number of interrelated matters. Each element in the rate is identified, and a cost for that element, prorated to the freighting unit (e.g., weight ton, measurement ton, or individual unit), is calculated as accurately as possible. There is no prescribed method for accomplishing this task; each contractor follows its own scheme of computation predicated upon the wages paid at any given time.

3. In breakbulk cargo operations, the contract contains a list of the commodities that will be handled and the charges per ton or other unit of each of the listed items. The fee is predicated upon normal working hours of the longshoremen and includes all necessary handling of goods, clerical work, checking cargo into or out of the ship, routine recoopering (sewing torn bags, securing loose boards in boxes and crates, and similar minor repair work), and watchmen service. A sample listing of different items handled in a breakbulk terminal follows:

Large unboxed automobiles	Charged per unit
Compact unboxed automobiles	Charged per unit
Bagged cargo stowing at more than 60 cubic feet per weight ton	Charged per 2,240 lbs. or per 2,000 lbs.
Cocoa beans in bags	Charged per 2,240 lbs. or per 2,000 lbs.
Dry skins in bales	Charged per 2,240 lbs. or per 2,000 lbs.
Copper slabs	Charged per 2,240 lbs. or per 2,000 lbs.
Cement in bags or strapped to pallets	Charged per 2,240 lbs. or per 2,000 lbs.

Many of the "old timers" in the stevedoring business used intuition, experience, and the barest minimum of rudimentary calculations to determine what they should charge to handle a particular commodity. Today, rates are made somewhat more scientifically and are computed to the fourth decimal place, reflecting the greater accuracy of the actual cost of performance under the contract.

Chapter 16. Containerization and Its Impact on Transportation

1. International Cargo Handling Coordination Association, *Journal* 2, special issue (September 1955): 16–49, passim.

2. McLean entered the long-distance trucking business in 1933, driving one truck. Over the next two decades, his transportation company grew into a multimillion-dollar operation. Headquarters were maintained in Winston-Salem, North Carolina, the state in which McLean was born.

3. In the United States, existing law regulating interstate commerce forbids the proprietor of one mode of transportation to own a competing method. For instance, until recently, no railroad was permitted to control an intercity trucking enterprise. A coastwise steamship company may not own a railroad that parallels its route and competes for the same business. The ideal of a single corporate unit controlling and using most efficiently the various kinds of transportation available in the United States therefore remained more of a dream than a reality until recently.

4. On January 21, 1955, McLean announced that he had acquired all the capital stock of Pan-Atlantic and at the same time had resigned the presidency of the McLean Trucking Company. (*New York Times,* February 13, 1955, part 5, 9.) The final separation of Pan-Atlantic from Waterman was accomplished on March 1, 1955 (*New York Times,* March 3, 1955, 55). McLean sold his stock in the trucking company in September 1955. (*New York Times,* November 28, 1956, 70.)

5. The first tanker acquired was the *Marine Leader,* purchased for $1,375,000 from Marine Navigation Co. of New York on April 5, 1956. After conversion, she was renamed *Maxton* in honor of the North Carolina city in which McLean was born. (*New York Times,* April 6, 1956, 46)

The *Ideal X* (ex *Potrero Hills*) and the *Almena* (ex *Whittier Hills*) were modified at the Baltimore shipyard of Bethlehem Steel Company, while the *Maxton* and the *Coalinga Hills* were adapted to the new service by Mobile Ship Repair, Inc., of Mobile, Alabama.

6. Quoted in the *New York Times,* November 28, 1956, 70. For a detailed account of McLean's participation in the container revolution, see Robert Mottley, "The Early Years," *American Shipper,* May 1966, 27–40.

7. For a complete description of the *Gateway City,* the first converted C-2 to enter McLean's service, see *Marine Engineering/Log,* December 1957, 67–9.

8. *New York Times,* November 23, 1958.

9. The following comparison between the operation schedules of the *Gateway City* (the first McLean ship to be converted to carry containers exclusively) and a conventional breakbulk ship of the same basic design with an identical power plant will demonstrate how the saving in stevedoring time benefitted the shipowner.

The *Gateway City* was assigned to sail between Port Newark and Houston, a distance of 1,928 miles. At her normal cruising speed of 14.5 knots, the one-way passage required 133 hours, without allowing for possible delays and the inevitable slow transit through inner harbor channels. In Houston, she used 14 hours to discharge and reload, and she then spent another 133 hours steaming back to Port Newark. Port time to discharge the northbound containers in the New Jersey terminal was 7 hours, bringing the total time for the round trip (from departure on voyage number one to start of loading of containers for voyage number two) to 287 hours (approximately 12 days). To ensure against breakdowns, it was established that the *Gateway City* would be withdrawn for maintenance purposes at the end of each 25-week period of operation. During the 50 weeks of the operating year, the ship was able to complete 29 round voyages. If every one of the 226 containers carried a full load of 20 revenue tons, ship earnings would be based on 4,520 tons per one-way passage.

The *Fair Isle,* a conventional breakbulk ship comparable in all respects to the *Gateway City,* was operated on the same route. Her sea time was identical with that of the containership, but discharging and reloading required 84 hours in Houston and a similar period in Port Newark. Total voyage time came to 434 hours. In 50 weeks, the *Fair Isle* completed 19.35 voyages. Her earnings also were based on carrying 4,520 tons per one-way passage.

Translated into fleet size, the calculations reveal that two containerships had the theoretical capability of maintaining sailings every 6.14 days through the 351 days of their operating year. The longer turnaround time for the breakbulk ship meant that three vessels would be required to make possible a sailing every 6.05 days. Because no more revenue would be earned by the three breakbulk ships than by the two containerships, it is obvious that the reduction in total voyage time was of major financial importance.

(The above calculations are entirely theoretical and do not reflect actual ship operations. The purpose of the computation is to show the disparity between the performance potential of the two types of ships and to suggest the relative earning power of the vessels.)

10. When Sealand Service, Inc., placed four diesel-powered and crane-equipped ships in service during 1978, McLean had no connection with that organization. The reason advanced by the owners for installing cranes was that the ships were to serve ports in the Middle East that had no facilities for handling containers. *New York Journal of Commerce,* May 5, 1978, 32.

11. For an excellent and comprehensive short history of the development of containerized shipping, see David Greenman, "Twenty-five Years of Container Ships," *Ships Monthly,* January 1992, 14–8 and February 1992, 28–31.

12. Up to this point, little attention has been devoted in these pages to the question of the sustained sea speed of containerships. One reason for this seeming neglect of an important subject is that the velocity of vessels is of less importance to both shippers and consignees than reducing the length of time the cargo has to be in the custody of the shipowner. When the *Gateway City,* which had a maximum speed of 14.5 knots, made her first voyage as a carrier of containerized cargo exclusively, she traveled at approximately the same speed as did all other cargo ships. What gave McLean a major advantage over his competitors was that his method reduced the time required to load the cargo aboard, remove it from the ship, and make it available to the consignee. It was as though he had raised the speed of the conventional breakbulk ship by at least 25%.

It was not until ships were designed and built to handle all their cargo in containers that significant increases were made in their cruising speed. As pointed out earlier, the fewer the days needed for a single voyage, the more revenue-producing trips a ship can complete in a year. There are, however, only two ways to reduce the duration of a voyage. One is to cut the time to discharge and reload. The other is to decrease the number of hours spent in transit between ports. To justify the cost of greater speed, it must be shown positively that the revenue earned by the additional voyage exceeds the cost involved. The speed of the container-carrying ship therefore must be related to the integrated transportation system and evaluated for its contribution to that system.

13. Statistics based on a study of dry-cargo container demand, published by UK-based CSR Consultants. *Cargo Systems International,* January 1993, 40–1.

14. Based on a survey of the total world fleet of containers in regular service at mid-1995. "Market Analysis," *Cargo Systems International,* January 1996, 4–5.

15. Most marine containers are made of steel in order to withstand the harsh conditions of sea service. In 1995, American President Lines and two other companies formed Ultralite Container Corporation to develop a lightweight marine container. The new containers are made of a composite material and are half the weight of steel marine containers. Company officials say the new containers need less maintenance than conventional steel

boxes, do not require painting, will not rust, and will have about a 50% greater useful life. Peter Tirschwell, "APL Enters Joint Venture to Make Lightweight Boxes," *Journal of Commerce,* May 2, 1995, 3B.

16. "Container Tracking," *Seatrade Review,* February 1995, 37–9.

17. "Global Alliances," *Lloyd's Ship Manager,* August 1995, 25–6.

18. "The Next Step is 15,000-TEU Containerships," *Fairplay,* November 19, 1998, 26.

19. "Ship Sizes Set to Rise," *Lloyd's Ship Manager,* August 1995, 29–33.

20. "Underwriters Differ on Open-Top Containerships," *American Shipper,* February 1996, 58–9.

Chapter 17. The Intermodal Transportation Concept

1. James Buckley, "Intermodal Transportation Needs Clear Definition," *Container News,* June 1988, 5.

2. For more information on acceptance and use of EDI, see John Crichton, "Kicking the Hard-Copy Habit," *Containerisation International,* June 1993, 36–40.

3. For more information on this subject see McKenzie, North, and Smith, *Intermodal Transportation—The Whole Story* (Omaha, Neb.: Simmons-Boardman Books, Inc., 1989), 243.

4. As early as 1923, a shipment of 7,500 bales of raw silk worth $8,250,000 was sent from Yokohama to Seattle and was transshipped into 2 special trains of 15 baggage cars each. These trains followed schedules equal to those carrying passengers (*New York Times,* January 7, 1923, 1). In 1926, a shipment of 10,000 bales of raw silk worth $11,000,000 arrived in New York just 17 days after it was loaded in Yokohama. The steamer used was the *Arabia Maru* of the Osaka Shoshen Kaisha fleet, which sailed from Japan on December 27, 1925. Two trains consisting of 11 and 12 baggage cars respectively were ready when the ship docked in Seattle; they departed on January 10, 1926, arriving in New York in the evening of January 13 (*New York Times,* January 14, 1926, 43). A record was claimed for the transcontinental run when a shipment valued at $5,400,000 was moved from Seattle to New York in 73 hours and 25 minutes; express passenger trains required 95 to 100 hours for the same trip. The demand for speed had two bases: the raw silk deteriorated rapidly, and interest charges amounted to about $1,000 a day. The "silk express" in 1925 handled 261,853 bales of new raw silk, valued at almost $700,000,000 (*New York Times,* September 26, 1925, section 8, 14).

5. "It is said that westbound traffic is three to four times heavier than eastbound trade, and that there is 'always' a shortage of containers in Nakhodka." *New York Journal of Commerce,* June 23, 1980, 22A.

6. In commenting on the long-held doctrine of "cargo naturally tributary" to a given port, the commission laid down two general principles for the future guidance of all concerned.

The first of these principles was that "certain cargo may be naturally tributary to a port, but any naturally tributary zone surrounding a port is constantly changing." In a particular case, the tributary zone would be determined by considering (1) the flow of traffic, including the points of origin or destination of the cargo, through the port prior to the introduction of the new practices of the carriers; (2) the relevant freight rates for inland transportation; (3) the natural or geographic patterns of transportation and the most logical and efficient use of those patterns; and (4) the needs of the shippers and the characteristics of the goods being moved.

The second principle was that "a carrier or port may not unreasonably divert cargo which is naturally tributary to another port." Judging by the factors listed under the first guideline, certain cargoes may be designated correctly as "naturally tributary" to a particular port. Should any or all of this cargo be diverted from that port, the logic and reasonableness of that diversion would have to be established. "Reasonableness" of an individual routing of cargo is to be determined by considering (1) the quantity of cargo being diverted, and whether substantial injury is being sustained by the bypassed port; (2) the cost to the steamship operator of providing direct service to the complaining port; (3) any practical and demonstrable difficulties in ship operations or other factors, such as the small quantity of cargo offered for scheduled sailings, or inadequate facilities for handling the proffered cargo, which would influence the water carrier's ability to provide direct service; (4) the competitive conditions existing in the trade; and (5) the fairness of the method or methods employed to effect the diversion, including, for example, the absorption of certain costs or the techniques of soliciting business.

The commission further noted that the contention that a region was naturally tributary to a given port "cannot be extended to the point where a port or a range of ports can claim a multi-state inland region as its exclusive 'territory.' This, however, is precisely what the complainants are attempting to do in this case."

Cargo was found to be originating in states far removed from the Gulf Coast. Observed the commission in its ruling:

> Even if it were assumed that all mini-bridge [mini-landbridge] cargo originates in Texas and Louisiana, the Gulf Coast ports all lay equal claim to those areas and no individual port has established an area locally tributary to it alone. . . . The theory that an entire region of the country might "belong" to a range of ports is not a tenable basis upon which to build a regulatory framework of fair competition between the interests of ports and carriers. Historical movements of cargo are not without some relevance, but it cannot be seriously maintained that Congress intended [the port-protecting] Section Eight of the 1920 Merchant Marine Act to freeze international transportation movements into their 1920 patterns.

An indication of the sense of financial injury that a port sustained by the diversion of cargo resulting from landbridge operations may be gained from that portion of the commission's decision dealing with the claim by Houston, Texas, that three-quarters of a $40-million bond issue had been assigned to build facilities to handle containers in the expectation that Sealand would continue to provide direct port-to-port service from Houston to Europe. The commission held that:

> Absent clear proof to the contrary, it must be assumed that a local investment decision of this magnitude was dependent upon a number of factors other than the unsecured assurances of continued vessel calls by a single containership operator. It has long been recognized that, absent unique circumstances, the Shipping Act does not require ocean carriers to provide service to a particular port.

A reexamination of this decision several months later prompted these comments from the vice chairman of the commission:

> Historical and geographical considerations (relating to naturally tributary cargo) may still be applied, but they should not serve as rigid criteria in defining any port's natu-

rally tributary zone. Competitive conditions existing in the trade, shipper needs, and the variety of transportation services available are equally valid criteria in determining naturally tributary cargo. . . . By questioning the notion that certain ports have proprietary right to certain cargo, we are increasing the need for ports to compete for their traffic and . . . increasing their incentive to develop innovative services to attract enough cargo to remain profitable. "Tributary Cargo Interpretation of FMC Receives Support," *New York Journal of Commerce,* December 4, 1978, 9.

7. "McAllister Doubles Container Capacity," *New York Journal of Commerce,* February 24, 1977. This service was discontinued before the end of 1977.

8. "Sea Container's 'Strider' Vessels," *The Motor Ship,* September 1976, 110–3. This is an excellent article describing these feeder ships, which could carry 330 20-foot containers and had a deadweight of 6,500 tons.

Chapter 18. How Freight Rates Are Made

1. Sletmo, *Liner Conferences,* 66–7.

2. "TWRA May Postpone July 1 Rate Hike," *New York Journal of Commerce,* June 6, 1985, 1A. "Rate Hikes Canceled by TWRA," *New York Journal of Commerce,* September 30, 1985, 3.

3. Sletmo, *Liner Conferences,* 114.

4. Ibid., 185–9; 252–4. The problems inherent in the "freight all kinds" rate are described in these pages.

Chapter 19. The Ocean Bill of Lading

1. *Benedict on Admiralty,* vol. 2-A, 3-1 and 3-2.

The duty of a private carrier is "to exercise such reasonable care and maritime skill as prudent navigators employ for the performance of similar service." See Saul Sorkin, *Goods in Transit,* vol. 1 (New York: M. Bender, 1994), 1–12.

2. The earliest case to define the term "common carrier by water" is *Coggs v Bernard,* reported in England in 1672. Justice Story in 1851 added that a common carrier "must exercise it [that activity] as a public employment; he must undertake to carry goods for persons generally; and he must hold himself out as ready to engage in the transportation of goods for hire as a business and not as a casual occupation *pro hac vice.*" Yung F. Chiang, "The Characterization of a Vessel as a Common or Private Carrier," *Tulane Law Review* 48 (1974): 304.

3. Material for this historical survey has been drawn from Alan Mitchellhill, *Bills of Lading: Law and Practice* (London: Chapman and Hall, 1982), 1; and Boris Kosolchyk, "Evolution and Present State of the Ocean Bill of Lading from a Banking Law Perspective," *Journal of Maritime Law and Commerce* 23, no. 2 (April 1992): 164–6, hereafter cited as Kosolchyk.

4. Quoted in Kosolchyk, 167.

5. Ibid., 168–9.

6. Reproduced in W. Bayard Crutcher, "The Ocean Bill of Lading: A Study in Fossilization," *Tulane Law Review* 45 (1971): 701.

7. Benjamin W. Yancey, "The Carriage of Goods: Hague, COGSA, Visby, and Hamburg," *Tulane Law Review* 57, no. 5 (June 1983): 1237.

8. A bill of lading issued by a common carrier prior to 1936 and cited by the House of Representatives in its hearings leading to the enactment of COGSA in 1936 set forth these exemptions:

> It is mutually agreed that the steamer shall have the liberty to sail with or without pilots, shall have the right to tow and assist vessels in distress and to deviate for the purpose of saving life or property and the ship is in no wise to be held responsible for delay, damage, or for any claims whatsoever, growing out of the ship's service in towing or assisting, deviation, or the like; that the carrier shall have liberty to convey goods in craft and/or lighters to and from the steamer at the risk of the owners of the goods; and, in case the steamer shall put into a port of refuge, or be prevented from any cause from proceeding in the ordinary course of her voyage, to transship the goods to their destination by any other steamer; that the carrier shall not be liable for loss or damage occasioned by perils of the sea or other water, by fire from any cause or wheresoever occurring; by barratry of the master or crew; by enemies, pirates, or robbers; by arrest and restraint of Princes, rulers, or people, riots, strikes, or stoppage of labor; by explosion, bursting of boilers, breakage of shaft, or any latent defect in hull, machinery, or appurtenances, or unseaworthiness of the steamer, whether existing at time of shipment, or at the beginning of the voyage, provided the owners have exercised due diligence to make the steamer seaworthy; by heating, frost, decay, putrefaction, rust, steam, smoke, coal dust, spray, oil, sweat, change of character, drainage, leakage, breakage, smell, taint, or evaporation from any other goods, vermin, or by explosion of any of the goods, whether shipped with or without disclosure of their nature, or any loss or damage arising from the nature of the goods or the insufficiency of packages; nor for land damage; nor for the obliteration, errors, insufficiency, or absence of marks, numbers, address, or description; nor for risk of craft, bulk, or transshipment; nor for any loss or damage caused by the prolongation of the voyage; nor for any damage to any goods, however caused, which is capable of being covered by insurance and that the carrier shall not be concluded as to correctness of statements herein of quality, quantity, gage, contents, weight, and value.

9. Marva Jo Wyatt, "Contract Terms in Intermodal Transport: COGSA Comes Ashore," *Tulane Maritime Law Review* 16 (1991): 182–3.

10. Peter D. Clark, "Court Places Portion of Box Weight Burden on Consignees," *New York Journal of Commerce,* June 17, 1994.

11. In 1936 the value of $500 was much greater than it is today. For many years an international debate has raged about changing the maximum liability from $500 to something more appropriate to our changing times. The two proposals put forward are the Hamburg Rules and the Hague-Visby Amendment. The Hague-Visby Rules, which have been ratified by 75% of the world's trading nations, increase the liability limit on packages to $1,000. U.S. shippers have favored the Hamburg Rules, which among other provisions make carriers liable during the entire time they have custody over shipments. Under COGSA, carriers are responsible only during loading and unloading and when the cargo is on board the ship.

12. United States courts have found it difficult to define categorically what constitutes a "package." As methods of packing change with newer technologies and the use of containers proliferates, the problems have increased. A particularly troublesome phrase in the statutes refers to "the unit of quantity, weight, or measurement of the cargo customarily

used as the basis for the calculation of the freight rate to be charged." Courts vary widely in their interpretation of these words. For instance, a container was loaded with 341 cartons of stereo receivers. The court ruled that each of the 341 cartons was a "package." In another instance a number of cartons of electronic gear were strapped to a pallet, and the ship's container was filled with these pallets. A different court decided that the pallet constituted the "package." In a third case requiring judicial interpretation, several locomotives were loaded aboard ship, and the freight charge assessed by the carrier was $10,000 per unit. The court ruled that each locomotive was a "package," and therefore the carrier's liability was limited to $500 per package. Yancey, "Carriage of Goods,"146–7 (footnote 36); Sorkin, *Goods in Transit* (vol.1) 1-12.

13. Crutcher, "Ocean Bill of Lading," 728.

14. Standardized bills of lading are examined clause by clause in Gram, *Chartering Documents* (London: Lloyd's of London Press, 1981), 85–196.

15. The acknowledgment of receipt by the carrier of goods in "apparent good order and condition" is prima facie evidence *only* of the condition of the shipment that is open to inspection and can be determined by the human eye. If the goods are in packages or other covers, some courts have held that the reference is only to the exterior appearance and condition of the packages. Nevertheless, it has been held that the acknowledgment of receipt in apparent good order and condition shifts the burden of going forward to the carrier. Sorkin, *Goods in Transit* (vol. 1), 2-94 and 2-98.

A bill of lading containing a clause stating that the term "apparent good order" does not mean that the goods were free from rust or moisture at the time the goods were received by the carrier, and further stating that on demand the carrier would issue a substitute bill of lading specifically setting forth notations as to rust and moisture without such restrictions as the words "apparent good order," is not a void bill of lading under COGSA. Ibid., 2-93.

A bill of lading stated: "Food, prepared, frozen, 0 [degrees] F. must be maintained," was held to show frozen condition at time of delivery to carrier sufficient to overcome negative import of standard entry, "contents of package unknown." Ibid., 2-95.

Chapter 21. Planning for a New Ship

1. Robert Taggart, ed., *Ship Design and Construction, Written by a Group of Authorities* (New York: The Society of Naval Architects and Marine Engineers, 1980), 11.

2. The original SD-14 was delivered in 1968 and had a deadweight capacity of 15,250 tons on a loaded draft of 28.5 feet (8.7 meters). Her service speed was about 14 knots. Several newer versions were developed subsequently by the shipyard and its designers. The SD-14 Mark IV had a deadweight of 15,000 tons, five holds and five hatches, four tween decks at one level, and a mean draft of 28.75 feet (8.8 meters). She was powered by a 5-cylinder diesel engine which gave her a speed of 15 knots on a fuel consumption of 25.5 tons of heavy oil per day. This model of the SD-14 was well suited to carry full cargoes of heavy grain, ore, coal, and timber. She fit easily into the packaged or general cargo trades by reason of her tween decks, her ten cargo derricks, and her quite adequate speed.

A total of 211 ships of this type were built. They appealed especially to Greek shipowners, whose fleets in the 1960s still included many Liberty ships, which were nearing the end of their useful lives. Two decades later, the demand for second-hand SD-14s was still significant. Robert Gardiner, ed., *The Shipping Revolution: The Modern Merchant Ship* (Annapolis, Md.: Naval Institute Press, 1992), 18.

3. Taggart, *Ship Design and Construction,* 8.

4. The distribution, by gradations of deadweight tonnage, of the dry-cargo bulk fleet in 1996 was as follows:

Size in Thousands of DWT	Number of Ships	Total DWT
10–30	2,101	47,100,000
30–50	1,553	59,400,000
50–80	904	58,200,000
80–100	33	2,800,000
100–150	254	33,600,000
150 and over	159	29,500,000

Drewry International Limited, *Shipping Statistics and Economics,* "Market Highlights," March 1996.

5. The *Regina Maersk* was 318.20 meters (1,044 feet) long overall, had a beam of 42.88 meters (141.7 feet), and a maximum draft of 14 meters (45.95 feet). She was driven by a diesel engine of 74,640 brake horsepower and had a service speed of 25 knots on a daily fuel consumption of 200 tons of heavy oil. She had special areas for explosive or dangerous cargoes below decks in the forward three holds; she also had explosion-strengthened sides and a sprinkler system.

6. W. L. Russo and E. K. Sullivan, "Design of the Mariner Type Ships," *Transactions of the Society of Naval Architects and Marine Engineers, 1953,* quoted in Taggart, *Ship Design and Construction,* 53. Quotation used by permission.

7. The *Jervis Bay* was built in 1992 by Ishikawajima Heavy Industries, Kure, Japan, for P&O Containers, Ltd. She was propelled by a Sulzer diesel engine of 42,116 brake horsepower. At service speed, she consumed 117.8 tons of high viscosity fuel oil per day.

8. The *Cape Hatteras* was built in 1992 by Schiffwerft GmbH of Wismar, Germany. On delivery by the shipyard, the vessel was registered in Cyprus and assigned to trade on the Madras-Singapore route. She was built to accept all sizes of containers in use in 1992–1993 and was given the technical designation of "multimeasurement container" (MMC) ship. Special mobile guides were installed, intended to accept containers between 20 and 49 feet in length. Of the 923 TEU capacity, 304 were stowed below deck. Reefer plugs were available for 204 containers. Her 11,964 brake-horsepower engine gave her a speed of 18 knots.

9. "First Panamax 'Open Hatch' Container Ship," *Nautical Magazine,* January 1992, 48.

10. "Cape Hatteras," *Ships Monthly,* April 1993, 17.

11. "Oost Atlantic Lijn: Containerization's Leading Lady," *Seatrade Review,* April 1993, 63.

Chapter 22. New Technology for the Maritime Industry

1. Michael Fabey, "FastShip Gaining Credibility," *Journal of Commerce,* September 18, 1995, A1.

2. "Into the Future," *Traffic World,* November 25, 1996, 6.

3. "Reefer Pallet Handling Goes Automatic," *Marine Engineers Review,* December, 1994, 58.

4. "Tractor Tugs Take Control," *Fairplay,* July 30, 1998, 32.

5. "Latest Box Boats Get Bigger Engines," *Pacific Maritime Magazine*, May 1999, 36.

6. For a full history of the development of the chronometer, refer to chapter 1 of the *American Practical Navigator,* originally by Nathaniel Bowditch. For the biography of John Harrison, who perfected the chronometer, see Dava Sobel, *Longitude* (New York: Walker & Co., 1995).

7. For a description of the various radio-navigation systems, refer to the chapter "Basic Radio-Navigation Systems" in *Dutton's Navigation and Piloting* by Elbert S. Maloney.

8. "Charts Plug into Modern Times," *Journal of Commerce,* December 11, 1996, 1B.

9. Ferries with speeds of 40 knots or more create a much more serious problem. For example, assume that two 40-knot ferries are approaching each other on reciprocal courses. The relative speed is 80 knots (92 mph). If the current radars are capable of picking up the other vessel at 18 miles, which (depending on aspect) is not likely, the ships have only 13.5 minutes to react before a collision.

10. "Nightsight Set to Be a Lifesaver," *Fairplay,* August 20, 1998, 52.

11. John La Dage and Lee Van Gemert, *Stability and Trim for the Ship's Officer,* 3d ed., (Centreville, Maryland: Cornell Maritime Press, 1983), 3.

12. "Is the Standard Up to Scratch?" *Fairplay,* October 1998, 8.

13. For a complete history of INMARSAT as well as detailed information on all types of satellite communication systems and services, refer to *Satellite Communications: Principles & Applications* by David Calcutt and Laurie Tetley. Edward Arnold, a member of the Hodder Headline Group, London, 1994.

14. Janet Porter, "New Maritime Distress System to Revolutionize Ocean Rescue," *Journal of Commerce,* February 3, 1992, 3B.

15. For detailed information on the GMDSS regulation and specifics on all of the equipment required along with their general operation, refer to J. Allen, *Introduction to the Global Maritime Distress and Safety System* (Panama City Beach, Fla.: Mercomms Unlimited, 1995).

16. John Zarocostas, "Edifact Gathering Steam, Global Experts Say," *Journal of Commerce,* March 22, 1993, 3B.

17. William B. Cassidy, "Year of Connectivity; Web Began to Mature, EDI Continued to Grow and Electronic Commerce Started to Reshape Business," *Trade World,* December 23, 1996, 43.

18. For general information on the different types of marine terminals, refer to chapter 14.

19. Philip Damas, "Robotics Catch On," *Containerisation International,* May 1995, 98–9.

20. Joseph Bonney, "Amtech Software Certified by ISO," *American Shipper,* September 1995, 66.

21. Ken Kelley and Ali Bologlu, "DGPS on the Waterfront: Tracking Cargo and Equipment in Maritime Terminals," *GPS World,* September 1995, 62–71.

22. "Post-panamax Cranes for Halifax," *Pacific Maritime Magazine,* August 1999, 23.

23. Information received from Web site of Daniel H. Wagner Associates, Inc. Development of the CCPS system by Wagner was funded by the Cargo Handling Cooperative Program, which is supported in turn by the U.S. Maritime Administration, while Sealand and Virginia International Terminals provided test cranes and installation support at facilities at Portsmouth and Norfolk, Virginia.

24. Jim Shaw, "NKK Stops Crane Swing," *Pacific Maritime Magazine,* March 9, 1998.

Glossary

ABS. American Bureau of Shipping. *See* classification society.

AEI. Automatic equipment identification. An equipment-tracking system that uses radio-frequency identification tags installed on all equipment and tag readers at strategic locations.

agent (vessel). A company or individual who represents the owner of the vessel in the vessel's various ports of call. Agents are engaged in the routines connected with the arrival, working, and departure of the ship.

AGV. Automated guided vehicle. A remotely controlled, self-contained, unmanned vehicle capable of moving containers around a terminal.

American Bureau of Shipping. See classification society.

AMVER. Automated mutual assistance vessel rescue system. An international program operated by the United States Coast Guard which provides resources to help any vessel in distress on the high seas.

AR. American rates.

arbitraries. Charges that are added to the freight rate to cover unusual circumstances involving the cargo carried.

ATRS. American tanker rate schedule

ballast. Any weight used to improve the stability of the vessel or to change the draft or trim of the vessel.

Baltic Exchange. Located in London near the Tower Bridge on the Thames River, this is the site where brokers who have been elected individually to membership in the exchange meet to work out charters for their principals.

bareboat charter. A contract between the owner of a vessel and the charterer whereby the owner transfers operational control of the vessel to the charterer. Also known as *demise charter.*

Beaufort scale. A scale of wind speeds ranging from 0 (calm) to 12 (hurricane). The scale was named after Admiral Sir Francis Beaufort, who devised it in 1806.

BIC codes. Four letter codes that identify owners of containers. Codes are assigned by Bureau International des Containers, a Paris-based organization.

BIFFEX. Baltic International Freight Futures Exchange.

bill of lading. A contract for the carriage of goods by a common carrier.

BIMCO. Baltic and International Maritime Council.

black trades. Tank vessels that carry only crude, residual, and darker oils up to the diesel grade.

boat note. See dock receipt.

BOG. Boil-off gas. Gas evaporated from the cargo on LNG carriers.

booking clerk. A senior member of the outbound department who controls the space in a breakbulk cargo ship, allocating that space to individual shippers as they make their requests.

breakbulk. Cargo that is moved as individual packages. This type of operation does not unitize the cargo.

bulker. Term used to describe a ship that carries goods (usually dry cargo) in bulk. A bulk carrier.

bunching. The overlapping of ship schedules in a fleet operation caused by cumulative delays of the various ships in the fleet.

bunkering. On a ship, the act of taking fuel oil aboard.

Bureau Veritas. See classification society.

cabotage restrictions. Laws that restrict the carriage of goods among a country's ports to carriers registered in that country.

cell. The actual space on a containership where a container can be stowed.

CFR. Code of Federal Regulations.

CFS. Container freight station.

charter party. A written agreement setting forth the terms and conditions under which the vessel owner makes a ship available to the shipper.

checkers. Terminal labor hired by the day to inspect, count, and measure cargo and to insert the appropriate data on the dock receipt.

class rates. A rate or charge assigned to a large number of unrelated commodities that have been studied individually and found to require the same revenue for their transportation.

classification society. A nongovernmental organization that certifies the ship's seaworthiness. These organizations inspect design drawings and specifications before construction begins; they supervise construction to ensure that standards are met and perform periodic surveys to determine continued seaworthiness of the ship. Principal societies are Lloyd's Register (England), American Bureau of Shipping, Det Norske Veritas (Norway), and Bureau Veritas (France).

clean trades. The more highly refined, clean-type oil products, such as gasoline, lubricating oil, and jet-engine fuels. These cargoes often require special care and handling.

CLP. Container load plan. A document that describes the cargo that is in a container and notes where it is stowed.

COGSA. Carriage of Goods by Sea Act.

commodity rates. A rate or charge for carrying a designated item such as, for example, granulated sugar in bags.

common carrier. A carrier that holds itself out to the public as one that, for a reasonable price, is ready, willing, and able to transport goods for anyone, without discrimination.

comptroller. Officer responsible for the fiscal control of a company. The comptroller is assisted by auditors and financial analysts.

conference. An association of common carriers operating on the same ocean route and using a common tariff.

conference (closed). A conference that limits membership to the number of carriers that will be sufficient to provide transportation for the proffered cargo.

conference (open). A conference that admits to membership any common carriers prepared to serve the trade routes covered by that conference.

consignee. The company or person ultimately receiving the cargo at the end of the trip.

container (marine). A metal cargo box that is built to ISO standards and can be loaded aboard ships, on truck chassis, or on railcars.

container rates. A rate or charge for carrying a whole container.

contract carrier. A carrier that operates as a private carrier hauling the goods of a single owner.

COW. Crude oil wash. A technique for cleaning tanks on a tanker. It uses crude oil drawn from the ship's cargo and is very effective in removing sludge.

cribs. Early cargo boxes that were developed from the standard wooden pallet and consisted of a base with lattice sides and a plywood top. The sides were collapsible for easier back-haul.

cross trades. Revenue-earning trade carried between two countries, neither of which is the country of registry for the ship carrying the cargo.

cubic cargo. Cargo requiring more than 40 cubic feet for stowage of a long ton.

currency adjustment factor. A freight rate adjustment factor that compensates the carrier who receives payment in foreign currency and then must convert to its own national currency at a loss.

CY. Container yard. A very large open area on a terminal where containers are stored.

daily cargo report. A stevedore's report of cargo work completed during the preceding twenty-four hours. The report covers these details: number of tons of cargo booked into the ship, tons of cargo actually delivered by shippers during the day, tons loaded, tons still to be loaded, hatches worked, number of men engaged, actual time men were employed, and commodities handled during the day.

danger zones. From a security standpoint, areas in terminals that pose the greatest risks. Generally these are areas where vehicles stop or paperwork is processed.

dead freight. The charge for the difference between the amount of cargo loaded and the amount of cargo booked (usually the ship's capacity) when the amount loaded was short through no fault of the vessel.

deadweight cargo. Cargo that stows in less than 40 cubic feet per long ton.

deadweight tonnage. The total weight that a ship can carry, including cargo, fuel, water, stores, and crew.

deferred rebate. Money paid by a conference to a shipper after a designated period of time during which the shipper's loyalty to the conference has been demonstrated.

delivery book. A book maintained by a marine terminal in which the drayman or other inland carrier signs for the cargo. It shows the date and hour when the ocean carrier released the goods.

delivery clerk. A key assistant to the terminal manager, the clerk is in charge of the office that keeps track of inbound cargo (cargo brought into the terminal by ship, then loaded onto inland carrier for delivery to the consignee).

demise charter. See bareboat charter.

demurrage. (1) The penalty assessed against the voyage charterer for holding the ship in port beyond the period specified for working cargo. (2) The charge against liner cargo left in the transit shed after free time has expired.

Det Norske Veritas. See classification society.

detention. Nonproductive time spent waiting to work cargo due to any cause beyond the control of the stevedoring contractor. This detention time will be billed by the contractor.

DGPS. Differential global positioning system. An electronic navigation system consisting of a constellation of 24 satellites and a differential correction transmitted locally to GPS receivers. This system permits positioning accuracy of less than one meter. *Also see* GPS.

dirty (oil) trades. See black trades.

dispatch. A premium payment made for reducing the time a ship must spend in port loading or discharging cargo.

dock receipt. A document prepared by the shipper that must accompany the cargo to the terminal. It contains these data: name of shipper and consignee; port of destination; description of the goods, including type(s) of package and weight; and the booking number.

dockman. Member of the longshore gang designated by the foreman to work alongside the ship.

domestic trade. Trade between two ports in the same country.

DOT. Department of Transportation.

draft. The depth of the ship below the surface of the water.

ECDIS. Electronic chart display and information system. A chart system consisting of layers of vector data that mariners can interrogate and customize as their navigational needs require.

EDI. Electronic data interchange.

EIR. Equipment interchange report.

exclusive patronage contract. A contract used by conferences in which the shipper is committed to give business only to carriers belonging to that conference.

FAK. Freight all kinds.

FCC. Federal Communications Commission. The agency responsible for regulating interstate and foreign communications by radio or satellite.

feeder vessels. Small, local vessels that transport cargo from outports to larger collecting ports (load centers) where the cargo is transshipped to larger vessels for transportation to distant destinations.

FIOT. Free in and out and trimmed. Refers to bulk cargoes loaded, trimmed, and discharged at charterer's expense.

fixture. Refers to a confirmed and signed charter party.

FMC. Federal Maritime Commission. A government agency responsible for the economic regulation of United States international waterborne commerce.

FOC. Flag of convenience.

freeboard. The vertical distance from the waterline to the top of the weather deck of a vessel.

free time. The number of days after the ship completes discharge during which the consignee may take delivery of his or her goods.

freight agent. Generally works under the freight traffic manager; directs the sales staff and handles departmental administration of the freight traffic department.

freight rates. The prices or rates charged for the services of water carriers.

freight tariffs. *See* tariffs.

freight traffic manager. Serves as a deputy to the vice president, traffic, and supervises the freight traffic department; ensures that departmental policies are carried out in the most effective manner.

fuel oil surcharge. A charge listed in the tariff and charged on every revenue ton of cargo to compensate for the extreme volatility of oil prices and the resultant instability of freight tariffs predicated upon these prices.

full and down. A vessel loaded in such a way that all cubic space is filled and the hull is immersed to the load line.

gangs. A group of longshoremen assigned to work as a unit.

gatehouse. The primary entry and exit point of a marine terminal.

GMDSS. Global maritime distress and safety system. An automated ship-to-ship and ship-to-shore distress alerting and safety system that relies on satellite and advanced terrestrial communication links.

GPS. Global positioning system. An electronic navigation system consisting of a constellation of 24 satellites locked into orbits 11,000 miles above the earth. This system permits positioning accuracy of less than 100 meters any time of the day.

gross form. A form of a voyage charter in which the owner of the ship pays for every item of expense, including loading, discharging, port fees, and all expenses in connection with the cargo, as well as the operating charges such as crew wages, subsistence, and fuel.

hatchtender. A longshoreman who acts as signalman and directs the winch operators. Using specialized hand signals, he or she serves as the communication link for cargo operations between the winch operators and the hold or the apron.

headhouse. The structure at the land end of a finger pier; it houses cargo receiving platforms and terminal management offices.

house flag. A flag designed by a shipping company which incorporates the company's colors and logo.

hustler. A yard tractor used to move containers on a container terminal.

ICTF. Intermodal container transfer facility. A facility where containerized cargo is transferred from one mode of transportation to another.

IMO. International Maritime Organization. A specialized, self-governing agency of the United Nations, autonomously supported by its member states.

IMPA. International Marine Purchasing Association.

industrial carrier. The marine transportation link in the process of manufacture or distribution (or both) of the materials used or produced by an industrial organization.

infrastructure. The foundation upon which growth is dependent; a railroad or highway net supporting a marine terminal; a system of communication linking suppliers and users.

intermodal transportation. A systems approach to transportation whereby goods or passengers are carried in a continuous through-movement between origin and destination using two or more modes of transportation in the most efficient manner.

inbound freight department. A section of the traffic department that is responsible for the consignee obtaining his or her cargo without delay and in an orderly manner.

inherent vice. The characteristics of a cargo that cause it to lose value during the voyage through no fault of the carrier. For example, fresh fruit may be accepted by a carrier in good condition but during the course of the voyage, it becomes overripe.

ISM. International Safety Management (Code). The commonly known name for the International Maritime Organization's "International Management Code for the Safe Operation of Ships and for Pollution Prevention."

ISMA. International Ship Managers' Association.

ISO. International Organization for Standardization.

ISSA. International Ship Suppliers Association.

jitney. A power unit, or tractor, used on a marine terminal to tow a train of two or more trailers loaded with palletized or loose packages or sacks.

jobber. A wholesale merchant who buys in very large lots and sells in quantities to retailers and heavy consumers.

jumbo boom. Shipboard cargo gear designed to lift heavy items.

landbridge. An intermodal transportation concept that utilizes a significant land mass to bridge two ocean routes. For example, a cargo movement from Japan to Europe utilizes water transportation from Japan to the West Coast of the United States, land transportation across the United States, and water transportation again from the East Coast to Europe. This has proven to be a timesaving alternative to the all-water route.

LASH. Lighter aboard ship.

lay days. (1) The period of days during which the owner must tender (or deliver) the vessel and make it available to the charterer. (2) The number of days allowed to load and discharge the cargo, as stated in a voyage charter.

LCL. (1) Less than car load (a railroad term). (2) Less than container load (a marine term).

limiting hatch. The cargo hatch that takes the greatest amount of time to work either because of the amount of cargo in the hold or the structural characteristics of the hatch. The limiting hatch determines the length of the ship's stay in port.

liner service. An ocean common carrier service that operates on an established route and has published sailing dates and published tariffs.

Lloyd's Register. See classification society.

LNG. Liquefied natural gas.

load center. Major ports where cargoes from outports are collected and consolidated for transshipment. Load centers improve the efficiency of ocean transportation by allowing ships to take advantage of economies of scale.

load line. Markings on the side of a ship showing the depth to which it can be loaded safely. Marks differ according to area of the world and season of the year.

long hatch. See limiting hatch.

long ton. Equal to 2,240 pounds.

longshoremen. Dock laborers who actually perform the loading and discharging of cargo from ships.

LOOP. Louisiana offshore oil port. An offshore terminal consisting of a single point mooring system for ships and a system of submarine pipelines connected to a storage facility ashore.

loyalty contract. See exclusive patronage contract.

marine terminal. A transfer point where goods are efficiently exchanged between a vessel and other modes of transportation. Consists of a berth for the vessel, cargo-handling equipment, cargo storage areas, and administrative offices.

Maritime Administration (MARAD). An agency within the Department of Transportation that is responsible for the promotion of United States commercial maritime interests.

MARPOL. An International Maritime Organization convention for the prevention of pollution from ships.

mate's receipt. See dock receipt.

metric ton. Equal to 2,204 pounds.

MSC. Military Sealift Command.

NCB. National Cargo Bureau. An organization dedicated to the safety of shipboard cargo-handling gear and to the safe loading, stowage, securing, and unloading of cargo on all vessels.

net form. A form of voyage charter in which the vessel owner pays all normal ship operating costs, and the charterer is responsible for charges accrued for loading and discharging the cargo as well as for port fees (except those related directly and solely to the crew) exacted against ship and cargo.

neutral body. An independent organization whose purpose is to police the obligations of a conference and its members.

neutral pools. A shorthand reference to a group of containers owned by leasing companies. These are used for one-way movements and then turned over to an agent. This agent places the containers in central collecting points where they form a pool from which individual units can be drawn to meet the needs of shippers within a geographical range of that central point.

notice of readiness. A document prepared by the master of a vessel and presented to the charterer indicating that the vessel is in all respects ready to receive the cargo or to comply with the orders of the charterer.

NTSB. National Transportation Safety Board. An independent agency of the United States government with the mandate to investigate transportation accidents, conduct studies, and make recommendations to government agencies and the transportation industry on safety measures and practices.

OBO. Oil-bulk-ore.

off hire. That moment when the ship's employment under a charter ceases and all payments under the charter are terminated.

off soundings. Refers to a ship in international waters and derives from the fact that its sounding equipment cannot measure the depth of the water.

on hire. That moment when the ship officially begins working under a charter and payments due under the charter begin.

operating department. A department in a ship operating company that is responsible for all matters concerning ship construction, operations, stevedoring, and labor relations.

O. S. and D. Over, short, and damaged cargo report.

outports. Smaller ports on the fixed route. Feeder vessels often transport cargo from the outports to load centers.

outbound freight department. The division of the traffic department that books cargo for the ship, processes bills of lading, and prepares manifests of all outbound cargo.

over-carried. Refers to cargo that has been carried beyond the port at which it was to be discharged.

Panamax (vessel). The largest vessels able to transit the Panama Canal.

parcels. In vessel operations, "parcels" indicate less than shipload lots.

permit clerk. A clerk who instructs shippers of large lots of cargo when to send their consignments to the terminal.

pier (finger). A marine terminal that projects into the waterway at an angle to the shore, thereby allowing ships to berth on both sides.

pile tag. One or more copies of the dock receipt left with the cargo when it is placed on the terminal. When the cargo is loaded aboard a vessel, this tag is given to the chief mate for record keeping and for planning cargo operations.

place utility. In economic terms, the idea that transportation adds value to a product by changing the location of the product.

pools. See neutral pools.

Port marks. A symbol applied to every box, bag, crate, or other container received for shipment to the same port. For example, Genoa might be designated by a red circle, while Istanbul would be symbolized by a green square.

post-Panamax (vessel). Vessels that are too large to transit the Panama Canal.

press up. To fill a tank to its maximum capacity.

private carrier. A carrier that transports only the goods of a single person or company.

productivity (of longshoremen). A measurement of the work accomplished by longshoremen in a given period of time. Generally productivity is stated in terms of the number of tons of cargo, or number of containers handled, per gang per hour.

purchasing agent. Person responsible for the procurement of stores and other material to meet all ship needs.

purser. This person serves as the shipboard agent of the freight and passenger department; often deals with manifests and other papers.

receiving clerk. A key assistant to the terminal manager. Supervises and records all deliveries of outbound cargo to the marine terminal. Issues the dock receipt to shipper acknowledging carrier's responsibility for custody and shows actual weight, measurement, and condition of cargo received for loading.

recoopering. Sewing torn bags, securing loose boards in boxes and crates, and doing similar minor repair work during cargo operations.

reefer. Shorthand term for refrigerated ships or cargoes.

RO/RO. Roll on/roll off.

roundsman. In a marine terminal, the foreman in charge of the security guards.

security chief. The person on a marine terminal who is responsible to the terminal manager for the physical safety of the facility and its contents.

self-sustaining. When referring to a ship, indicates that the ship can load and unload with its own gear.

ship chandler. Companies or individuals who supply the miscellaneous small lot items needed by a ship.

ship husbandry. The procurement of stores, spare parts, supplies, and services for ships.

short ton. Equal to 2,000 pounds.

short delivered. Refers to cargo which, at delivery, is less than the quantity shown on the manifest. Often, the missing cargo has been mistakenly discharged at a port where the ship called before coming to the port of destination.

slips. In a fleet schedule, the delays of a ship along its route.

SOLAS. Safety of Life at Sea. An International Maritime Organization convention that addresses safety equipment and practices aboard ships.

space chartering. The practice of one shipping company chartering a block of space in another shipping company's ship; usually done by companies within a single conference.

specialized carrier. A carrier designed for the express purpose of carrying, usually in shipload lots, a particular type of cargo.

spotted. Cargo delivered to ship's side at the exact location where it will be loaded aboard.

STB. Surface Transportation Board. The agency responsible for the economic regulation of the United States domestic transportation modes.

STCW. Standards for Training, Certification, and Watchkeeping. An International Maritime Organization convention that addresses standards for training and competence of crewmembers.

stowage factor. The number of cubic feet required to stow one long ton of a given cargo.

stripping. The act of unloading goods from a container.

stuffing. The act of loading goods into a container.

surcharge. An additional charge (usually a fixed percentage) added to the freight rate.

taking exception. Recording of defects or discrepancies in cargo received. Refers to the phrase in the bill of lading that cargo is accepted for shipment "in apparent good order and condition, except as noted hereon."

tanker. A ship designed to carry liquid bulk cargo.

tariff. (1) A detailed listing of freight rates and services provided by a carrier. (2) Duty on goods imported.

tender. To deliver a vessel to the charterer.

TEU. Twenty-foot equivalent unit.

third party. Any person not contractually related who has some interest in the transaction. For example, a ship broker, who brings a shipowner and a charterer together and facilitates the negotiation of a charter for the vessel.

through rates. A single rate charged for shipments originating with one ocean carrier and transferred to connecting carriers at intermediate points.

time charter. A contract between the shipowner and the charterer for use of the ship for a specific period of time.

time utility. In economic terms, the idea that transportation adds value to a product by timing when a product arrives at a market.

timekeeper. Clerk at a marine terminal who keeps detailed records of the employment of every laborer hired on an hourly basis.

topping off. Refers to the final steps in finishing the loading operations of a tanker.

traffic department. A department in a shipping company responsible for dealing with customers using the ship for export or import cargoes.

traffic study. A systematic compilation of data concerning one or more of the many problems related to selling the service of ships.

tramp shipping. A shipping service where the carriers contract to haul cargo in shipload lots between ports designated by the charterer.

transit shed. A large covered space on a marine terminal used temporarily to store cargo to be loaded on a ship or delivered to the consignee.

turnaround time. The length of time the ship must spend in port to work her cargo.

unit trains. A train consisting of identical cars and a single type of cargo. For example, a coal train will have only cars carrying coal, and an intermodal unit train will have only cars carrying containers. Normally unit trains consist of specialty cars.

upland area. An outdoor storage area on a traditional breakbulk marine terminal.

USCG. United States Coast Guard.

VLCC. Very large crude carrier. A designation applied to tank vessels of 200,000 tons deadweight or larger.

voyage charter. A contract of affreightment covering the movement of a shipload of a particular cargo from one designated area to another at a stipulated rate per ton of cargo loaded.

VTS. Vessel traffic system. A traffic advisory system used in many large ports and in congested waterways to prevent groundings and collisions.

warranties. Stipulations made by the owner of the vessel as to the details of a ship's characteristics and performance.

wharf. A marine terminal whose face lies parallel to the shoreline.

wharfage report. An inventory of all cargo on which demurrage is payable because it has been left on the terminal beyond the allowed free time.

WNA. Winter North Atlantic. A load line assigned by a classification society to ships not over 100 meters long when trading in the North Atlantic Ocean.

WS. World scale.

Index

Page numbers in italics indicate photographs.

About the Authors

Lane C. Kendall was born in New Orleans, Louisiana, on May 11, 1912. Among his earliest memories were riding the ferry across the Mississippi River and hearing the whistles of steamboats and steamships. When he was eight years old, his mother took him and his sister on an ocean voyage from New Orleans to Le Havre, and that voyage ignited his lifelong interest in ships and the maritime business. He earned both a bachelor's and a master's degree from Tulane University and pursued graduate studies at the University of California (Berkeley) and Princeton University. His long and distinguished career in shipping began with Grace Line and included duty as a combat cargo officer in the U.S. Marine Corps. He was a faculty member at the U.S. Merchant Marine Academy and a commercial shipping advisor to the commander of the Military Sealift Command. Among other awards, Kendall received the Navy's Superior Civilian Service Award and the Naval Institute's Award of Merit. Lane Carter Kendall died on March 2, 1999, in Oakland, California.

James J. Buckley graduated from the California Maritime Academy in 1971 with a bachelor of science degree in nautical science. He began his sailing career as an able seaman aboard a U.S. flag merchant vessel. In 1976 he received his unlimited master's license and has sailed as master for eight years on tramp and liner vessels. Captain Buckley earned endorsement for first-class pilotage for San Francisco Bay as well as the degree of a master of business administration. Ashore, he has worked for a terminal operator and stevedoring company. In 1985 he joined the faculty at California Maritime Academy and currently holds the academic rank of professor in the Department of Maritime Management. At the academy, he has been Department Chair and chief mate and training captain on the training ship *Golden Bear.* In the fall of 1998 he became a graduate student in the doctorate program of Transportation Technology and Policy at the University of California (Davis). Captain Buckley resides in Vallejo with his wife Pam.

ISBN 0-87033-526-X